Restoring Nature

AMERICA'S PUBLIC LANDS

Series Editor
Char Miller
Pomona College

Advisory Board
Douglas Brinkley
Rice University

Jackie Gonzales
Historical Research Associates Inc.

Patricia Nelson Limerick
University of Colorado Boulder

RESTORING NATURE

The Evolution of
Channel Islands
National Park

Lary M. Dilsaver and
Timothy J. Babalis

UNIVERSITY OF NEBRASKA PRESS   LINCOLN

© 2023 by the Board of Regents of
the University of Nebraska

All rights reserved

The University of Nebraska Press is part of a land-grant institution with campuses and programs on the past, present, and future homelands of the Pawnee, Ponca, Otoe-Missouria, Omaha, Dakota, Lakota, Kaw, Cheyenne, and Arapaho Peoples, as well as those of the relocated Ho-Chunk, Sac and Fox, and Iowa Peoples.

Library of Congress Cataloging-in-Publication Data
Names: Dilsaver, Lary M., author. |
Babalis, Timothy, author.
Title: Restoring nature: the evolution of Channel Islands National Park / Lary M. Dilsaver and Timothy J. Babalis.
Description: Lincoln: University of Nebraska Press, 2023 | Series: America's public lands |
Includes bibliographical references and index.
Identifiers: LCCN 2022019481
ISBN 9781496233363 (hardback)
ISBN 9781496233554 (paperback)
ISBN 9781496234018 (epub)
ISBN 9781496234025 (pdf)
Subjects: LCSH: Channel Islands National Park (Calif.) | Channel Islands (Calif.)—Environmental conditions | Conservation of natural resources—California—Channel Islands | Restoration ecology—Government policy—United States | BISAC: NATURE / Ecosystems & Habitats / Oceans & Seas | NATURE / Environmental Conservation & Protection
Classification: LCC F868.S232 D55 2023 | DDC 333.95/160979491—dc23/eng/20221003
LC record available at https://lccn.loc.gov/2022019481

Designed and set in Adobe Text Pro by L. Auten.

Frontispiece: The *Ocean Ranger* at East Anacapa Islet is one of the diverse boats the National Park Service needs to manage the park's five islands. Photographer Robin Dilsaver, 2018.

CONTENTS

List of Illustrations	vii
List of Maps	ix
Acknowledgments	xi
Introduction	xiii
1. The Channel Islands of California	1
2. A Monumental Task	29
3. Legislative Protection for the Islands and the Sea	67
4. Resource Management in the Early Years	91
5. Building the New Park	117
6. Growth of the Natural Resource Management	139
7. Managing the Resources on Santa Rosa Island	171
8. New Owners on Santa Cruz Island	201
9. Restoring Nature	231
10. Channel Islands National Park in the New Century	267
Conclusion	309
Notes	317
Bibliography	371
Index	385

ILLUSTRATIONS

Frontispiece. The *Ocean Ranger* at East Anacapa Islet — ii
1. Aerial view of Santa Cruz Island — 4
2. Caliche on San Miguel Island — 7
3. Aerial view of San Miguel Island — 39
4. Pinnipeds on San Miguel Island — 45
5. Frenchy's structures at the cove on Middle Anacapa Islet — 54
6. The pier at the Landing Cove on the north side of East Anacapa Islet — 55
7. Gary Davis and Bill Ehorn — 73
8. Russell Vail, John Gherini, Pier Gherini, Carey Stanton, and Al Vail — 75
9. Santa Barbara Island Quonset huts — 75
10. I&M step-down diagram for Channel Islands National Park — 99
11. Damage from rabbits on Santa Barbara Island — 105
12. A diagram of marine habitats in the Santa Barbara Channel — 108
13. Former coast guard structures on East Anacapa Islet — 118
14. Vail & Vickers using traditional techniques to herd cattle — 129
15. Torrey pine (*Pinus torreyana*) — 131
16. The Main Ranch in the Central Valley of Santa Cruz Island — 134
17. I&M step-down diagram for the NPS — 144

18. The kelp forest looking toward the surface — 153
19. A seafloor decimated by purple sea urchins — 157
20. Fog covering the higher portions of Santa Rosa Island — 175
21. A stand of Island live oak (*Quercus tomentella*) on Santa Rosa Island — 175
22. A western snowy plover — 183
23. Lobo Canyon on Santa Rosa Island — 198
24. Sheep on Santa Cruz Island — 203
25. The Central Valley of Santa Cruz Island looking east — 208
26. An island fox — 242
27. Island fox enclosures at the Windmill Site on Santa Rosa Island — 250
28. Superintendents of Channel Islands National Park 1974–2018 — 268
29. NPS botanist Clark Cowan rolling up ice plant on East Anacapa Islet — 279
30. Oblique aerial photo showing Prisoners Harbor as designed by the Stantons — 286
31. Prisoners Harbor after reconfiguration and restoration of the wetland — 286
32. Aerial photo showing eucalyptus along the Cañada del Puerto — 287
33. The Cañada del Puerto area after Park Service removal of the eucalyptus grove — 288
34. Technology used in managing the five islands — 306

MAPS

1. The eight Channel Islands — xiv
2. The five islands of Channel Islands National Park — 2
3. Santarosae Island and California coast during the late Pleistocene era — 3
4. Santa Cruz Island — 4
5. Santa Rosa Island — 6
6. Anacapa Island — 8
7. Ocean currents — 9
8. Sea temperatures — 10
9. Division of Santa Cruz Island — 25
10. 1966 Gherini development plan — 63
11. Park and marine sanctuary boundaries — 89
12. Landownership on Santa Cruz Island, 1978 — 134
13. Kelp monitoring sites at Channel Islands National Park, 1984 — 155
14. Marine Protected Areas around Channel Islands National Park, 2020 — 168
15. Isthmus portion of Santa Cruz Island — 230

ACKNOWLEDGMENTS

Former Park Superintendents William "Bill" Ehorn, Russell Galipeau, and Charles "Mack" Shaver provided valuable input on park management and resource issues. Current and former park employees Ken Convery, Timothy Coonan, Kate Faulkner, Chris Horton, David Kushner, Derek Lohuis, Paula J. Power, Dan Richards and Ian Williams helped with research on natural resources. Other NPS officials who also provided important data and assistance include former assistant regional director Holly Bundock; former Department of the Interior solicitor Barbara Goodyear; Greg Gress, chief of the NPS Pacific Land Resources Program; and fire specialists Derek Hartman and Robert Taylor at Santa Monica Mountains National Recreation Area.

Channel Islands National Marine Sanctuary officials who provided information and support for understanding the complex marine resources in the park waters include Lindsey Peavey, Chris Caldow, Chris Mobley, Michael Murray, and Carol Pillsbury. Annie Little of the U.S. Fish and Wildlife Service and Kathryn McEachern of the U.S. Geological Survey supplied vital data. Robert "Bob" Hansen, Peter Schuyler, and Lotus Vermeer helped with the complicated story of the Nature Conservancy on Santa Cruz Island. Other important contributions came from Peggy Dahl of the Santa Barbara Museum of Natural History Archives, John Gherini of Santa Cruz Island, Dr. Lyndal Laughrin of the University of California Research Center on Santa Cruz Island, Mark Oberman of Channel Islands Aviation, Marla Daily of the Santa Cruz Island Foundation, and the staff of Island Packers who transported the authors to the islands. Special thanks go to John and Carol Grenfell of Ventura and Paul Petrich of Goleta, who graciously hosted Lary Dilsaver during his research trips and made the project economically feasible.

Finally, special credit and thanks go to five individuals who made extraordinary contributions to this project. Chief of Cultural Resources Laura Kirn managed the project with aplomb and competence. Former chief scientist Gary Davis spent many hours in conversation, interviews, and manuscript reviews to bring the stories of the marine resources, the Inventory and Monitoring program, and natural science in the park to fruition. Cartographer Rockne Rudolph supplied a number of excellent new maps that grace the pages of this book. Of particular note was former chief of cultural resources Ann Huston who conducted numerous interviews with current and former park employees, located illustrations, and extensively reviewed the drafts of the administrative history that led to this book. Finally, Robin Dilsaver helped every step of the second phase of research, supplied one of the photographs, proofed the manuscript, and offered excellent constructive criticism.

INTRODUCTION

Eight discrete islands and a number of associated rocks make up California's Channel Islands. The northern five form Channel Islands National Park. In the early sixteenth century, all of these islands supported a portfolio of terrestrial species, scores of them endemic, that had managed to reach the islands on their own or with Native American transportation. The ancestors of the Chumash had been in the region for at least thirteen thousand years. As occurs on islands, some species had grown larger than their mainland relatives and others had shrunk. Some, such as the pygmy mammoth, had become extinct about the same time humans arrived, during the waning of the Pleistocene ice age. Others, such as the diminutive island fox, diverged into multiple subspecies, one to an island. In the sea surrounding the islands, two ocean currents created a circulatory pattern marked by a broad range of water temperature and extensive upwelling that feeds myriad species of fish, birds, and aquatic mammals. Otters, pinnipeds, and whales proliferated. The sea offered a bounty of food to prehistoric inhabitants from both the islands and the mainland.

In the first half of the nineteenth century, the Spanish, Mexicans, and Americans arrived as the Chumash were moved away. With them came all the tools, land-use systems, and flora and fauna of their ancestral homes in the Old World. Sheep, cattle, pigs, horses, burros, rabbits, cats, and rats fed on native plants and animals while distributing the seeds and spores of exotic and invasive vegetation. Other newcomers raided the bird nests for eggs, decimated the otter and fur seal populations, and harvested the fish and other marine life at an ever-increasing level. By 1933, the larger islands were inhabited and used for agriculture. The smaller islands were

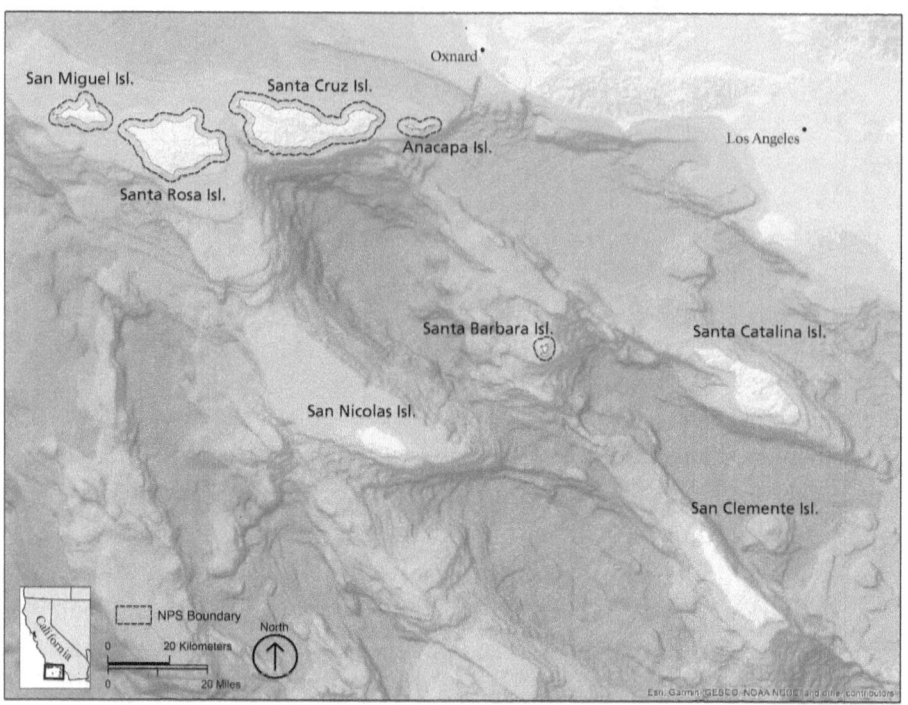

Map 1. The eight Channel Islands showing the contours of the Pacific Ocean floor. Cartography by R. Rudolph, CINP.

overgrazed by lease holders' animals. That year, the U.S. Lighthouse Bureau offered the smaller islands to the National Park Service (NPS). It took five more years for the agency to secure only the two smallest islands—Anacapa and Santa Barbara. After forty-two more years the agency secured park status and significant management responsibility or cooperation on the three larger islands in the northern archipelago.

The NPS has sought to reestablish and reinforce the native species and eradicate the exotic flora and fauna from the five islands it controls or shares with the U.S. Navy and the Nature Conservancy. As the years passed, that mission has intensified as science evolved and discovered how much damage had been done to the delicate habitats of these small fragments of land and to the surprisingly threatened sea around them. Two processes have been necessary to restore the ecosystems of the park's land and sea. The first has been a complex and often bitterly controversial campaign to actually acquire the property. As of 2022, the NPS still only completely controls 53 percent of the five islands' land and, technically, none of the sea. Yet it has worked with other agencies to have a strong input into the management of their territories.

The second process has been the extirpation of nonnative species and protection or reestablishment of native ones. This too has been deeply controversial, and the NPS has faced virulent criticism from animal rights groups and proponents of the 150 years of Euro-American land uses. In the process, Channel Islands National Park has played a major role in the scientific advances that led the NPS to focus on the integrity of its ecosystems rather than simply protecting individual species. In a recent review of NPS resource management policies, the National Park Service Advisory Board defined the goal of park managers: "Ecological integrity describes the quality of ecosystems that are largely self-sustaining and self-regulating. Such ecosystems may possess complete food webs, a full complement of native animal and plant species maintaining their populations, and naturally functioning ecological processes such as predation, nutrient cycling, disturbance and recovery, succession, and energy flow."[1]

This book explains how and why this story of natural resource management happened and offers it as a lesson on restoration ecology and public land management. It is drawn from a much larger administrative history report on Channel Islands National Park completed for the National Park Service in 2021 by the same authors.[2] That lengthy report considered many other topics, including cultural resources, interpretation, law enforcement, maintenance, and personnel issues. Many of those issues are important to the National Park Service for its future management responsibilities but are overly detailed and of less interest to outside readers. Our purpose for this book is to educate students, scholars, and the public about the complexities and controversies that accompany efforts to protect natural resources and restore ecological integrity to both the land and the sea. Channel Islands National Park, on the doorstep of twenty million people, is the perfect case study of these processes. It tests the motives and realities of overcoming traditional uses to restore the ecosystems on and around what many have called "America's Galapagos Islands."

Restoring Nature

The Channel Islands of California   1

At the same latitudes as mainland California running from Santa Barbara to La Jolla lies an archipelago of islands known as the Channel Islands. They consist of eight main islands and an aggregation of small isles and rocks that encircle each. They occur in two clusters that roughly parallel the mainland shores. In the north lie four islands—Anacapa, Santa Cruz, Santa Rosa, and San Miguel—the remaining highlands of a larger, Pleistocene era island geologists call Santarosae, a western outlier of California's Transverse Ranges. The nearest, Anacapa, lies only twelve miles southwest of Ventura. The furthest, windswept San Miguel, is 25.7 miles from Point Conception but 64 miles from Ventura. This group makes up the bulk of Channel Islands National Park. The four southern islands—Santa Barbara, Santa Catalina, San Clemente, and San Nicolas—are much farther apart and lie like the corners of a rumpled trapezoid. Santa Barbara on the northeast corner is the smallest of all eight islands and the final piece of the national park. Southeast of it lies the privately owned island of Santa Catalina, by far the most famous of all with its decades of high-profile tourism. Westward lie the last two islands, both controlled by the United States Navy. San Nicolas Island, the farthest of all eight from any point on the mainland at fifty-three miles, achieved fame due to the fate of an early nineteenth-century Native American, who was left alone there for eighteen years after her people were removed to the mainland, and whose story formed the basis of Scott O'Dell's novel *Island of the Blue Dolphins*. Finally, San Clemente Island, southeast of San Nicolas, houses another navy base and is one of the nation's last target islands for naval gunnery and missile practice.

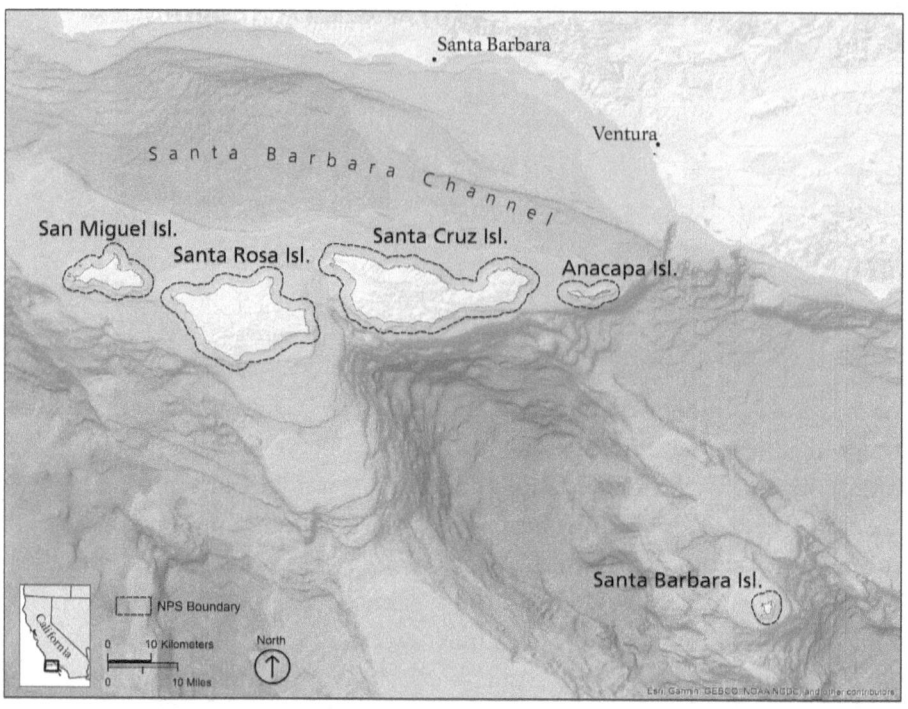

Map 2. The five islands of Channel Islands National Park. Cartography by R. Rudolph, CINP.

Physiography of the Land and Sea

California's Channel Islands as well as the Southern California Bight in which they lie have been formed by plate tectonics. From the Miocene Period, some thirty million years ago, three plates have shaped the western edge of North America. An oceanic segment of the crust known as the Farallon Plate converged on the westward-moving, continental North American Plate, driven there by the northwesterly moving Pacific Plate. Between twenty-seven and eighteen million years ago the Farallon plate completely subducted under the North American Plate. Thereafter the Pacific plate plucked off pieces of the continental plate. Beginning eighteen to twenty million years ago, one piece of the continent was oriented north-south along the coast, with the material that forms San Miguel Island lying near San Diego. As that piece of the continent moved

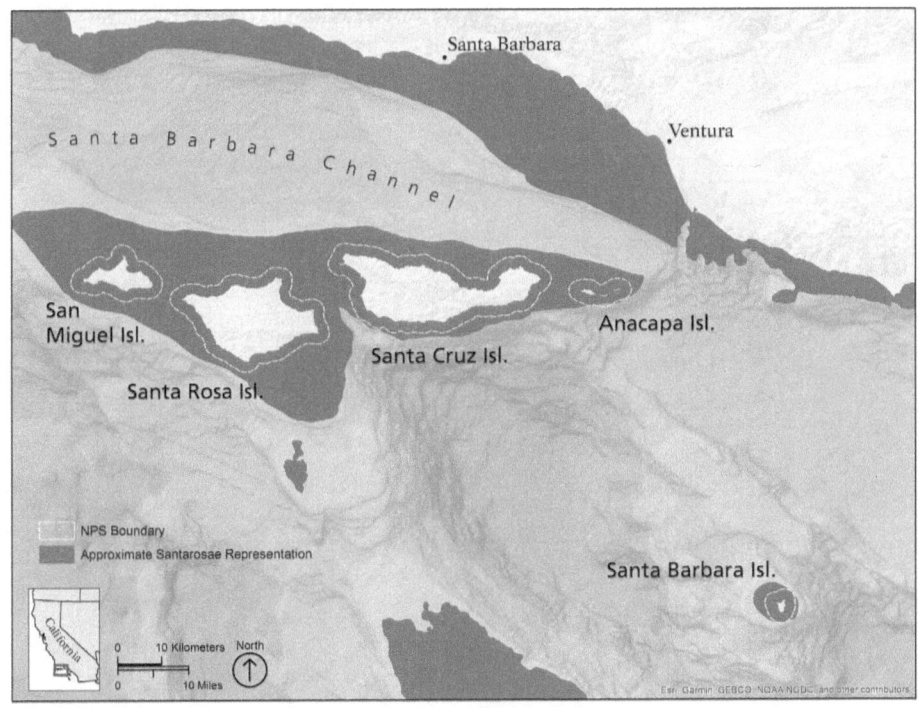

Map 3. Santarosae Island and California Coast during the late Pleistocene era. Cartography by R. Rudolph, CINP.

north it "docked" back onto the continent and its southern end rotated clockwise approximately 110 degrees to its current east-west orientation. South of the rotating block, a gap opened, creating the space now occupied by the Southern California Bight and the Los Angeles Basin. From Point Conception the shoreline juts eastward but the continental shelf continues due south with its edge along the Patton Escarpment. By the latitude of Los Angeles, the edge of the shelf is nearly 120 miles west of the mainland beaches. This marine region consists of a complex array of southeast-to-northwest-trending basins and ridges.[1] The four southern islands are the highest portions of the submarine ridges.[2]

Coupled with Pleistocene tectonic uplift, the fluctuation of sea level during periodic glacial advances and retreats created ancient shorelines that now form marine terraces at multiple elevations. During the last

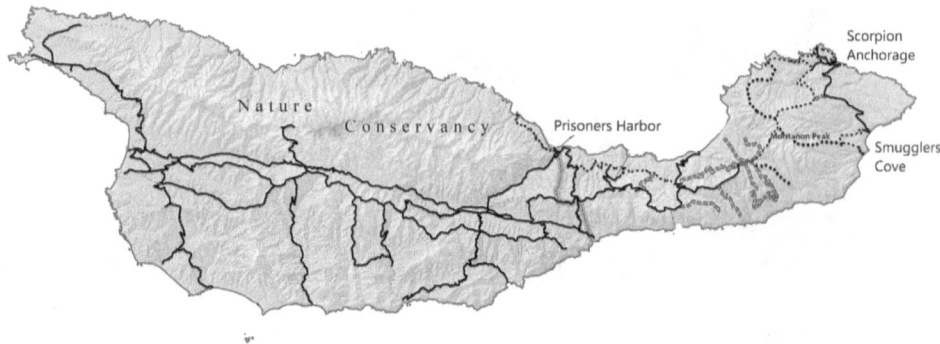

Map 4. Santa Cruz Island. Cartography by R. Rudolph, CINP, and L. Dilsaver.

Fig. 1. Aerial view of Santa Cruz Island. Photographer and date unknown, CINP Digital Archives, No. 199908_009.

Ice Age, which ended about eleven thousand years ago, sea level was approximately 400 feet (122 meters) lower than it is today. During that period, the four northern islands formed the large island Santarosae. The modern islands comprise only 30 percent of the acreage that Santarosae once had. Many marine terraces from that glacial era are now underwater and contain thousands of submerged archaeological sites.[3]

THE INDIVIDUAL ISLANDS

Santa Cruz is the largest island within the northern archipelago of the Channel Islands. It is approximately ninety-five square miles in size, or just over 60,752 acres (24,585 ha). The Park Service owns 14,764 acres (5,975 ha) and the Nature Conservancy (TNC) owns the remainder.[4] The bulk of the island, comprising the TNC's 76 percent of the total area, lies to the west of an isthmus that pinches it into two distinct parts. The eastern 10 percent of the island is physically divided from the remainder of the island by an arid range of steep, rocky hills called the Montañon that run perpendicular to the length of the island like a defensive wall. West of the Montañon, the island is defined by the Santa Cruz Island Fault and the Cañada del Medio (Central Valley) that lies along it.[5] North of the fault, the island is dominated by volcanic rock and south of it by an assortment of sedimentary or metamorphic material ranging from sandstone to schist.

Santa Rosa Island is the second largest of the Northern Channel Islands at 53,364 acres (21,596 ha) in area. Geologically, much of Santa Rosa Island is composed of sedimentary rock overlain with more recent Pleistocene marine deposits. This friable, easily eroded material gives the island an overall gentle profile with rounded hills and many broad, open plains. Like its larger neighbor, it has an east-west fault that separates it into differing northern and southern geologic blocks. The north is relatively open and level, the fault dominated by expansive marine terraces with deeply-incised stream channels while south of it the topography is more rugged. The highest point on the island, Soledad Peak at 1,574 feet, is located here.[6]

San Miguel Island is a tilted tableland lying at the western end of the northern chain. It is just under fifteen square miles or 9,536 acres (3,859 ha). It is underlain by Cretaceous, Tertiary, and Quaternary marine sed-

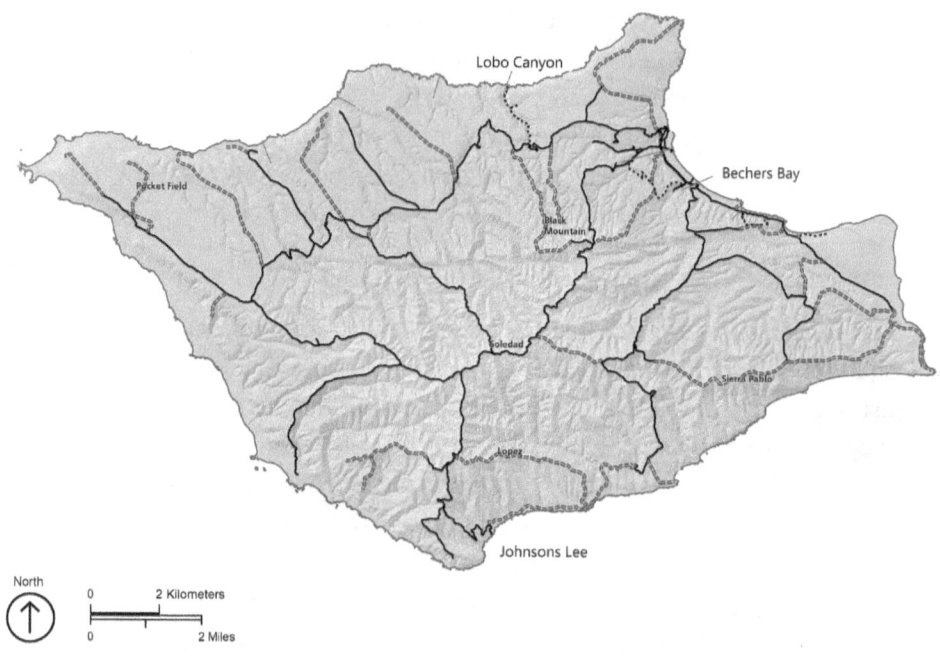

Map 5. Santa Rosa Island. Cartography by R. Rudolph, CINP, and L. Dilsaver.

iments, volcanic rocks, and eolianite deposits. It once boasted trees, but sheep grazing in the nineteenth and early twentieth centuries defoliated most of the island and exposed it to strong, cool winds sweeping southward around Point Conception. This northwestern wind has formed parallel dunes aligned into narrow, northwest-southeast trending ridges and swales interspersed with barren erosion pavement. Point Bennett is a sandy flat at the western tip of the island that supports one of the largest pinniped rookeries in the world.[7] One of the notable features of San Miguel Island is a calcium-carbonate-cemented soil that formed in its semiarid climate. This dissolved calcium carbonate collected and solidified lower in the soil profile where it bound the soil into a hard, cement-like substance called caliche. On San Miguel Island, the deep roots of trees that grew in centuries past became sheathed in calcium carbonate that remained as a hollow form after decomposition or left molds of the roots that filled with windblown sand and calcium carbonate. In both cases,

Fig. 2. Caliche on San Miguel Island was formed by dissolved calcium carbonate that collected around the roots of early vegetation, hardened, and then became exposed when strong winds blew away the softer surrounding material. Photographer and date unknown, CINP Digital Archives.

the caliche "forest" of San Miguel Island was created when strong winds blew away the uncemented sandy soil surrounding the caliche casts and the root sheaths.[8]

Anacapa Island is an exposed Miocene-era volcanic ridge separated into three linear islets—East, Middle, and West Anacapa. The three-part island is approximately five miles in length but is only 1.1 square miles, or nearly 700 acres (283 ha), in area. Anacapa is composed of a gently north-dipping sequence of volcanic rocks overlain by sedimentary deposits. Vertical cliffs surround the island, except for a lowland at the eastern end of Middle Anacapa, an area known today as Frenchy's Cove. East Anacapa is the most uniformly level of the islets and has seen significant human development over the last two centuries.[9]

Santa Barbara Island, smallest of all the eight islands, is slightly over one square mile in area (652 acres or 264 ha). It is located approximately thirty-eight miles west of the Palos Verde peninsula on the mainland. The

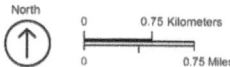

Map 6. Anacapa Island, showing Frenchy's Cove and the Landing Cove. Cartography by R. Rudolph, CINP, and L. Dilsaver.

island is composed primarily of basalts that were deposited underwater. Santa Barbara Island is the eroded top of a submerged seamount exposed most recently in the late Pleistocene. Near its southern edge is the highest elevation at 634-foot Signal Hill. The eastern and western portions of the island slope to broad marine terraces.[10]

THE OCEANIC FEATURES

Fully one half of Channel Islands National Park consists of the waters within one mile (1.6 km) of the five islands. Water circulation around the Channel Islands is complex, resulting from the interaction of large-scale ocean currents, seasonal temperature changes, and diverse marine habitats. The California Current flows south along the west coast of North America, bringing cool water from the northern Pacific Ocean toward the equator. It is strongest during summer. After passing Point Conception, it bifurcates with its eastern flow going toward the shore where it meets a deeper current of warmer water moving poleward, known as the Southern California Countercurrent. The mixture of these waters creates a marine transition zone with a striking temperature gradient and a number of small eddies. Near the Northern Channel Islands, these

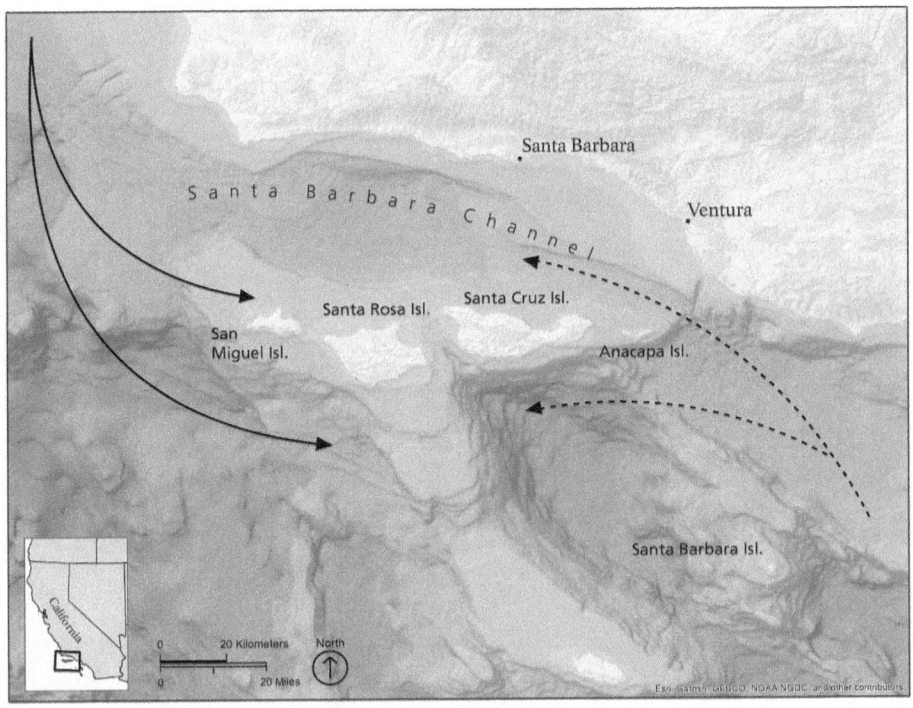

Map 7. The southward flowing California Current and the northward flowing Southern California Countercurrent create a temperature gradient and upwelling that support a great variety of marine life. NOAA, cartography by R. Rudolph, CINP.

currents create the much larger counter-clockwise-flowing Santa Barbara Gyre, which causes upwelling of water and nutrients from greater depths. Northern and southern marine species overlap, creating a transition zone between the Oregonian and Californian marine biogeographic provinces supporting a wealth of marine plants and animals.

A variety of habitats support more biodiversity than the terrestrial portions of the park. They include sandy beaches, rocky shores, kelp forests and rocky reefs, shallow sandy seafloor, and pelagic zones that are home to a diverse group of algae, plants, invertebrates, fish, and marine mammals.[11] Rocky seafloor habitats are often characterized by dense patches of kelp, a form of marine algae. One third of Southern California's kelp

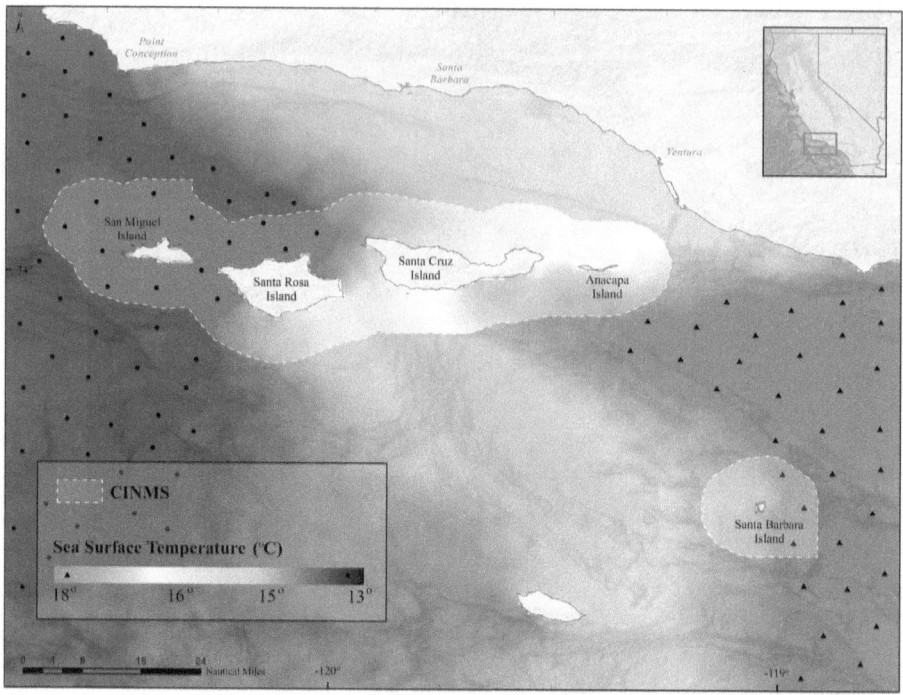

Map 8. The sea temperature gradient from Santa Barbara Island in the south to San Miguel Island in the north. The boundaries around the islands are those of the Channel Islands National Marine Sanctuary. NOAA, cartography by R. Rudolph, CINP.

forests are found within the park and Channel Islands National Marine Sanctuary (CINMS) waters down to depths of more than 100 feet (31 meters). Increasingly frequent El Niño events bring warmer water that suppresses the upwelling and decreases the amount of nutrients in the upper level of the water column.[12]

CLIMATE

Channel Islands National Park has a Mediterranean-type climate. A high-pressure cell over Southern California with descending, dry air over the summer creates desert-like conditions at the surface. In the winter, the cell moves south exposing the islands to a belt of cooler, westerly winds that bring precipitation off the Pacific Ocean. Approximately 95 percent of the rainfall in the Channel Islands occurs between November and April. The marine location of the Channel Islands moderates temperatures with the result that summers are milder and winters warmer than the mainland interior. The moist ocean air also brings an increase in nighttime humidity and frequent fog, especially at San Miguel and Santa Rosa Islands. Because of their wide spatial distribution and concomitant variation in sea temperatures and wind regimes, significant differences in temperature, fog, and rainfall prevail among the islands. Regional rainfall patterns are highly variable and unpredictable. Long periods may occur between storms in a single season, and substantial variation exists in yearly rainfall totals. Extended multiyear droughts punctuated by moderate to wet years are common.[13] Throughout the year, winds are primarily from the northwest, tending to increase throughout daylight hours and becoming easterly at night when the land develops higher air pressure than the sea. Periodically, Southern California experiences high-velocity easterly winds from the mainland, locally called Santa Anas, that dramatically increase temperature and decrease humidity. They are the primary driver of wildfires in Southern California shrublands. Although Santa Ana winds can occur in any month, they predominate from September to December.[14]

One other factor has a powerful effect on the weather and marine conditions around Channel Islands National Park—the periodic appearance of El Niño and La Niña. They are opposite phases of a natural climate pattern across the tropical Pacific Ocean. This shifting pattern is called the El Niño-Southern Oscillation. It can manifest three states—El Niño, Neutral, or La Niña. El Niño (the warm phase locally) and La Niña (the cool phase) lead to significant differences in average ocean temperatures, winds, surface pressure, and rainfall across parts of the tropical Pacific. During El Niño, the surface winds across the entire tropical Pacific are weaker than usual. Ocean temperatures in the eastern tropical Pacific are warmer than average and rainfall is above average. The frequency and intensity of these events has increased since the early twentieth century from 7–20-year intervals to 5–7-year intervals with higher El Niño maximum temperatures. This is significant because higher temperatures contain less nitrogen for kelp growth and reproduction, so the marine forests decline and impact other habitat species.[15]

FLORA AND FAUNA

The California Channel Islands contain extraordinary biological diversity with more unique marine and terrestrial taxa than most temperate islands of the world. Several factors influence the flora and fauna of the islands. First, they are distant from mainland populations and limited in size and resources. Second, climate change has allowed some relict species to survive when their mainland populations succumbed to harsher conditions and more stringent competition. Third, the convergence of cold- and warm-water ocean currents draws deep, nutrient-rich waters toward the surface near the Channel Islands sustaining a high biomass and diversity of phytoplankton, zooplankton, marine algae, and the animals that depend upon them. Fourth, strong air and water temperature gradients exist across the island archipelago driven by these regional currents. Plants and animals to the northwest are exposed to year-round wind and fog while air and water temperatures are higher in the southeastern part of the park. Finally, the separation of the five islands allowed each one to evolve its own subspecies from the mainland species that arrived through time.[16]

The park supports two categories of terrestrial flora—a native one that includes many rare and endemic species and a nonnative one primarily introduced since the 1840s. Because of their isolation, the islands support fewer plant species than grow in areas of similar size on the mainland. About 570 plant taxa are native and 205 are nonnative. Major plant communities include coastal dune, coastal bluff, coastal sage scrub, grasslands, chaparral, island oak woodlands, mixed hardwood woodlands, pine stands, and riparian areas. Mixed broadleaf woodland stands, oak woodlands, and pine stands are scattered through the islands on sheltered slopes and canyons, or on ridges exposed to frequent moist fogs. Smaller but no less significant vegetation communities include coastal dune, Baccharis scrub, caliche scrub, and wetlands.[17]

Some of the island native endemics are relicts, representing species that occurred on the mainland when climates were cooler. Of the 570 native plant taxa known to grow in the park, 64 species, subspecies, or varieties are endemic to the park. Of these, twenty-three are found on only one island. Each of the five islands has endemic species, composing from 4 percent to 10 percent of the total taxa. Many of the islands' endemic species are considered rare, and fifteen are listed federally as threatened or endangered. Three notable arboreal endemics are Island oak (*Quercus tomentella*), Torrey pine (*Pinus torryeana ssp. insularis*) and island ironwood (*Lyonothamnus floribundus ssp. aspleniifolius*).[18]

Because of their isolation and remoteness, the Channel Islands support fewer native animal species than similar habitats on the mainland. Species that reached the islands could fly, swim, raft across the water on debris, or were introduced by aboriginal people. Endemic animal species include the island deer mouse (*Peromyscus maniculatus ssp.*), island night lizard (*Xantusia riversiana*), island fox (*Urocyon littoralis ssp.*), and island scrub-jay (*Aphelocoma insularis*). The islands also provide critical habitat for seabird nesting and marine mammal birthing. A total of sixty-eight native terrestrial vertebrate species have been recorded in the park, including three amphibian, six reptile, two rodent, two carnivore, eleven bat, and forty-eight breeding landbird species. These numbers do not include migratory birds. Over time some vertebrate species evolved into distinct subspecies on the islands. The deer mouse and island fox are recognized as distinct subspecies on their respective islands. Twenty-three endemic terrestrial animals in the park are Channel Island subspecies or races, including eleven landbirds. Relatively little data exists on the terrestrial invertebrate fauna populations on the islands. However, a 1989 survey reported 137 species of insects and arthropods on Anacapa Island alone.[19]

Park ornithologists have recorded thirty species of shorebirds that use the islands. Santa Rosa Island is a particularly important wintering area and stopover point. Nine raptor species live in the park and are primarily seen on Santa Cruz and Santa Rosa Islands. Hawks and owls also occur intermittently on Anacapa, San Miguel, and Santa Barbara Islands, which have limited habitat to support them. Several bird species disappeared from the park during the twentieth century. The Santa Barbara Island population of the Channel Island song sparrow (*Melospiza melodia graminea*) was driven to extinction due to habitat destruction by introduced rabbits, a 1959 fire, and predation by feral cats. Bald eagles (*Haliaeetus leucocephalus*) and peregrine falcons (*Falco peregrinus*) disappeared, but both species are making a comeback due to reintroduction efforts.[20]

Collectively, the islands constitute a major seabird breeding area in the northeastern Pacific with half of the world's population of ashy storm petrels (*Oceanodroma homochroa*) and western gulls (*Larus occidentalis*), 95 percent of the U.S. breeding population of Scripps's murrelets (*Synthliboramphus scrippsi*), and the only major breeding population of California brown pelicans (*Pelecanus occidentalis*) in the western United States. Thirteen species breed on the park's islands, but many more species use its land and waters during migrations and in the winter. Western gulls are the most abundant breeding seabird in the park, with a population estimated at more than fifteen thousand pairs, followed by Cassin's auklet (*Ptychoramphus aleuticus*), brown pelican, Brandt's cormorant (*Phalacrocrax penicillatus*), and Scripps's murrelet.[21]

Of the eleven bat species, three are breeding, year-round residents—Townsend's western big-eared bat (*Corynorhinus townsendii townsendii*), pallid bat (*Antrozous pallidus pacificus*), and California myotis (*Myotis californicus caurinus*). Four other terrestrial mammals live on the islands—five subspecies of Channel Islands deer mouse (*Peromyscus maniculatus ssp.*), the Santa Cruz Island harvest mouse (*Reithrodontomys megalotis santacruzae*), the Island spotted skunk (*Spilogale gracilis amphiala*), and the island fox (*Urocyon littoralis*). The latter is a relative of the mainland gray fox and is the largest native land mammal that lives in the park. Three subspecies live in the park—the San Miguel Island fox (*U. l. littoralis*), Santa Rosa Island fox (*U. l. santarosae*), and Santa Cruz Island fox (*U. l. santacruzae*). Island foxes occur in virtually every habitat on the three islands. They eat a wide variety of plants and animals, are territorial, generally monogamous, and breed once a year. Island foxes are relatively inquisitive and docile and show little fear of humans.[22]

MARINE SPECIES

Channel Islands National Park supports one of the largest and most varied population of pinnipeds (seals and sea lions) in the world. Four species of pinnipeds breed on the islands, while a fifth, the Guadalupe fur seal

(*Arctocephalus townsendii*), hauls out but rarely breeds in the park. The California sea lion (*Zalophus californianus*) is the most common species and has established breeding colonies or haul-outs on all of the islands. Sea lion numbers have generally increased throughout the Channel Islands since the 1970s, though the population has experienced low reproductive success in recent years. Northern elephant seals (*Mirounga angustirostris*) are the second most common species and breed, or haul out, on all of the islands. Elephant seals were virtually extirpated from the park islands due to human hunting but survived on Isla Guadalupe in Mexico. After cessation of the hunting, their numbers in the park increased steadily from the 1930s. Harbor seals (*Phoca vitulina*) are also common and breed on all of the islands. Northern fur seals (*Callorhinus ursinus*) appear only on San Miguel Island. The Guadalupe fur seal, a federal- and state-threatened species, occurs in very small numbers, usually from one to three individuals, and occasionally breed on San Miguel Island. The Steller sea lion (*Eumetopias jubatus*) formerly bred on San Miguel Island and Santa Rosa Island. Steller sea lions have largely abandoned these and other southern haul-outs, perhaps due to warming ocean temperatures favoring California sea lions, although a few individuals have been recently spotted on San Miguel Island.[23]

The varied oceanographic conditions and the transition between them, the diversity of habitats ranging from sheltered bays to exposed open coasts, and the relatively undisturbed location of the islands support a wide variety of invertebrates, fish, sea turtles, seaweed, marine plants, marine mammals, and seabirds. The sea surrounding the islands supports at least 492 species of algae and four species of seagrasses known to occur from among the 673 total species described for all of California. The total number of invertebrate species in southern California may be in excess of five thousand, not including micro-invertebrates. Common and ecologically important invertebrates in the park and in the marine sanctuary that surrounds it include abalone, anemones, barnacles, clams, crabs, mussels, prawns, scallops, sea cucumbers, sea slugs, sea stars, sea urchins, spiny lobster, and squid. More than four hundred species of fish have been documented around the islands, a greater species richness than nearby coastal regions, largely due to the presence of kelp.[24]

Humans Arrive on the Islands

Humans have been present on the Northern Channel Islands for at least thirteen thousand years. The oldest radiocarbon date from the islands is from a femur found by archaeologist Philip Orr in 1959 on Santa Rosa Island. Known as "Arlington Man," the bone dates to that time. Nearly one hundred sites dating from eight thousand to twelve thousand years BP have been found on Santa Cruz, Santa Rosa, and San Miguel islands. Other sites from the precontact and contact periods are well distributed and provide evidence of cultural and technological evolution and maritime adaptations.[25] These early inhabitants of the islands were ancestors of the modern Chumash, first encountered by European mariners in 1542 with the expedition of Juan Rodríguez Cabrillo. At the time of European contact, the Chumash were the most populous of California's hunter-gatherer societies, occupying a large area along the northern half of the Southern California Bight, including much of the Transverse Ranges, and north of Point Conception to the region around Morro Bay. Although mainland Chumash inhabited inland as well as coastal sites, most were oriented to the sea and highly dependent on marine resources. Coastal communities possessed a sophisticated boat-building technology that allowed them to access offshore resources as well as maintain close communication and trade with neighboring Island Chumash. As early as 1,500 years ago, they constructed wooden plank canoes called *tomols* for fishing and harvesting in the seas around the islands. Chumash society was characterized by a high level of political and economic complexity. Some archeologists consider the Chumash, at the advent of the historic period, to have been among the most complex hunter-gatherer societies in the world.[26]

The Island Chumash developed a trading economy based on manufacturing and exporting shell beads that were used as currency and importing mainland products such as grass seeds, acorns, roots, and bows and arrows. They mined the islands' rich deposits of chert to make microblades for drilling holes in the shell beads. Fish bones recovered from archaeological deposits at Daisy Cave on San Miguel Island indicate that "early Channel Islanders fished relatively intensively in a variety of habitats using a number of distinct technologies," including the earliest known uses of boats, hook-and-line technology, and basketry found on the Pacific Coast of North America. The islands' archeological record has produced "some of the oldest evidence of maritime adaptations in the New World," according to archeologist Jon Erlandson, who, with his associates, has dated fish bones found at Daisy Cave as far back as 11,500 years BP.[27] San Miguel, Santa Rosa, and Santa Cruz Islands supported an estimated three thousand Island Chumash in the seventeenth and eighteenth centuries. Anacapa and Santa Barbara Islands, lacking fresh water and other necessary resources, were used seasonally for food gathering and toolmaking.

Early contacts with European mariners began in 1542 and influenced life among the Chumash through the introduction of new trade goods and exotic diseases. However, the decisive impact came with permanent Spanish settlement along the mainland coast after 1769. In 1782, Franciscan priests established Mission San Buenaventura just across the Santa Barbara Channel from the islands. Over the next two decades, all of the remaining Island Chumash were removed to the mainland missions, spurred in part by a major earthquake that strongly affected the islands. By the late 1820s the Northern Channel Islands were vacant.[28]

Exploitation by Europeans and Americans

When presented with an island, a typical Euro-American response has been to put domesticated animals on it. In some cases, this was done to prevent human starvation in the event of a shipwreck. More often it was done to make money. When presented with marine resources that have sustained small populations of natives for centuries, the typical response has been to apply superior technology to maximize harvests and trade. In both cases, significant environmental impacts follow. When the Europeans encountered the Channel Islands, these two processes began. They rapidly intensified once Americans took political control.

Juan Rodríguez Cabrillo, the European discoverer of Alta California, happened upon the Channel Islands in 1542, an encounter that became fateful for Spain and fatal for him. Cabrillo arrived in the Americas in 1520 and participated in conquests by Cortez in Mexico and other conquistadors in Central America. Two decades after Cabrillo's arrival, Spanish

Viceroy Antonio de Mendoza sent two exploratory expeditions out into the Pacific, one to head west and the other north, up the coast. In 1542 Mendoza appointed Cabrillo to take charge of the northern expedition "to discover the coast of New Spain." After making the first landfall in what would become the western United States at modern San Diego, the small fleet explored the Channel Islands, giving a confusing mix of redundant names to most of them. The Spaniards met Chumash on both the islands and the mainland, admired their *tomols*, and soon began fighting with some of them. During a melee, possibly on San Miguel Island, Cabrillo suffered an injury that soon turned gangrenous. He died days later and was buried on one of the islands.[29]

Russian incursions from its new territory in Alaska brought the Spanish into California beginning in 1769. The Russians and their Aleut hunters focused on the teeming populations of otters and fur seals and for the next eight decades marine resources drew the attention of Spanish, Mexican, English, and American seafarers. The Spanish tried to protect their interests, regulate against killing otter pups, and keep out poachers, but they had neither the boats nor the men to patrol the islands. Soon, English and American companies and individuals outfitted their ships with experienced Aleut hunters who, using their watertight kayaks, harvested three thousand to five thousand otter pelts per trip out. Each sea otter pelt could bring up to one hundred dollars in the Chinese market. San Miguel and Santa Barbara Islands had the greatest concentrations of otters. Captain Winship of the *O'Cain* employed enough Aleuts in 1811 to hunt the islands and then sell 3,952 pelts in Canton. Inevitably, by the 1820s, the otter boom waned, and by 1870 only a few men could support themselves from the sea otter trade. By then, scarcity had pushed the price up to $475 on the London market.[30]

In 1821 Mexico gained its independence from Spain and soon thereafter secularized the missions. The new, young country allowed some foreigners to own land if they became citizens and converted to Catholicism. Some Americans deserted from visiting ships and took advantage of the opportunity. Not long thereafter, Yankee frontiersmen came to California by land and joined the profitable hunts upon arrival at the coast. One was George Nidever who was part of the Joseph Walker party that made the first east-to-west crossing by Americans of the Sierra Nevada, in 1833. Nidever, who had trapped beaver, fought Indians, and shot game for food and grizzly bears for fun, soon moved to the Santa Barbara area. There he became a proficient otter hunter in the Channel Islands under the license of Mexican citizen William Goodwin Dana. In the 1850s, Nidever constructed an adobe house on San Miguel Island and participated in early sheep ranching on that island.[31]

Other marine mammals drew the attention of the hunters as well. The Euro-Americans quickly learned of the commercial possibilities of pinnipeds. In the early 1800s, they began to stalk not only fur seals for their rich pelts but elephant seals to render oil from their layers of fat. Fur seals were slaughtered by the thousands in California between 1790 and 1835. Whalers first took elephant seals in the 1880s. When the gray whales were gone in the summer, whalers went after elephant seals for oil. Sea lions supplied several useful products, including a silky skin for luxury items and the sex organs of bulls, which Chinese purchased as a cure for impotence. During the late 1870s, oil from sea lion blubber sold for fifty cents per gallon. Later the Channel Islands became a prime source of sea lions for circuses and zoos around the world.[32]

The Chinese were the first outsiders to develop a commercial abalone fishing industry in the latter half of the nineteenth century. By 1853 they began harvesting abalone to feed their compatriots in San Francisco and from there, started shipping them to the home country. Chinese merchants operating in Santa Barbara's Chinatown formed several companies that enjoyed financial success. Some Chinese built camps on the islands where they would fish from skiffs. The Chinese abalone industry peaked on the four Northern Channel Islands from 1892 to 1895. In 1900, however, local counties passed ordinances that made it illegal to gather abalones from less than 20 feet (6.1 meters) of water. This curtailed the operation in the twentieth century, although Japanese divers replaced the Chinese by securing the abalone from deeper waters.[33]

Two other marine resources drew Americans to the waters around the Channel Islands—fishing and harvesting kelp. The extraordinary richness of the fish species and populations around the Northern Channel Islands, particularly near the Santa Barbara Gyre, sustained a huge fishing fleet based from Santa Barbara to San Diego. Commercial operations dominated fishing prior to World War II. After it ended, recreational fishing underwent a meteoric rise in popularity. Beginning in the late nineteenth century, several companies harvested kelp from around the islands to be used for fertilizer, consumption, and myriad other purposes. Because the plant grows so fast, nobody in those early days thought there would ever be a problem with its distribution and abundance.[34]

During the Mexican period, which ended in 1848 with the Treaty of Guadalupe-Hidalgo, the authorities granted lands on Santa Rosa and Santa Cruz Islands to worthy citizens.[35] Development of island sheep and cattle ranches began in the 1840s. Sheep became more common because they were less susceptible to feed shortages and didn't require as much water to survive. Serious droughts occurred, especially in the 1870s, during which thousands of sheep were slaughtered to prevent overgrazing and consequent starvation. Contemporary chroniclers recorded erosion and denudation that showed that overpopulation of sheep was the norm and some of these periodic kills came too late to protect the islands' native flora. A more insidious threat came from nonnative plants brought in by the animals or in their feed. Many forage plants were imports dating back to the time of Spanish occupation.[36]

The Pre-Park Development of the Individual Islands

Each of the islands played a part in the development of marine and terrestrial industries. While stock raising, fishing, and hunting dominated the uses of the islands, each had its own specific history, predicated on environmental differences and particular human activities. Anacapa Island saw a limited amount of exploitation due to its lack of water and ruggedness, yet a few people and plenty of sheep inhabited it for decades. In 1854 President Franklin Pierce reserved the entire island for lighthouse purposes.[37] During the rest of the century, a variety of entrepreneurs sought ways to make a living from the resources of Anacapa Island. In 1890 the *Ventura Free Press* reported that a party of boaters encountered an encampment of Chinese abalone hunters and fishermen. Egg hunters scaled the steep cliffs where they found seabird eggs to sell in San

Francisco. Perhaps, the oddest excitement was raised in 1873 and again in 1895 with reports of gold on the island in richer deposits than those in California's Mother Lode region. Although some locals on the mainland hurried to buy mining equipment, nothing came of these mythical "strikes."[38]

The wreck of the *Winfield Scott* in 1853 directed attention to the need for a navigational aid on Anacapa Island almost as soon as it had become United States property. Yet the expense of building a lighthouse on the island delayed appropriations for nearly half a century. The Bureau of Lighthouses finally lit the Anacapa Light for the first time on March 25, 1932. It was the last new light station established on the California coast.[39] The Bureau of Lighthouses had awarded a five-year lease to graze sheep on Anacapa Island thirty years earlier as required by law. Ranchers used Frenchy's Cove between West and Middle Anacapa Islets for the main headquarters of their operations. Sheep survived on Anacapa year-round, but marginally. The island is lush after winter rains, but arid and lacking in forage the rest of the year. To improve forage, sheep ranchers introduced exotic grasses. By the 1930s, the sheep had destroyed most of the edible native plants and had begun to eat San Miguel Island milk vetch (*Astragalus miguelensis*). This endemic plant poisoned many of the sheep and ended commercial grazing on the island. Belated recovery of the island's flora then began. Congress ended the Lighthouse Bureau's lease program with Public Law 74–351 on August 27, 1935.[40]

Once Frenchy's Cove lost its function as the sheep manager's center, the man after whom it is named arrived in 1928. Raymond "Frenchy" LeDreau, an immigrant from Brittany, France, took up residence. A well-educated widower, LeDreau lived the life of a hermit, fishing, gathering abalone and lobster, and trading his catches for supplies and liquor with passing boat crews. He was a jovial and gracious character despite his penchant for solitude and hosted many visitors. When the National Park Service came to Anacapa Island in 1939, he so impressed Roger Toll, the lead investigator, that he recommended that LeDreau be given informal caretaker status. He fulfilled this role for the Park Service until an injury forced him to leave the island in the 1950s.[41]

SANTA BARBARA—HISTORY

Santa Barbara Island also had a limited use except for lighthouse purposes. No grants were made during the Spanish and Mexican periods, so the island passed directly to the U.S. government following the Treaty of Guadalupe-Hidalgo. On August 24, 1905, President Theodore Roosevelt issued an executive order that reserved Santa Barbara Island for lighthouse purposes. The order allowed for leases of five-year duration to interested members of the public.[42] On June 16, 1914, Alvin Hyder obtained a five-year lease. He and his two brothers, along with their families, moved out to the island and brought about three hundred sheep the following year. They also introduced hundreds of black-and-white Belgian hares to the island to release, then trap and sell the meat and pelts. At the time, feral cats roamed the island and feasted on the rabbits. The Hyders left by 1922, and in February 1932, Superintendent H. W. Rhodes requested permission to transfer authority for both Anacapa and Santa Barbara Islands to the National Park Service.[43]

SAN MIGUEL ISLAND—HISTORY

San Miguel Island, being the farthest to the west and featuring the harshest climate, saw its vegetation stripped by decades of sheep grazing to the point of being called a huge sand dune. George Nidever purchased a schooner in San Francisco in early 1850 and "bought out the interest of a man by the name of Bruce" who had been grazing sheep on the windswept island. Nidever imported forty-five head of sheep, seventeen head of cattle, two hogs, and seven horses. By 1862 he had six thousand sheep, two hundred head of cattle, one hundred hogs, and thirty-two horses on the island, totals far higher than the carrying capacity of the island.[44]

The unidentified Bruce and then Nidever established sheep ranching on the island, but it was their successors, owners of the Pacific Wool Growing Company who transformed it into an industry. Visitors to the island in the 1870s described a sheep operation out of control as the animals grazed the vegetation down to the sand. U.S. Coast Survey employee and archeologist Paul Schumacher spent four days on the island and wrote about the starving sheep, calling the island "a barren lump of sand."[45]

Ensuing decades saw the lease pass to Captain William G. Waters, who sublet it to Robert L. Brooks and J. R. Moore, and finally into the hands of Brooks alone. Herbert Lester, a wartime friend of Brooks, moved to the island in 1929 as manager and soon made it his goal to acquire the island lease for himself. Lester brought a bride to San Miguel and the two had a pair of daughters. They became a "Swiss Family Robinson" saga for the local and eventually the national media. On November 7, 1934, President Franklin D. Roosevelt transferred the jurisdiction of San Miguel Island to the U.S. Navy. The military stationed three sailors on the island who had nowhere to go but the Lester household. Friction with them led Lester to frustration, an unfortunate woodchopping accident, and deep depression. On June 18, 1942, Lester wrote a note to his wife explaining where searchers could find his body and committed suicide. Lester was buried on the island, his family left for the mainland, and Brooks looked for a way to continue his fading operation.[46] In 1948 the navy revoked the lease and ordered Brooks to remove his sheep from the island within seventy-two hours so that it could be used for practice bombing and guided missile tests. Brooks had to leave over five hundred sheep and four horses behind. A few feral sheep were finally eradicated in the 1960s. The armaments subsequently dumped on or fired at the island by the military made its later use by the National Park Service (NPS) difficult but had less impact on its biotic recovery.[47]

SANTA CRUZ ISLAND—HISTORY

Not only is Santa Cruz Island the largest and most biologically diverse of the islands, it also has the most complicated history. The island had been granted by the Mexican government to prominent *ranchero* Andrés Castillero in 1839. In 1857 he sold it to American immigrant William E. Barron, when sheep were introduced.[48] In 1869 William Barron sold the island to a group of ten San Francisco investors, one of whom was French immigrant Justinian Caire. These men established the Santa Cruz Island Company (SCIC) to manage the island. By 1887 the company, as well as the island, had become the property of Justinian Caire.[49]

Caire's management of Santa Cruz Island was a model of enlightened scientific farming for that period, and he was enormously successful. He developed the island ranch on the principle of diversity, producing a variety of high-quality products ranging from beef cattle and dairy to wine, but sheep constituted the mainstay of his operation. Caire improved the original herd of sheep with purebred Rambouillet Merino, which proliferated rapidly to more than fifty thousand by 1890. He invested heavily in the physical infrastructure of the ranch, and most of the surviving buildings on the island today date from the years of his management.[50]

In 1897 Justinian Caire died shortly after transferring his shares in the Santa Cruz Island Company to his wife Albina. At various times Albina gifted shares in the company to her children. As a result, two Caire sons and two unmarried daughters received more shares than the two married daughters, Amelie and Aglae. In 1911 the Santa Cruz Island Company failed to pay its annual license tax, which led to the forfeiture of their corporate charter. Taking advantage of this forfeiture, Amelie and her husband Edmund Rossi sued for liquidation of the company and distribution of its assets among all of the family members. Edmund was represented in this suit by his brother-in-law, attorney Ambrose Gherini. In 1913 the courts ruled in Edmund's favor, but the rest of the family, except Amelie's married sister Aglae Caire Capuccio, appealed. The subsequent litigation created an emotional rift in the family that never healed. In 1921 the courts finally upheld Edmund Rossi's suit and agreed to divide Justinian Caire's property equally. The Rossi and Capuccio families were given parcels six and seven on East Santa Cruz Island, which was separated from the main mass of the island by the Montañon. This was a useful barrier to place between the hostile factions of the deeply divided family.[51]

In 1926 Aglae Capuccio sold her share to her sister Amelie's children. Daughter Maria and her husband, attorney Ambrose Gherini, made the decision to focus exclusively on sheep.[52] By 1932 the Gherinis had bought out the various interests held by the other children of Amelie Rossi.[53] Ambrose Gherini maintained the ranch as a supplement to his principal business, which remained law. When Ambrose Gherini was no longer able to manage the ranch himself, his older son, Pier Gherini, took over. Later, Francis Gherini, Pier's younger brother, took over from him.

Following the partition of the Caire family's property in 1925, all of the area west of the Montañon, including the isthmus, remained with Justinian

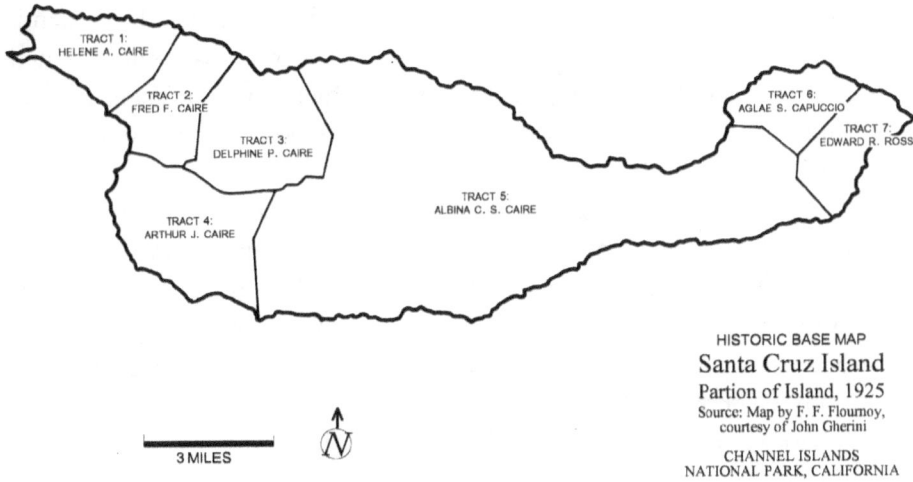

Map 9. The division of Caire's Santa Cruz Island estate resulted in seven distinct tracts. The two easternmost tracts, bordered by the Montañon, became known as East Santa Cruz Island. It was owned later by the Gherini family and acquired by the NPS in 1997. Provided by John Gherini.

Caire's widow, Albina, her two sons and two unmarried daughters. These five parcels comprised 90 percent of the island's total area and included the Central Valley with the Main Ranch complex. In 1937 the surviving heirs sold all of these parcels as a single unit to Los Angeles businessman Edwin L. Stanton, who transformed the old Caire ranch into a successful beef cattle operation.[54]

SANTA ROSA ISLAND—HISTORY

Like Santa Cruz Island, Santa Rosa was also given as a land grant, to brothers Carlos and Jose Antonio Carrillo in 1839. Four years later, they sold their grant to American immigrants John C. Jones and Alpheus B. Thompson, who had both married daughters of Carlos Carrillo. The Americans developed the earliest commercial livestock operation on Santa Rosa, importing cattle, sheep, and horses in 1844. These were the first exotic animals known to have been introduced to the island.[55] Thomas Wallace More and his brothers incrementally purchased livestock and assets starting in 1858, and by 1870 they had legal control of the island. During the More years on Santa Rosa Island, sheep stocking rates reached sixty thousand in a given year. After nearly a half-century of sheep grazing under the Mores, the environmental degradation of Santa Rosa Island had become obvious.[56]

It was within this context that Walter Vail first considered taking over the debt-ridden assets of the More family at the turn of the twentieth century. Vail was already an established cattleman in the rural west, and he recognized that Santa Rosa Island held economic potential if managed correctly. He bought the island from the failing More estate in 1901. Over the ensuing years, he and his business partner, John Vickers, phased out the Mores' sheep and replaced them with high-quality beef cattle. The last of the now-feral sheep were rounded up and slaughtered in the 1950s. When Walter Vail died in a streetcar accident in 1906, his family assumed primary responsibility for the cattle operation on Santa Rosa Island over the next two generations. Walter Vail's eldest son, Nathan Russell (commonly known as "N.R."), managed the island ranch from 1908 until his death in 1943. N.R.'s younger brother, Ed, then took over as ranch manager until 1961, when N.R.'s son Al Vail took over. His twin brother, Russ Vail, managed the business side of the operation from a small office in Santa Barbara. The Vickers family heirs remained silent partners in the Vail & Vickers Company.[57] The Vails improved Santa Rosa Island's forage and operated a scientifically informed grazing operation that became recognized around the country for its enlightened range management.[58]

ALIEN SPECIES

Islands generally are vulnerable to invasion of nonnative plants. In the case of Channel Islands National Park, many nonnative species became established and spread rapidly on the islands during the past 150 years. About 197 taxa not native to California have been introduced into the park islands since European contact. In addition, some species native to the California mainland have been introduced to the islands. All of the islands have nonnative species, ranging from 38 species on Santa Barbara to about 170 species on Santa Cruz. Eleven of the latter's 88 plant families and 82 of its 348 plant genera are nonnative taxa. These nonnative species have changed the overall composition and ground cover of many of the vegetation communities and now cover approximately two-thirds of the park's land surface.[59] Currently, the most extensive vegetation communities on the islands are nonnative grassland and coastal sage scrub with significant areas of chaparral on Santa Cruz and Santa Rosa Islands.

In general, the understories of the native scrub communities are invaded by a variety of annual and perennial nonnative grasses and herbs. Annual grasses have spread over all of the islands and are the most widespread nonnatives. Between 35 percent and 75 percent of each island is covered by nonnative grasslands dominated by Mediterranean annual grasses, including brome (*Bromus*), barley (*Hordeum*), fescue (*Vulpia*), and oats (*Avena*). Five species of perennial iceplant (*Carpobrotus edulis, C. chilense, Malephora crocea, Mesembryanthemum crystallinum,* and *M. nodiflorum*) are common and cover large areas of Santa Barbara, East Anacapa, and San Miguel Islands in carpet-like mats. Two ice plant species are hard to replace because they accumulate salt in their tissue that is released into the soil upon their death. The salt level of the soil becomes too high to be tolerated by many other plants, including most of the native species. Several opportunistic exotic species, including bull thistle (*Cirsium vulgare*), Russian thistle (*Salsola iberica*), and spiny cocklebur (*Xanthium spinosum*), rapidly colonize available habitat and form dense monotypic stands, completely excluding native island species.[60]

Several slow-spreading weed species also grow on the islands, including black mustard (*Brassica nigra*), tamarisk (*Tamarix aphylla*), kikuyu grass (*Pennisetum clandestinum*), rice grass (*Piptatherum miliacea*), Bermuda grass (*Cynodon dactylon*), and tall fescue (*Festuca arundinacea*). These species are very persistent once they become established and can form dense populations. Their seeds are spread through animal feces, mud on vehicle tires, or animals' feet. Kikuyu grass is particularly aggressive and has taken over large areas of wetlands and riparian banks on Santa Cruz. Among the most noticeable to visitors are the thick stands of fennel (*Foeniculum vulgare*), particularly on Santa Cruz Island along Cañada del Puerto Creek from Prisoners Harbor toward the Main Ranch on the Nature Conservancy property and from the Scorpion anchorage area.[61]

Human enterprise had a dramatic impact on the flora of Santa Barbara Island. Several unique plant species, such as Santa Cruz Island buckwheat (*Eriogonum arborescens*), Creamcups (*Platystemon californicus*), and a species of *Dudleya*, suffered grazing by sheep and feral rabbits to the brink of extinction. According to botanist Ralph Philbrick, between 1940 and 1970 the native California seablite (*Suaeda californica*), giant coreopsis (*Coreopsis gigantea*), and others have been drastically reduced and largely replaced by the invasive exotic ice plant (*Mesembryanthemum crystallinum*) and annual grasses dominated by barley grass *Hordeum* and wild oats *Avena*.[62]

A Monumental Task 2

The National Park Service considered the idea of making Santa Cruz Island a national park as early as 1924, but Director Stephen Mather felt that the island would be more appropriate as a state park.[1] In 1928 the state of California seriously entertained this idea when its newly formed state park commission, headed by landscape architect Frederick Law Olmsted Jr., included Santa Cruz Island among its 320 proposed units.[2] However, the commission did not include the island in its final proposal and the stock market crash less than a year later eliminated any further public investment in parks.

The issue came up once more four years later, this time in connection with the five government-owned islands—San Clemente, San Nicolas, Anacapa, Santa Barbara, and San Miguel. The three largest islands—Santa Catalina, Santa Cruz, and Santa Rosa—were all privately owned. At that time, all of the government islands were administered by the Bureau of Lighthouses. San Clemente, San Nicolas, and San Miguel were also leased to private ranchers for livestock grazing. In June 1932, the Commissioner of Lighthouses, George R. Putnam, notified NPS director Horace Albright that his bureau wanted to transfer some of its California property and wondered if the NPS would be interested in taking over some of the islands to administer as parks. Putnam believed that the only islands that might interest the Park Service were San Clemente, San Nicolas, and San Miguel, since Anacapa and Santa Barbara Islands comprised fewer than 1,000 acres each.[3]

Director Albright repeated Stephen Mather's recommendation that the islands would be more appropriate as state parks. In October 1932, he informed William Colby of the California State Conservation Commission of Putnam's offer and subsequent agreement to extend this offer to the state. Although Albright did not think the islands were nationally significant, he warned that something would have to be done relatively soon to ensure such protection, since "[the people at the Lighthouse Service] tell us that they are being pressed quite hard by parties interested in establishing private hunting clubs on the islands and other groups who are interested in exploiting the islands for gas and oil purposes."[4]

The Toll Report

By January 1933, the NPS and state park officials had organized a site inspection. Roger Toll, superintendent of Yellowstone National Park and the agency's primary field inspector of proposed parks, and Thomas Vint, chief landscape architect from the San Francisco field office, represented the Park Service. W. A. S. Foster, assistant chief of the state park system, represented the state. The Lighthouse Service provided transportation, with H. W. Rhodes, superintendent of lighthouses, playing host. Roger Toll, who preceded his companions to Southern California by a few days, met with park supporters on January 14 in Santa Barbara. Many of the participants had extensive first-hand knowledge of the islands and were able to provide Toll important information. They included Dr. David Banks Rogers, archeologist and director of the Santa Barbara Museum of Natural History (SBMNH), who had spent years studying and collecting artifacts from the Northern Channel Islands; Frank Flournoy, a civil engineer who had conducted the court-appointed topographical survey of Santa Cruz Island for the partition of the Caire family estate in 1923–24; and Earle Ovington, a pioneer aviator who had settled in Santa Barbara and possessed an intimate bird's-eye knowledge of the islands.

On January 25, Toll and his party crossed the Santa Barbara Channel to San Miguel Island and proceeded to steam east and south over the next three days, viewing each of the islands in succession except distant San Nicolas. The group put ashore at Santa Cruz, Anacapa, San Clemente, and Santa Catalina Islands. Santa Barbara was believed to be "nothing much more than a big rock," according to Foster. Santa Rosa, surprisingly, drew little comment. Toll had nothing to say about it, while Foster acknowledged that it possessed good pasturage but was not suitable as a park. The islands that elicited the greatest interest from all members of the expedition were privately owned Santa Cruz and Santa Catalina. Both Toll and Foster seemed to agree that the government islands would only be desirable in conjunction with one or more of these larger islands but by themselves did not warrant designation as a park or monument.[5]

W. A. S. Foster wrote up his final report shortly after returning, and his conclusions reflected the immediate impressions that expedition members had formed on the trip without the benefit of further consideration or research. He was convinced that a park could not be justified without first acquiring one of the big islands to anchor it, preferably Santa Cruz Island, which he believed to be the most interesting of all the islands after Santa Catalina. Of the other big islands, Santa Rosa had failed to attract anyone's attention, while San Clemente was dismissed out of hand for its desolation and comparative remoteness. Unless Santa Cruz Island could be acquired, or some other resource possessing similar significance, Foster believed there was little reason to pursue the proposal any further. Thomas Vint corroborated that this was the consensus of the group at the conclusion of the expedition, later writing, "We found that the islands now owned by the Government are quite bleak and barren in their general aspect, and that the islands themselves have no outstanding value to warrant National Park or National Monument use."[6] However, both Vint and Toll decided to consult scientific experts on the islands before Toll wrote up the final report for the NPS delegation. By that time, Toll's recommendation concerning establishment of a park or monument in the Channel Islands, although less than enthusiastic, was far more positive than Foster's.

One of the first scientists to be consulted by Toll and Vint was Dr. William A. Setchell, chair of the department of botany at the University of California, Berkeley (UCB). Setchell and other members of his department were already well aware of the Channel Islands, and the chairman responded with enthusiasm to the idea of protecting the islands as a park or monument.[7] He acknowledged landscape architect Vint's assessment of the barren and non-picturesque character of the islands, especially the smaller government-owned islands, but insisted that they possessed considerable biological significance because much of the terrestrial flora was unique to these islands. This was particularly the case of the larger islands, such as Santa Cruz. Setchell believed that this uniqueness represented an earlier stage of plant evolution that was preserved on the islands by their comparative isolation from mainland influences and wrote, "The Channel Islands represent a surviving relic of the flora of California as it probably existed in late Tertiary times." This relictual island endemism had been observed by many other California botanists. The islands also supported examples of autochthonous (indigenous) endemism, representing the ongoing but divergent evolution of populations long separated from a source species.[8]

William Setchell was even more excited about the marine resources of the Channel Islands. This may be why Vint, who saw greater park potential in the watery portion of the islands than the terrestrial, contacted him. Among Setchell's professional interests was marine botany. He had written his graduate thesis on kelp, and he was intimately familiar with the large kelp beds that grew offshore of the islands.[9] He considered these submarine masses of vegetation to have "no counterparts elsewhere in the Northern Hemisphere." Not only were these submarine forests of giant kelp noteworthy in themselves, but they supported an abundance of other animal and plant life. Setchell recommended that they be protected in order to limit public access and prevent private exploitation. He noted that the Channel Islands kelp beds had already been harvested during World War I for the production of nitrates and acetones needed in the war effort, and correctly predicted that the practice would resume.

Setchell contacted a colleague at UCB, wildlife biologist Joseph Grinnell, to ask his opinion about the significance of the islands in terms of their fauna. Grinnell was director of the university's Museum of Vertebrate Zoology and already had close ties with the National Park Service. Assistant director of the NPS Branch of Research and Education Harold C. Bryant, at that time, had been his student.[10] Grinnell strongly agreed that the islands should be protected as a national park or monument. He described the abundant fauna that the islands supported as rare or endemic species including island foxes, several species of landbirds, and the island night lizard. Grinnell also noted that many marine mammals and pelagic birds depended on the islands for critical habitat. He considered all of these populations and endemic species at risk from adverse human impacts and recommended that conservation measures be taken to protect them.[11]

Vint and Toll also sought the opinion of archeologists and historians on the cultural significance of the islands. Although the full significance of the Channel Islands' 13,000-year record of human occupation was not yet known, many scholars already suspected the value of these resources based on the density and quality of archeological deposits. Speaking of Santa Cruz Island, David Banks Rogers informed Toll that "scientifically it is a tremendous value, as it once supported a teeming prehistoric population of sea-faring people whose origin is shrouded in mystery."[12]

This and other reports from scholars familiar with the Channel Islands finally persuaded Vint and Toll that the islands should become a national park or monument. In his final report, Roger Toll recommended that the proposed park should be oriented primarily toward the waters surrounding the islands rather than the islands themselves. "The value of such a project would not be dependent upon the scenery of the islands nor their land features, but primarily upon the interest and value of the marine features, including plant and animal life."[13] It would be, in Toll's words, an oceanic national park. No other such park yet existed within the national park system.

Toll's enthusiasm for the proposed park, however, was dampened by the fact that the three largest and most significant of the islands were privately owned and unavailable to be included in a park. However, he suggested, "It seems quite possible either now or at some future time to develop an area of remarkable interest in connection with the Channel Islands, using as a starting point the islands that are now owned by the Government and adding in the future such parts of the privately owned islands as might be made available."[14]

Channel Islands National Monument

Despite Roger Toll's endorsement of the proposed monument, the Park Service failed to take any action for another four years. In the interim, the Lighthouse Service went ahead with its plans to dispose of excess property by transferring San Nicolas Island to the U.S. Navy in January 1933, followed by San Clemente and San Miguel Islands in November 1934. Only tiny Anacapa and Santa Barbara Islands remained within the authority of the Department of Commerce. The Lighthouse Service still had active aids to navigation on both of these islands and even maintained a small residential compound on East Anacapa, but it needed only a portion of the island land area for these purposes and had no interest in keeping the rest. Both islands were too small to be of use to the navy but remained attractive to various private interests. Before offering the islands up for private sale, however, the Department of Commerce repeated its earlier offer to transfer the islands to the NPS, notifying Secretary of the Interior Harold Ickes by letter, dated February 5, 1937.

Still unsure about the value of this offer, despite Roger Toll's 1933 report, the Park Service arranged another site visit. This time Assistant Director Harold Bryant was sent from the Washington DC office. Bryant seemed an appropriate choice, given his past experience in California and his close acquaintance with scientists familiar with the Channel Islands. Bryant made a one-day excursion to the islands on September 20, 1937, accompanied by Deputy Chief Forester Lawrence F. Cook and Acting Assistant Regional Director Bernard F. Manbey from the Park Service's regional office in San Francisco. The park men rode a coast guard ship to Santa Cruz Island and met with Edwin L. Stanton who had just bought all but the eastern end of Santa Cruz Island a few months earlier. Bryant made it clear that he believed Santa Cruz Island ought to be managed by the NPS, and he was disappointed when Stanton assured him he was not interested in selling and intended to continue raising sheep.[15] Thereafter, the expedition departed Santa Cruz Island and steamed to Anacapa and Santa Barbara Islands to view them through binoculars from the deck of the coast guard ship.[16]

The report that Harold Bryant submitted a few months later contained little information that Toll's report had not provided. However, Bryant included a manuscript and accompanying letter of support from Dr. Theodore D. A. Cockerell, a biologist from the University of Colorado who was working on a synthesis of the biological resources of the Channel Islands.[17] Cockerell's manuscript appears to have been the principal source of information that was later used to support the establishment of the monument. Like the other scientists whom Toll and Vint had consulted in 1933, Cockerell pointed to the high number of endemic species occurring on the islands and emphasized the scientific significance of this phenomenon. He described both autochthonous and relictual endemics and attributed their occurrence to past sea-level rise, which had cut the islands off from the mainland sometime during the late Pleistocene epoch. Geologists later rejected this idea of an ancient peninsula extending from the mainland, but recognized that the northern islands were once united as the single large island Santarosae. Cockerell also noted that the geologic record preserves evidence of a much different climate than the present one, containing fossils of woody flora such as Douglas fir (*Pseudotsuga menziesii*) and Gowen cypress (*Cupressus goveniana*) that are now found further north.

The information supplied by Cockerell supported Harold Bryant's conclusion that the principal significance of the Lighthouse Service's remaining Channel Islands lay in their value to science. He agreed with Cockerell and the other scientists that the vulnerability of the islands' natural resources to private spoliation justified protection, the same assessment offered by Roger Toll four years earlier.[18] His report differed from Toll's by its curious failure to mention marine resources.[19] Bryant was the only one in the inspection party to recommend that the Park Service accept Anacapa and Santa Barbara Islands from the Lighthouse Service, but he suggested that they remain undeveloped and be used solely for scientific research.[20] Bryant, like Toll before him, held out hope that the monument might eventually grow beyond these two islands and become more than an undeveloped nature reserve. He clearly was thinking of Santa Cruz Island, which he was careful to note "would make an ideal national park."[21]

Even before Bryant's final report was submitted, NPS director Arno Cammerer met with Secretary Ickes on October 20, 1937, to discuss, among other matters, a proposed Channel Islands National Monument. Using the Antiquities Act of 1906, the president could unilaterally proclaim a national monument. That act originally was intended to protect archeological resources from the depredations of amateur collectors and pothunters. In its final form, however, it was broad enough to allow the protection of both cultural and natural resources possessing scientific significance. Many of the nation's early monuments were proclaimed on the basis of unique natural features, including Devils Tower, Petrified Forest, Lassen Peak, Muir Woods, and Grand Canyon, all of which were established in the first two years of the act.[22] The Antiquities Act was not intended to protect scenic or recreational values, even though NPS administration meant that visitors would have to be allowed access in order to fulfill the agency's legal mandate.[23]

Ickes approved the proposal, instructing Cammerer's office to draft a proclamation for the president's signature.[24] Presidential Proclamation No. 2281 establishing the eighty-fifth national monument was signed by Franklin Roosevelt on April 26, 1938. The monument included only Santa Barbara and Anacapa Islands, encompassing approximately nine-tenths of the former (581.76 out of 652 acres) and just over three-fourths of the latter (538.22 out of approximately 700 acres total). The remaining land area was retained by the Lighthouse Service for its aids to navigation. The statement identifying the monument's significance and purpose was as brief as it was problematic: "Whereas certain public islands lying off the coast of Southern California contain fossils of Pleistocene elephants and ancient trees, and furnish noteworthy examples of ancient volcanism, deposition, and active sea erosion, and have situated thereon various other objects of geological and scientific interest."[25]

No mention is made of the unique and vulnerable biological resources that inspired the Park Service's initial support for the monument. Only geologic processes are described. Confusing also is the reference to "fossils of Pleistocene elephants and ancient trees," neither of which were found on the two monument islands. This confusion may have resulted from an overly-hasty reading of Harold Bryant's report by Washington DC staff, who were unfamiliar with the islands and failed to appreciate the differences between them. There were other problems as well. The monument boundaries began at the "high-water line" and included no marine resources despite Roger Toll's recommendation. This omission suggests that the *Bryant Report* may have been the only source consulted by the NPS staff who drafted the proclamation. The new boundaries failed to include much of the marine mammal haul-out sites, which made it impossible for the Park Service to protect these animals from poachers, a problem that soon became apparent.

Managing the Monument

Faced with the tiny size of the new monument, the NPS immediately sought to increase its area. In August 1938, E. K. Burlew, acting secretary of the interior, asked the secretary of the navy whether he would transfer San Miguel Island to the NPS or at least cooperate with the agency in managing it. The secretary of the navy, however, responded that his service wished to keep San Miguel, even though it had no present use for the island and was, in fact, leasing it to a sheep rancher. The navy claimed that it was providing adequate protection for the "scientific values" found there, but Interior officials were alarmed to learn that the navy was allowing livestock to graze on this fragile landscape. Believing that this was a recent development, they were highly critical of the navy for authorizing the practice.[26]

On December 2, 1938, Acting Secretary of the Interior Harry Slattery wrote to the secretary of the navy requesting that sheep grazing on San Miguel Island cease and that the island with its adjacent offshore rocks "remain free from all but scientific and emergency use." He also repeated Interior's request that San Miguel Island be transferred to the Park Service if the navy should no longer need it for national defense purposes.[27] Acting Secretary of the Navy William Leahy responded a few weeks later, explaining that the navy had inherited an existing grazing lease from the Lighthouse Service when it obtained the island in 1934. The navy chose to renew this lease, and would continue to do so, but required its lessee to gradually reduce his stocking rate. Leahy was baffled by Secretary Slattery's suggestion that these practices would, in a short time, destroy the island's natural ecology, since sheep grazing had been introduced nearly one hundred years earlier by George Nidever. According to records possessed by the navy, San Miguel had been covered with dense brush up to that time, but the increase in Nidever's stock eventually denuded it. Continuation of grazing over subsequent years had kept island vegetation in a depauperate state up to the present time. Secretary Leahy closed his correspondence to Slattery with a request for the Interior's opinion on the impact of continued grazing in light of this information. The remark was a poignant reminder that the NPS needed to know more about the Channel Islands if it was to manage them responsibly and avoid further embarrassment in its dealings with the navy.[28] Within a matter of weeks, Director Arno Cammerer instructed his regional office in San Francisco to organize a detailed inspection of Channel Islands National Monument as well as San Miguel Island.[29]

THE FIRST SUMNER REPORT

The Park Service's first official inspection of the new monument was conducted by two wildlife biologists from San Francisco, E. Lowell Sumner Jr. from the NPS regional office, and Richard M. Bond from the Soil Conservation Service. The expedition left San Pedro on April 14 and spent two days each on Santa Barbara, Anacapa, and San Miguel Islands.[30] Sumner inventoried plant and animal species on the three islands and later compared his data with historical inventories in order to learn how much had changed over the last century with the introduction of exotic species and loss or diminishment of native ones. As brief as the expedition was, Sumner's survey was remarkably comprehensive and provided the Park Service with essential baseline data for the monument islands. Sumner called attention to key resources that were particularly significant or vulnerable, such as the breeding colony of brown pelicans (*Pelecanus occidentalis californicus*) on Anacapa Island, the endemic Channel Islands song sparrow (*Melospiza melodia graminea*), and the high number of endemic plant species on all of the islands.[31] These observations helped shape many of the park's future management priorities.

Sumner also identified significant problems or threats to the islands. Livestock grazing had denuded island vegetation, resulting in the erosion of topsoil, documented by Richard Bond, and the destruction of habitat for many native species. In describing the much-reduced song sparrow habitat on Santa Barbara Island, for example, Sumner quoted a historical account from 1890 that described the island as covered in "long coarse grass that grows thick and tangled everywhere, making walking difficult."[32] The song sparrow was extremely abundant in this dense vegetative cover,

Fig. 3. This aerial photograph taken by the U.S. Navy in the late 1960s shows that San Miguel Island remained heavily altered by the sheep removed two decades earlier and then extensively covered by windblown sand. CINP Digital Archives.

which contrasted markedly from the relatively sparse cover evident during Sumner's inspection. Indeed, further reduction in native vegetation contributed to the extinction of the song sparrow by 1958. The most severe changes observed by Sumner and Bond had occurred on San Miguel Island, where historic grazing rates had been the most intense. Richard Bond wrote, "Exposed to the destructive force of accelerated run-off and gale-like winds, the sandy soil, stripped of its vegetation and deprived of its humus, gives the impression of disintegrating almost everywhere."[33]

The scientists submitted two versions of the *Sumner Report*. The first, which was submitted to the NPS director on July 28, 1939, was authored entirely by Sumner and intended primarily for internal use. It included a list of practical recommendations at the end of each section meant for guidance of park administrators and resource managers. The second version of the report was slightly longer and included additional sections on soil conditions authored by Richard Bond. It omitted most of Sumner's management recommendations, suggesting that it may have been intended for a wider audience.[34] Sumner's recommendations concerning the monument islands included the following main points: (1) Place the monument under the administration of one of the existing national parks on the mainland; (2) secure the assistance of the Coast Guard Service and the State Division of Fish and Game in patrolling the islands and adjacent waters; (3) post the island, informing visitors that it was a national monument and thus discouraging egg collecting and the slaughter of marine mammals; (4) remove or exterminate exotic house cats and Belgian hares on Santa Barbara Island; and (5) appoint hermit Raymond "Frenchy" LeDreau as custodian or caretaker on Anacapa Island and allow him to continue living there.[35]

Although San Miguel Island was not part of the monument, Sumner also included recommendations for its management. This island attracted Sumner's greatest interest. After noting the various reasons for its significance to science and scholarship, he observed that "the custodianship of the Federal Government certainly should include a conscientious attempt to check further destruction and restore it as nearly as possible to its original productive condition."[36] Sumner recommended a restoration program that would involve successive plantings of native species following the removal of all sheep. Herbert Lester was grazing about 1,100 head at that time.[37]

Victor Cahalane, the acting chief of the Park Service's wildlife division, quoted extensively from Sumner's report in an August 14 memo for the NPS director in Washington DC.[38] Repeating most of Sumner's recommendations, Cahalane emphasized the need for greater protection of the islands' marine mammals and nesting sea birds and the extermination of exotic species like cats. Sumner's recommendations became the monument's de facto first resource management plan. His report, with its detailed management guidelines, represented an important precedent for future management.[39]

Responding to Cahalane's memo, Acting Regional Director Colonel John White instructed Eivind Scoyen, superintendent of Sequoia National

Park, to assume administration of Channel Islands.⁴⁰ Management by Sequoia's superintendent followed the wishes of President Roosevelt whose interest in the islands had been spurred by his Smithsonian friends and who wished to avoid congressional inquiries about funding the new monument.⁴¹ Although the arrangement was meant to be a temporary expedient, Channel Islands National Monument remained under the nominal authority of Sequoia until 1957. The regional office proposed that an annual budget of $515 be allocated for the purpose of administering the monument. This small sum was designed to support only a minimal Park Service presence to protect essential resources. Small though it was, this budget was not approved until the 1941 fiscal year.⁴²

Probably the leading concern for NPS managers during the monument's first decade was protecting its wildlife from destruction by visiting fishermen, poachers, and collectors. The slaughter of marine mammals was of great concern to park managers. It was still common at that time to fire on the animals from passing boats or hunt them on shore. Commercial fishermen considered sea lions a nuisance, believing that they competed for economically valuable fish or fouled nets. The California Department of Fish and Game (CDFG) was authorized to cull sea lion populations periodically to support commercial fishing interests. Some poachers still hunted the animals, while others simply killed them for fun. Lowell Sumner encountered a party of hunters on Santa Barbara Island during his 1939 inspection. Realizing that they had come ashore to shoot the marine mammals, he warned the men that this was not permitted within the boundaries of a national monument. The men professed ignorance and departed without complaint. Sumner reasoned that signage might stop the shooting and the common practice of raiding sea bird nests for eggs. Numerous nesting colonies of sea birds made both of the monument islands popular destinations for gathering eggs. Anacapa's greater accessibility to the mainland made it more vulnerable, but Santa Barbara Island was also targeted. Most of these eggs were probably taken for food, but some were also gathered for private collections or sold to museums. Sumner mentioned that bald eagles were particularly susceptible to this practice.

Effective deterrence would require active patrols and, ideally, a physical presence on the islands. The Park Service had neither the staff nor the equipment to conduct patrols, so it sought assistance from other agencies that did have these resources. On June 29, 1939, Regional Director Frank Kittredge wrote to Herbert C. Davis, the head of the CDFG, explaining the situation and asking whether his agency could provide support. Kittredge noted that he had received reports, some from CDFG sources, that shootings were occurring on the monument islands and might be expected to continue if something was not done to intervene.[43] Davis agreed to provide the patrols, but in return, he asked that the Park Service, in the interest of reciprocity, allow his agency to conduct periodic culling of the sea lion herds within monument boundaries. Davis reminded Kittredge that the state had a responsibility to "manage the size of the herds so that they will be preserved for their aesthetic value, but not allowed to multiply to where they are an unnecessary predator on our commercial and game fishes."[44]

This offer underlined how different the values of the NPS and the CDFG were regarding wildlife and suggested that the state would be a questionable ally in the protection of marine mammals. Nevertheless, Kittredge referred the offer to Lowell Sumner, who was concerned that this might set a precedent for allowing outside agencies to manage wildlife within national park units, a practice that the NPS had consistently opposed up to that time.[45] In the end, Sumner referred the decision up the chain-of-command to Washington DC, where the proposal was rejected. The Washington office not only agreed with Sumner's concern over precedent, it also noted that the state's policy was under criticism, and the NPS did not want to be implicated in a controversial practice that might soon be rejected.[46]

The Park Service also sought assistance from the U.S. Coast Guard. Sumner strongly recommended this alternative in his report and later followed up in Washington DC.[47] It was an obvious suggestion in most respects, since the coast guard already conducted sea patrols, had a good working relationship with the Park Service in the Channel Islands, and now shared the two monument islands with the NPS after its merger with the Lighthouse Service in 1939. In mid-March 1940, Captain S. V. Parker, commander of the coast guard's San Francisco District, contacted the NPS regional office in that city to offer his assistance. The regional director responded by outlining a minimal patrol of monthly aircraft overflights, supported by surface vessels as needed.[48] Although this agreement remained in effect until the outbreak of World War II, by early 1941 Lowell Sumner wrote that the park's minimum patrol requirements still needed to be met.[49]

Another management priority identified by the *Sumner Report* was exotic species. Sumner had described the devastating effects that introduced mammals had on the island ecosystems. Sheep had caused most of the damage to the native vegetation on all of the islands.[50] On Santa Barbara Island, grazing had ceased by about 1930, and native vegetation was beginning to recover, but introduced Belgian hares and domestic cats were still causing considerable damage.[51] The hares fed on native plants such as the giant coreopsis (*Coreopsis gigantea*) and might have posed a more significant threat if not for predation on them by the cats.[52] However, the cats preyed on more than just rabbits. They also hunted sea birds that used Santa Barbara Island as nesting habitat. By the time Sumner visited the island in 1939, historic nesting populations of Cassin's auklet (*Ptychoramphus aleuticus*) and Scripps's murrelet (*Synthliboramphus scrippsi*, formerly known as Xantus's murrelet) had been entirely eliminated.

Sumner recommended that the cats be eliminated as soon as possible, a sentiment that was shared by Victor Cahalane.[53] Neither of the scientists discussed the Belgian hares, which were not yet an urgent problem due to predatory cats. They may not have contemplated what might happen once predation pressure from cats was removed. Sumner consulted with various experts at the UCB and CDFG to determine how the cats might be controlled. He proposed several potential treatments for consideration by the Washington office. These included biological control with the introduction of five or six male bobcats or a similar number of male coyotes. Under this scenario, the introduced predators would harass and kill the domestic cats, then eventually die off themselves without being able to reproduce and become naturalized on the island. Whatever the likelihood of success, the risks involved seemed considerable, and Cahalane rejected this option. Sumner also proposed using poisoned bait. This had the advantage of being target specific and unlikely to result in unforeseen collateral damage. Sumner's only hesitation was over a matter of principle, since the use of poison, he pointed out, was "contrary to the usual policy of this service."[54] No attempt at controlling exotic species would be made until the park could place staff on the islands themselves.

GATHERING INTEREST

The single greatest problem facing the NPS in the administration of Channel Island National Monument was not having a physical presence on the islands or any practical way for NPS staff to access them on a regular basis. This handicap prevented the agency from effectively addressing any of Sumner's management concerns. His recommendation to grant custodian authority to Raymond "Frenchy" LeDreau was clearly not an adequate solution and did nothing to address management of Santa Barbara.[55] The young monument needed a dedicated NPS ranger and, if possible, a boat to provide transportation and marine patrols. Regional Director Kittredge indicated as much in a memo to Eivind Scoyen of Sequoia not long after the superintendent assumed authority for the monument. His highest priority was placing a ranger for at least part of the year on Santa Barbara Island, where the threat from sea lion poachers was greatest. Although Kittredge did not mention it, an on-site ranger would also be able to implement resource management objectives such as control of the exotic cats. Superintendent Scoyen, however, had a low opinion of the new monument and was reluctant to commit any resources to it without a dedicated budget.[56]

Despite his initial reservations, Scoyen agreed to visit the Channel Islands to learn more about them. The trip took place over the week of May 13–18, with Scoyen accompanied by Sequoia's naturalist, Frank Oberhansley, and two rangers. Richard Bond from the Soil Conservation Service again joined the NPS party in Los Angeles. The coast guard provided transportation out of San Pedro, taking the group first to Santa Barbara, where two days were spent exploring the island. Scoyen estimated that they saw about 1,200 sea lions as well as six elephant seals (*Mirounga angustirostris*) hauled out on a beach. These large pinnipeds had only recently returned to California waters after being hunted close to extinction during the previous century.[57] The party made a similar

Fig. 4. Point Bennett supports thousands of visiting pinnipeds, including at least four different species that nest there. Photographer unknown, November 2003, CINP Digital Archives, "Cultural Resources."

exploration of Anacapa Island, camping at Frenchy's Cove, where they enjoyed the company of Frenchy LeDreau. Superintendent Scoyen was deeply impressed by his tour of the islands, and his earlier low opinion of the monument was "completely reversed." The discovery of the rare elephant seals on Santa Barbara had convinced him of the importance of protecting the island as a reserve for threatened wildlife. Anacapa was similarly important, he realized, for the protection of nesting sea birds, especially the large colony of brown pelicans. But Scoyen also enjoyed the scenic opportunities of the Channel Islands. "With all due respect to Yellowstone's grizzly show, and other things of this kind which I have seen in the national parks," he wrote, "I never had more real fun than about an hour spent watching a colony of about sixty sea lions gambol and play in the ocean off the west coast of Santa Barbara Island." He concluded his brief report with the exuberant comment, "Boy! We've got something out there in the Channel Islands."[58]

Superintendent Scoyen was far more interested in making a commitment to manage the Channel Islands after his May visit. When a budget was finally approved for the monument the following fiscal year, Scoyen assigned a Sequoia ranger to Santa Barbara Island from May through early July 1941. Ranger Clarence Fry quickly demonstrated the importance in having a ranger posted on the island. During his stay, he kept a record not only of wildlife but also of human visitors, adding significantly to the park's knowledge of how the island and surrounding waters were used, how often they were visited, and by whom. For example, during the month of his residence, Fry counted eighty-six commercial fishing vessels in the immediate vicinity of Santa Barbara Island. He was also able to document threats to resources, as when he intercepted and warned off some of these fishermen attempting to harvest a meal from the numerous gull nests on the island.[59]

Fry's successful deterrence of these egg foragers was further justification for having a ranger on-site. Although he did not witness any attempts to assault sea lions or other marine mammals, Fry was aware that periodic raids occurred. The captain of a visiting coast guard patrol boat described one such incident when "hundreds were slaughtered" by commercial fishermen. A final important contribution made by Ranger Fry to the management of Santa Barbara Island was the elimination of the feral cat population. He did not mention the hares.[60]

Colonel John White, who had been regional director, returned to Sequoia National Park to replace Scoyen in May 1941, and he also assumed authority over Channel Islands National Monument.[61] White first traveled to the Channel Islands during the following September. Like Sumner and Bond in 1939, he included San Miguel in his itinerary, visiting Point Bennett on the west end of the island, where he enjoyed watching thousands of seals and sea lions hauled out on the beach.[62] The Park Service remained strongly interested in San Miguel Island and still believed it ought to be included in the monument.

The United States entered World War II on December 8, 1941. Locally, the United States quickly responded by organizing a system of coastal defenses with lookout stations located on all eight of the islands. All of the coastal lookout stations were manned by small garrisons of military personnel.[63] National defense temporarily replaced all other considerations in the Channel Islands, and nobody from the NPS visited the monument again until after the war ended. One action that the military took on Santa Barbara Island with later consequences for the NPS was the introduction of Red New Zealand rabbits to provide food in the event the island forces were cut off from communication with the mainland.[64]

In the decade following World War II, the American economy grew dramatically, with gross national product nearly doubling by 1955 and per capita income rising nearly as rapidly.[65] The national parks figured prominently in the leisure plans of many, and greater numbers visited the parks than ever before. Nevertheless, the Park Service budget remained stagnant over that decade, and increased visitation placed great stress on park resources. The Park Service as a whole could not respond to national trends in park visitation, owing to a lack of adequate funding, and management in the Western Region could not keep up with the surge in popularity of the Channel Islands. Lacking any staff presence on the islands, the NPS was only dimly aware of the changes that were occurring and the effects they might be having on monument resources. In the absence of good information, the regional office considered fact-finding inspections a high priority.

On April 20, 1948, Lowell Sumner accompanied Regional Director Owen Tomlinson and Superintendent Scoyen in an aerial survey of the Channel Islands from a coast guard observation plane. In his final report, Sumner reiterated many of the themes he had discussed prior to the war, but now with even greater urgency.[66] His chief concern was the destruction caused not by new visitors but by existing livestock. "This unique and originally beautiful group of islands," Sumner wrote, "has been almost unbelievably vandalized for about one hundred years by overgrazing."[67] Although he noted that Anacapa and Santa Barbara had both begun to recover following the cessation of grazing more than a decade earlier, all of the other islands showed visible signs of ongoing deterioration as a result of livestock still being pastured on them. San Miguel Island appeared to have suffered the greatest impact, with conditions "so bad that by contrast severely eroded areas on the mainland seem relatively good. Probably only the Dust Bowl of the Middlewest, during its worst days, is in a more miserable condition."[68]

Sumner had a great deal to say about Santa Rosa and Santa Cruz Islands, both of which were privately owned and still actively ranched. As previous NPS inspections had already concluded, Santa Cruz Island was the more significant of the two, in terms of natural resources and recreational opportunities, and Sumner was very critical of what he characterized as a legacy of poor management.[69] He also believed that private ownership was similarly destroying Santa Rosa Island, which offered excellent recreational and scientific potential. This was the first enthusiastic assessment of Santa Rosa Island by a member of the Park Service. It may have resulted from Sumner's aerial vantage, which revealed far more of the island than the previous views from passing boats.

The 1948 aerial reconnaissance resulted in two decisions for further action. The first of these was to resume negotiations with the navy over the subject of continued livestock grazing on San Miguel Island and the possibility of transferring the island to NPS jurisdiction. Although the navy had already rejected requests to transfer San Miguel prior to the war, the NPS regional directorate thought that with the war over, the island might now be surplus to military needs. The directorate was apparently unaware of growing concerns within the Department of Defense over the perceived communist threat, which would escalate into active fighting in Korea two years later. In May 1948, Acting Regional Director Maier sent a memo to the Washington DC office summarizing the conclusions of the aerial survey and asking the director to take steps to begin negotiations with the navy over management of San Miguel Island and possible transfer of ownership. To support the first of these proposals, Maier noted that the navy had recently agreed to manage some of its strategic possessions in Micronesia as natural reserves and hoped that this might serve as a precedent for future management of San Miguel Island as well.[70]

A few months later, Acting Director Hillory Tolson notified the regional office that its request was being forwarded to the navy through the secretary of the interior. However, he expressed doubt that the navy would consider relinquishing San Miguel, because it was already contemplating "directed missile experiments in that vicinity." This was news to the regional office, which was not yet aware that the navy was increasing its activities in the Channel Islands rather than scaling them back.[71] As Director Tolson expected, the secretary of the navy responded a few weeks later denying the request for transfer of San Miguel Island, but the navy was willing to terminate livestock grazing and work closer with the NPS over management of resources.[72] Apparently unknown to the secretary of the navy, local naval authorities had already terminated the remaining permit on San Miguel in July, when lessee Robert Brooks was given seventy-two hours to remove his sheep from the island.[73]

In addition to opening dialogue with the navy, inconclusive though it was, the 1948 aerial reconnaissance also confirmed the importance of conducting regular tours of the islands to assess their condition and to support NPS management prerogatives. At that time, the federal presence in the monument was limited to a handful of coast guard personnel stationed on east Anacapa Island, and a coast guard tender that visited Santa Barbara Island about once every three months to fill the oil reservoirs on its two automatic lights.[74] Over the next few years, Superintendent Scoyen tried to make at least one aerial reconnaissance each year.[75] These overflights were supplemented by the occasional land inspection, beginning in 1950 when Scoyen, Regional Naturalist Dorr Yeager, and Lowell Sumner visited Anacapa to assess the island in connection with a concession proposal.[76]

Apart from these infrequent official inspections, the NPS relied on private individuals, especially scientists who maintained an active interest in the islands and made occasional research visits to them. Their reports provided valuable information about existing natural and cultural resources as well as the impact of recent human activities. Some of these reports were highly critical of federal mismanagement of the islands. For example, in 1949 archeologist Phil Orr, curator of the SBMNH, accused the navy of killing island foxes and sea lions while the NPS tried to protect them.[77]

EXTENDING THE SEAWARD BOUNDARY

On March 25, 1946, the Park Service issued a *Boundary Status Report for Channel Islands*. The document focused attention on the inadequacy of the monument's boundary. Among other things, it noted that Gull Island (also known as Sutil Island), a small islet located about 2000 feet off the shore of Santa Barbara Island, was not included within the monument, because the monument's boundaries had been defined by proclamation as the high-water line.[78] As a matter of resource management and protection, this was a crucial omission, since the islet's high cliffs protected the habitat of native flora and fauna, lost or severely damaged on the larger, more accessible islands. When the matter was brought to the attention of Lowell Sumner, he explained in a memo to the regional director that:

> "Gull Island" has unique features which render its inclusion within the Monument unusually important. The reason for its importance is that neither cats, rabbits, nor domestic sheep, which in times past have ravaged the main island, appear ever to have reached "Gull Island." Consequently, the latter now constitutes the only remnant of Santa Barbara Island where some of the murrelets remain that once nested in great colonies in burrows on Santa Barbara Island proper. Similarly, it is believed that exotic weeds, which overran the main island during the years that sheep grazed there, are absent from "Gull Island," and that the original island flora has been undisturbed by sheep or domestic rabbits.[79]

Sumner believed that the monument boundary needed to be adjusted to include this valuable asset. He pointed out that poachers might use Gull Island as a vantage point from which to shoot at the sea lions on nearby Santa Barbara Island.[80] Regional Director Owen Tomlinson agreed with Sumner and wrote to Director Newton Drury recommending an amendment to the monument proclamation to adjust the boundaries accordingly.[81]

The proposal was hardly new. Not long before the war, then-superintendent Eivind Scoyen had written to the director wondering how far seaward NPS jurisdiction extended. "If we do not have jurisdiction [seaward]," he continued, "do you think it would be possible to extend the monument boundaries so that they would include one-half or a mile ocean strip around the entire group?" Scoyen was concerned not only with the need to include marine resources within the monument's boundaries, but also the smaller islets and offshore rocks.[82] Scoyen's query was referred to the Solicitor's Office, which responded that NPS jurisdiction unambiguously ended at water's edge and recommended that action be taken to include outlying rocks and islets through a supplemental presidential proclamation. Nothing was said about jurisdiction over the water and submerged lands. The solicitor also recommended that the NPS confirm its authority to manage resources on coast guard reservations within the monument.[83] This discussion was interrupted by the war, but Director Drury now brought it up in response to Sumner's concern over Gull Island. Drury contacted the Bureau of Land Management (BLM), which had de facto authority over all unreserved offshore rocks and islets. He asked about the feasibility of extending the monument's boundary to include such features within a one-mile radius of each of the monument islands. BLM director Fred W. Johnson responded favorably to this proposal and even offered assistance in preparing the necessary proclamation to implement it.[84]

Drury also wished to learn whether the coast guard had any excess property in the Channel Islands and sent his regional chief of lands to southern California to make inquiries. The coast guard, it turned out, had nothing it was willing to transfer to the NPS, but Commander O. A. Peterson of the Eleventh Coast Guard District shared some additional news that alarmed the Park Service representative. He had recently heard that the navy was planning to expand its guided missile program at Point Mugu and might need to declare a broad restricted zone that would encompass all or most of the northern islands, including all of the national monument. The navy would install observation posts at the coast guard reservations on Anacapa and Santa Barbara Islands to monitor its missile launches. The details and full extent of this proposed program, which would become the Naval Air Missile Test Center (NAMTC), were classified and remained vague, but the implications for the future of the national monument were potentially grave.[85]

In transmitting this information to Director Drury, Regional Director Tomlinson questioned the advisability of continuing with plans to expand the monument until the navy's intentions were fully known, but Drury insisted that the Park Service move forward as quickly as possible. He hoped that extending monument boundaries to surrounding offshore rocks would enhance protection for the wildlife and other resources within the monument. He also supported a suggestion proposed by Lowell Sumner that the NPS enter into a cooperative agreement with the navy to have its personnel protect wildlife on the monument islands or at least refrain from molesting them.[86] Sumner's proposal was not immediately implemented, but the idea remained interesting to both agencies.

Director Drury's concerns over this new threat to monument resources resulted in a revision of the *Boundary Status Report*, completed on January 16, 1948, that proposed that the monument encompass offshore rocks and islets within a one-mile radius of each island as well as the intermediate areas.[87] This was consistent with recent developments in legal theory concerning offshore jurisdiction. Prior to 1937, all submerged lands extending at least three miles from the continental shoreline and from offshore islands were understood to belong to the adjoining state, not to the federal government. This was why the 1938 proclamation of Channel Islands National Monument established its boundary at the high-water line. However, doubts over the principle of state authority within the three-mile coastal margin led to a court case—United States v. California (332 U.S. 19)—before the Supreme Court in 1947. The justices ruled that the three-mile coastal margin lay within federal jurisdiction, based on a principle of paramount rights.[88] This meant that the monument's boundaries could now be extended to a one-mile radius by a simple presidential proclamation without appeal to the state. On February 9, 1949, President Truman signed Proclamation No. 2825 increasing the boundaries of Channel Islands National Monument accordingly.[89] Throughout this discussion, the navy offered no objection to the boundary change once it received assurances from the National Park Service that its missile test program would not be affected.[90]

Following the Supreme Court decision, states could no longer challenge federal ownership of submerged lands in court, but they could appeal to Congress to make changes in the law itself. In 1953, only four years after the monument's boundaries were extended, Congress passed Public Law 31, commonly known as the Submerged Lands Act.[91] This granted jurisdiction to the states over the submerged lands three miles seaward of their coastline (or three leagues, in the case of the Gulf states). The

Submerged Lands Act did not conflict with the Supreme Court's decision in United States v. California because the federal government was, in effect, ceding federal lands to the states, consistent with its constitutional rights.[92] The Park Service was unaware of this legislation and its implications for Channel Islands National Monument. Neither NPS nor state officials realized that the 1949 proclamation expanding the monument had been effectively annulled. It would be more than two decades before this fact was appreciated, and then only after further clarification by the U.S. Supreme Court.[93]

PLANS FOR THE MONUMENT IN THE 1950S

Between 1952 and 1957, the regional staff prepared a series of documents outlining a plan of development that would facilitate greater visitation. This development outline constituted the monument's first formal master plan. It proposed concentrating a development at Frenchy's Cove on the north side of Anacapa Island. The plan's proposed development would be confined to the middle islet. Later, the NPS developed a new access point at Landing Cove, where visitors can climb a steep stairway to the East Anacapa Islet plateau. Although recreation was now an official part of the monument's management objectives, it remained subsidiary to resource protection, as the master plan made clear, "the theme of development should be the preservation of the biological and ecological aspects of the islands with the least possible impact upon the area by the presence of visitors."[94]

Later additions to the master plan included an assessment of island vegetation prepared by forester W. C. James. He described the destructive effects of past livestock grazing, which had resulted in erosion and the introduction of exotic weeds. James also observed how the islands had steadily recovered following the cessation of grazing. This recovery, however, had been interrupted recently on Santa Barbara Island by the growing population of rabbits. Scarcely ten years after the war, the rabbits were estimated to number as many as fifty thousand. In 1955, efforts to control these animals intensified when Cabrillo National Monument chief ranger Don Robinson began dropping bags of poisoned barley and carrots from navy aircraft. The program never entirely eliminated the

Fig. 5. Frenchy's structures at the cove on Middle Anacapa Islet named for him. Photographer unknown, CINP Archives, ACC. 217, CAT. 3191.

rabbits, but it kept the population at manageable levels so long as the practice continued.[95]

In September 1940, Newton Drury received an unexpected letter from Edwin Stanton, an old classmate of his from UCB. Stanton explained that he was owner of the majority of Santa Cruz Island, since his purchase of it from the Caire family in 1937, and expressed his desire to see the property ultimately protected as a public park.[96] Although this was less than a forthright offer, Stanton seemed to be implying that he was willing to sell. This is how Acting Director Demaray, who received the letter, interpreted his intent. Unfortunately, both Drury and Demaray knew that Congress was unlikely to appropriate funds to purchase the ranch, no matter how great its significance, and Demaray wrote back to Stanton regretfully informing him of this fact.[97]

Ten years later, NPS efforts to expand the sea boundaries of the monument may have been the source of rumors that began circulating around

Fig. 6. The pier at the Landing Cove on the north side of East Anacapa Islet is the second most visited access to the park's islands. Photograph by Bill Ehorn, December 2008, CINP Digital Image Files.

local communities that the Park Service was interested in acquiring one or more of the privately owned islands for the monument.[98] While the interest was certainly there, nobody in the Park Service believed at this time that any of the islands not already in federal ownership would be acquired anytime soon, if ever. Nonetheless, the rumors encouraged Stanton to phone Director Drury in June of 1950. Drury reminded Stanton that the Park Service's interests in Santa Cruz Island dated to 1928, when the State Park Commission had recommended protecting the island as a public park, "but that no feasible way of acquiring it had ever been devised." He went on to state that he was personally in favor of making Santa Cruz Island an addition to Channel Islands National Monument, "if the lands were tendered to the Federal Government," but that the Park Service would not be able to purchase the island outright owing to a lack of sufficient funds and the unlikelihood of any congressional appropriation to provide them. Efforts by the state to acquire the Stanton Ranch had proven similarly futile, since the state was even less able to afford such a major purchase than the federal government.[99]

Although Stanton indicated to Drury that he would be willing to cooperate with any interested groups wanting to raise funds to acquire his property, he left it clear that he would not be willing to make an outright donation. Drury had no choice, therefore, but to decline Stanton's offer again, but he was nonetheless excited by the possibility that Santa Cruz Island might someday be added to the monument.[100] Despite Drury's enthusiasm, the Park Service did not have the financial means to acquire any significant new property until the budgetary appropriations of Mission 66 were implemented nearly a decade later. By that time, Edwin Stanton had relinquished responsibility for the Santa Cruz Island Ranch to his son Carey, who did not share his father's interest in selling the island or seeing it become a public park.

MISSION 66 AND THE CHANNEL ISLANDS

Conditions in America's national parks continued to decline well into the 1950s as the NPS budget remained stagnant while visitation exponentially increased. Growing public attention to the crisis finally inspired Park Service Director Conrad Wirth to propose major changes.[101] Wirth assembled special committees to develop a prospectus of what was needed most by the parks. The result was an ambitious plan of upgrading and modernization that he called Mission 66, after the target date for the plan's completion on the agency's fiftieth anniversary.[102] Wirth presented the Mission 66 prospectus to President Dwight Eisenhower in January 1956 and received the president's personal endorsement. Congress followed shortly afterward and voted an increase in the Park Service budget that would ultimately total nearly $1,000,000. The funds made it possible to implement the largest and most comprehensive development program since the creation of the Park Service four decades earlier.

Mission 66 touched nearly every corner of the national park system in one way or another. Its effect on Channel Islands National Monument was indirect but profound. The expansion of the NPS budget after 1956 combined with the enthusiasm and boost in morale brought about by the initiative encouraged park staff throughout the region to begin thinking once more of expansion and growth. Within this positive environment, thoughts returned to the idea of a greater Channel Islands National Monument with an addition of new lands and possibly redesignation as a national park. Even before introducing Mission 66, however, Director Wirth had given new hope for protecting coastal and seashore areas such as the Channel Islands. In 1954, he implemented a series of studies designed to inventory and assess the remaining undeveloped coastal areas possessing significant resource values and opportunities for public recreation. Channel Islands was among several locations on the Pacific coast that received great attention as a result.

Director Wirth's seashore surveys were modeled after earlier series conducted by the NPS during the 1930s. Those prewar studies identified twelve seashore areas on the Atlantic and Gulf of Mexico coasts that were determined significant enough to be designated units of the national park system and thirty areas deserving protection under state park systems. In 1937 these recommendations resulted in congressional authorization of the nation's first national seashore at Cape Hatteras in North Carolina and its establishment in 1953.[103] Rapid economic development following the war had removed a number of the recommended sites from consideration. Wirth decided, therefore, to conduct an updated survey of the

Atlantic and Gulf coasts in 1954. The study, funded by the Avalon and Old Dominion Foundations, resulted in a report entitled *Our Vanishing Shoreline*, published in June 1955. Surveys of the Pacific coast and Great Lakes shorelines were undertaken shortly after the eastern program.[104]

While these coastal surveys were still underway, the NPS learned of a 1957 congressional proposal, House Resolution 8935, to establish a naval petroleum reserve on San Miguel, Prince, and San Nicolas Islands, all of which were under naval jurisdiction. Eivind Scoyen was acting for Director Wirth at that time, and his personal familiarity with the Channel Islands helped prompt immediate action. After requesting that the Department of the Interior (DOI) delay its report to Congress on the proposed bill, Scoyen instructed the regional office in San Francisco to gather as much information as it could on San Miguel Island. The resulting report was submitted to the directorate in November 1957. It provided a detailed description of the island's resources and an assessment of their value. The report found that the island's natural resources, primarily its flora and fauna, were highly significant and in need of "absolute protection by a qualified governmental body."[105] Based on these observations, the Park Service recommended that San Miguel Island be excluded from H.R. 8935 and instead added to Channel Islands National Monument. Although nothing ultimately came of the petroleum reserve, the perceived threat and NPS response to it elicited further attention. In 1958 the federal government's Advisory Board on National Parks, Historic Sites, Buildings, and Monuments concurred with the NPS Directorate's high opinion of San Miguel Island and also recommended that the secretary of the interior make the island an addition to the monument. But the advisory group went a step further and recommended that other islands in the archipelago be added as well, if and when they became available.[106]

The following year, the final report of the West Coast seashore study was published.[107] It carried the unimaginative title *Pacific Coast Recreation Area Survey*. Like *Vanishing Shoreline*, its purpose was to inventory the remaining undeveloped coast line and report on areas of potential value for public recreation. More than 1,700 miles of shoreline were covered, and the team identified 527 miles that remained largely undeveloped and possessed significant public values. This was divided into seventy-four individual sites, each of which was assessed separately. Seven of these sites were determined to possess outstanding significance, with five warranting protection as national parks: Cape Flattery, Oregon Dunes, Point Reyes, San Miguel Island, and Santa Cruz Island.

The Channel Islands comprised 241 miles, or nearly 14 percent, of the Pacific coastline and accounted for some of the most significant resources encountered by the survey team, who concluded that "there is, in fact, nothing comparable found along the entire Pacific Coast in the way of maritime ecology which is still relatively untouched."[108] The report concluded that "careful consideration should be given to any future opportunity to acquire or preserve for public purposes any or all of the Channel Islands group."[109] Scientific values predominated in this assessment, which clearly implied that the existing monument was not sufficient to protect these values and that one or more of the larger islands needed to be acquired.

The national seashore idea received further impetus when President John F. Kennedy included it in a special message to Congress in February 1961. Kennedy's purpose was to ask for improved conservation of natural resources, but among the resource values he listed was outdoor recreation. He urged Congress to enact a wilderness protection bill—passed three years later under President Lyndon Johnson's administration—but also "legislation leading to the establishment of seashore and shoreline areas such as Cape Cod, Padre Island, and Point Reyes for the use and enjoyment of the public." Kennedy was primarily interested in Cape Cod but was urged by staff to balance this request with proposed seashores on each of the other two major coastlines.[110] The proposal was sufficiently broad to allow other seashore areas to be considered as well, and this inspired California supporters of an enlarged Channel Islands. They now began thinking of a potential Channel Islands National Seashore.[111]

Among the most vocal and well-connected supporters of a new park or national seashore in the Channel Islands was *Santa Barbara News Press* editor Thomas Storke. He became enthused with the idea of transforming the islands into a grand theme park where visitors would encounter a romanticized mock-up of old Spanish California, interpreted by costumed rangers with guitars.[112] Less enthusiastic about the proposed park were the private land owners who would be required to sell their ranches on Santa Cruz and Santa Rosa Islands.[113] Storke lobbied California senators Thomas Kuchel and Claire Engle to introduce a Channel Islands bill. Although the senators supported the idea, they were reluctant to introduce the bill at this time because they feared it would divert attention from the Point Reyes National Seashore Bill (S. 476), which they had introduced to Congress in January. Both senators felt that passage of the Point Reyes bill was far more urgent, because real estate development was already threatening this northern California peninsula, while the Channel Islands had some protection in place with the monument and were not confronted by any imminent threat.[114]

Responding to the growing interest among local supporters in a Channel Islands National Park, the NPS hastily put together an illustrated booklet entitled *A Sea-Dominated National Park: Its Prospect and a Proposal*, which appeared in 1963.[115] The proposal was for a marine national park comprising five of the Channel Islands—the existing two monument islands plus San Miguel, Santa Cruz, and Santa Rosa. The brief publication represented no original research, but instead summarized information obtained from recent surveys. Descriptions of each of the five islands were included, though field studies had not been conducted on the two privately owned islands, so the conclusions regarding their merits were somewhat speculative.[116]

That same year, the advisory board strongly endorsed the establishment of a major new national park in the Channel Islands, and before the year was out, the first of several park bills was introduced to Congress by Senator Claire Engle and Representative Edward Roybal.[117] The bill (S. 1303) proposed establishing a Channel Islands National Seashore, in keeping with the momentum that had begun with the seashore surveys of the previous decade and President Kennedy's 1961 message to Congress. The NPS itself preferred the national park designation. The distinction between the two was confusing to many and often used interchangeably, with the more common designation of national park preferred by most. Another reason for the national seashore designation in the Senate bill was the recent passage of the Point Reyes National Seashore Act, which had been signed into law the previous September. This legislative success was an encouraging precedent, but it did not lead to a successful expansion and redesignation as seashore or park for Channel Islands.[118]

ENHANCED MANAGEMENT OF THE MONUMENT ISLANDS

In 1962 the U.S. Coast Guard initiated plans to automate the Anacapa Island Light Station. Completed in 1968, the automation allowed the coast guard to support the new equipment through periodic visits. The coast guard began demolishing the buildings on East Anacapa until Superintendent Robinson notified them that he would like to retain the complex for NPS staff use. The coast guard agreed to retain the remaining structures if the NPS was willing to maintain them.[119] By 1970 a formal agreement was signed between the DOI for the NPS and the Department of Transportation for the coast guard, formalizing the negotiations that the Park Service would manage the majority of the islet as part of the national monument and all of the remaining buildings and structures.[120]

Another important development in 1963 was a Memorandum of Agreement (MOA) between the NPS and the navy over the management of San Miguel Island. The agreement theoretically allowed the Park Service to conduct research needed to develop a program for conservation of the island's significant natural and cultural resources. While the navy remained unwilling to relinquish its authority over the island, citing its need for greater access in the event of a future military escalation, it finally was amenable to allowing Park Service management of the island resources. The navy, however, insisted that the island must remain closed to the public. This later rendered the agreement meaningless after the NPS Solicitor's Office determined that the Park Service could not spend appropriated funds on lands owned by another agency that were not open to the public for recreational use. The stipulation made it impossible for park staff to conduct any research or resource management on San Miguel Island and even prevented the preparation of a resource management report that was required by the agreement.[121]

In spite of the technical problems with the MOA, the NPS and the navy cooperated in a few resource-related activities. In June 1966, the Park Service sent a report to the navy entitled "A Suggested Plan for the Management and Protection of Values of San Miguel Island" that requested elimination of the feral sheep left on the island after Robert Brooks's last attempt to remove them in 1950. From July 17 through 20, research biologist James K. Baker of Joshua Tree National Monument, a ranger, and several navy personnel shot 148 sheep, finally clearing the island after a century of overgrazing. In the meantime, San Miguel remained unmanaged and was protected largely by its isolation and the threat of periodic training bombardments by naval aircraft.

On May 12, 1967, the NPS separated the joint administration of Channel Islands and Cabrillo National Monuments. Donald Robinson became superintendent of Channel Islands. The small staff set up shop in an office building in downtown Oxnard with a bare-bones budget.[122] The following year, the Island Packers Company began providing public transportation to the islands, which increased visitation and the need for a Park Service presence on the islands. The monument stationed rangers seasonally on Anacapa and Santa Barbara Islands to orient visitors and campers, provide guided walks and information, conduct marine patrols around the islands to protect the resources, and provide assistance where needed.[123] With such a small staff, the rangers also were responsible for maintaining the island facilities, clearing trails, repairing their boats, shooting rabbits, assisting island researchers, giving talks in the community, and helping to staff an NPS field office in Los Angeles.[124] The rangers also made occasional patrols out to San Miguel Island under the 1963 agreement with the Navy.

THE GHERINI DEVELOPMENT PLAN AND PROPOSALS FOR NATIONAL PARK STATUS

On September 5, 1965, the NPS formally announced its intention to seek national park status for the Northern Channel Islands.[125] A Park Service study team made a ground reconnaissance of Santa Rosa later that year, the first time that NPS staff had ever visited this island. The inspectors concluded that the island did not warrant becoming part of the national park system, but they did not prepare a full report of its negative assessment.[126] Later in 1965, the park proposal received a boost when Pier Gherini presented plans to the Santa Barbara County Planning Commission to develop his family's property on East Santa Cruz Island. The plans envisioned a recreation-oriented development covering approxi-

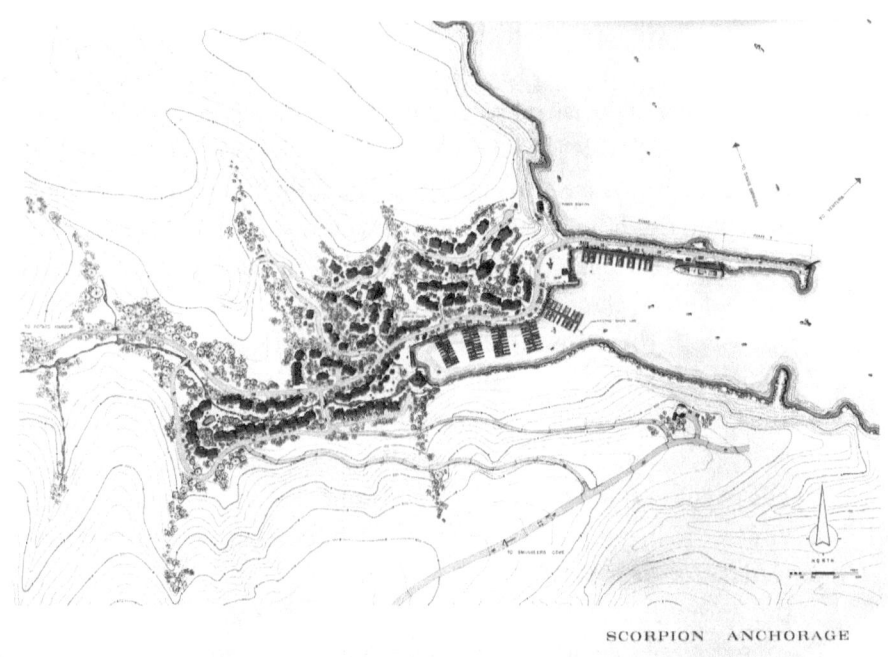

Map 10. In 1966 Pier Gherini proposed a plan to develop a residential complex at Scorpion Anchorage. The NPS opposed it. Provided by John Gherini.

mately 6,000 acres but concentrated in two villages—one at Scorpion Valley and the other at Smugglers Ranch—with a combined population of three thousand people. Both villages would include a boat pier, while Scorpion would also have a marina with slips for 150 vessels. Since the proposed action would require an amendment to the county's General Plan, which at that time designated the entire island for agricultural and open space purposes, the Planning Commission opened the proposal to public debate in a series of four hearings.[127]

The Park Service and environmental groups like the Sierra Club and the Nature Conservancy opposed the plan, but many private landowners and local businessmen supported it. In response, the Park Service's Western Office of Design and Construction hurriedly prepared its own

A Monumental Task   63

"Preliminary General Management Plan" for Santa Cruz Island. This was not based on any first-hand reconnaissance and reflected only a general understanding of the island itself, but it revealed the agency's own interest in recreational development.[128] The Park Service was represented at the Planning Commission hearings by Assistant Regional Director Leo Diederich, who explained that the agency's own plan would provide nearly the same recreational amenities, located in the same or similar places, but would not include residential development. The greatest difference was access. The NPS development would be open to everyone, while the Gherini project was essentially a private resort.[129]

The County Planning Commission approved the Gherini plan on January 12, 1966, and the County Board of Supervisors rezoned the island from agricultural to commercial and residential use. The Gherinis were legally free to begin building their resort, but the proposed development proved far too expensive to implement. The most important consequence of the entire affair was the attention it drew to the island, both from the general public and from the Park Service. It also greatly increased interest in establishing a national park there. During the following three sessions of Congress, from 1966 through 1970, a total of eleven bills were introduced to establish a Channel Islands National Park.[130] The lack of first-hand information about the two largest islands became the most significant obstacle stymieing legislative progress. Acknowledging this need, Senator Alan Cranston of California introduced a study bill in 1970 to the Ninety-first Congress. In a letter to NPS director George Hartzog, Cranston emphasized what was required for significant progress to be made—access to the islands themselves, which could only be obtained with the cooperation of existing landowners.

Superintendent Don Robinson made efforts to meet with the owners of Santa Cruz and Santa Rosa Islands. He had enjoyed a good relationship with Edwin Stanton, then owner of 90 percent of Santa Cruz Island.[131] But with Edwin's death in 1963, his son Carey assumed management of the island operations and moved to the Main Ranch. On a visit to the island, Robinson pondered the expensive antique furnishings and original artwork and made a comment on where the superintendent's office would be once the NPS took over the island. This deeply antagonized Carey Stanton, who had formed a poor opinion of the Park Service when he visited Anacapa Island and found it closed with a lot of trash scattered around. Robinson's thoughtless remark reinforced Stanton's negative opinion of the monument and the National Park Service. Nor had Robinson endeared himself to Francis Gherini, whose family owned the east end of Santa Cruz Island.[132]

With relations between the NPS and the private landowners rapidly deteriorating during Don Robinson's superintendency, access to the larger islands became so tense that Secretary of the Interior Stewart Udall quipped that he would have to watch out for anti-aircraft fire during an aerial reconnaissance.[133] The situation deteriorated further a few years later when the NPS supported an amendment to a park bill that would have given it "legal authority to enter on private property against the owner's will for the purpose of collecting data."[134] This threat served only to anger private property owners, especially Carey Stanton. Although the bill failed, it would be years before the Park Service's relations with Carey Stanton recovered.[135]

As the National Park Service sought ways to expand the monument and develop visitation on the islands it had, management changes did occur. Toward the end of Robinson's tenure, the Ventura Port District, in a bid to attract business to the newly constructed marina, offered the monument the use of a three-bedroom house in its harbor, along with berths to moor the monument's boats. Following a period of great staff discontent and a regional investigation into ethics violations, Don Robinson retired in April 1974 and John O. Cook took over as acting superintendent until the arrival of Superintendent William H. Ehorn on June 23.[136]

Legislative Protection for the Islands and the Sea　3

Rapid growth in California's population and economy during the postwar years greatly intensified development, especially along the coast near urban centers such as San Diego, Los Angeles, and the San Francisco Bay Area.[1] The resulting crowding as well as pressure on natural resources underlined the need for better-regulated, regionally-coordinated planning. A popular backlash formed in reaction to some of the more excessive development schemes, such as the Reber Plan, which would have filled in most of San Francisco Bay. It resulted in the Bay Conservation and Development Commission in 1965 that served as a precedent for more comprehensive, regulatory and planning efforts throughout the state's coastal areas.[2]

Federal efforts to provide comprehensive planning for the development of coastal marine resources began in 1966 when Congress established the Commission on Marine Science, Engineering and Resources, popularly known as the Stratton Commission after its chairman.[3] The commission produced a report titled *Our Nation and the Sea: A Plan for National Action* in 1969 that included an entire chapter on management of the coastal zone.[4] It recommended that the coastal zones should continue to be managed at the local level through state coastal zone authorities empowered to manage the coastal waters and adjacent land.[5]

That same year, an event with national consequences occurred off the Southern California coast. Nine oil-drilling platforms had been installed off Santa Barbara County between 1958 and 1966. Despite local protests, oil companies acquired the first federal Outer Continental Shelf lease in the Santa Barbara Channel south of Carpinteria in 1966. Union Oil began drilling at Platform A six miles off the coast shortly thereafter.[6] On January 28, 1969, that platform suffered a blowout that began what was at the time the worst oil spill in U.S. history. The spill continued for eleven days, with lesser leaks continuing for months thereafter. Sea birds, pinnipeds, dolphins, kelp beds, and miles of beaches were coated with crude oil. In the end, an estimated eighty thousand to one hundred thousand barrels leaked out. Winds and swells spread it over hundreds of square miles of open water, and it eventually impacted mainland shorelines from Pismo Beach north of Santa Barbara to San Diego.

Oil surrounded Anacapa Island, including the tidepools at Frenchy's Cove, and also hit beaches on Santa Cruz, Santa Rosa, and San Miguel Islands. It clogged the blowholes of some dolphins causing their lungs to hemorrhage. Other animals that ingested the oil were poisoned. Wildlife rescuers at one point counted some 3,600 dead ocean-feeding seabirds. A number of poisoned seals, sea lions, and some dolphins washed up on the shorelines. The spill killed innumerable fish and intertidal invertebrates, ruined kelp forests, and displaced many endangered birds. *Life Magazine* reporters visited San Miguel Island and counted over one hundred dead California sea lions and other pinnipeds on one stretch of oil-covered beach four months after the blowout.[7]

Environmentalists, politicians, and scientists arrived in Santa Barbara, and all had plenty to say about the weak regulations that ruled the oil industry. Secretary of the Interior Walter Hickel resisted a demand to remove all offshore drill rigs by a new environmental protest group, "Get Oil Out" (GOO). Union Oil's president, Fred Hartley, dismissed their concerns by pointing out that no people had died, which compared favorably to the murders that routinely happened in Washington DC. But the environmental catastrophe set off a spark in the national populace. Over the next three years an amazing series of environmental laws were passed both nationally and in California. The National Environmental Policy Act (NEPA) and its state version, the California Environmental Quality Act (CEQA), were among the legal products of the increased environmental activism energized by the oil spill. A decade of other laws to protect the sea and its denizens have also rewritten the ways that companies and governments can affect the marine environment.[8]

In 1972, three years after the Stratton Commission published its report and the oil spill riveted attention on Southern California beaches, Congress enacted the Coastal Zone Management Act (CZMA), putting into effect most of the Commission's recommendations relating to the management of coastal areas.[9] President Nixon followed its most important recommendation with the creation of a new federal agency, the National Oceanic and Atmospheric Administration (NOAA) in 1970. Among its responsibilities was the administration of the CZMA, which provided incentives for states to establish their own programs for managing their coastal areas.[10] A notable feature of the CZMA, with significance to NPS management of the Channel Islands, stipulates that any federal action that might have an effect on resources within the state's coastal zone must be consistent with the standards and policies established by that state in its coastal plan.[11] The state has the authority to review the proposed actions of federal agencies for consistency with its management plans.[12]

Shortly thereafter, the Marine Mammal Protection Act of 1972 and the Endangered Species Act of 1973 passed. The Marine Mammal Protection Act established a moratorium on the taking of all marine mammals within U.S. waters and by U.S. citizens on the high seas. It is administered primarily by the National Marine Fisheries Service (NMFS), the division of NOAA that later administered fishery management plans.[13] Administration of the Endangered Species Act was divided between NMFS, which is responsible for marine and anadromous species, and U.S. Fish and Wildlife Service (USFWS), which is responsible for terrestrial and freshwater species.

California also completed its Comprehensive Ocean Area Plan in 1972. Shortly thereafter, California voters approved Proposition 20, the Coastal Zone Conservation Act, establishing a Coastal Zone Conservation Commission that assumed responsibility for planning activities that involve marine and coastal resources. Temporary at first, it was reauthorized as permanent with greater responsibilities as the California Coastal Commission in 1976.[14] The Coastal Act required that all cities and counties having a portion of their areas located within the coastal zone must prepare a Local Coastal Plan (LCP). This comprehensive management document includes a Land Use Plan and all relevant zoning ordinances, maps, and other legal instruments needed to implement the plan. Each LCP must be reviewed and approved by the Coastal Commission before it can go into effect. This, and subsequent oversight to ensure compliance, meant no development could legally occur within the coastal zone until the local government's LCP had been approved.[15]

This requirement had significant impact on the Northern Channel Islands. Planners for Santa Barbara County, which includes all of the Northern Channel Islands except Anacapa (Ventura County), developed a draft LCP starting in early 1977, which the county board of supervisors adopted in January of 1980, and submitted it to the Coastal Commission for review. At that time, the Channel Islands National Park bill that would expand the national monument to include all of the northern archipelago was approaching its final form in Congress and was considered certain to pass. In this context of growing interest for the natural and scenic values of the islands, the Coastal Commission refused to approve the county's plan that designated the Channel Islands within its Agriculture II land use zone, which would also allow construction of new houses in clustered developments with densities of one dwelling for every two acres of land. This would have amounted to as many as 2,300 new houses that could be built on both Santa Cruz and Santa Rosa Islands. This zone would also allow oil and gas development. The Commission did not consider this level of development appropriate for the Channel Islands with their unique scenic values.[16]

The Coastal Commission's concern about further development of the Channel Islands was more than just hypothetical. The Vail & Vickers Company, which owned all of Santa Rosa, had recently applied to the county for permission to allow residential development of the island.[17] While this may have been a strategy to raise the appraised value of their property in anticipation of future sale to the federal government, it nevertheless represented a legitimate threat to the preservation of the archipelago's rural character. Moreover, the county generally supported this and similar development proposals, in contrast to the Coastal Commission, and later threatened litigation against the state following pressure from the private landowners. Although Santa Barbara County modified its land use plan to reduce potential residential development on the Channel Islands to densities of no more than one dwelling per 320 acres, the Coastal Commission still refused to endorse the proposal. After the park bill passed, the Commission certified the county's LCP only as it applied to the mainland coastal zone.[18]

The CZMA and the National Marine Sanctuaries Act of 1972 protected coastal resources, but other legislation was needed to protect marine resources.[19] In 1976 Congress passed the Fishery Conservation and Management Act, more commonly known as the Magnuson-Stevens Act.[20] It limited or excluded foreign competition within the Exclusive Economic Zone of the United States, which extends two hundred miles offshore, and established the NMFS as the single federal regulatory authority. It also introduced a comprehensive planning process implemented through eight regional fishery management councils. Each council was required to prepare a fishery management plan establishing standards and protocols for commercial harvest. Once approved, these standards would be enforced by the NMFS.[21] Although the Magnuson-Stevens Act did not apply to state waters within the three-mile boundaries of the territorial sea and therefore did not apply directly to the waters surrounding the Channel Islands, it did affect management of marine resources within the Santa Barbara Channel and further offshore, having a significant effect on the activities and livelihood of Southern California commercial fishermen.

The Supreme Court granted jurisdiction over the near-shore waters around the Channel Islands to the state in 1978. Protest from scientists familiar with the Channel Islands and its natural resources, prompted the California Department of Fish and Game (CDFG) to designate state ecological reserves in the waters within one nautical mile of Anacapa, Santa Barbara, and San Miguel Islands. The state legislature had already designated the state-owned waters surrounding the islands as an oil and gas sanctuary administered by the California State Lands Commission. All mineral development within these critical offshore areas was prohibited.[22] The new ecological reserves essentially corresponded to the marine areas previously administered by the National Park Service. A cooperative agreement between the NPS and the State of California in 1979 allowed federal rangers to coordinate with state game wardens in order to enforce the ecological reserve regulations. Even with the active participation of NPS rangers, however, many park staff and scientists familiar with the park's resources believed that the ecological reserves were inadequate, because state regulations were lenient and provided little meaningful protection.[23]

Superintendent Bill Ehorn

In 1974, the year that Don Robinson retired, most of the private landowners criticized the Park Service's poor management of the monument and opposed a greater role for the agency in the Channel Islands. This attitude began to change with the arrival of a new superintendent, William "Bill" Ehorn. He vastly improved the quality of management and encouraged better relations with the monument's neighbors. Equally important among Superintendent Ehorn's early accomplishments were his efforts to build the monument's infrastructure and establish a strong foundation of staff morale. He realized these objectives through projects ranging from improving the facilities on the islands and natural resource management to essential capital improvements such as the construction of a new visitor center. The greater respect his administration brought to Channel Islands National Monument, both within and outside the NPS, was an essential precondition for its eventual designation as a national park. A Channel Islands National Park that encompassed all the northern islands had been desired since the earliest NPS reconnaissance in 1933. Ehorn did more than any other person to realize its creation.

BUILDING RELATIONS WITH THE COMMUNITY

Ehorn arrived in Ventura with enthusiasm and an impatience to get things done that proved to be characteristic of his professional career. He began almost immediately to implement plans for a new visitor center in the Ventura Marina. By October 1974, Congress passed P.L. 93–477, with the support of Congressman Robert Lagomarsino and Senator Alan Cranston, allowing the NPS to accept a donation of land from the Ventura Port Authority for 2.5 acres to be used for the proposed facility. The law also authorized an appropriation of just under $3 million for construction.[24]

Among the most important and daunting challenges that Bill Ehorn undertook after arriving at Channel Islands was improving relations with

Fig. 7. Dr. Gary Davis preparing to dive while in conversation with Superintendent William "Bill" Ehorn. Photographer and date unknown, CINP Digital Archives, photograph 000010000001.

the private landowners on the islands. Ehorn possessed a natural talent for this sort of diplomacy. The first fruits of his efforts came with Dr. Carey Stanton's grudging approval to allow Ehorn to visit Santa Cruz Island in 1976. This was the first time that any Park Service staff had been allowed to come to the Stanton Ranch since Don Robinson's fateful visit. The occasion was arranged by the U.S. Navy's Ted Green, who had a good relationship with Stanton. Carey Stanton agreed that Ehorn and Green could visit the Mt. Diablo site with his ranch manager Henry Duffield. This was the first time Ehorn had ever seen Santa Cruz Island up close, and he was deeply impressed. Following the visit, Ehorn sent a thank-you note to Stanton, who invited Ehorn to meet for lunch on the mainland. At lunch, Ehorn invited Stanton to come visit Anacapa Island and arranged for helicopter transportation for Stanton and Duffield to come to the island for lunch. Stanton reciprocated by inviting Ehorn and his guests NPS director Gary Everhardt, Regional Director Howard Chapman, and the park's chief ranger Charles "Mack" Shaver to come for cocktails and lunch at his Main Ranch in the Central Valley. Stanton also invited Al Vail, part owner and principal manager of the Vail & Vickers Cattle Company on Santa Rosa Island. This was Ehorn's first encounter with Al Vail, and the two men quickly became friends.[25]

Ehorn's success in winning over the island ranchers had much to do with his management record during the previous two years. The most noticeable change was simply the attention that the islands now received. Ehorn set about repairing and cleaning up the facilities and renovated small visitor centers on East Anacapa Islet and Frenchy's Cove on Middle Anacapa Islet. He also renovated the old Quonset hut on Santa Barbara Island and added a small visitor center and ranger station to it.[26] All of these sites had been criticized by local private landowners for their general disarray and poor maintenance under Superintendent Robinson.

During lunch at the ranch house on Santa Cruz Island, Director Everhardt asked Dr. Stanton if he would be willing to sell or donate his share of the island to the Park Service. Stanton refused, but his response was no longer as angry as it had been when Don Robinson had announced that he would enjoy the ranch house when it belonged to the government. In essence, the Park Service succeeded in gaining the cooperation of Dr. Stanton, even though it did not obtain his property. This success became evident during the legislative hearings for the park bill a few years later, when Dr. Stanton withheld any objection that he might have had to the inclusion of Santa Cruz Island within the proposed park boundaries.[27]

Superintendent Ehorn also made important progress on San Miguel Island during his first few years. Prior to that time, little had been done to manage that island's valuable and fragile resources despite the 1963 Memorandum of Agreement (MOA) signed with the navy that directed the Park Service to assume management responsibilities. Within his first year as superintendent, Bill Ehorn visited Point Bennett on the western tip of San Miguel Island where the NMFS maintained a research station under the direction of Dr. Robert DeLong.[28] Ehorn remembers walking across the island to Point Bennett, where Dr. DeLong explained to him the significance of what he was seeing. This was the only place in the world where six species of pinnipeds (seals and sea lions) would haul out

Fig. 8. Island owners (*left to right*) Russell Vail, John Gherini, Pier Gherini, Carey Stanton, and Al Vail. Photograph provided by John Gherini.

Fig. 9. A steep climb to wartime Quonset huts was available to visitors on Santa Barbara Island. Photographer and date unknown, CINP Archives, ACC. 217, CAT. 3247.

on an annual basis. As Ehorn viewed the noisy rookery, he realized that he was witnessing a sight that was unequaled anywhere else in the world.

Superintendent Ehorn's first action toward this end was to address the 1963 MOA with the navy. The original agreement had been reached with the intent of allowing the Park Service to manage San Miguel Island's resources while the navy maintained titular authority over the island itself. Shortly after Ehorn arrived at the monument, he discovered that this agreement had never been acted upon—in fact could not be acted upon—because the navy had insisted that the Park Service develop a report on the resources of the islands together with recommendations for their continued protection and management.[29] Until this report was completed, the navy insisted on keeping the island closed to public access. The report was never written, so the island remained closed. NPS solicitors insisted that the agency could not spend money where public visitation was forbidden. Ehorn's staff quickly completed the required report and then negotiated a compromise with the navy to allow public access under the guidance of a park ranger. This agreement also provided for the transfer of San Miguel Island to the National Park Service if the navy ever determined that the island was surplus to its own needs. The new agreement was approved on October 20, 1976.

Later that year, Superintendent Ehorn also addressed the lack of any formal management policy for San Miguel Island by organizing a Management Advisory Committee, which included Dr. A. Starker Leopold, who then sat on the president's Marine Mammal Commission; Dr. DeLong; Dr. Dennis Power, director of the Santa Barbara Museum of Natural History (SBMNH); Carey Stanton; and representatives of the U.S. Navy; the CDFG; the University of California, Santa Barbara; and the NPS. These experts were brought together for a two-day meeting and field trip in January of 1977 to determine how visitation would be controlled and resources protected.

At the meeting, the committee issued fourteen recommendations including classification of San Miguel and Prince Islands as an Environmental Protection Subzone; placement of a permanent island ranger and a seasonal ranger at a site near Cuyler Harbor; maintenance of the existing "road" as a trail; use of a small boat to patrol the harbor area;

inauguration of a program to allow small parties of permitted visitors to tour limited sections of the island with a ranger; formation of an advisory committee to screen potential researchers; and continuation of flights for NPS personnel, preferably by helicopter, but not for visitors.

In late 1978, Bill Ehorn, Regional Director Howard Chapman, and the base commander of Point Mugu signed the resulting Statement for Management. It divided the islands into two zones. On San Miguel a Natural Environment Subzone consisted of a one-acre site for the existing Marine Mammal Research Center hut, staffed by NMFS researchers; the sixty-foot-wide "trail corridor"; and a five-acre helicopter pad "where landings can be spread out to reduce impact." All the rest of the two islands and the surrounding state waters were classified as an Environmental Protection Subzone managed to "perpetuate their unique ecological and scientific values."[30]

Channel Islands National Park Act (P.L. 96-199)

The event that decisively moved Bill Ehorn to pursue park status for Channel Islands National Monument was the Supreme Court's decision in 1978 to grant the state of California authority over the waters within the one-mile boundary of the monument. The Park Service had introduced regulations limiting commercial fishing within the monument in 1972. Resource staff from the Western Regional Office (WRO) had become concerned over the decline in abalone, spiny lobster, and some fish species around the islands and implemented closures in order to protect the remaining populations. All commercial take of abalone and lobster was prohibited from the waters on the north side of Anacapa Island and the east side of Santa Barbara. The new regulations also prohibited the taking of any invertebrate marine life from the intertidal zone.[31] These rules angered commercial fishermen who resented being denied access to a resource they had long harvested. Some also questioned the right of the National Park Service to regulate fisheries within these waters, because the state had jurisdiction over coastal waters elsewhere. Eventually, a group of fishermen appealed to the state of California to challenge the federal authority. The fishermen knew that the CDFG would be more supportive of their interests than the NPS.

The kelp harvesting industry also challenged the NPS. Those companies harvested extensive populations of giant bladder kelp (*Macrocystis pyrifera*) that grow within coast areas throughout the Southern California Bight. Dense forests of bladder kelp occur widely around the Channel Islands, creating habitat for more than 750 species of fish and marine invertebrates. Bladder kelp anchors itself to rocks on the seafloor at depths as great as 100 feet (30.5 meters), sending its long stipes and broad, leaf-like blades to the surface, where they float in thick mats suspended by the species' bladders. In optimal conditions, like those present around the Northern Channel Islands, kelp can grow more than a foot per day. These underwater forests are largely responsible for the unique abundance and diversity of marine life in the park. But kelp is also a source of a commercially valuable chemical called algin, which is used for a wide variety of applications in the production of both foods and medicines. Since algin is difficult to synthesize, it must be collected from natural sources. It was first harvested off Southern California between 1916 and 1918 for production of chemicals like acetone and iodine during World War I. Production fell off with the conclusion of the war until the 1930s, when new commercial applications were discovered for algin. Thereafter, a number of small companies began harvesting along the Southern California coast on leases from the state. One of these, the Kelco Company, expanded its operations to the Channel Islands in 1950 after kelp populations along the mainland coast declined.[32]

By the 1970s, Kelco had become a division of the multinational pharmaceutical firm Merck & Co. and employed about five hundred people in its San Diego processing plant. The company used large, barge-like harvesting boats with cutters mounted on a rack at the forward end. The cutters sheared off the upper four feet of the kelp, where the biomass was thickest, and a conveyor carried the harvested material onboard. These ungainly but effective boats moved through the kelp forests like sea-going lawnmowers. They typically harvested each bed three or four times a year. Kelco derived about 12 percent of its annual harvest from the Channel Islands.[33]

The Southern California fishermen eventually convinced the state of California to sue the Department of the Interior, challenging the Park

Service's authority to regulate fisheries within monument boundaries. The state claimed that the 1953 Submerged Lands Act had given California exclusive jurisdiction over all waters and submerged lands within three miles of the island shorelines, including those waters within the one-mile boundary of the monument. The suit eventually made its way to the U.S. Supreme Court, which upheld the state's claim on grounds that the NPS had not exercised its right to reserve the lands in which it had a prior interest when the Submerged Lands Act was passed in 1953. Had the agency done so, it could have reserved the submerged lands (and overlying waters) within the monument's one-mile seaward boundary. Although it mattered little to the court, the reason the Park Service had failed to exercise these rights back in 1954 was due to the neglect of the monument itself, which at that time had no staff of its own. When the Supreme Court announced its decision on May 15, 1978, Bill Ehorn was on Santa Barbara Island. Chief Scientist Gary Davis later recalled when a Kelco boat approached the island and cut through the forest Ehorn openly wept with frustration.

Ehorn resolved to expand the monument and gain park status in order to prevent further damage to Channel Islands, and perhaps even to regain some of what had been lost.[34] The moment could not have been more opportune to pursue a park bill. Even as the Supreme Court was debating the monument's jurisdiction, Carey Stanton was engrossed in negotiations with the Nature Conservancy (TNC) over the sale of his land on Santa Cruz Island. In September of 1978, Stanton told Ehorn that he had just sold his property to the conservancy. Ehorn responded to Stanton that he was pleased to know that most of Santa Cruz Island would now be protected through the stewardship of an organization "that has policies that are closely aligned with those of the National Park Service."[35]

Another strong inducement to pursue the Channel Islands-park bill at this time was the interest that had been aroused in nearby Los Angeles County by Congressman Anthony Beilenson. He was elected to the House as representative of California's Twenty-third Congressional District in January 1977. One of the first things Beilenson did after arriving in Washington was submit a bill to include the Santa Monica Mountains within the national park system. Representative Robert Lagomarsino, whose

Thirteenth Congressional District lay just north of Beilenson's, had submitted a Santa Monica Mountains National Park bill only a few months earlier.³⁶ But Lagomarsino had been reluctant to support a similar bill for the Northern Channel Islands, even though they lay within his district. His feelings changed, however, when Beilenson proposed a combined Santa Monica Mountains and Channel Islands National Park.³⁷ This incident may have convinced him of the likelihood that some action would eventually be taken and that it was better for him to get behind it rather than stand aside. Lagomarsino was aware that the best way to steer any proposed bill in the direction he wanted it was to author the bill himself. He had several reasons to be concerned. Beilenson's proposal would have given ownership of the waters around the islands to the National Park Service, but Lagomarsino believed these should remain under state jurisdiction. He also wanted to protect the interests of the private landowners, many of whom were personal friends. Indeed, his own brother worked as a hunting guide on Santa Cruz Island, and his family had close ties with many of the island ranchers as a result.

Representative Lagomarsino introduced the earliest version of his Channel Islands bill, H.R. 2975, to the House on March 26, 1979. Bill Ehorn had gone to Washington DC to help Lagomarsino and his aides draft the bill. The legislation would eliminate the existing monument, establish a national park in its place, and authorize the NPS to acquire all properties within the designated boundaries, but only with the willing cooperation of both private and federal land owners. Of great significance later, this earliest version of the Channel Islands National Park bill contained the stipulation that the Park Service develop a "natural resources study report" that included "(1) an inventory of all terrestrial and marine species, indicating their population dynamics, and probable trends as to future numbers and welfare; and (2) recommendations as to what actions should be considered for adoption to better protect the natural resources of the park."³⁸

Of more immediate consequence to most interested parties were the bill's stipulations concerning the Park Service's relationship with private landowners. In his original draft, Representative Lagomarsino specified that the lands belonging to the Vail & Vickers Company on Santa Rosa

Island and to TNC on Santa Cruz Island could not be acquired through condemnation. The bill also specified that private owners who agreed to sell their lands could retain a twenty-five-year reservation of use and occupancy (RUO), which could be terminated only if the former owners exercised an incompatible use. Lagomarsino included in his bill the following clause: "Existing uses of any property acquired under this Act (including, but not limited to, grazing activities and operations and the control and management of feral and non-native animals by selective control techniques used before the date of enactment of this Act) shall not be treated as incompatible uses."[39] If the owners chose not to obtain an RUO, they would still be able to request a "leaseback." The latter was an agreement that would allow the former owners to continue an existing use of the lands, though now for a fee paid to the Park Service and subject to the agency's conditions.

Testimony for the bill was heard in the House National Parks Subcommittee on April 30, where the bill was marked up. On May 4, H.R. 3757, a procedural bill that had been introduced by Representative Philip Burton, was reported from the Committee on Interior and Insular Affairs, and Lagomarsino's Channel Islands bill now became Title II of H.R. 3757. During this markup period, the representatives made a number of changes to Lagomarsino's original bill. Most significant were changes in the language concerning the rights of private landowners. The clause in the original bill describing RUOs was considerably modified and now included the right to remove nonnative animals from the island "not to exceed a *fifteen-year period* [authors' emphasis]." This clarified Vail & Vickers' right to continue their economically important commercial hunting operation. These rights would be subject to termination if the secretary of the interior determined that the uses were incompatible with the administration of the park, but in the event that an RUO was abrogated for these reasons, the amended bill now required that monetary compensation be awarded. Leases were also subject to termination, especially if the lessee introduced incompatible uses. Of much greater significance, Lagomarsino's clause specifying that existing practices would not be construed as incompatible was removed. Instead, the secretary would now have full latitude in determining whether a use was compatible or not. Condemnation of TNC lands on Santa Cruz Island and Vail & Vickers' property on Santa Rosa remained forbidden as in the earlier bill.

Most of these changes were directed at Vail & Vickers and were not as solicitous as Lagomarsino had been with his original proposal. Nevertheless, the amended bill still offered the ranchers considerable assurances—they would not be forced to sell their lands, and if they did choose to sell, they would be able to retain a twenty-five-year RUO that would allow them to continue ranching. They would also be able to continue their hunting operation, but only for fifteen years. Counterbalancing these assurances, however, the Vail & Vickers Company operations would be subject to scrutiny by the NPS. But the House bill was sufficiently clear in its definition of allowable activities that it would be difficult for any right of use to be terminated during a twenty-five-year RUO so long as it did not deviate substantially from existing practice. Moreover, the assurance of monetary compensation in the event of termination reduced the possibility that the NPS would act capriciously.

On May 7, 1979, the U.S. House of Representatives considered and passed H.R. 3757, as amended. Shortly thereafter, the bill was introduced to the Senate as S. 1104 by Senator Alan Cranston of California. The Senate Subcommittee on Parks, Recreation, and Renewable Resources held hearings on July 19, 1979. Representative Lagomarsino introduced the amended House bill to the Senate with a letter that remained very solicitous of the Vail & Vickers interests.[40] He reiterated these sentiments in his opening statement to the Senate subcommittee on the morning of July 19, but clarified that Vail & Vickers expected to make necessary upgrades and improvements in their operation in order to remain economically competitive.[41]

Vail & Vickers were still opposed to selling their land and would support the bill only if it did not require them to do so. As inholders, Vail & Vickers feared that any modification in ranching practice might trigger a hostile condemnation and force them to sell the island against their will. The company encouraged the committee to "clarify the language in the bill to provide condemnation only when the Secretary of Interior determines a property is undergoing or about to undergo a significant change in use which on the basis of documentation is clearly inconsistent with the purposes of the park."[42]

The NPS defined a "change in use" that might constitute grounds for condemnation as, "any activity not historically related to ranch operations currently existing [including] development of residential or commercial facilities, or drilling for oil or any use that would have an impact on natural or cultural resources."[43] This statement illustrated the Park Service's willingness to allow continued ranching on Santa Rosa Island at that time as a private inholding, at least in principle, but also its demand for control of how the ranching operation would be conducted. NPS director William Whalen, during his testimony, described unacceptable change in use on land owned by the park as subdivision, mineral extraction, and possibly overgrazing. Respecting the last, he explained that present grazing levels were acceptable but that the park would want to work with the landowner to determine appropriate animal units per acre in the future.

Vail & Vickers members testified before the subcommittee that their chief concern remained the threat of condemnation, but made some additional suggestions regarding how this problem might be addressed. Al Vail proposed that any use judged incompatible should trigger a temporary restraining order rather than outright condemnation. He also proposed that any such determination be reviewed by a federal district court. This would give the family an opportunity to respond before a neutral arbiter and prevent the Park Service and the secretary of the interior from using their authority inappropriately. These suggestions illustrated how deeply the Vails' mistrust of the National Park Service already ran, despite the best efforts of Superintendent Ehorn.

Although the property interests of private landowners like Vail & Vickers were the principal focus of the subcommittee's attention, other concerns were also expressed. Many senators worried about the effect that the proposed park might have on the state's authority over the waters surrounding the islands. Representative Lagomarsino had raised this issue when he introduced the House bill to the Senate, noting that his version of the bill contained explicit assurances that the state would retain its authority over the waters and submerged lands within three miles of each island's shoreline.[44] Kelco submitted a written statement protesting the park bill as currently written on the assumption that, if passed, it would return authority over the near-shore waters to the NPS.[45] The company recommended that the bill be amended to assure continuation of lawful commercial activities if authority over the marine component of the proposed park were transferred from the state to the federal government. Such an amendment proved unnecessary, however, because most of the senators preferred to retain the state's authority over these waters.[46]

The Park Service continued to address concerns about whether Santa Rosa Island should be included in the proposed park or not. Acting Director Daniel Tobin wrote a lengthy account of the unique natural resources of the island, but also wrote that the Vail & Vickers ranch "represents one of the best opportunities to preserve and interpret historical ranching operations." Bur Low in the NPS Director's Office emphasized that the proposed bill would allow condemnation of their property only in response to incompatible use and that it specifically cited grazing operations as a compatible use.[47] Nevertheless, on November 7, 1979, some four months after the Senate subcommittee hearings took place, Vail & Vickers submitted a letter to Congress stating that the Park Service's response had not reassured them. The company proposed one of two alternatives—either Santa Rosa Island be excluded from the proposed park boundaries or the Vail & Vickers' property be condemned at the earliest possible time and the company be compensated at the existing market value. In this event, Vail & Vickers' recent appraisal of the subdivision value of their ranch would represent an important negotiating position.[48]

The first alternative was not really a viable option. A park bill that did not include Santa Rosa Island or Santa Cruz Island would be unlikely to pass Congress. Vail & Vickers were aware of how much momentum had already been built behind the bill by this time and realized that it was unlikely to be abandoned, so, in fact, only their second alternative was intended as a serious proposition. This would allow them to preserve the economic value of their property, even if it meant losing the property itself. Selling the ranch was not a desirable option until passage of the proposed bill began to appear inevitable. Bill Ehorn met with Al and

Russ Vail in Washington DC the night before the subcommittee hearings and stressed his and Lagomarsino's belief that the expressions of support from Congress would ensure they could continue ranching after selling through the RUO or leaseback options.[49] The Vails had considered the possibility of a sale and made efforts to ensure the best possible terms. Now they needed an assurance that the federal government would buy their property *as soon as possible*.

Urgency was important for two reasons. In order to obtain the full market price for their property, Vail & Vickers believed that the sale would have to be completed before Santa Rosa Island became an inholding within the proposed park. The land value would be diminished unless a sale was legislatively required on the basis of market value prior to the passage of the bill. Vail & Vickers had secured an appraisal made in anticipation of the park debate. The highest value for which the property was currently appraisable assumed that the island could be developed for high-end residential subdivision, but the existing park bill would allow the Park Service to initiate condemnation procedures if this sort of development was ever seriously considered. Acknowledging that they could not avoid becoming part of the proposed park, they wanted to ensure that they would be bought out before the anticipated devaluation of their property.[50] Urgency was also needed in selling Santa Rosa Island because both Vail & Vickers families were concerned about the inheritance tax, which would require them to pay a substantial percentage of their land's value as members of the present generation died.[51]

If the ranchers kept the island, commercial hunting was still a rich source of funds. Vail & Vickers had introduced elk to Santa Rosa Island in 1912 and deer in 1929 in order to provide an opportunity for large game hunting.[52] In addition to the wild pigs, which were already abundant, the deer and elk had successfully naturalized within their new environment and were proliferating so rapidly by the late 1970s that periodic culling was needed in order to maintain a manageable population and prevent overgrazing. Al and Russ Vail's sister Margaret Woolley recognized the potential for commercial hunting as a revenue source for the island and ultimately formed an agreement with Wayne Long of Multiple Use Management to run the hunting operation.[53]

The Senate Committee on Energy and Natural Resources adopted the subcommittee markups on November 29, 1979, but introduced several changes of its own. The most significant of these was made in response to the letter submitted by the Vails expressing their dissatisfaction with the prospect of becoming an inholder within the proposed park. In deference to Vail & Vickers' concerns, the Senate committee replaced the non-condemnation provision of the original bill with a new clause requiring the NPS to secure Santa Rosa Island first: "the acquisition of these lands shall take priority over the acquisition of other privately owned lands within the park."[54]

On February 20, 1980, it was sent back to the House for review and concurrence. Representative Keith Sebelius expressed strong regret that the Senate had bowed to pressure from the state. He believed that the proposed park was substantially diminished by the abdication of the Park Service's authority over its marine resources. To compensate for the loss of protection, Sebelius encouraged the Park Service to place greater emphasis on the bill's mandate to inventory the park's terrestrial and marine species that had survived from Lagomarsino's first bill. He stated, "This should at least serve as an early warning system for any jeopardy that may come to these species resulting from any adverse impact brought upon them due to commercial fishing, kelp harvest, oil drilling, space technologies activities and the like."[55] The result was Section 203a of the final act that expanded the stipulation to study and monitor marine resources and set further precedent for an inventory and monitoring program throughout the park system.

The prospect of swarms of destructive visitors had been one of Carey Stanton's objections to park status, and one of several reasons why he sold his property to the Nature Conservancy in 1978. Representative Lagomarsino agreed to sponsor a bill only with the stipulation that any future park be managed on a low-intensity basis.[56] Hence, the final bill included the following important stipulation: "The park shall be administered on a low-intensity, limited-entry basis. . . . In recognition of the special fragility and sensitivity of the park's resources, it is the intent of Congress that the visitor use within the park be limited to assure negligible adverse impact on park resources. The Secretary shall establish appropriate carrying capacities for the park."[57]

After these comments were recorded, the House voted its concurrence with the Senate amendments, and H.R. 3757 was enrolled. On March 5, 1980, President Jimmy Carter signed the bill, which was recorded in the Federal Register as P.L. 96–199, and the nation's fortieth national park was established. The act called for the first inventory of terrestrial and marine species in two fiscal years, a general management plan coordinated with the state of California and TNC within three fiscal years, and a report to the president on wilderness suitability also within three fiscal years. The NPS had much work to do.

Channel Islands National Marine Sanctuary (1980)

When Channel Islands National Park Act passed, it reaffirmed state jurisdiction over the near-shore waters around the newly added Channel Islands as well. Immediately after the 1978 Supreme Court decision, protest from scientists familiar with the Channel Islands and its natural resources, had prompted the CDFG to designate the waters within one nautical mile of Anacapa, Santa Barbara, and San Miguel Islands as state ecological reserves.[58] A year earlier, the state of California had tentatively nominated a large marine area within the Santa Barbara Channel for designation under the Marine Sanctuaries Act. The proposed sanctuary, as originally defined, would have extended twelve nautical miles from the shorelines of the three monument islands. The nomination was considered during a long public scoping process that also considered potential marine sanctuaries in other parts of the state. Eventually, four areas within the state's coastal waters were chosen, with Channel Islands National Marine Sanctuary (CINMS) the first to be established, in September 1980, only seven months after passage of the Channel Islands National Park bill. The original state proposal was later modified to include only six nautical miles, rather than twelve, but was also extended to encompass the waters around Santa Cruz and Santa Rosa Islands in response to the anticipated national park expansion. The resulting sanctuary comprises 1,470 square miles.

Within this area, the sanctuary provided limited protection for all marine life as well as artifacts of cultural value. Its jurisdiction overlapped the legislative boundaries of the national park, the state ecological reserves, and the state-owned waters within the three-mile territorial limit as well as extending an additional three nautical miles into federally owned Outer Continental Shelf (OCS) waters. By and large, the regulations first established for the CINMS did not specifically provide protection of the biological resources within this large area, on the assumption that existing federal and state laws would do so. Early regulations were concerned instead with potential development or intrusions near the Channel Islands and included restrictions on seabed construction, aircraft overflights, vessel traffic, dumping of waste, and the development of new oil and gas leases.[59]

NOAA, the NPS, and the CDFG shared administration of the Marine Sanctuary. Overlapping jurisdictions within the sanctuary boundaries and the limited staffing available to NOAA necessitated cooperation. Three other federal agencies had vested responsibilities within the sanctuary boundaries—the U.S. Coast Guard, which maintained aids to navigation on Anacapa and Santa Barbara Islands; the U.S. Navy, which still owned San Miguel Island and maintained missile tracking facilities on Santa Cruz Island; and the Minerals Management Service, an agency within the Department of the Interior, which oversaw leases on the OCS to the oil and gas producing industries.[60]

A few months later, on July 17, 1981, the National Park Service signed an interagency agreement with NOAA and CDFG that formally identified the responsibilities each agency would assume in the administration and management of the new marine sanctuary.[61] CDFG agreed to provide the law enforcement and a boat to carry it out. The NPS agreed to design and implement research for sanctuary management, provide supply office space in the park headquarters for a sanctuary manager, and produce interpretive displays relevant to the sanctuary. In exchange for these services, NOAA provided funding for a contract to design a seabird monitoring protocol and partially funded the kelp forest monitoring program designed by NPS chief scientist Gary Davis. The Park Service funded ten multiyear design studies and then implemented the protocols with

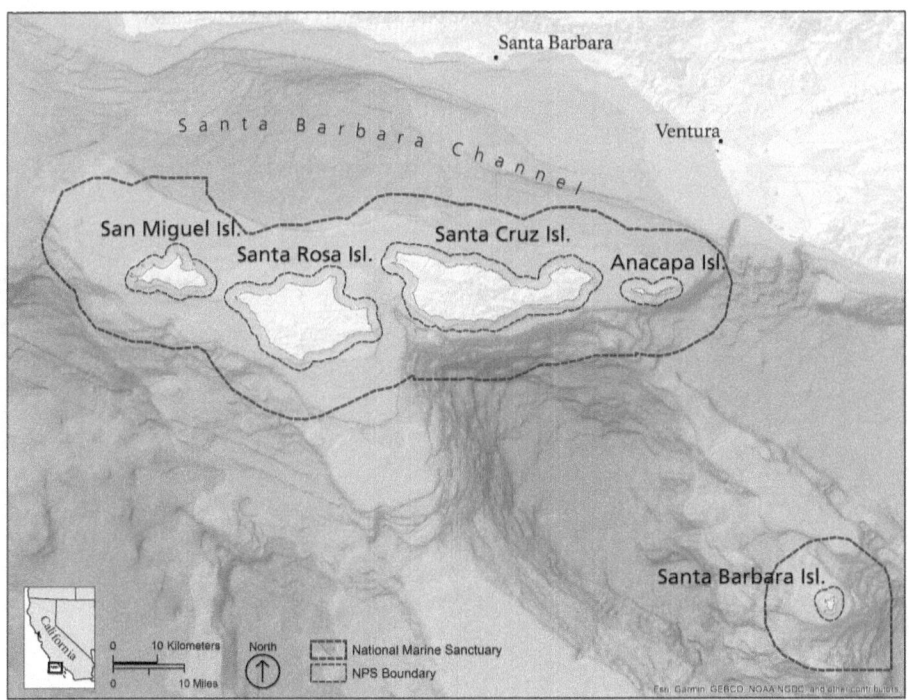

Map 11. Boundaries of the national park and marine sanctuary after their enabling acts. Cartography by R. Rudolph, CINP.

personnel and support. Initially the marine sanctuary manager was a NOAA employee who received primary direction from the director of the Marine Sanctuaries Office in Washington DC but received direct supervision from the park's superintendent. Some NOAA funds were used to hire a small staff to assist the sanctuary manager. Like the manager, these seasonal employees worked at the national park headquarters. In 1987 NOAA appointed its own manager and moved the CINMS headquarters to Santa Barbara. Despite the separation, the two staffs continue to work together for the preservation of the marine resources surrounding the Channel Islands.

Resource Management in the Early Years

The natural resource management program at Channel Islands National Park dates back to the late 1960s, when the monument was required to prepare a natural resource management plan (NRMP). This policy for all units with natural resources was a response to the findings and recommendations of the *Leopold Report*. Secretary of the Interior Stewart Udall had appointed the committee in response to pressure from scientists and resource managers who were concerned that the agency had neglected its natural resources during more than three decades of recreation-oriented development culminating with Mission 66.[1] The *Leopold Report* made two crucial points, which it presented as objectives for future management. The first was the idea that parks represented vestiges of nature relatively undisturbed by human intervention. Where this still appeared to be the case, the report recommended that those primitive conditions be maintained. Where it was not, it recommended that these conditions be the objective toward which management aimed. The authors wrote, "A national park should represent a vignette of primitive America."[2]

The other point the report emphasized was the need for sound research as a prerequisite to proper management. This was integral to the goal of maintaining or restoring primitive conditions, for it often required serious study to determine what those conditions were. The report observed that most research currently being done in the parks served interpretive rather than management purposes and urged that this emphasis be changed by replacing naturalists with professional scientists.[3] Secretary Udall immediately endorsed the *Leopold Report*, requiring the Park Service to adopt its recommendations.

Parks were ordered to promptly prepare NRMPs that would adapt the principles outlined in the *Leopold Report* to their specific situations and needs. Each plan required three essential elements: (1) an inventory and description of existing biotic communities, natural processes, and land use practices; (2) an inventory and description of biotic communities and natural processes under conditions when Europeans first arrived; and (3) processes for managing or restoring existing conditions to the original primitive state where it was possible to do so. Each of these elements required sophisticated knowledge of the resources. The NPS director's guidelines proposed establishing an extensive research program to accompany each stage of the management plan.[4] So closely attuned was research to resource management, in fact, that no research project could be undertaken if it was not first identified in the park's resource management plan.[5]

Channel Islands National Monument (CINM) was hindered from responding immediately by its neglect at that time under coordinated administration with Cabrillo National Monument as well as the lack of adequate baseline knowledge of its natural resources. These challenges began to be addressed in 1967 following the separation of the two monuments and assignment of permanent staff to Channel Islands. Rangers stationed on Santa Barbara and Anacapa Islands soon prepared rudimentary resource management plans. Valuable as they were, however, these early reports reflected the practical experience of generalist rangers rather than the professional analysis of trained scientists and were not based on any systematic inventory or study of the resources themselves.[6] Senior NPS officials acknowledged this deficiency and addressed it the following year. James K. Baker of the Park Service's Office of Natural Sciences initiated a basic data survey for a Channel Islands NRMP. Field work was conducted by scientists from local research institutions including the University of California, the Natural History Museum of Los Angeles County, and the Santa Barbara Botanic Garden.

The findings of these scientists allowed the NPS staff to complete the monument's first comprehensive NRMP in 1975.[7] The plan recommended eight research projects, seven management programs, and two hydrologic programs. It emphasized the treatment of exotic terrestrial species. The scientists strongly recommended complete eradication of rabbits from Santa Barbara Island, reduction in the numbers of rats on Anacapa Island, and control of invasive exotic plants. Ice plant (*Mesembryanthemum crystalinum*) on Santa Barbara Island was the only plant they specifically identified, but they also called for further study of other potentially noxious species. The plan also identified priorities for marine resources, including the further study of marine mammals, evaluation of the intertidal zone to assess potential visitor impacts, and inventory and evaluation of commercial and sport fisheries, all to develop best management practices. Management guidelines were also needed for the recently designated Research Natural Area on West Anacapa Island to protect breeding California brown pelicans.

In July 1977, park staff began work on a general management plan (GMP) for the monument in anticipation of congressional legislation that would require such plans for all NPS units.[8] A GMP required baseline data for both natural and cultural resources as well as information relevant to other aspects of monument operations. That plan was completed in 1980, a few months after enactment of the park bill. However, the park now needed further research to inventory all of the resources on just-added Santa Cruz and Santa Rosa Islands. Resource managers worked closely with the park's legally mandated science program to develop accurate and comprehensive baseline inventories of natural resources throughout the park. Key to that work and to the future of both Channel Islands and the entire national park system was the development of a groundbreaking inventory and monitoring program.

Gary Davis and Long-Term Monitoring

Public Law 96–199 establishing Channel Islands National Park in 1980 gave powerful impetus to scientific research with its explicit mandate in Section 203(a) to inventory the new park's terrestrial and marine species in order to determine present conditions and probable future trends in species populations. To do this it would be necessary to monitor these inventories over time and to accumulate long-term datasets that were capable of revealing individual changes too subtle to be clearly manifested in the short term, or larger patterns that would only be recognizable after many years. Implementing a monitoring program to achieve these objectives was the intent of this section of the park bill. It had been proposed by marine biologist Dr. Gary Davis, who at that time was still employed as the chief scientist at Everglades National Park but was a friend of Superintendent Bill Ehorn. Over the years, Ehorn and Davis had stayed in touch, and Ehorn had tried to hire Gary Davis as Chief Ranger at Channel Islands in 1977. Davis declined but told Bill to get back in touch with him if he ever needed a chief scientist. A year later, as Ehorn watched the Kelco Company harvester cutting swathes through the kelp forest off Santa Barbara Island, this need became glaringly apparent. He realized that the only way he could challenge such abuse was through the authority of legitimate scientific research. Ehorn recognized the need for a chief scientist on his staff and his thoughts soon returned to Gary Davis, but not until the park bill had already been set in motion.[9]

In the meantime, Davis himself, through a fortuitous chain of circumstances, had become involved with the Channel Islands already. In 1979 he was contacted by a man named Clay Peters, who at that time was employed as a congressional staff member and was busy drafting language for a bill to convert Biscayne National Monument to a national park. Since Biscayne was located in southern Florida not far from where Gary Davis was stationed, Peters naturally turned to Davis for advice. Peters had once been employed as a ranger in the National Park Service and had served with both Gary Davis and Bill Ehorn at Lassen Volcanic National Park during the 1960s. Coincidentally, Peters was working on a draft of the Channel Islands park bill at the same time and happened to mention this to Davis. Because both men were old friends of Bill Ehorn, their conversation soon turned to the proposed legislation and how it should be worded. Davis was able to introduce the section on natural resource inventory and recommendations to the park bill, with significant consequences both for the park and his own career. He had come to appreciate the importance of long-term monitoring and suggested that it be incorporated into the bill as a legislative mandate.[10] Monitoring, however, was not a popular concept at the time, because it was considered too open-ended. No politicians would agree to fund a proposal that appeared to offer no measurable returns within the lifespan of their political tenure.

Davis compromised by avoiding the term "monitoring" and agreed to set definite limits to the proposed program. The result of this compromise was the ten-year population dynamics study described in the final park bill. Davis hoped that, once this short-term monitoring program was set in place, it would show practical results to justify continuing as the long-term monitoring program he envisioned.

Gary Davis had learned the value of long-term datasets and ecosystem management from his experience in southern Florida between 1971 and 1980. His chief influence here was Dr. William B. Robertson who monitored pelagic birds like the sooty tern (*Onychoprion fuscatus*). Research on the habits and population dynamics of this species had been carried on since the 1930s, when experiments with banding and monitoring their seasonal movements first began. Robertson expanded this research at Everglades.[11] The most significant result, however, was the longevity of the dataset accumulated. By the time Davis left Florida, the sooty tern had been carefully and comprehensively monitored for a full half-century.

Among the favorite foods of sooty terns are juvenile bluefin tuna. This species is highly valued among both commercial and sport fishermen and was harvested in great numbers during the time that Robertson and his predecessors were collecting monitoring data on the birds. Many years before any decline was noticed in the tuna fishery, the tern data showed a significant change in the birds' diet with the juvenile tuna all but disappearing. Another twenty years passed before the fishery began to notice any decline in mature tuna, but the origins of this decline had been presaged in the disappearance of juvenile fish in the terns' diet. These juvenile fish had been overharvested by the commercial fishery. By the time the effects of overharvesting were noticed, the entire population began to collapse. The key lesson for Davis was the value of having long-term datasets, such as that on the terns, to predict changes where a population may not exhibit an immediate, measurable response to a cumulative adverse effect.

After Gary Davis laid the foundation for a long-term monitoring program in the park bill, Bill Ehorn invited him to become chief scientist at the new park in early 1980. Davis arrived fully committed to implementing the principles of ecosystem management and long-term monitoring. He made this clear in a presentation before the annual convocation of the Western Region's research scientists and their regional supervisors later that year. The other scientists on the committee were less than enthusiastic about his proposal, believing that monitoring of the sort he described was not true research. Nevertheless, he was strongly supported by Bill Ehorn, who had become convinced of the need for reliable data on population dynamics as a result of his failure to prevent the commercial exploitation of marine resources around the islands after the transfer of jurisdiction to the state in 1978.

As noted, Section 203(a) appeared in the earliest version of the park bill introduced by Representative Robert Lagomarsino in the spring of 1979 and remained unchanged and unquestioned throughout the remaining legislative process.[12] Lagomarsino and other political supporters of the bill were willing to accept Davis's proposed research and monitoring program because they were acutely aware of the park's vulnerability within the heavily used maritime corridor of the Santa Barbara Channel. The reality of the threats confronting the new park had already been demonstrated by the historic hunting of marine mammals, the increasing pressure on marine resources from the fishing industry, the oil spill from the blowout on Platform A in 1969, and contamination of the marine food chain from industrial pollutants like the DDT and PCBs released into the coastal waters up until 1972. Past research had shown the importance of scientific monitoring to determine whether such threats were having a negative impact. Another concern was that establishment of the park would bring crowds of visitors, who could damage the islands' resources that were previously protected by limited access under private ownership. The legal requirement that the park be administered on a low-intensity, limited-entry basis could not be done effectively without an accurate assessment of the park's natural resources and their vulnerability to the impacts of human visitation.[13]

IMPLEMENTING THE INVENTORY AND MONITORING PROGRAM

The first challenge for Gary Davis at Channel Islands was to identify what natural resources the park actually had. Individual scientists and research institutions had published their work on the Channel Islands, but this material needed to be reviewed and the information compiled in a single source that would be easily accessible to park researchers. Any gaps in the body of knowledge could then be identified and filled through additional field work. The literature review initiated in 1979 produced an annotated bibliography containing more than four thousand entries by 1981. Based on this review, the park was able to compile a comprehensive list of species and species assemblages with enough contextual information to begin prioritizing their significance for monitoring purposes.

The research team then began developing protocols for key species. Monitoring a species required individual population dynamics including their abundance, distribution, population age structure, reproduction, recruitment, growth rate, mortality rate, population sex composition, and phenology (seasonal patterns).[14] This posed substantial practical challenges. Section 203(a) boldly instructed the park to inventory and monitor *all* terrestrial and marine species. But as Davis pointed out, the park at that time was known to possess "nearly 1,000 macroscopic species of marine plants and animals, at least 69 species of breeding birds, over 100 endemic terrestrial plants, and hundreds of other terrestrial plants and animals."[15] It would be absurdly difficult to consider all of these species, and impossible to do so within two years when the first biennial report to congress was due. Therefore, Davis proposed selecting a smaller, more manageable number of representative species, grouped within several broad categories.

Criteria for the selection of these species took into account a variety of ecological, social, economic, legal, and political factors. Endangered or threatened species or those specifically protected, such as marine mammals, had to be included as a matter of law and policy. Other priorities included species that were endemic to the park, harvested species, species that were major elements or indicators of critical habitat for endangered species, exotic or feral species, species that were dominant or characteristic components of major park ecosystems, and other highly visible or charismatic species. Eventually, nearly five hundred species were selected for long-term monitoring. Davis also added a few categories representing background conditions or activities because of their close relationship to the population dynamics of significant individual species. These included human patterns of impact through park visitation and fishery harvest, and environmental factors such as weather and water quality.

By 1982, when the first biennial report was submitted, Davis and his colleagues had identified fifteen categories of species or environmental conditions to monitor. Each category represented a distinct research project or task. The development of the data management system, already implemented, formed a sixteenth category. These projects were ranked numerically according to their priority. Pinnipeds were at the top of the list. This demonstrated either the relative importance of marine mammals to the park, or the fact that a well-established pinniped monitoring program already existed at Point Bennett, or both. All sixteen projects, as well as the component or intermediate tasks needed to implement them, were diagrammed on a hierarchical "step-down plan" that showed the order in which the program would proceed.[16]

Each of the fifteen monitoring projects was broken down into five distinct tasks: (1) review and summarize existing information on population dynamics, (2) design sampling techniques using historical precedents whenever appropriate, (3) design a system for routine analysis of the resulting data, (4) design a system for routinely archiving and reporting the results of the data analysis, and (5) field test the sampling techniques and demonstrate the analytical and reporting systems using actual data. One of the major accomplishments of the initial research program was to systematize these tasks for all of the project categories. The result of this effort was a series of handbooks that provided detailed monitoring protocols for each assemblage of species or environmental condition being studied. These protocols could then be used by resource managers to continue long-term monitoring when the program passed from a purely research and design phase to its implementation. Although resource management officials would play an increasingly greater role in the monitoring program, the science division would still be responsible for directing it and for conducting primary research. Gary Davis, therefore, remained just as busy as ever. In 1983 the NPS Regional Office hired Dr. William Halvorson through the University of California, Davis, Cooperative Education Studies Unit to oversee design of monitoring protocols and to conduct research. Halvorson was duty stationed at Channel Islands along with Gary Davis.[17]

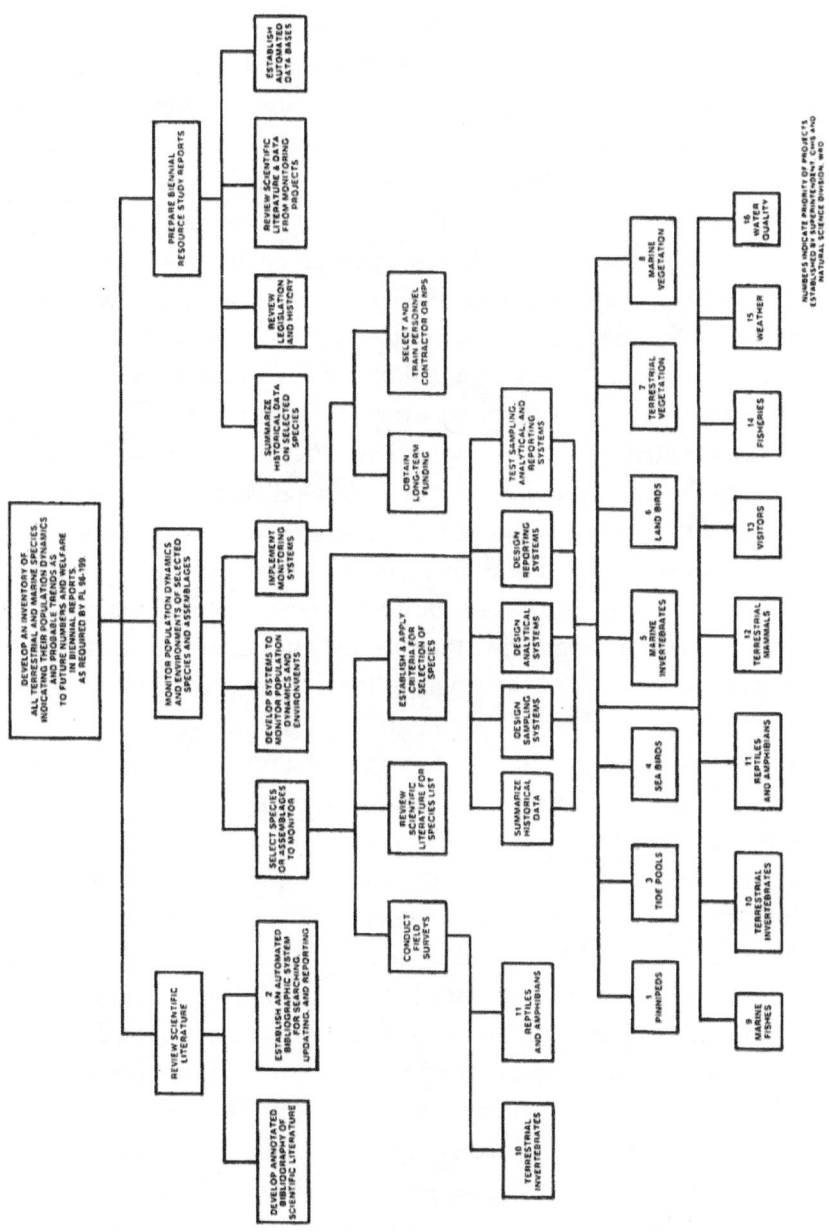

Fig. 10. I&M step-down diagram for Channel Islands National Park. Provided by Gary Davis.

As early as 1984, Davis had begun to compare the Channel Islands' inventory and monitoring program to a Health Maintenance Organization (HMO), in which doctors provide regular checkups on members to assess their physical condition according to predefined indicators, or vital signs, of health and fitness. Whereas a doctor might monitor such vital signs as blood pressure, cholesterol level, and nerve reflex, scientists and resource managers at Channel Islands monitored population dynamics of the nearly five hundred species identified in their protocols as well as a few broader conditions such as weather, visitation, and fishery pressure. The long-term monitoring of these natural indicators allowed managers to assess the health of the entire ecosystem over time in order to detect negative trends early and possibly treat them before they became too advanced.[18]

By 1988 the developmental stage of Channel Islands' inventory and monitoring program was largely complete. Inventories had been made of all known species within each of the monitoring categories defined by the program. Ten protocol handbooks were compiled, establishing detailed guides for monitoring the selected vital sign indicators within these categories. Four of the original fifteen categories from the step-down plan were combined into a single kelp forest handbook, authored by Gary Davis, while the herpetofauna and mammal components were combined into a single protocol. Eventually, protocols were written for terrestrial invertebrates (insects) and sandy beaches.[19] What remained was implementation of the long-term monitoring itself, which would be undertaken on a regular basis and continued indefinitely. Although some programs would be managed outside the Park Service, such as the National Marine Fisheries Service (NMFS) monitoring of pinnipeds at Point Bennett, most of the monitoring protocols were designed to be accomplished by the park's resource management staff. This required substantial increases in staff numbers and the base funding to pay them.

Gary Davis and Bill Halvorson estimated in 1987 that the annual operating costs for the monitoring program as designed would be $822,000. By that time, the total cost of the research design phase had come to $1,764,000.[20] However, park requests for base funds to implement the designed monitoring protocols were not competitive in the NPS budget system. If the program was to succeed, Davis realized he would have to find support from outside Channel Islands, and he began visiting other parks and regional offices around the country to propose a service-wide inventory and monitoring program.[21]

Tackling the Problem of Exotic Animals

From the earliest days of the national monument, exotic animals were recognized as invasive and damaging to the habitats of the islands. Roger Toll, Harold Bryant, and Lowell Sumner all described the disastrous effects that these animals had on the delicate island habitats. Superintendent Bill Ehorn recognized his responsibility to protect those resources and took steps to respond. In so doing, he demonstrated his penchant for summary action with positive biological results but also political risks.

BURROS ON SAN MIGUEL ISLAND

In early 1977, while Ehorn was organizing an advisory team for San Miguel Island, he decided to eliminate a small herd of burros that had become naturalized there. The burros had originally been brought to the island by ranchers.[22] By the 1950s, they had become feral and grown to a sizeable herd despite the navy's attempts to eliminate them through aerial gunnery. The burros contributed to a serious erosion problem by grazing its sparse vegetation, creating trails along hillsides, and by the physical action of their large hooves. Particularly worrying to resource managers was the impact that the burros might be having on the fragile caliche forests, which could not sustain trampling. Ehorn learned that veterinarian Dr. Charles Douglas of the University of Nevada, Las Vegas, had assisted Death Valley and Joshua Tree National Monuments and Grand Canyon National Park with their burro issues. At Ehorn's request, Douglas examined the burros during the winter of 1976 and found them in poor health with "grotesquely elongated hooves that hampered walking or running." This is a problem with many ungulates when they are confined to soft, sandy environments where few hard surfaces are available to abrade their ever-growing hooves. Douglas also observed few old individuals in the San Miguel herd, suggesting a high rate of mortality.[23]

These concerns inspired Ehorn to proactively address the problem, accompanied by Chief Ranger Mack Shaver, Dr. Douglas, and an assortment of firearms. Ehorn had one of his staff at park headquarters prepare an environmental assessment under the recently-passed National Environmental Policy Act (NEPA) complete with alternatives and a Finding of No Significant Impact (FONSI), even as he and his companions were tramping about the island with rifles in hand. As they dispatched the burros, Dr. Douglas aged and sexed them, took blood and tissue samples and noted their weight, measurements, and general health. By noon, the three men had shot about half of the burros and settled down for lunch, when Ehorn received a call from his secretary at park headquarters warning him that the navy had learned what he was up to and wanted him to hold off until they could run it through the proper channels. Ehorn instructed the secretary to reassure their navy contact (Wes Maylen at Pt. Mugu) that he would personally contact the admiral and take responsibility for his actions. After signing off, Ehorn decided to use this encouragement to finish the job as quickly as possible, and the three men proceeded to dispatch another dozen or so burros before concluding that they could return to the mainland. The thirty dead burros were left to decompose where they fell.

Ehorn assumed that this was the end of the story, but two further developments over the next few weeks proved otherwise. First, a pilot making a routine overflight of the island observed at least one live burro still standing and informed Ehorn of this fact. Second, and far more disturbing, Ehorn got a call from the California Department of Fish and Game (CDFG) office in Santa Barbara, notifying him of a complaint they had received from a woman who had been fishing illegally on San Miguel Island and had come across the rotting carcasses of the burros. She was deeply disturbed. It required little effort to infer the cause of this morbid discovery, and word quickly reached the press. Soon Ehorn was talking to an editor named Dick Smith from the *Santa Barbara News-Press* who, according to Ehorn himself, "chewed me up one side and down the other." Smith was a well-known Santa Barbara conservationist and wilderness advocate. Attempting to mollify Smith, Ehorn invited him to come out to the island the following week to learn about the resource management issues the monument faced. The environmentally-active editor readily agreed and promised to bring along representatives of local animal rights groups. In the interim, Ehorn flew back out to San Miguel Island and shot the remaining burro, which turned out to be a pregnant female.

This jenny proved to be the last surviving burro on the island, so Ehorn was finally successful in dispatching this issue, but he faced a much more daunting problem with the media. In preparation for his approaching press visit, he contacted A. Starker Leopold and Ralph Philbrick, members of the recently-organized Management Advisory Committee, who expressed their support for his actions and promised to stand behind him during the anticipated lawsuits and media assault. A call to the Park Service's Western Regional Office in San Francisco elicited a more equivocal response, well short of actual support. On the day of the planned press visit, Ehorn arrived early at park headquarters to prepare lunches for the trip over to San Miguel Island. Dick Smith was supposed to arrive at 8:00 a.m. At 8:30, Ehorn received a call notifying him that, incredibly, the editor had died in bed the night before. The press visit was canceled. Smith, it turned out, had been the instigator of the opposition to Ehorn's actions, and the story died with him. Ehorn was aware that this incident might have cost him his job, but the absence of any media follow-up allowed his superiors to dispense with disciplinary actions and bury the story. This was uncanny luck, but it also took a great deal of audacity on Ehorn's part just to get to this point.[24]

RABBITS ON SANTA BARBARA ISLAND

Another incident that illustrates Bill Ehorn's characteristic attitude toward bureaucratic process, and his good luck, was the eradication of exotic rabbits on Santa Barbara Island. During the war, U.S. Navy personnel operating a Coastal Lookout Station on Santa Barbara Island introduced Red New Zealand rabbits to provide food in the event the island was cut off from communication with the mainland.[25] When the military left at the end of the war, the rabbits remained, albeit in small numbers. Lowell Sumner counted only a handful during an inventory in 1950. Just a few years later, however, Sumner returned to witness a dramatic explosion of this population and an equally dramatic degradation of native vegetation. Sumner explained his observations:

It is typical of such irruptions that they begin unobtrusively but after several years commence to snow-ball in their effects. The present one has now reached disastrous proportions. The rapidity with which such biological changes can take place on small islands where predators are largely absent illustrates the danger of allowing several years to elapse between biological inspections. Also illustrated is the manner in which the military, when unsupervised, can erase without a thought fifteen years of conservation efforts by our Service.[26]

Sumner noted that the island was in deep trouble. The once-dense grove of the native giant coreopsis (*Leptosyne gigantea*) had a stricken aspect, with an impoverished understory that was everywhere crisscrossed by rabbit trails. The old hay field looked as if it had been run over with a mowing machine. Bare ground showed through the carpet of denuded and dying vegetation. Park personnel claimed there were so many rabbits that the animals had no thickets to hide in and sat crouched on the bare ground. Sumner advised an immediate response but was forced to leave on an assignment to Alaska before he could implement anything.

With Sumner's return in the fall of 1954, the rabbit removal program finally began. That October, Sumner and three others spent six full days hunting rabbits with shotguns and .22 rifles, making two or three drives across the same areas each day. Sumner recorded 400 kills and between 150 to 200 survivors. He took photographs to compare with ones he had taken in 1950, illustrating the decimation of the vegetation by rabbits. One photo showed the "Grizzly Giant" in its 1950 glory, the largest giant coreopsis known to the NPS, toppled by rabbits in 1954. Each fall the control program continued, with poison bait introduced as well. A controversy soon arose when newspapers reported that the Park Service was "bombing" the island with poison, thus endangering native fauna. The controversy was resolved when the Park Service explained that the poisoned bait was only delivered to the island by aerial drop for rangers to distribute by hand directly to the target species.[27]

In 1955, 2,500 rabbits were killed. The next year, about 600 were killed, and in 1957 the number was about 250. Rabbit foraging had caused the exotic ice plant to spread, and by 1958 this species covered over half the

Fig. 11. Damage from rabbits was extensive on Santa Barbara Island. Photographer and date unknown, CINP Digital Archives, "Cultural Resources."

island. Since the rabbits could not penetrate the ice plant, they were forced out into the open. Sumner reported that the fall eradication season, begun in September of 1958, was so successful that only ten of the six thousand rabbits estimated in 1953 remained. The last of the feral cats had also been eliminated.

This initial success was not followed up, however. Over subsequent years, the Park Service presence on Santa Barbara Island was too sporadic to ensure consistent resource management, and the exotic rabbit population gradually recovered, while natural resources suffered commensurately. This was a matter of great concern to the Santa Barbara Botanic Garden, because of the loss of native species like the giant coreopsis. Ralph Philbrick, the director of the garden, began complaining to Bill Ehorn soon after the new superintendent arrived at the monument. Ehorn had the resident island ranger equipped with a firearm and assigned him rabbit hunting as a collateral duty. Even explosives and poison gas were attempted, but all of these measures could only manage the problem; they were never enough to actually eliminate the rabbits.[28] It was several years before Ehorn could find a successful solution. This happened in 1980, after Ehorn convinced Gary Davis to come to Channel Islands. One of his first tasks for Davis was the eradication of the Santa Barbara rabbits.

Since no one method had ever proven entirely successful, Davis began by setting up an experiment to test a variety of different methods. He divided Santa Barbara Island into a grid so that a different technique could be tried in each section and compared. The rabbit population was assessed by measuring the quantity of scat. After an initial period of trial and error, the most effective method proved to be spotlighting. Rangers, including Bill Ehorn, would walk the island at night with powerful, handheld lights. The rabbits, which were generally more active at night, would be immobilized by the beam. Scores at a time could then be dispatched relatively easily with a single shotgun blast. After only a few weeks of this treatment, the rabbit population on Santa Barbara Island was nearly gone, and Ehorn was so elated that he resolved to devote as many staff resources as necessary to finishing off the remainder.

At about this time, Ehorn happened to run into Regional Director Howard Chapman at a training workshop and bragged to him about his recent success on Santa Barbara Island. Instead of being pleased, however, Chapman was mortified that Ehorn had gone ahead without conducting environmental compliance as required under NEPA. Chapman warned Ehorn to hold off until an environmental assessment could be prepared. Ehorn quickly assured Chapman that the remaining rabbits would not be exterminated until this was done. By this time, however, the only remaining rabbits on Santa Barbara Island were two that had been captured as pets and were being kept in a cage in the ranger station. Ehorn telephoned back to headquarters as soon as he could and told his staff to take good care of those rabbits. Meanwhile, Ranger Nick Whelan was instructed to prepare an environmental assessment with a FONSI for Chapman's signature as soon as possible. When Chapman eventually signed off on this dubious compliance, the two pet rabbits—affectionately named for

Chapman and NPS director Russ Dickenson—were sent to a new home on the mainland, and Santa Barbara Island was finally free of rabbits for the first time in nearly eighty years. The native vegetation began showing signs of recovery almost immediately.[29]

Managing the Habitat and Resources of the Sea

Marine life represents the most extensive and diverse biological resource associated with the Channel Islands. However, the marine environment is less accessible than the terrestrial one, and research in this area lagged considerably behind land-based research. Some exceptions existed where there was an economic interest that could support scientific research, sometimes in an advocacy role. For example, early studies of giant kelp (*Macrocystis pyrifera*) conducted by the Scripps Institute of Oceanography were made possible largely as a result of fees paid by private harvesting companies.[30]

Nevertheless, in 1966, CINM's annual fisheries report expressed alarm at the intensification of fishing pressure with the introduction of purse seines and gill nets. It concluded that "until such [an ecological] study is undertaken and completed we cannot begin adequate and meaningful management of the waters which constitute the Channel Islands National Monument's raison d'etre."[31] Superintendent Don Robinson initially ignored this warning. Most of the information on marine resources came in the form of personal observations by recreational fishermen operating within the monument's one-mile seaward boundary. Data on commercial activities became available only after a permit system was introduced with special regulations implemented in April 1972.[32]

In 1969 the CDFG, with assistance from the park staff, had established underwater transects around Anacapa and Santa Barbara Islands in order to monitor the effects of the blowout on Union Oil Company's Platform A. Superintendent Robinson used the state's monitoring program to justify closing these waters to commercial fishing. This action helped convince the NPS Directorate of the need to monitor population dynamics of commercially valuable marine species in order to better manage them. Among the more noteworthy of these projects because of their scale and duration, were marine mammal studies on San Miguel Island, conducted

Fig. 12. The diversity of marine habitats in the Santa Barbara Channel are shown in this diagram from Channel Islands National Marine Sanctuary's *Condition Report, 2016*.

under the authority of the Bureau of Commercial Fisheries (later the NMFS) and seabird studies conducted primarily on Santa Barbara Island by scientists from the University of California.[33]

Superintendent Ehorn's natural resource management plan of 1975 repeated the emphasis on the need for marine ecological research and led to three important research projects. Mark M. Littler of the University of California, Irvine, inventoried the intertidal zone at selected sites throughout the Southern California Bight.[34] The purpose of this study was "to establish quantitatively reliable and reproducible baseline assessments of the distribution and abundance of rocky intertidal organisms." Also in 1975, Dana Seagars of San Diego State University began a study of sea urchins (*Strongylocentrotus purpuratus*, et al.) on Anacapa Island. Concern over the growing market for sea urchins and its possible adverse effects on the population motivated his study.[35] Mark Littler also conducted a third marine project, an Assessment of Visitor Impact on Anacapa Island Tidepools. It became the long-term Rocky Intertidal Monitoring Program under the park's early inventory and monitoring program in 1982.[36]

After the Supreme Court's 1978 decision overturned the monument's 1949 seaward boundary extension, authority for the marine environment off the monument islands was managed by the CDFG. The monument ceased collecting data on commercial and recreational fishery harvests, and scientific research by the NPS halted. In 1980, with the establishment of the national park, Gary Davis reimplemented research in cooperation with CDFG to monitor the population dynamics of subtidal biota. This Marine Ecosystem Dynamics Monitoring Project established sixteen sampling sites in deeper waters around all of the park islands. Sampling continued over successive years in the expectation that long-term monitoring of population trends would improve NPS and CDFG management of the natural resources of the park.[37] This monitoring program, now called the "Kelp Forest Monitoring Program," has been collecting annual data at these original sixteen sites from 1982 to the present.

MARINE MAMMALS, HISTORY, AND CONDITIONS

Preservation of marine mammals and associated marine species, such as seabirds, was Roger Toll's leading justification for the establishment of a national monument in 1933. Although this was not formally included in the 1938 proclamation, it was understood by senior Park Service managers and often stated explicitly.[38] Simply enforcing this commitment became a controversial task for Park Service staff because it was common practice at that time for fishermen, boaters, and the CDFG itself to shoot these animals.[39] No legal protection existed for marine mammals until passage of the Marine Mammal Protection Act in 1972. NPS policies prevented shooters from doing this within monument boundaries, though in 1942 the state requested permission to enter the monument to reduce the number of Steller sea lions by killing 50 percent of all males and pups. The NPS denied the request even after the state appealed and cited a wartime need to protect the fisheries.[40] One of the principal reasons the

Park Service sought to extend the monument boundaries around Santa Barbara and Anacapa Islands in 1949 was to increase the area of federal protection for marine mammals, not only against the random depredations of private hunters and fishermen but also against the official management practices of the state.

At one time, California's coastal waters teemed with an extraordinary abundance of marine mammals, including sea otters, pinnipeds, and cetaceans (whales). Russians began hunting sea otters in the Bering Sea and off the coast of Alaska during the late eighteenth century. The sea otter (*Enhydra lutris*) was abundant, with its original range extending from the Bering Sea to Baja California.[41] Among several favorite hunting grounds was San Miguel Island, where large numbers of otters frequently congregated.[42] The total number taken from this region during the heyday of this activity was estimated at approximately two hundred thousand animals.[43] By 1870 the sea otters had been extirpated from these waters and were believed to be extinct. However, a small number escaped the hunt and survived in complete obscurity until about one hundred were discovered in 1938 off the mouth of Bixby Creek near Monterey.[44]

By the late 1970s, approximately 1,650 sea otters lived off the central California coast. Although this represented a robust gain from 1938, biologists worried about the limited range of the population. More than one hundred million barrels of oil traveled by tankers through these same waters every year, and biologists feared that a single accident could eliminate the entire California sea otter population. This concern together with the listing of the California subspecies in 1977 as threatened under the Endangered Species Act (ESA) led to the proposal to establish a separate population outside the area vulnerable to shipping traffic. This proposal became an integral part of the recovery plan that was legislatively mandated under the terms of the ESA. Congress approved a recovery plan in November 1986 to have the U.S. Fish and Wildlife Service (USFWS) biologists capture sea otters around Monterey Bay and relocate them to San Nicolas Island. San Nicolas was selected for the new population both because of its remoteness and because it logistically supported the program as an active U.S. Naval base. USFWS eventually brought a total of 138 animals there.[45]

The program was controversial from the start. Commercial and sport fishermen feared competition from the voracious animals and fiercely opposed expanding their range. In deference to the interests of the fishermen, Congress established a "no-otter zone" as part of the 1986 recovery plan. This legislatively excluded sea otters from all coastal waters south of Point Conception, with the exception of San Nicolas Island. Any otters that wandered into this zone, which included the national park, would have to be captured and relocated north of Point Conception. This stipulation exacerbated criticism of the plan from nearly every party, since it was widely and correctly believed that the no-otter zone would be nearly impossible to enforce.[46]

Six species of pinniped occur around the Channel Islands, including the northern fur seal (*Callorhinus ursinus*), the Guadalupe fur seal (*Arctocephalus townsendi*), the Steller sea lion (*Eumetopias jubatus*), the California sea lion (*Zalophus californianus*), the harbor seal (*Phoca vitulina*), and the northern elephant seal (*Mirounga angustirostris*). Just as valuable to European hunters as the sea otter was the fur seal. The northern species of this pinniped was found in great abundance on the Pribilof Islands in the Bering Sea and extended as far south as the Channel Islands, where it overlapped with the northern range of the Guadalupe fur seal. Like the sea otter, the fur seal was valued for its soft, fur-covered pelts, which were used to manufacture a variety of luxury items. By the 1850s, Russian and American fur traders had extirpated the fur seal from its California range although as many as four million were estimated to remain around the Pribilof Islands in 1867 when the United States acquired Alaska. Under American laissez-faire practices, the hunt reduced the herd to a meager 132,000 by 1910 when a census was made. In response to this alarming result, the North Pacific Fur Seal Convention was ratified by the United States, Great Britain, Russia, and Japan in 1911, banning the practice of hunting from deep-water vessels and granting jurisdiction to the U.S. federal government to manage onshore hunting. In 1966, the Fur Seal Act banned all commercial hunting of fur seals, permitting only subsistence take by native Aleuts and Inuits. Two years later, a small colony of northern fur seals was discovered once again breeding on San Miguel Island after an absence of one hundred years.[47]

Similar to the northern fur seal is the Guadalupe fur seal, though it has a much more limited range and prefers warmer waters. Originally, these animals were found from the Farallon Islands off San Francisco south to the central Baja California peninsula. One of the largest breeding colonies was found on Guadalupe Island, from which the species takes its common name. Fur traders regularly sailed the area and hunted the Guadalupe fur seals indiscriminately. As early as 1825, the species had been extirpated from Alta California waters.[48] By the early twentieth century, the species was thought to be extinct, but in the early 1950s a small breeding colony had reestablished itself on Guadalupe Island. Nonbreeding adults began to appear annually on San Miguel Island after 1969.

The northern elephant seal is the largest of the pinnipeds found on the California islands. The bulls weigh up to six thousand pounds and average about three times larger than the females. The original breeding range of the northern elephant seal extended from Point Reyes to the middle of the Baja peninsula. As late as 1870, Scammon noted that they still numbered in the thousands on the California islands from San Miguel south into Mexican waters.[49] However, their numbers were in steep decline, owing to the commercial desirability of the oil that could be rendered from their body fat. By the late nineteenth century, elephant seals had been extirpated from California, and only a few remained in Mexican waters around Guadalupe Island and San Cristobal Bay, where they were now legally protected.[50] They were not seen again on the Northern Channel Islands until 1938, when Paul Bonnot observed four yearlings on San Miguel Island. By 1948, a small number had also returned to their historical rookeries on Santa Barbara Island.[51]

Two species of sea lions originally overlapped at the Channel Islands. The Steller sea lion is a northern species that typically bred along the Pacific coast of Siberia and Alaska and down the North American coast to Southern California. The Channel Islands were the southernmost breeding grounds of this species. The California sea lion prefers warmer waters, and its breeding range is confined to the coast of Mexico and the southern half of California. With the decline of the more economically valuable species of marine mammals, European and American hunters intensively targeted the sea lions. This occurred in spite of the animal's marginal value for oil and for their "trimmings," the male sexual organs sold to the Chinese as a traditional aphrodisiac. This exploitation effectively reduced California's once vast herds to only a few thousand by the early twentieth century. Beginning in the early twentieth century, many sea lions were also captured for zoos and marine parks. The California sea lion was preferred because of its intelligence and relative docility.[52]

The harbor seal is one of the smaller pinniped species and the least pelagic, preferring to remain close to shore, often within estuaries, bays, and harbors, from which the species derives its common name. The harbor seal is also the most widely distributed of the pinnipeds, with populations found throughout the northern hemisphere in both the Atlantic and Pacific Oceans. The subspecies that occurs within the eastern Pacific along the shores of California is *P. vitulina richardii* and ranges from the arctic shores of Alaska in the far north to the southern tip of Baja California. Harbor seals lack the dense coats of fur that were so appealing to hunters during the nineteenth century and were a poor source of oil.[53] Nevertheless, harbor seals were hunted throughout the nineteenth century, often for food to support the hunters who were engaged in harvesting more economically important marine mammals.[54] One observer writing toward the end of that century also noted that the harbor seals' habit of hauling out in bays and harbors near human settlement made them vulnerable to idle potshots, who "make a mark of every animal they see, whether they can use it or not."[55]

With the declining commercial importance of marine mammals by the end of the nineteenth century, there was little interest in studying them. However, in 1927 Paul Bonnot of the U.S. Bureau of Commercial Fisheries, the ancestor of the NMFS, investigated complaints from fishermen in California about the alleged depredations of seals and sea lions. The resulting study, which Bonnot completed the following year, was noteworthy for being one of the earliest attempts at a scientifically based investigation of California pinnipeds that included population censuses.[56] Although Bonnot's investigation took in most of the California coastline, he encountered only three species, the Steller sea lion, the California sea lion, and the harbor seal, all of which were present on the Northern Channel Islands.

Bonnot investigated the activities that continued to affect pinniped herds on the Channel Islands and throughout California during the early decades of the twentieth century. Interest in the animals had been renewed in 1899, when local fishermen persuaded the CDFG to consider managing sea lion populations. State commissioners agreed with the fishing industry that sea lion populations needed to be reduced, though they had no data to support this conclusion. Because many of the largest colonies were located on lighthouse reservations, the Department of the Treasury granted permission to the state to hunt its sites. Protests from the U.S. Fish Commission, the Department of Agriculture, and the New York Zoological Society led to cancellation of the order, but state game wardens proceeded to cull sea lions from non-federally protected locations along the coast.

Not long after 1900, these systematic culls appear to have ended, possibly owing to their initial success in reducing the size of the sea lion herds. Nevertheless, hunting by private individuals continued even after the official culling had ended. Bonnot reported that in 1907 and 1908 hunters killed nearly all of the sea lion bulls of breeding age on San Miguel Island. Natural history societies urged the state legislature to pass a bill in 1909 that protected sea lions in the Santa Barbara Channel and on the Channel Islands. This was the first legal protection to be afforded these marine mammals in California waters. The commercial fishing lobby continued complaining until after 1927 when Bonnot began an investigation. He discovered that bounty hunters from Oregon who had exhausted their supply in that state wanted to extend their hunt to California. They had convinced California fishermen that the sea lions threatened commercial fish stocks and that they should petition the state to offer a bounty as Oregon had.

Bonnot realized that the fishermen's allegations were based on little or no evidence and rejected their rationale for the fishery decline. If marine mammals were having a significant impact on commercial fish stocks, he believed it reflected the diminished state of the stocks themselves due to overfishing. He insisted that such hunts be supported by reliable data gathered from regular censuses of the sea lion populations and made periodic surveys of California pinnipeds over the next two decades. His efforts, assisted by other researchers from the Bureau of Commercial Fisheries and the CDFG, represented the first attempt to study population trends of marine mammals in California coastal waters.[57]

In 1958, George Bartholomew, a biologist with the University of California, Los Angeles, made a systematic survey of marine mammals throughout the Channel Islands. He found small breeding colonies of the northern elephant seal. Ten years later, Richard Peterson and Burney LeBoeuf of the University of California, Santa Cruz, discovered a small breeding colony of northern fur seals on San Miguel Island. The Guadalupe fur seal was also observed as an occasional visitor to the Northern Channel Islands, but this species did not establish a breeding colony here. These discoveries brought the total number of pinniped species using the Northern Channel Islands to six, with five establishing active breeding colonies at Point Bennett. Smaller colonies also existed on Santa Barbara Island.[58] The response to this discovery was the establishment of the research station at Point Bennett in 1969 under the direction of marine biologist Robert DeLong. The research activities of this station have continued up to the present.[59]

A few years later, in 1975, the San Miguel Island colonies received additional support when members of the Marine Mammal Commission, who were there to observe a permitted capture of sea lions for commercial use in zoos, accompanied Superintendent Bill Ehorn. Sea lions had been taken for this purpose since the beginning of the century, but the Marine Mammal Protection Act had introduced new standards governing the treatment of these animals, and the commission members were present to make sure that the activities did not violate these standards. One of the commission members was Dr. A. Starker Leopold. Several men came ashore and herded the sea lions into a tight group. They then threw a net over the individual they wished to capture. All of the animals appeared visibly distressed by these actions and stampeded across the beach. Seeing this, Dr. Leopold ordered a stop to the operation and revoked the permit.

Afterward, Leopold expressed his desire that San Miguel Island be fully protected, with only small numbers of people allowed controlled access to witness the marine mammal rookeries at Point Bennett. Ehorn explained that the navy could ensure protection for the island and that the Park Service, through its cooperative agreement with the navy, could provide the sort of management that Leopold envisioned. Dr. Leopold approved of this arrangement, and his support encouraged Ehorn to proceed toward finalization of the cooperative agreement with the navy in 1976 that allowed the Park Service to assume responsibility for managing the island's cultural and natural resources. This had significant consequences for the marine mammal colonies because it resulted in the permanent presence of a protection ranger on the island who helps the semipermanent researchers at Point Bennett discourage illegal harassment of these animals.[60]

Building the New Park   5

Passage of the park's enabling legislation in 1980 dramatically increased the boundaries of the new park but did not result in an immediate increase in land ownership. Much of the new park still had to be acquired, or cooperative management responsibilities defined where property titles could not be transferred. This proved to be a time-consuming and difficult process that followed a different course on each island. The simplest transfers of authority to the National Park Service (NPS) involved lands and property owned by other federal agencies, such as the U.S. Coast Guard (USCG) on Anacapa Island. Properties held by private owners presented greater challenges. Not until these properties were either acquired or formal agreements were negotiated between the interested parties could the park begin to exercise any management responsibility for the islands' resources.[1]

The 1975 Anacapa Island agreement between the Park Service and the coast guard worked well enough for immediate purposes, effectively preserving some of the historic structures and providing park staff with access to the eastern islet. However, the park's enabling act of 1980 authorized the NPS to acquire any lands within the legislative boundaries of the new park unit.[2] Shortly after its establishment, the new national park sought a public land order to transfer the remaining 160-acre surplus property on East Anacapa Islet from the USCG to the NPS. This still would give the coast guard access to service its now-automated aids to navigation. The USCG finally agreed to transfer all but the easternmost promontory of East Anacapa Islet in 1983.[3] The actual transfer was delayed until January 2009 by communication problems among the USCG, the Bureau

Fig. 13. Former Coast Guard structures on East Anacapa Islet serve Park Service residential, maintenance, and revegetation purposes. Note the many western gulls that now nest there after the eradication of rats. Photograph by L. Dilsaver, August 2018.

of Land Management (BLM), and the NPS, as well as hazardous material surveys and environmental clearances for the fuel oil spills around the underground fuel tanks and lead contamination around the water tank building. When the transfer took place, the NPS assumed control over all the coast guard property on East Anacapa including the promontory with the lighthouse and fog signal building.[4]

The Land Protection and General Management Plans

The park's enabling legislation required a new general management plan (GMP) by October 1, 1983, but park officials chose to prepare a supplement mainly focused on Santa Cruz and Santa Rosa Islands rather than rewrite the existing plan from scratch. The key issues that the supplemental GMP had to address fell into three broad categories: land acquisition, resource management, and visitor use. Despite the advances in resource management planning and the start of the inventory and monitoring program

(I&M) procedures, park resource managers and planners knew little about the resources on the two new islands. The Santa Barbara Museum of Natural History organized an islands symposium that same year and brought together more than 400 scientists, government employees, and interested laymen to discuss and share knowledge about all of the California islands.[5] However, despite the maturation of research, gaps still existed in knowledge about the two largest islands. Private owners denied requests for access, forcing park planners and resource managers to rely on less accurate methods such as aerial surveys of archeological middens and broadly defined vegetative associations.[6]

Of the three issues addressed by the GMP, visitor use depended almost entirely on the other two. It was also affected by the legislative requirement that the islands be managed on a limited-entry, low-intensity-use basis.[7] Recreation carrying capacities could not be established until the affected resources were identified and their potential impacts accurately described. These limitations led the planners to adopt a conceptual approach in their preliminary draft. This proved disastrous when presented to the public during workshops held in June and July of 1982. Hoping only to stimulate discussion, the planners provided a broad range of alternatives, including options for development that appeared excessive. Many participants at the workshops mistakenly assumed that these were actual proposals and reacted with alarm. Their comments, however, proved valuable since they helped define what the local public and private landowners considered acceptable.[8]

During the time that this conceptual plan was being prepared, the Department of the Interior (DOI) initiated a critical review of NPS land acquisition and protection practices. Secretary of the Interior James Watt, recently appointed by President Ronald Reagan, advocated private property rights and objected to federal practices that relied too heavily on eminent domain and fee-simple purchase to acquire property.[9] With the encouragement of Watt, the General Accounting Office (GAO) prepared a report, *Federal Land Acquisition and Management Practices*, that questioned why the government had relied almost entirely on fee-simple acquisition instead of other methods for protecting park resources. The recommendations of this study were supported by a similar report resulting from a congressional workshop on public land acquisition conducted by the Senate Committee on Energy and Natural Resources in July 1981.[10]

In response, the NPS initiated eight service-wide studies to explore alternatives to fee-simple purchase. Each study examined how resource protection might be achieved through conservation easements, transfer of development rights, or other nontraditional methods applied instead of, or in combination with, outright acquisition. Channel Islands was chosen as one of these studies, resulting in a June 1982 report entitled *Resource Protection Case Study*. One important consequence of this study was an improvement in trust between the Park Service and the private landowners of Santa Cruz and Santa Rosa Islands. Believing that they now shared common, or at least not antithetical, interests, the landowners granted permission in February of 1982 for the Channel Islands case study team, including planners, to visit Santa Rosa and East Santa Cruz Islands. The planning team was able to refine its concepts for future use and management based on this brief reconnaissance.

The research conducted for the case study was helpful, but a GMP was still necessary to determine visitor use and resource management strategies. Without such information, the nature and extent of ownership required to protect these resources could not be accurately determined. As a result, the case study authors recommended that future land protection research be conducted only after the GMP was done. However, the report did identify four priority acquisition options that would allow the NPS to acquire the lands in question. In the first option, oil leases on the Outer Continental Shelf that were managed by the Minerals Management Service would be granted to private developers in exchange for a comparably valued parcel of land within the island inholding. Although this option would require modification of some existing laws, it provided a ready funding source that did not demand further congressional appropriations.[11]

A second option would offer concession rights in exchange for the land, either in part or in full. This provided an economical means of offsetting the original cost of purchase and might create an incentive for infrastructure development to support visitor activities. However, the report also noted that it would be difficult to enforce NPS policy among concession holders with practices on the islands predating the Park Service presence.

It also might be difficult to develop enough business capacity to make the concessions financially worthwhile, especially on Santa Rosa Island, which could not expect to receive much visitation given its distance from the mainland. A third option involved a land exchange with comparably valued property owned by the BLM or the GAO. The chief disadvantage of this option was the bureaucratic complexity of the process itself, which could be time-consuming and expensive. BLM officials still resented the many time-consuming tasks they had to perform for numerous exchanges of this sort at Joshua Tree National Park.[12] The final option was direct purchase with funds appropriated by congress.

Following review of the eight land protection case studies, the DOI issued guidelines for preparation of land protection plans (LPPs) for all parks containing private inholdings. To prepare such a plan for Channel Islands, further access to these properties was essential. Once again believing that this process was in their interest, the Vails and the Gherinis granted permission, though only for a few weeks. A multidisciplinary team of NPS scientists, managers, and planners was allowed to visit Santa Rosa Island in December 1982 and April 1983 and East Santa Cruz Island in April of 1983. The team concentrated its efforts on areas of sensitive resources and probable visitor use to provide direction for both the LPP and the GMP.[13]

As a result of these studies, the NPS prepared and released a detailed land protection plan in February 1984.[14] It reiterated that fee-simple acquisition of the private lands was the most desirable option. The question was not whether the lands should be purchased by the Park Service but how. The LPP proposed implementing a schedule of staggered acquisitions based on areas with resources of highest priority to the NPS. First, 10 percent of Santa Rosa Island would be purchased, then 45 percent of East Santa Cruz, then 80 percent of Santa Rosa, then 55 percent of East Santa Cruz, and finally the remaining 10 percent of Santa Rosa. The advantage of this method was that it allowed the Park Service to begin acquiring land immediately with the limited funds it already had.[15] Vail & Vickers immediately lodged a formal protest arguing that this plan would constitute a violation of Sec. 202(c) of the park enabling act that stipulated that acquisition of Santa Rosa Island must take priority over that of any other private inholding. This summarily ended consideration of the "phased acquisition" method.[16]

The NPS concluded that the federal government needed to acquire the Vail & Vickers and Gherini private inholdings in the park as soon as possible. Formal negotiations with them could not begin until appraisals had been completed on their lands. These were underway even as the planning studies were being conducted, but the earliest would not be completed for another year. In the meantime, the GMP was approved in 1985. It emphasized management on a limited-entry, low-intensity-use basis, consistent with the park enabling legislation. Limited development would be allowed at only three visitor entry points—Bechers Bay and Johnsons Lee on Santa Rosa Island and Scorpion Harbor on East Santa Cruz where historic development already existed. Planners deferred further wilderness studies and recommendations for all of the islands. In the meantime, natural areas would be managed as wilderness to the extent feasible.[17]

The Sale of Santa Rosa Island

The biggest and most complicated land acquisition for Channel Islands National Park was Santa Rosa Island, owned by the Vail & Vickers Company.[18] A great deal of controversy followed the ranchers' sale of the island to the federal government, in late 1986, and the arrangements associated with that sale. By 1985 the government had completed its formal appraisal of Santa Rosa Island, estimating its value at $29,500,000. This was considerably higher than the original estimate of $19,000,000 made six years earlier during the congressional hearings on the park bill and was more acceptable to the Vail & Vickers Company. The additional acquisition funds provided that year allowed negotiations with the company to begin soon afterward. Although Vail & Vickers wanted to expedite the sale as quickly as possible, questions remained concerning the details of the proposed transaction.

The congressional deliberations and the text of the park's enabling legislation, P.L. 96–199, offered Vail & Vickers two options: a reservation of use and occupancy (RUO) or a "lease agreement." A reservation of use and occupancy applies to a property that has been purchased by the National Park Service but with a stipulation that allows the former owner to continue using it for a specified length of time. A retained *right of occupancy* is specified in the deed and a negotiated charge is deducted from the payment to the former owner.

A "leaseback," or just "lease," was defined in the NPS management policies of 1978 that stated agency rules and practices: "In the case of any property acquired by the Secretary pursuant to this subchapter with respect to which a right of use and occupancy was not reserved by the former owner pursuant to this subsection, at the *request* of the former owner, the Secretary may enter into a lease agreement with the former owner under which the former owner may continue any existing use of such property which is compatible with the administration of the park and with the preservation of the resources therein" (emphasis added).[19] The significance of this choice is that the owner receives the full price of the sale from the U.S. government and can only request a leaseback, pay a fair market value rent for the duration of the lease, and continue to use the land as before.

Negotiations were carried on between the Lands Division of the Western Regional Office (WRO), the DOI's Office of the Solicitor, and Vail & Vickers through their attorneys. The Lands Division carried out extensive planning and calculated several options for the duration of a leaseback. Throughout this process, park superintendent Bill Ehorn remained in touch with Al and Russ Vail, who respected him as a friend and relied on his advice. Ehorn recommended to the Vail brothers that they accept an RUO for the residential core of the ranch but negotiate a lease for the rest of the island. He assured them that the consequences, as far as their ranching operation was concerned, would be the same, but they would benefit in the short term by receiving a smaller deduction from the full appraised value of their property than for a reserved right on all of the island. According to an appraisal prepared by the Lands Division in May 1986, the Vails would receive $26,000,000 if they retained an RUO for the entire island but $3,500,000 more if they retained only the 7.6-acre ranch complex.[20]

On December 29, 1986, the Vail & Vickers Company sold Santa Rosa Island to the National Park Service for $29,580,250 and retained only the small RUO at Bechers Bay.[21] This allowed family members residential use of the Main Ranch area for a period of twenty-five years, along with reasonable access to the property by means of the pier, the airstrip, and associated roads. The sale was rushed through, even though the terms of a lease agreement had yet to be established, in order to avoid an additional tax burden resulting from changes to the capital gains rate with the Tax Reform Act of 1986 that were scheduled to go into effect at the beginning of the following year. Although the attorneys for both sides were forced to work through the holiday week, Vail & Vickers saved several million dollars in taxes.[22]

NEGOTIATING A LEASE OR SPECIAL USE PERMIT (1987)

The NPS gave the ranchers a three-month lease to continue its operations after the sale while negotiating for a longer-term lease, but it soon stretched to nine months as the Vail & Vickers Company sought the most beneficial deal. Ehorn later explained that he believed that the laudatory comments by legislators six years earlier were essentially a directive to allow ranching on the island.[23] Western Regional appraiser Jack MacDonald, Ehorn, and Al and Russ Vail had surveyed the island on April 17, 1986, and Macdonald prepared an "appraisal supplement" for Vail & Vickers that estimated annual fair market rental values for a lease agreement at $313,500 per year for the cattle operation and $100,000 per year for commercial hunting. This figure for the ranch assumed that the average daily inventory of cattle over the course of a year would not exceed 5,500 head and calculated their rental value based on an estimate of $6.79 per animal unit month (AUM). An animal unit month is a standard measure of stocking rates used by rangeland managers and is defined as the amount of forage needed by a mature one-thousand-pound cow grazing for one month. The Park Service thought a rent based on $6.79 per AUM was reasonable when compared with average mainland values, which could range between $8.00 and $10.00 per AUM. Allowing for the additional transportation costs associated with the remote island location, the NPS appraisal was believed to fall within that range.[24] In case this sum appeared onerous, MacDonald noted that Vail & Vickers would also benefit from the NPS assuming maintenance costs for the airstrip, the pier, and some of the roads as a condition of sharing operations on the island.

Vail & Vickers responded through their attorneys that the cost was "far in excess of what can be supported today by a ranching operation."[25] The company sought support for a much cheaper lease while insisting that it was for a limited period so they could phase out its operations. In response to an appeal from the Vails, Senator Pete Wilson wrote to Interior Secretary Donald Hodel, drawing his attention to their concerns and requesting that the Park Service be asked to reevaluate its appraisal.[26] Senator Wilson also suggested that it was in the best interest of the government to see Vail & Vickers continue cattle ranching on Santa Rosa Island. Not only was the cattle operation, in his opinion, "a crucial interpretive and management resource," but he also pointed out that the Park Service would incur considerable costs if it had to assume full responsibility for managing the island and relocating Vail & Vickers' property and their tenants. During the year of negotiations, Superintendent Ehorn wrote to the *Santa Barbara News-Press* that "Santa Rosa Island . . . is still being used as a working cattle ranch by its recent owners, Vail & Vickers, and they have the option of leasing back the entire island to continue their ranching operation *for several additional years*" (emphasis added).[27] Congressman Lagomarsino also wrote on behalf of Vail & Vickers requesting they be permitted to "continue operation of the cattle ranch on approximately 51,000 acres for a *five- to ten-year period*" (emphasis added).[28]

As negotiations continued, Ehorn suggested to Al and Russ Vail that they could negotiate a special use permit (SUP) for the rest of the island. Former NPS solicitor Barbara Goodyear later defined the SUP that was available to Vail & Vickers: "A special use permit grants no property interest to the permittee. It is a mere license to use property that is revocable by the permitting entity at any time. No compensation is due for its termination. There is also no guarantee that subsequent permits would be issued."[29] Ehorn assured them that their operations would be preeminent on the island throughout a five-year SUP. In a 2019 interview, Ehorn stated that he was so happy to gain the island for the park and make it immediately available to visitors that he believed the agency could allow a limited duration of ongoing ranching and hunting while developing infrastructure for the complete takeover at the end of the permit.[30] In addition, the money earned through permit fees would remain with Channel Islands and could be reinvested in resource protection and facilities development on Santa Rosa Island.[31]

Vail & Vickers expressed an interest in the SUP option if the cost could be reduced. By September 1987, the NPS had prepared a new proposal that still entailed the protection of threatened natural resources and provisions for public visitation, both of which could conflict with the operations of a private cattle ranch and a hunting concession. In consideration of these objections, the new appraisal reduced the proposed assessment by more than half to $3.00 per AUM. This would result in an annual rent of approximately $162,000, though the figure could vary depending on the number of cattle actually stocked in a given year.[32] Although $3.00 was considerably less than the base range determined by the Park Service one year earlier, Vail & Vickers argued that it was still too high. They had a separate appraisal prepared by their own advisor, James Nofziger, challenging the government report and the estimates the NPS had derived from it. This rebuttal was submitted to the park in early December, necessitating further negotiation of the proposed rent before any permit could be finalized. Ultimately, the park's chief of operations, Tim Setnicka, who was not an appraiser, and the Vails agreed upon a rate of $1.48 per AUM, resulting in an annual fee of approximately $80,000.[33] This was scarcely a fourth of the estimated fair market value as originally determined by NPS appraisers, and critics such as the National Parks and Conservation Association (NPCA) later argued that the difference represented a substantial federal subsidy for cattle ranching on public park lands.[34] The Park Service agreed to the terms, and a five-year renewable SUP was finally signed on December 29, 1987, exactly one year after the sale of the island.[35]

The exact details of what Ehorn told Vail & Vickers through the year of negotiations remain unclear. Later, various media sources reported that Ehorn had verbally informed the Vails that he expected the five-year SUP terms would be renewed until the RUO for the residential complex that Vail & Vickers had chosen ended in 2011. Ehorn strongly denies that he ever promised the Vails a twenty-five-year operation on the entire island or shook hands on the deal as the local press claimed.[36] This debate was the crux of all the controversy that ensued. If Ehorn had promised the Vails that they would be able to continue ranching for the duration of their twenty-five-year RUO on the ranch site, it would have had no basis in law because nothing was ever written down and the superintendent did not have the authority to represent the Park Service in making such a broad agreement.[37] The Vails and their supporters in the local media maintained that, as old-fashioned cattlemen, they were accustomed to finalizing agreements on an unwritten basis and saw nothing unusual in placing their trust in a man they respected.[38] At the same time, they also insisted that the will of Congress supported their interest in continuing the ranch for the duration of their active lives.

One other incident has a bearing on these different versions of the story: On October 25, 1987, the *Chicago Tribune* quoted a Channel Islands employee (either a naturalist or a ranger-interpreter who was not named in the article) saying, "Negotiations continue with the Vail and Vickers Co., which previously owned the island and retains the right to ranch it for up to 25 years." This would have been the case if the ranchers had signed a RUO or a lease and paid the required amount. As the negotiations entered their final stages in late October, this seasonal employee stated that the ranchers had a twenty-five-year "right" to continue operations. That suggests that this duration was expected by the some of the park's personnel at that time. But the ranchers never had a "right" to an SUP, and when they rejected the lease option, they lost even its minimal contractual protection.[39]

MANAGING A PARK ON A RANCHING ISLAND

The special use permit allowed the Vails to continue ranching as they always had. They were allowed to run cattle over nearly 53,000 acres of the island. An earlier study by Gary Davis and Bill Halvorson had recommended a number of other parcels to be off-limits to grazing, including Johnsons Lee, where park operations were to be centered; two parcels of Torrey pine trees; three oak woodlands on Soledad Peak; the caliche area at Sandy Point; a small lagoon between Skunk Point and East Point; and three dune areas extending from Cluster Point to just north of Bee

Canyon along the southwest shoreline. However, these restrictions did not make it into the first SUP or any subsequent ones. The park promised to minimize use of the roads from Johnsons Lee to Soledad Peak to access the oak woodlands and from the ranch pier at Bechers Bay to the Torrey pine forest for public visitation. In addition, the ranchers were allowed to dictate priority use of the pier for their cattle operation. Although the barns, corrals, and pier were outside of Vail & Vickers RUO, the ranchers objected to visitors off-loading on the pier and walking through the ranch, potentially disturbing their ranch operations. In effect, this occasionally prevented the NPS from using the pier and forced visitors to off-load on the beach instead.[40]

Rent was to be paid monthly to the NPS, based on a stocking animal number not to exceed 5,900 head, a slight increase from the total originally proposed one year earlier. In 1993 Superintendent Mack Shaver gave responsibility for renewing the SUP to Chief of Operations Tim Setnicka who then reduced the rate to $1.00 per AUM.[41] Deer and elk, which provided a substantial supplemental income to the Vails through hunting leases, were not originally factored into the AUM limits. Later they were included, but that did not reduce the total allowable cattle units per year.[42]

The Soil Conservation Service confirmed the stocking regimen allowed by this permit, which remained more or less unchanged from before the sale of the island. After visiting Santa Rosa Island in the spring, District Conservationist Lynn Brittan wrote that the island "appears to be grazed carefully, even in this year of below normal rainfall." Optimal utilization of the island would require additional fencing, water development, and cattle movements but would not be cost-effective. Brittan also observed that "the forage on Santa Rosa Island is a valuable resource and has been carefully managed over the years" but recommended that a resource management plan be drafted with an emphasis on grazing practices.[43]

The NPS, with the concurrence of the Vail & Vickers Company, complied with this advice and contracted specialists from the University of California system to prepare a range management plan.[44] Completed on April 1, 1992, the plan stipulated: grazing would be allowed year-round; the cattle inventory would not exceed 4,500 AUMs per year; other

Fig. 14. Vail & Vickers continued using horses, homemade wrangling equipment, and traditional techniques to herd cattle on Santa Rosa Island. Photograph by Bill Ehorn, date unknown, CINP Digital Archives, "Cultural Resources."

elements might be considered that were consistent with "good range management"; stray livestock would be promptly removed from any of the eleven reserved NPS parcels [which were never adopted]; and salt would "be placed in a location where water supplies will not be affected." These criteria reflected rangeland values at the expense of the natural habitat. Although the range conservationist also implemented a water quality monitoring program, park management generally gave priority to commercial ranching over natural resource preservation.[45] The park's resource management staff, visiting scientists, and environmentalists complained that this conflicted with the mission of the Park Service itself. To these observers, the park's solicitous attitude toward the ranchers was not only inappropriate but destructive, especially since the NPS now owned Santa Rosa Island.

With completion of this sale, the Park Service began moving staff to Santa Rosa Island in May of 1987 and established a small operations area near an abandoned air force station on the southern coast at Johnsons Lee. The GMP identified Johnsons Lee as a site for park operations because Vail & Vickers insisted that the NPS remain distant from the ranch headquarters operation at Bechers Bay. The latter was one of the concessions to the ranchers that later resource managers, environmentalists, and other critics decried. The NPS owned the island but allowed the former landowners to insist that their operations should be paramount in cases where they clashed over location and schedule with park activities. The rudimentary Park Service facility consisted of four travel trailers that were placed on existing cement pads approximately fifty yards away from most of the abandoned military buildings. Both water and fuel had to be brought to the site, requiring difficult and expensive transportation.[46]

Beginning Memorial Day weekend, May 23–25, 1987, the park opened Santa Rosa Island to public visitation. Because of the extensive regional and local media coverage, interest in visiting the island was great from the beginning. In response to this demand, the concession boat operator, Island Packers, began running seasonal public trips to Santa Rosa in July. However, visitation was strictly controlled due to the desire to avoid interfering with ranching operations. Persons wishing to go onto Santa Rosa Island had to obtain a free landing permit, meet the island staff person, and remain in his or her company for the duration of their visit. Visitors could select one of two areas to land, either at Officer's Beach near Johnsons Lee for a walk to nearby canyons and coves or near Bechers Bay for a walk to the Torrey pine forest. The Bechers Bay alternative proved the more popular choice. As a result, NPS personnel stationed at Johnsons Lee had to drive to Bechers Bay on the days visitors landed. Because the distance between the two sites was thirteen miles over a primitive dirt road, the trip averaged one hour each way.[47]

Carey Stanton and Santa Cruz Island

The Park Service hoped to eventually own all of Santa Cruz Island, despite Carey Stanton's strong opposition to this idea. NPS hopes may have been bolstered by memories of Edwin Stanton's two overtures to sell his ranch to the Park Service decades earlier.[48] After purchasing the Santa Cruz Island ranch, Edwin Stanton introduced sheep, which promptly went

Fig. 15. A Torrey pine (*Pinus torreyana*) on the north slope of Santa Rosa Island. The species only occurs in one other small area near San Diego. Photograph by L. Dilsaver, October 2017.

feral. The most economically valuable pastures on the ranch had to be fenced off to prevent overgrazing.[49] Stanton then turned his attention to cattle, and he eventually developed a successful beef operation, introducing high-quality, polled Hereford stock. This remained the principal economic basis of the Stanton Ranch until augmented in 1965 by sport hunting through paid excursions. Edwin Stanton benefitted immensely from the expertise and practical intelligence of his ranch manager, Henry Duffield, whom he had hired in a spontaneous act of generosity or foresight after Carey Stanton met him while vacationing in Mexico.[50]

Edwin Stanton and his wife, Evelyn, had two children, Edwin Jr. and Carey. The parents assumed that their elder son would take over the ranch on Santa Cruz Island, while Carey would follow a professional career in medicine. But Edwin Jr. was killed during the invasion of Normandy in 1944. A son, Edwin III, was born while Edwin Jr. was away in Europe. Carey Stanton now inherited the management of the Stanton Ranch in place of his older brother.[51] Carey's father died six years later, and ownership of the island and related assets were shared between Carey and his mother Evelyn. In 1964, the two reincorporated Justinian Caire's old Santa Cruz Island Company (SCIC), which had been dissolved at the wish of its original shareholders in 1946.

On the basis of his father's will, Carey received two-thirds of the company shares and became the principal owner and decision-maker of the Santa Cruz Island Company. He began contracting with the Santa Cruz Island Hunt Club in 1965. This business was operated by William E. Huffman and Richard A. Lagomarsino, the brother of Congressman Robert Lagomarsino. In 1966, Carey leased a small parcel of land in the Central Valley just west of his Main Ranch to the University of California, Santa Barbara (UCSB) for a research station. The station was managed later by resident caretaker Dr. Lyndal Laughrin. At the recommendation of Henry Duffield, who continued as ranch manager after Edwin Stanton's death, Carey finally abandoned the sheep operation, turning out the remaining sheep to become feral. Most wandered to the north side of the island, where they were targeted by the hunt club.[52]

Carey's mother, Evelyn Stanton, died in 1973. Her one-third share in the Santa Cruz Island Company went to Edwin III, Carey's nephew, but young Edwin was still a minor and Carey held the shares for him in trust. That same year, Carey met Marla Daily, who became a close working assistant for the remainder of his life, and afterward, a loyal defender of his legacy. Her official duty was to catalogue Stanton's personal library, but in fact, she was responsible for any number of tasks that came up in the course of managing the ranch or Stanton's elaborate social events.[53] Later, Edwin III criticized his uncle's management of the island ranch, in which he had no part. He had inherited his one-third share of the Santa Cruz Island Company, but as a minority shareholder, he had little influence in how it was managed. On November 12, 1976, he filed a lawsuit against his uncle's company charging that he was being excluded from sharing in its benefits. He alleged that Carey and his grandmother, before her death, had been "using the corporation for their own selfish purpose of keeping the island for their personal power, vanity, pleasure and aggrandizement without regard to profit motive or benefit to the minority shareholder."[54] Edwin also claimed that the cattle operation had been losing money since 1965, while his uncle had been living an extravagant lifestyle at the expense of the Santa Cruz Island Company and, by implication, his own expense.[55]

Carey Stanton knew that whatever the outcome of this suit, it would prove costly to him and probably ruin the island ranch. By this time, he had come to love Santa Cruz Island and was fiercely protective of its interests, but the ranch was a great burden and suffered under considerable financial liabilities, not least of which was the inheritance tax that Stanton had been required to pay following his mother's death. This was exacerbated by falling livestock prices. Stanton had come to depend, to an increasing degree, on the various rental incomes he received. The most lucrative source of revenue was the lease to the Santa Cruz Island Hunt Club. While these incomes were sufficient to maintain the ranch and to service existing debt, they would not be able to sustain Stanton through a protracted lawsuit, and he began to consider other alternatives, including sale of the ranch itself.[56]

The Park Service had approached Stanton about purchasing the property several months earlier at the lunch that Stanton hosted for NPS director Gary Everhardt, Western Regional director Howard Chapman, and Superintendent Bill Ehorn. When Director Everhardt asked Stanton if he would be willing to sell the ranch, Stanton's answer was still an emphatic "no." Stanton opposed selling to the federal government in principle as well as precedent. Marla Daily recalls that Carey Stanton frequently complained of the government's inability to provide consistent, responsible management of its resources owing to its ever-changing political leadership. He also objected to existing NPS policies, which he believed placed too much emphasis on providing public access and recreational development, all of which he thought would adversely affect the character of Santa Cruz Island.[57]

THE NATURE CONSERVANCY

Carey Stanton briefly considered selling his ranch to the University of California but decided that the state university system was also subject to political vicissitudes with the governor on its board of directors and would therefore prove equally unreliable. In the end, Stanton chose to sell to a private, nonprofit organization and began negotiations with the

Fig. 16. The Main Ranch in the Central Valley of Santa Cruz Island has served as the home of Justinian Caire and Carey Stanton and as the headquarters for the Nature Conservancy. Photograph by L. Dilsaver, August 2018.

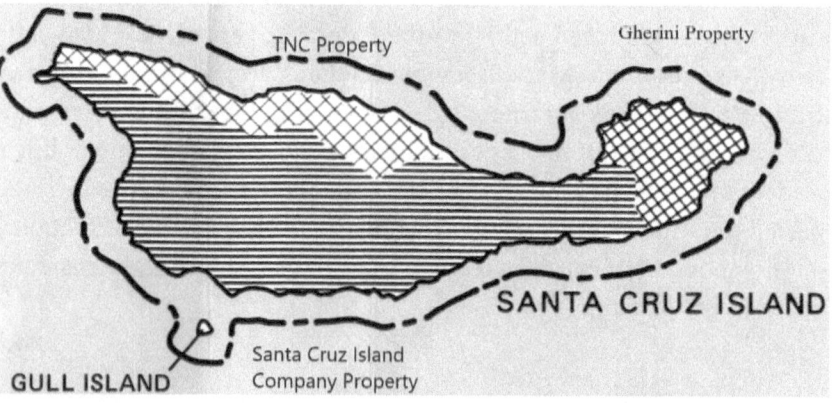

Map 12. A Park Service landownership map shows Santa Cruz Island with the Gherini property on the eastern edge and the northern section of the island purchased outright by TNC in 1978. From NPS, *Land Management Plan*, CINP, February 1984.

Nature Conservancy (TNC) in January of 1977. Incorporated in 1951 by a group of scientists from the Ecological Society of America, TNC was committed to protecting significant natural places through strategic land purchases and conservation easements.[58] The organization was already aware of Carey Stanton and his Santa Cruz Island Ranch through board member Jake Chittle, a wealthy Southern California rancher who had bequeathed his own property in the Santa Ynez Mountains to TNC in 1975. Chittle contacted Marla Daily to arrange a meeting, but Daily, well aware of Stanton's sensitivity on this subject, advised Chittle not to contact him directly. Instead, she proposed bringing Stanton to a public presentation that was being planned by TNC at the Santa Barbara Museum of Natural History. Unaware of the elaborate choreography that was occurring behind his back, Stanton agreed to go and was pleased with TNC and its staff. During the discussion that followed the presentation, he indicated his willingness to consider selling to the organization.[59]

By September 1978, Carey Stanton and TNC reached an agreement and were ready to sign a deed of sale. The terms of the agreement were complex and surprisingly low. TNC paid $2,524,000 for the sale. This included $900,000 to buy out Edwin III by purchasing all of his one-third share in the Santa Cruz Island Company. It came at a time when his own child was ill and he was consumed with worry and faced with potentially serious medical costs. As part of the agreement to settle the lawsuit, the amount of money paid to Carey Stanton had to match that paid to Edwin III. Hence, another $900,000 purchased half of Carey's two-thirds share. Carey Stanton was left with outright ownership of one-third share in the company as well as proxy status for his nephew's shares, allowing him to remain the majority shareholder in the company for voting purposes, despite TNC's majority ownership of the island. The balance of the money from the sale went to repay the company's outstanding debts. A complex division of the island was also made, with TNC receiving about 12,000 acres, approximately one-fourth of the ranch property on the island's northwestern side. This was subsequently leased back to the Santa Cruz Island Company. The company, and therefore Carey Stanton, retained nominal control of the entire ranch for the time being. However, he also agreed to bequeath the entirety of his shares in the company to TNC upon his death, or in 2008, whichever came first.[60]

East Santa Cruz Island

At the time the park enabling act passed in 1980, East Santa Cruz Island was equally divided among the four children of Ambrose and Maria Gherini. In 1930, the couple had purchased the interest of Maria's siblings and became the sole owners of the east end of the island, thenceforth known as the Gherini Ranch.[61] Ambrose raised between three and four thousand sheep, using Scorpion Ranch as his base of operations and Smugglers Ranch as a seasonal outpost. After their deaths, East Santa Cruz Island was divided equally between the Gherinis' four children, Pier, Francis, Ilda McGinness, and Marie Ringrose. Both Pier and Francis had grown up helping their father on the ranch during summers, and they now shared in the management of the operation, though each had his own legal practice on the mainland as well. The two sisters were less involved in the ranch, though they maintained their legal interests.

Raising sheep on East Santa Cruz Island was an arduous task, and its profitability steadily diminished in the decades following World War II. In response, the Gherini family considered other ideas for developing their property. This included an unsuccessful 1963 plan for an extensive recreational and residential resort that stimulated interest in establishing the national park.[62] The Gherinis were not simply looking for ways to make more money from their land. They were also trying to get out of the difficult business of running an island sheep ranch. Failing to find an economic alternative, they entered into an agreement in 1979 with William (Pete) Peterson to operate the ranch for a small fee and a percentage of Peterson's profits. East Santa Cruz Island would remain a sheep ranch, but now the Gherinis would be relieved of the responsibility of personally running the operation.

Pete Peterson and his young wife, Michel, managed the sheep ranch with great enthusiasm and ingenuity, but little profit, for the next five years. In 1984, however, Pete Peterson was seriously injured in a plane crash while returning to the island, and while he recuperated in the hospital, Francis Gherini made arrangements with outdoorsman Jaret Owens to operate a hunting club called Island Adventures on East Santa Cruz Island. This was finalized through an operational agreement signed by all of the Gherini family members.[63] Owens proposed to host excursions for paying customers, who would be allowed to hunt the island's semi-feral sheep. For $1,000, plus expenses, each hunter would be allowed to shoot one ram and two ewes. This was a far more lucrative, if less sustainable, operation than traditional pastoralism. Under the agreement, the Gherinis would receive 25 percent of the profits. Precedent for the Owens' hunting club already existed on Carey Stanton's side of the island, where the Santa Cruz Island Hunt Club had been operating since 1965.[64]

Jaret Owens was assisted in setting up Island Adventures by his parents, Duane and Doris Owens. The elder Owens moved out first to Smugglers Adobe and then the Scorpion Ranch House and spent the next two years making them habitable after years of neglect and vandalism by passing boaters. Owens then requested and received permission from Francis Gherini to begin hosting guests at the improved ranches. By this time, Pier Gherini's health had begun to fail, and his brother assumed most of the responsibility for managing island affairs.[65]

The ever-present threat of vandalism by passing boaters convinced Francis Gherini of the need to maintain a resident caretaker at each of his remote ranches. Duane and Doris Owens looked after Scorpion, but Smugglers remained vulnerable, since the Owens' hunting parties were present only intermittently. Francis Gherini therefore proposed an arrangement with the Park Service to post a ranger on East Santa Cruz Island to prevent trespassers from landing on the island and damaging property. Superintendent Ehorn consulted with the DOI's solicitor's office about the legality of this action because the NPS did not yet own any of the property. The solicitor agreed that the park legislation allowed it and Ehorn consented to the proposal because he knew it was in the best interest of the park to maintain the island resources in good condition. He also appreciated the importance of maintaining good relations with the Gherinis in order to facilitate the eventual sale of East Santa Cruz Island to the NPS, which by this time the park administration considered inevitable.[66]

Park maintenance staff Kent Bullard and Earl Whetsell modified a Conex shipping container to serve as a ranger residence and sent it over to the island on the park boat. It was offloaded at Smugglers by a helicopter in 1984. This solution became the permanent residence and office of the newly established East Santa Cruz Island and established a precedent for park housing on the other islands. Despite the good relations between NPS ranger Mark Senning and Francis Gherini, the latter continued to oppose the NPS acquisition of his property. Francis voiced his opposition on August 14, 1989, writing that he "strenuously" objected to the sale of his brother's interest to the Park Service.[67]

Relations were also positive at that time between the NPS and Island Adventures. Superintendent Ehorn periodically visited the island and would stop by to see the Owenses at Scorpion Ranch. He always had good things to say about the work that Duane and Doris were doing on the property and encouraged them to continue. Ehorn even arranged for Duane to become a VIP (volunteer in park), allowing him to use the ranger's ATV to assist in patrolling East Santa Cruz Island.[68] These warm relations continued while Ehorn remained superintendent, but they changed dramatically after he left the Channel Islands.

Growth of the Natural Resource Management   6

The 1985 general management plan (GMP) emphasized the need for enumeration and analysis of natural resources. The I&M procedures designed by Gary Davis provided these data. Assisting with that program and with preparation of the park's planning documents were the highest priorities for the resource management program in the 1980s. Channel Islands National Park staff had completed a new resource management plan (RMP) in 1982 as part of the preparation of the new GMP focused on the two recently added islands.[1] Although these activities occupied much of the program's time and energy, ongoing efforts to control exotic species on the islands also continued. Resource management at this time was still primarily a collateral duty of the island rangers.[2]

In August 1983, Frank Ugolini transferred to Channel Island to lead the park's newly independent resource management division. Shortly after arriving, Ugolini initiated a complete revision of the recently issued 1982 RMP. His early objectives included eradication of black rats on Anacapa Island, establishment of a monitoring program for the caliche forest on San Miguel Island, and monitoring tidepools to measure visitor impact.[3] He completed the final draft in January 1984. By this time, many of the baseline inventories and monitoring handbooks were finished. The program began its second phase with implementation of long-term monitoring by resource management staff. The responsibilities of the research program and the park's resource management division were to be fully integrated and work in tandem with appropriate uses of the respective skills of research scientists for baseline inventories and resource managers for long-term monitoring.

After Gary Davis and Bill Halvorson estimated that the monitoring program would cost roughly $822,000 in 1987, inflation and other issues meant it was only "three-quarters of what was required to actually run the program as it was designed."[4] The funding shortfall encouraged Gary Davis to seek greater authority and funding for the vital signs program on a national level. In turn, this had a profound impact on the growth and relative status of the natural resource management program at Channel Islands. The park's I&M program was one of three prototype parks when the National Park Service sought to apply it to the entire system. This in turn expanded the natural resource program in both funds and staff. Park administrators felt the best way to implement the prototype program was to fully integrate it into the natural resource management program, not to create a "stand-alone" work unit. The outcome of this structural decision was a blend of purpose, personnel, and funds among monitoring, restoration, compliance, and all the myriad functions of park resources operations. Hence, the money was not earmarked and was available for resource management as well as for research.[5] However, Davis found that at Channel Islands it still disappeared into other places. The NPS then established a board of directors composed of park superintendents to oversee how that money is spent. With that centralized control, if the money started to wander off, it could be brought back for monitoring.[6]

Inventory and Monitoring Service-Wide

Gary Davis had long realized that the long-term monitoring program he had initiated at Channel Islands might become a model for similar programs at other national parks and protected areas. He had proposed this as early as November 1982.[7] But it was not until Davis became frustrated with the park's inability to fund his long-term monitoring protocols that he began to seriously pursue the idea of a national program.[8] By that time, there was growing interest at several other parks and regional offices for such a program. In October 1986, Alaska regional director Boyd Evison convened a two-day workshop in Seattle, Washington, comprising NPS field scientists including Gary Davis, resource managers, and representatives from the U.S. Forest Service (USFS) and several universities.[9] This resulted in a draft policy statement, the *Evison Report* for developing a service-wide I&M program using Channel Islands as a model.

The Evison task force emphasized the importance of collecting baseline inventory data of park natural resources and monitoring them over time. The need for inventory and monitoring had long been appreciated by many resource managers, who had already implemented programs in piecemeal fashion elsewhere in the park system. What was lacking, according to the Evison group, was a comprehensive and systematic approach with effective policy guidance from the highest levels of NPS administration. The group also insisted that the budget to support such a program be made as stable and long-term as the program itself.

After being passed around among Park Service senior administrators and receiving their comments and modifications, the *Evison Report* was eventually published as the *Natural Resources Inventory and Monitoring Initiative* in 1987. The report included a strong justification for the implementation of a service-wide I&M program in policy, noting that legislative precedents already existed. The National Environmental Policy Act (NEPA) of 1969 requires managers to have adequate knowledge of resources in order to determine the effects of management actions. This implies the need for baseline inventories, and to the extent that effects are assessed, it also implies a degree of monitoring. The Forest and Rangeland Renewable Resources Planning Act of 1974 (P.L. 93–378) set a more explicit precedent for the USFS by requiring the inventory and monitoring of economically valuable forests and rangelands under its administration.[10] The roots of this legislation dated back to late nineteenth-century conservation practice with its principles of multiple-use management for sustained yields.

Probably the strongest argument in support of the I&M initiative was a report submitted to the NPS in February of 1987 by the General Accounting Office (GAO) criticizing the agency for failing to make an adequate response to its own *State of the Parks* report of 1980. That document identified more than three hundred threats facing the natural and cultural resources of twelve parks that the GAO had sampled. When it visited the same parks in 1986, it found that 80 percent of these threats remained unresolved and more than 40 percent had not even been documented.

Staff members in the parks often lacked sufficient data to respond to the investigators about the threats. Although the Park Service had committed itself to implementing RMPs for all of its park units in response to the 1980 report, the GAO found that most of these plans were inadequate or incomplete. The problem stemmed from insufficient funding, even though the NPS budget for resource management had more than doubled during the first half of that decade.[11] The GAO criticized all of the RMPs for lacking comprehensive baseline data and failing to accurately measure changes in resource conditions over time. What was missing was an adequate inventory and monitoring program to support resource management planning, a criticism with which the Park Service itself fully concurred.[12]

In response to this growing problem, the NPS Directorate issued a draft *Standards and Guidelines* for implementing the proposed I&M initiative by the end of 1987.[13] However, after more than a year of peer review, the Directorate concluded that the document did not provide practical guidance for implementing I&M programs at the park level. Details were not fleshed out, objectives were not clear, and standards were inconsistent.[14]

While the Washington Office wrestled with these ideas on the programmatic level, similar discussions took place within the parks themselves. At the Spring 1989 meeting of the Western Region's Natural Resources and Research Advisory Group, park resource managers proposed developing a regional I&M program in place of the still unwritten service-wide program. The obvious model for it was the program already functioning at the Channel Islands. The advisory group therefore appointed Davis and Halvorson to lead a team of twenty-four park-based scientists and managers and charged them with developing a draft "Ecological Monitoring Program" over the next few months. Team members completed the proposal by the end of summer, and it served as the focal point of discussion at a workshop that they hosted at Channel Islands that September.[15] A select group of interested superintendents, research scientists, park resource managers, and representatives from both the Western Regional Office and the Washington Office attended the workshop. Most importantly, six members of Dr. Gene Hester's staff were also present.[16]

Gene Hester was the Washington Office's associate director for natural resources and the man chiefly responsible for trying to implement Boyd

Evison's proposal over the previous eighteen months. The *Standards and Guidelines*' deficiency was that it had been developed on a conceptual level to address programmatic concerns rather than on practical realities. But here was a model that was based on an existing program at an actual park. The Channel Islands model lacked nothing in detail. In fact, Davis and Halvorson presented an elaborate step-down diagram that contained even more detail than the original version Davis had developed for Channel Islands in 1982. It also represented the experience of nearly ten years of development at the park.

Later that year, Hester assembled a task force charged with developing a workable plan for implementing the programmatic I&M initiative based on the Channel Islands model. Of course, Gary Davis was one of the twelve task force members. Between December 1989 and March 1990, they developed a service-wide inventory and monitoring plan. It had the same goals and policy statements as those in the earlier *Standards and Guidelines* and the *Evison Report* but differed because it acknowledged the inadequacy of existing inventory data. These deficiencies had to be addressed as they had been at Channel Islands. First, the agency needed a review of literature conducted over a one-year period, the results of which would be compiled in a single electronic database. This would reveal gaps in existing knowledge. Second, field surveys were crucial to collect baseline data to fill those gaps. These surveys were expected to be completed over a period of ten years. Together, the literature reviews and field surveys would constitute the inventory phase of the overall I&M program.

Monitoring would be introduced in stages through a park-based, rather than service-level, approach. The present plan acknowledged the complaint made by reviewers of earlier proposals that each park's natural resources and physical conditions were unique and could not be addressed through a generalized methodology. Therefore, each park, or in some cases a group of parks that were closely related, should develop its own monitoring protocols appropriate to local conditions. In principle, long-term monitoring could begin after the conceptual design for these protocols had been completed, peer-reviewed, and approved. However, as Channel Islands had already discovered, long-term monitoring depended on effec-

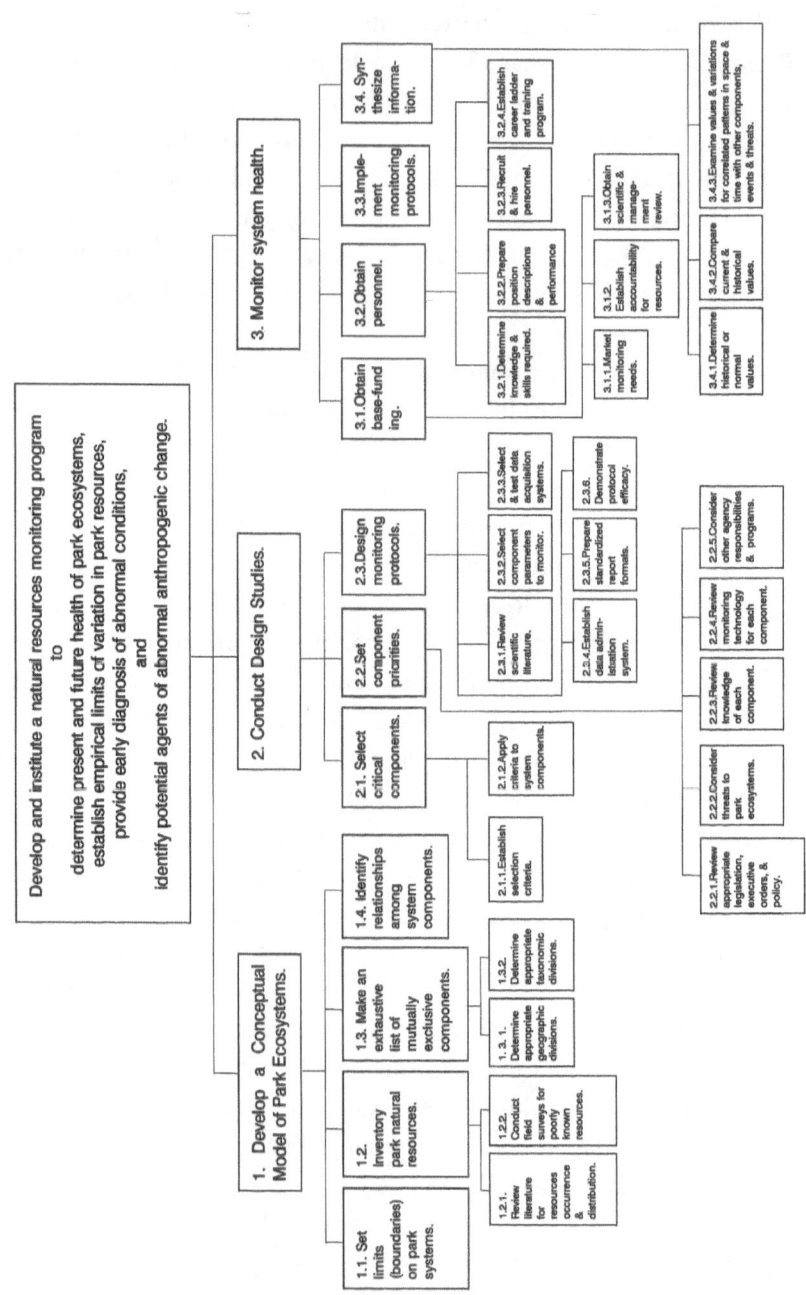

Fig. 17. I&M step-down diagram for the NPS. Provided by Gary Davis.

tive budgetary planning because it required permanent staff increases in order to maintain the program indefinitely. Inventories could be done on a project-funded basis with temporary staff, but the monitoring phase of the I&M program needed significant base outlays from the NPS budget. Park Service leaders decided that these would be made on an incremental basis to a small group of pilot parks that could test the program. The first two pilot programs would be implemented in 1992, and two additional parks would be added every year until 1995, with a total of eight pilot parks proposed. Naturally, Channel Islands was chosen as one of the first two pilot parks in the long-term monitoring program.

In 1992 the Park Service finally published the "Inventory and Monitoring Guideline" as NPS-75. This was a director's order that was intended to provide detailed and consistent policies for implementing inventory and monitoring programs service-wide. The Channel Islands program now became a model for the entire agency. In the 1998 National Parks Omnibus Act, Congress ordered I&M to be carried out throughout the park system.[17]

Major Changes after Bill Ehorn Departs

In July 1989, Bill Ehorn left Channel Islands National Park to become superintendent of Redwood National Park in northern California. His departure brought changes many had not expected. Assistant Superintendent Tim Setnicka served as acting superintendent of the park during the four-month interval between Ehorn's departure and the arrival of the new superintendent in November 1989. Ehorn had elevated Setnicka from chief ranger to chief of operations and then to assistant superintendent since the latter's arrival at the park in 1987. Setnicka's highly unorthodox style was as decisive as Bill Ehorn's but far less positive.[18]

Setnicka proved adept at managing operations and was well respected by many of the rangers he supervised, but he had an unusual way of interacting with people, often testing them to see how far they could be pushed. Ehorn successfully exercised a firm hand in supervision, paying close attention to what was happening in the park and providing quick response to any trouble before it could escalate out of hand. Administrative officer Chris Horton played the invaluable role of "eyes and ears" for his administration, placing her knowledge of the field and her concern for other people to good use. The success of the park's administration, however, rested ultimately on the effective authority of the superintendent. Setnicka proved to be a capable supervisor under Ehorn's, leadership and Horton's watchful eye but would later become controversial as a leader.[19]

Former chief ranger Charles "Mack" Shaver succeeded Ehorn as superintendent. Upon his return to the island park, Shaver faced renewing the Special Use Permit for the Vail & Vickers Ranch, initiating a development plan for NPS facilities on Santa Rosa Island and working toward the acquisition of East Santa Cruz Island, as well as managing the park operations and time-consuming regional office commitments. The NPS experienced seismic changes during Mack Shaver's five years as superintendent of Channel Islands. Director Roger Kennedy reorganized the agency, reducing staff throughout the nation, changing regional boundaries, and moving superintendents, all with the goal of saving money. These actions negatively affected employee morale. At the same time, House Speaker Newt Gingrich and his "Contract with America" shut down the government, which closed Channel Islands National Park for three weeks over Christmas, when the visitor center and Anacapa Island traditionally welcomed higher-than-normal visitation.[20]

Because of Kennedy's ill-conceived agency reorganization, Shaver also served as one of the principals on the Regional Leadership Committee, supporting other national park areas in the newly reorganized Pacific West Region. As a result, he worked in other parts of the country for at least a week every month and relied on Setnicka to shoulder the management issues at Channel Islands during these times. Shaver knew, if closely supervised, Setnicka's skills could be harnessed into park achievements. However, he also knew Setnicka could be a divisive force. He told Setnicka, each time he left him in charge as acting superintendent, before making any decision, "Ask yourself whether I would do what you are even thinking of doing."[21]

One critical problem that Shaver faced was how to keep park scientist Gary Davis working on park issues after his transfer to Secretary of the Interior Bruce Babbitt's new National Biological Survey (NBS). With his transfer to the NBS, the NPS lost line authority to the scientist and his ground-breaking work. When Shaver announced that his retirement would occur in March 1996, Regional Director Stan Albright asked him if Setnicka should be promoted to superintendent. "Absolutely not," Shaver responded. Yet, Albright and Shaver were backed into a corner in order to get Davis back to the park. Setnicka would have to become superintendent so Gary Davis could occupy the now vacant deputy superintendent FTE (full-time employee). The latter position was then abolished and Setnicka was named superintendent.[22]

Natural Resource Management Dominates

By the end of the 1980s, resource management at Channel Islands remained understaffed and limited in what it was capable of doing, but compared to the monument days, considerable progress had been made. Lacking, however, was the resource management staff to implement these protocols. As the prototype inventory and monitoring park, Channel Islands received an additional $800,000 in its 1992 and 1993 fiscal year budgets, with $622,000 intended specifically for long-term monitoring and the remainder for ecosystem restoration. Although the purpose of this funding was to support Channel Island's role in the I&M program, the money was allocated to the resources management division in order to hire additional park staff to assist in long-term monitoring. With the money distributed to the resource management budget, it would be difficult or impossible to disentangle what belonged to management and what belonged to monitoring, thereby making it easier to justify committing the time of management staff to monitoring activities. But critics of this arrangement feared that it could allow I&M funds to be diverted to other, non-resource-related purposes. Their concerns were justified when Setnicka was reprimanded for transferring funds allocated for resource management to operations. Other parks received I&M funds through a separate Washington-based account to prevent this form of abuse.[23]

Despite this inherent danger, one benefit was the resulting growth in the resource management division. Money allocated through the I&M initiative allowed several new positions to be established exclusively for resources management, resulting in profound changes to the park's management priorities. Prior to 1992, the entire resource division had accounted for a relatively small percentage of the total park staff. It was managed by Kate Faulkner, who replaced Frank Ugolini after he retired in 1989. The resources division also utilized project-based funding for seasonal technicians on a year-to-year basis. The park also continued to benefit from Gary Davis and William Halvorson, who filled the park's research mandate.[24]

Following the budget increases of 1992, the resource management division grew to include more than a third of all base-funded positions. By 1995 the division comprised 16.4 FTEs out of the park's total of 46.5. The increase in seasonal and temporary positions made the resource division the most visible component of the park. But it also became increasingly dominated by a natural rather than cultural emphasis. The cultural resources program remained stable with archeologist Don Morris as the only permanent employee. The growing imbalance in FTEs between natural resources and cultural resources, as well as other divisions in the park, was natural given that the funding increases for that year went largely to the I&M program.[25]

The park's predominant focus on natural resource protection reflected a growing professionalism of the resource management division and the increasing sophistication of scientific research that both caused and accompanied it. The I&M program was one expression of this. Another was the decision to hire Kate Faulkner in 1989 to head the resource management program. As an experienced biologist, Faulkner emphasized ecosystem restoration and the removal or eradication of nonnative species. This management approach was opposed by some staff members, especially Tim Setnicka, who believed that it was excessive and unnecessary. Underlying Faulkner's emphasis was the knowledge gleaned from the I&M program that much of the island's native habitat was already degraded or greatly imperiled. These concerns would lead her to question the existing special use agreement with Vail & Vickers on Santa Rosa Island.

FIRE MANAGEMENT

Fire has been a factor in the Channel Islands since well before humans arrived. Research at San Nicolas Island showed that at least twenty-four major fires occurred between thirty-seven thousand and twenty-five thousand years BP.²⁶ When scientists and resource managers came to the islands, they had two separate research agendas—determining the fire regimes of the past to understand the evolution of the islands' ecosystems and calculating how to cope with the changes that would come with eradication of nonnative ungulates. Sediment cores on Santa Cruz and Santa Rosa Islands showed that fires happened between one and nine times over the millennium prior to the arrival of Americans 160 years earlier. Thereafter, the introduction of sheep, cattle, and other grazers reduced vegetative cover and transformed the vegetation communities on the islands. Nonnative plants, particularly annual grasses, replaced shrubland and woodland communities.

With reduced vegetative cover, natural ignition diminished, but human behavior led to more frequent burns. Santa Barbara Island seems to have suffered the largest impact. Between 1917 and 1921 the island was burned every year to clear land for agriculture. Two large fires also occurred on the small island, one in 1959 that burned 400 acres and another in 1976 that torched even more land. The largest fire in history on one of the five park islands occurred on the north shore of Santa Cruz Island on lands now managed by the Nature Conservancy (TNC). It consumed 7,575 acres in 1932. The largest fire on lands the park now manages was accidentally ignited on San Miguel Island on November 1, 1967, by a navy flare and burned an estimated 3,200 acres. Another on San Miguel charred 650 acres on January 22, 1976.²⁷

After 1980, as part of the requisite land planning, Superintendent Bill Ehorn contacted Carey Stanton and the Vails on the two privately owned islands to secure their permission for Santa Barbara County fire crews to access their property in case of fire. This was the opening step in a planning process to develop an official fire management plan as required of all units in the park system.²⁸ The owners submitted their permission statements, but legal confusion delayed implementation when first the county and then the state of California refused to take the lead role in fire suppression on the private islands. It took until 1993 for an interagency agreement to be adopted by the park and Los Padres National Forest giving the NPS a more dependable partner in case of fire on the islands.²⁹

In 1988 the park received $2,500 to accelerate planning and preparation for its fire program, and in July 1989 a group of fire management specialists visited the three larger islands to survey the fuel loads and help design a startup fire management program. The team emphasized the importance of this program because of the ongoing ecological restoration plans stating:

> The visit and the emphasis on developing a Fire Management Plan are very timely because a radical change in fuel conditions is imminent, albeit planned, for most areas of the islands. Many decades of heavy domestic livestock grazing and foraging is coming to a negotiated end as the park takes ownership and progressively assumes resource management emphasizing natural plant communities. Although the removal of grazing will not readily return the vegetation to prehistoric conditions, the regrowth of the existing plants, especially grasses, will be very rapid. From limited information on one large animal enclosure, it is clear that even a poor growing will produce a substantial, largely uninterrupted fuel mosaic capable of supporting fires of moderate to high intensity with high rates of spread.[30]

After two more years of planning and study, the NPS released a "Fire Management Plan" as an amendment to the natural resource management plan (NRMP) of 1982. Two major decisions shaped the plan's policy. First, total suppression would be the response to fires, both natural and human caused. This was to be an "interim policy" until restoration of the native ecosystem had reached the point where "fire use" would be consistent with its survival. Planners recognized the detrimental effects of fire suppression on some vegetation but argued it would continue until research brought a better understanding of its impacts on both natural and cultural resources. The other decision was consistent with the overall policy of the National Park Service in performing prescribed burns under carefully monitored weather and fuel conditions to reduce the fuel load. The goals of the plan in descending order of priorities were to prevent the loss of human life; prevent damage to park facilities and property owned by visitors and island owners; and ensure that the fire programs protect natural, cultural, and historical values of the park. The objectives of the plan in descending order of priorities were to maintain an active fire suppression program capable of responding to 90 percent of the fire starts in the park; create an interpretive program to reduce "person-caused" fires; protect cultural resources; protect threatened and endangered plant and animal species from damage by a fire or by suppression methods; maintain a park fire committee; and provide training to personnel.[31]

During the 1980s and early 1990s, several fires broke out on the islands, but none posed a major threat. In 1985 a 15.5-acre fire occurred on San Miguel Island. Two years later, the first lightning-caused fire in more than thirty years ignited on TNC/Carey Stanton property. The latter was suppressed by Bill Ehorn and his crew at the request of Stanton. In 1989 two small fires began on Santa Cruz and Santa Rosa Islands but were quickly suppressed. Another caused by human error erupted on Santa Rosa in 1994. Prescribed fires were part of the plan, but the first two deliberate burns were on TNC property on West Santa Cruz Island with approval by the NPS in 1993 and 1994.[32] During the 1990s, TNC conducted twelve prescribed burns on its property with most concentrated in the lower Central Valley and near Christy Ranch. Yet 1997 brought scrutiny and controversy to the prescribed fire procedure when the park released a plan to burn 600 acres, including Old Ranch Canyon on the eastern portion of Santa Rosa Island. This came amid the most intense controversy over grazing on the island and the fate of Vail & Vickers operations there. The Park Service secured the approval of the U.S. Fish and Wildlife Service because the burn would include an area occupied by Santa Rosa Island live forever (*Dudleya blochmaniae ssp. insularis*), a rare endemic perennial. Fortunately, the plant does not show above ground during mid to late June, the window of time planned for the burn. The NPS issued a Finding of No Significant Impact on June 16, 1997, and carried out the burn, which grew to 812 acres.[33]

Interagency Cooperative Management of Resources

The management of marine resources continued to be a complex process for the National Park Service at Channel Islands. The lack of jurisdictional control by the agency led to a few conflicts and exceptional efforts to craft cooperative agreements. In December 1987, an incident occurred that tested the relationship between Ehorn and the U.S. Navy. One of the targeted ships the navy used for bombing practice, the USS *Tortuga*, ran aground on San Miguel Island. It created a visual blight as well as a danger for pinnipeds and other marine species. Because the navy owned the island, the NPS had to request that it be removed. The navy balked at doing so, citing an expense of more than $2,500,000. Not long after that, Gary Davis and members of the Channel Islands National Marine Sanctuary staff visited the site in time to see a bull sea lion impale itself on an exposed steel beam. When word of the incident got out, the navy reluctantly removed the wreck. The possibility that the wrecked ship could be a safety hazard for divers and even contain unexploded ordnance mandated action regardless of cost.[34]

Another change in resource management that took place on San Miguel Island affected visitors more than the resource. The National Marine Fisheries Service (NMFS) and the NPS studied the pinniped viewing areas at Point Bennett in order to make sure that the animals were not disturbed by noisy or visible people. NMFS decided to restrict visitors to a new viewing location farther away from the hauled-out pinnipeds. The former viewing area was close to nest sites for gulls, and the scientists believed that people might disturb the gulls and start a cascade effect whereby frightened birds would disturb the pinnipeds. Groups of up to fifteen people would be allowed at the new visiting site, although the ranger leading them could reduce that number depending on the visitors' behavior. Later, the standard number of visitors was reduced to ten.[35]

One of the early purposes of the I&M program was its evaluation of ecosystem integrity in the sea around the Channel Islands.[36] Kelp forests provide important habitat for more than 750 species of fish and invertebrates.[37] California's renowned giant kelp forests rise from depths of 80–100 feet (25–30 meters) over rocky reefs and cover thousands of acres in the park with canopies like those of tropical rainforests. The thick kelp canopy acts as a shelter from predators and nursery habitat for juvenile fish. The density and extent of giant kelp (*Macrocystis pyrifera*) around the park islands is a result of suitable rocky substrates around the islands. The giant kelp that appears in the intertidal zone is only drift, broken from the parent plants by storms or boat propellers.

Fig. 18. The kelp forest looking toward the surface. Photograph by Gary Davis, August 2004.

Commercial and recreational fishing strongly affect several types of popular marine animals. Proper management of their populations is a vital responsibility of the state of California and careful monitoring by the NPS is key to exercising it. The California spiny lobster is one of the most important and recreationally popular fisheries. Although it is an important component of the park's marine environment, the spiny lobster's apparent resilience made it an object of lesser concern for park scientists. Yet, despite its relatively healthy populations, scientists have observed significant fluctuations in the past. The species is at the northern edge of its geographic distribution in the park. The major source of larval production is in Mexico, but the larvae can travel thousands of miles over periods of up to nine months before settling into a benthic existence where they can grow to a marketable size. Urban coastal development on the mainland destroyed much of its littoral kelp habitat and raised concern because declining mainland availability might intensify lobster exploitation by fishermen at the islands.[38] In spite of fluctuations, spiny lobster populations in the park have not shown signs of stress from overharvesting to date.

Abalone have suffered a very different fate. Six species of abalone occurred naturally in the park's waters. California's abalone species suffered serial depletion beginning when red abalone (*Haliotis rufescens*) landings began steep declines in the 1950s, followed by landing declines of pink abalone (*H. corrugata*) in the 1960s, green abalone (*H. fulgens*) by the early 1970s, and white abalone (*H. sorenseni*) by the time monitoring protocols were implemented by the park in the 1980s. Based on data from landings by commercial and sport fishermen, the period of greatest decline for white abalone occurred during the 1970s, after depletion of the shallower abalone populations.[39] The availability of scuba gear following World War II, along with innovations, such as neoprene wet suits and repetitive dive tables in 1957, made this relatively deep-water species more easily accessible. The full extent of the fishery's impact, however, was not recognized for some years, until monitoring revealed the abundance, distribution, and relative size of the surviving population in its natural environment.[40]

The I&M that began in 1982 consisted of a sampling process designed to measure changes in population dynamics of a suite of more than seventy marine species that inhabit the kelp forest ecosystem. It revealed population abundance, distribution, and size structure in addition to presence or absence. In 1985, long-term monitoring of the rocky tidal ecosystem expanded beyond Anacapa to San Miguel, Santa Rosa, and Santa Barbara Islands. The expansion included the establishment of forty fixed plots to monitor black abalone (*H. cracherodii*) within the lower intertidal zone. Each plot measured approximately 3 square meters (10 square feet) and was monitored every spring and autumn by park resource staff. Along with fixed photo plots to monitor key algae and sessile invertebrate organisms, researchers measured abundance and size of black abalone in the larger plots.[41]

Researchers also sampled red and pink abalone in the subtidal kelp forest, conducting twelve randomly selected 3 x 20-meter (10 x 65 feet) band transects at each of the kelp monitoring sites every year.[42] Over four

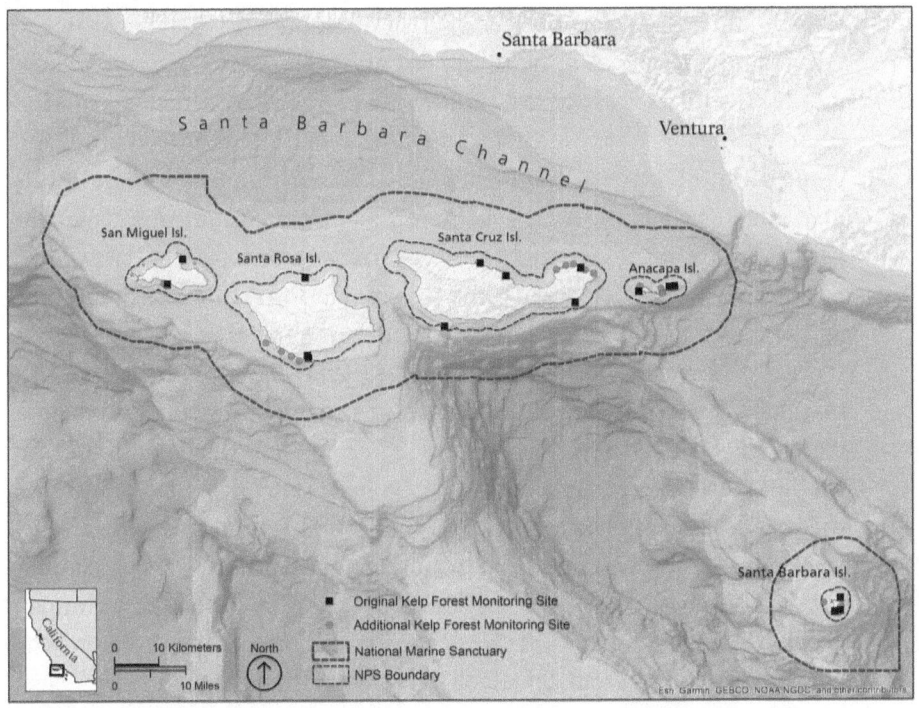

Map 13. Kelp monitoring sites at Channel Islands National Park in 1984 and those added during subsequent years. Cartography by R. Rudolph, CINP.

consecutive years of monitoring, park staff observed that black abalone abundance fell by 96 percent at four of the islands, although only 39 percent off San Miguel; red abalone fell by 97 to 98 percent; and pink abalone fell by 51 to 94 percent. These numbers far exceeded the range of natural population variance and suggested anthropogenic causes. Fishery take was capable of reducing population densities of breeding abalones to such low densities that reproductive collapse could cut off the supply of juveniles to unsustainable levels given the capacity of the fishing fleet and market demand.[43]

NPS scientists Gary Davis and Dan Richards and the California Department of Fish and Game (CDFG) scientists Peter Haaker and David Parker hypothesized that a variety of factors, some natural and some human, had conflated to bring down the abalone populations. Human take of abalone reduced the reproductive capacity of populations and their resilience to withstand cyclical warming of the sea and the subsequent loss of kelp as a food source. In 1957 mystified oceanographers recorded a period of much warmer than normal water in the Santa Barbara Channel and along all the Southern California Coast. Later, the phenomenon was identified as an El Niño. It was the most severe case of this recurrent phenomenon in the twentieth century to that point. However, an equal or greater episode occurred in the Channel Islands region between 1982 and 1984. It brought exceptionally warm waters and severe winter storms to the California coast. The storms swept away much of the kelp forest on which the abalone depended for food and habitat, while the warmer waters encouraged a proliferation of sea urchins. Both abalones and sea urchins were impacted the same way by food reduction, but in addition to loss of food, small purple sea urchins (*Strongylocentrotus purpuratus*) were released from competition by human take of their primary competitors, red sea urchins and abalone, and released from predation by human take of fishes and lobsters. This allowed purple urchins to dominate the benthos and graze virtually all macro algae, including giant kelp. Warm El Niño waters were also nitrogen poor and prevented robust growth of kelp needed to support recruitment of juvenile abalone and hindered the regeneration of the kelp forests. The resulting lack of adequate food resources may have caused the abalone to starve. Each one of these factors, and possibly others, contributed to the abalone's sudden collapse, but ultimately, the scientists believed it was human agency that made the species unusually vulnerable to this chain of natural events by destabilizing the marine ecosystem in which the abalone lived.[44]

White abalone, which were not directly monitored because their deepwater habitat was generally beyond safe diving limits, were no longer seen on survey dives, and the scarcity was alarming. Although direct harvesting of white abalone by commercial and sport fishermen may have exacerbated the abalone's decline, reducing pre-1980s populations to the point where a natural chain of events could prove devastating, harvesting was only part of the problem, and regulating the take of individual species by fishermen would not have prevented it. Despite robust efforts to regulate the fishery including a prohibition on fishing during the spawning sea-

Fig. 19. A seafloor that once supported a kelp forest shown decimated by purple sea urchins. Photographer and date unknown, CINP Photo Archives.

son, bag limits for recreational fishermen, limited entry to fishing areas, and permit fees, the species continued to decline until fewer than two thousand adult individuals remained by the end of the 1980s. CDFG had to close the fishery entirely in 1996 to prevent the species' extinction.[45]

What was "upset" in this case was the integrity, resilience, and capacity for renewal of the ecosystem. The abnormally long recovery time for the black, red, and pink abalone following the El Niño years seemed to confirm the scientists' suspicion that the ecosystem itself was now far more vulnerable to catastrophic but short-term natural events than it would otherwise have been. Davis and Richards observed: "There are strong indications that stochastic physical environmental factors, such as storms, now appear to be the principal agents of change in this system, rather than the biological components which previously buffered the system against extreme, long-lasting fluctuations. The reduction of this buffering capacity and subsequent shift of control from probabilistic biological factors to unmanageable deterministic physical factors, paradoxically, will make the system more predictable but less manageable."[46] Davis argued that management objectives had to be reoriented to address the entire ecosystem rather than individual species, since it now seemed clear that the declining populations of the latter were not isolated phenomena but symptoms of the declining resiliency of the environment itself. This realization became an important justification for the establishment of strong marine protected areas, based on the national marine sanctuary that already existed, but with greater authority to restrict access and regulate use.

By the end of the decade, Gary Davis actively pursued this idea through a proposal to establish "marine harvest refugia" (no-harvest zones) within the boundaries of the national park and national marine sanctuary.[47] Although Davis conducted a multiyear study of this idea with funding from the State Department's Man and the Biosphere Program, the refuge itself was never implemented. The project was designed to test the viability of concentrating adult abalone in historic densities within a protected area to promote reproduction as a population recovery strategy.[48] One thousand adult pink abalone were procured from a live abalone wholesaler and placed in the marine protected area on East Anacapa Island, below the island ranger's quarters to ensure maximum surveillance. The California Abalone Association, a political lobbying group of commercial abalone divers, strongly opposed the project, and it terminated after one year. The transplanted abalone disappeared within a few months thereafter.

This evolution in resource policy objectives from managing for individual species to managing entire ecosystems was one of the more immediate and significant results of the I&M program at Channel Islands. It had demonstrated the inadequacy of existing regulation of the abalone fishery based on harvest limitations alone, and it provided crucial data about the condition of the broader environment that helped to explain why those regulations were not working. The I&M program also proved its value as an early detection system, alerting resource managers to the sudden decline of the abalone populations even as it was happening. A final, tragic confirmation of the value of early detection through systematic monitoring came in 1986 with the discovery of a withering syndrome in black abalone. This resulted from invasion by a pathogen that causes the fleshy body of the abalone to shrivel up inside its shell, usually resulting in death.[49]

Although monitoring could do nothing to prevent this disease, it did alert resource managers early on to the existence of the problem and allowed them to identify regulatory measures to protect surviving black abalone and other abalone species that were also affected by the syndrome.

Unfortunately, the California Fish and Game Commission (CFGC) ignored the early warnings. It protected surviving black abalone populations only after they had declined to critically low densities, closing fisheries only after the populations had collapsed, island by island, over a period of years. Monitoring made it possible for scientists to follow the course of the epidemic disease from the moment of its earliest expression and assisted them in understanding its nature and how it might ultimately play out.[50] Too late, the National Oceanic and Atmospheric Administration (NOAA), which has the authority to apply the Endangered Species Act for fish and marine invertebrates, issued a rule in early 2009 to list the black abalone under that law.[51]

Establishment of State Marine Reserves

Despite the establishment of Channel Islands National Marine Sanctuary (CINMS) in 1980, the status of marine resources was poor by the late 1990s, as demonstrated by nearly two decades of monitoring data. After the 1978 Supreme Court case gave California the right to manage within three miles of the islands' shores, the CFGC agreed to maintain some reserved areas but not to the depth that the NPS had protected. The state agency also cooperated in the efforts to monitor kelp forests and other marine resources once the national park and marine sanctuary were established. Nevertheless, between 1980 and 1998 the park waters lost 80 percent of its kelp forest and four of its five abalone species. The data from monitoring showed that protection of habitat and water quality alone had not sustained ocean ecosystems or fisheries.[52]

The CFGC closure to fishing on the north side of Anacapa protected lobsters, sea urchins, and other species living on the rocky reefs and kelp forests of the area. Monitoring begun in 1981 by Gary Davis and carried out for two decades showed that kelp forests were denser and lasted longer, lobsters were more plentiful, and sea urchins were larger than in unprotected areas nearby. In 2002 a consortium of scientists from four universities called the Partnership for Interdisciplinary Studies of Coastal Oceans (PISCO), reported that "the ecosystem protected in the Anacapa Island reserve now contains most of its animals and plants in a relatively natural state."[53] Subsequent studies produced abundant evidence showing that within areas protected from fishing, rapid increases in abundance; size; biomass; and diversity of animals occur regardless of where in the world the reserves are sited.[54]

During the 1990s, Gary Davis and others on the park staff began working on a proposal to CFGC to have it establish marine reserves as no-fishing zones in order to determine whether relief from fishing would result in recovery of the endangered species. At the same time, a group of private fishermen, primarily long-term residents who had seen their catches diminish over the years, approached the NPS asking if it would assist them in doing something to rectify the situation. Most of the members were older people who had the financial means to own boats and fish the Santa Barbara Channel for recreation. They remembered the halcyon days of the 1950s when the fish and crustaceans were plentiful. Now, as they took their grandchildren to fish, the returns were comparatively meager.[55] They organized a local campaign with the Ventura County Fish and Game Commission and created the Channel Islands Marine Resource Restoration Committee (CIMRRC) that met monthly for more than a year. They drummed up support among local and regional fishing clubs, yacht clubs, charter boat operators, and local news outlets.

In April 1998, both the NPS and the CIMRRC presented their proposals to the California Fish and Game Commission. Gary Davis had worked with the recreational fishing group to "train them in civics," that is, how to work with the government to get something passed into law. The upshot was that the CIMRRC's plan was virtually identical to that of the Park Service. Davis later recalled that the CFGC's members largely ignored the appeal of the NPS but responded enthusiastically to the same program when presented by the local fishermen. The NPS wanted reserves over 50 percent of the sea within the park boundary. This was strongly recommended by marine biologists as necessary for recovery. They believed that seriously endangered fishery species could not be saved without half the coastal water restricted. However, 20 percent was the common proportion in various reserves around the world and what the National Marine Fisheries Service and the South Atlantic Fisheries Management Council had proposed in bands along the Atlantic Coast from North Carolina to Florida. Recognizing the political futility of proposing 50 percent coverage, the NPS and CIMRRC used these precedents to ask for 20 percent.[56]

The CFGC agreed with the proposal but did not know how to identify which zones around the islands to include and what rules to apply to each one. Yet a solution was readily at hand. In 1998, CINMS had established a community-based Sanctuary Advisory Council (SAC). It comprised ten government seats and ten nongovernment seats, representing commercial and recreational fishermen, divers, conservationists, businesses, tourism, and some citizens at large. Sanctuary director Edward Cassano offered to incorporate into it a working group that would negotiate for reserves or other solutions to the crisis. It would identify critical issues, research objectives and educational opportunities, and establish a framework for considering specific reserves. NOAA's mission included developing an informed constituency to increase awareness and understanding of the purpose and value of the sanctuary. It was the appropriate agency to undertake this complicated role. CINMS and CDFG developed a joint federal and state partnership to co-chair a Marine Reserve Working Group (MRWG) of stakeholders to consider the establishment of marine reserves in the sanctuary.[57] The following year, the state legislature facilitated the process by passing the California Marine Life Protection Act, which required CDFG to reevaluate all existing marine protected areas and design new units that together would function as a statewide network.[58]

In the spring of 1999, the MRWG consisted of a core of the five SAC members, a Sea Grant Extension marine advisor, and a representative of the CDFG. Ten additional members were selected to represent a range of community perspectives (e.g., sport fishing, commercial fishing, and kelp harvesting).[59] The working group formally adopted ground rules for consensus that required members to offer positive alternatives if they disagreed with a group proposal or to withdraw from the process. The SAC selected a sixteen-member Marine Reserves Science Panel to provide scientific guidance and a five-person Socioeconomic Team to help the working group evaluate the social and economic implications of marine reserves. The group considered only scientists with no published "agenda" on marine reserves.[60]

Beginning in early 2000, a task group within the MRWG formulated a statement of the problem and a list of goals and objectives within each goal to solve it. The former was straightforward: "To protect, maintain, restore, and enhance living marine resources, it is necessary to develop new management strategies that encompass an ecosystem perspective and promote collaboration between competing interests. One strategy is to develop reserves where all harvest is prohibited."[61]

After several drafts, the MRWG set forth five goals with objectives on December 14, 2000, that were straightforward but also ambitious: (1) an Ecosystem Biodiversity Goal: to protect representative and unique marine habitats, ecological processes, and populations of interest including multiple levels of diversity (e.g., species, habitats, biogeographic provinces, trophic structure) and to set aside areas that provide physical, biological, and chemical functions that enhance long-term productivity; (2) a Socioeconomic Goal: to maintain long-term socioeconomic viability while minimizing short-term socioeconomic losses to all users and dependent parties; (3) a Sustainable Fisheries Goal: to achieve sustainable fisheries by integrating marine reserves into fisheries management to facilitate rebuilding harvested populations and enhancing spillover into non-reserve areas; (4) a Natural and Cultural Heritage Goal: to maintain areas for visitor, spiritual, and recreational opportunities that include cultural and ecological features and their associated values; and (5) an Education Goal: to foster stewardship of the marine environment by providing educational opportunities to increase awareness and encourage responsible use of resources.[62]

The Science Panel had to decide what criteria should be used to decide where to establish marine reserves and how large they should be. Among the desirable criteria were (1) biogeographic representation: including different regions characterized by different sets of habitats; environmental conditions; and species, including the Oregonian zone of cold, south-flowing water around San Miguel Island and northern shores of Santa Rosa Island and Santa Cruz Island; the Californian zone around Anacapa Island that is affected by the north-flowing, warmer Southern California Countercurrent; and a transition zone of mixing waters from the southern shores of the two big islands to Santa Barbara Island; (2) habitats including rocky shores, sandy bottoms, kelp forests, eelgrass beds, and estuaries; (3) rare or vulnerable habitats susceptible to stresses; (4) vulnerable life stages such as breeding, juvenile, or migration periods; (5) areas for species of concern such as abalone, lobster, and California sheephead; (6) sufficient size of a reserve necessary to promote population recovery; (7) linkages connecting ecosystems through plants, animals, and nutrients; (8) reserve networks linked by movement of animals and plant propagules; (9) human threats, including pollution and extensive recreation use; (10) natural catastrophes, including storms and climate change; and (11) social and economic values of the local and regional communities. This final criterion would lead to the most controversy, both in the working group and among the public.[63]

Gary Davis summed up further recommendations to the list. He suggested that at least 30 percent of park waters be reserved with boundaries clearly defined by physical features, natural or built, that would run in cardinal directions for easy recognition by fishermen. He reiterated that the reserves should represent all three biogeographic zones, with at least two reserves per zone, and each reserve should have at least six miles of shoreline. They should protect key biological features, such as rookeries, and include the west end of San Miguel Island, Prince Island, Gull Island, Scorpion Rock, West Anacapa Island, and southeastern Santa Barbara Island. Finally, he thought no reserves should be placed at major anchorages, but some should lie at smaller sites to provide data on the effects of disturbance.[64]

MRWG members soon learned how difficult their task would be. At a major meeting held September 26–27, 2000, the science and socioeconomic panels presented their findings and ideas. Reporter Melinda Burns of the *Santa Barbara News-Press* wrote that they introduced fishermen and environmentalists to "rough waters ahead." The Science Advisory Panel issued its official summary of the data and recommendations it had compiled in a report entitled *Estimating Reserve Size for Conservation and*

Fisheries Management, dated January 17, 2001. Its conclusions presented stark choices for fishermen:

> Given the available empirical data, a minimum reserve size of 30% of the suitable habitat in a management area would sustain approximately 80% of the species for which data are currently available. To meet the minimum habitat requirements for all species, the fraction set aside in reserves would need to exceed 70% of the suitable habitat in the management area. If reserves are designed for fisheries enhancement and sustainability, numerous theoretical studies and limited empirical data indicate that protecting approximately 35% of fishing grounds will maximize catches. Thus a reserve area of 30–50% of an area of interest will achieve some measure of protection for both conservation and fisheries goals.[65]

Burns wrote, "For every rocky reef, sandy plateau, eelgrass bed, kelp forest and underwater canyon that conservationists wanted to save, it seemed someone from the fishing community had an objection." Urchin divers, lobstermen, squid boat operators, sport fishing outfits, and beach fishermen all had different areas they would not sacrifice.[66]

The socioeconomic panel struggled to match the hard data presented by the science panel. Relying on CDFG statistics on fishery catches helped, but measuring nonconsumptive uses such as no-take diving and general marine tourism was nearly impossible. Vernon R. Leeworthy and Peter C. Wiley presented a cost-benefit breakdown of their findings three days after the Science Panel's official release. It began with summaries of the potential benefits for nonconsumptive users, scientific values, nonusers, and improving fishery stocks both in and out of the reserves. Benefits to science included further opportunities for monitoring and research. For fisheries they predicted a "long-term increase" in harvest, consumer products (food), and jobs because of greater recruitment (reproduction) within the reserves. For nonusers there would be value in knowing that the resources were there if they ever wanted to use them in the future.

Leeworthy and Wiley followed with a list of potential costs to commercial and recreational fisheries. These included lost harvest and income to fishermen, a consequent drop in income and jobs in the community, loss to consumers due to rising prices for fish, user conflicts in overcrowded areas outside the reserves, loss of local harvest knowledge that might support sustainable fishing practices, social disruption due to loss of income and jobs, lost income to businesses that serve fishermen, loss of tourism and its income, and loss of overall resource populations due to overfishing in non-reserve areas.[67] Two studies challenged the socioeconomic report from opposite camps in the controversy. Environmental Defense conducted its own analysis of the economic influences of marine, resource-based industries in Santa Barbara and Ventura Counties. To nobody's surprise, its authors found that the economies of the two counties were stronger than that of California as a whole, that primary industries employed a miniscule proportion of the population, that the growing labor force would find few opportunities in those fields, and that the local catches of highest value were exported, which blunted the arguments for the multiplier effect and local consumer benefits. They noted that measuring tourism was complicated and that recreational fishing could help but admitted they could not predict its future.[68]

On March 7, 2002, the American Sports Fishing Association in cooperation with the United Anglers of Southern California released a report developed by Robert Southwick of Southwick Associates Inc. of Fernandina Beach, Florida, entitled *The Economic Effects of Sportsfishing Closures in Marine Protected Areas: The Channel Islands Example*. The report's stated goal was to broaden understanding of the economic issues related to the proposed Marine Protected Areas within CINMS. However, even Leeworthy and Wiley accused its authors of applying "blatantly bad science in what can only be described as 'pure advocacy analysis.'"[69] Subsequently, Gary Davis pointed out that when the socioeconomic team calculated potential economic losses, they assumed all future landings would remain at previous mean levels, even though it was clear they would not, because some fisheries, such as abalone, had collapsed and other landings had declined.[70]

The difficult job of compromise began in earnest after the September meeting. As different specific resource and use issues arose, the membership of the forces for and against a recommendation shifted. One's strongest ally at one meeting might become a bitter foe at the next. Five members who represented fishing groups opposed or sought to minimize the reserves. Locky Brown claimed to represent diving groups, but the MRWG received a letter at its last meeting, signed by more than ten prominent leaders in diving clubs, angrily complaining that Brown had not represented their interests. It seems he was a competitive spear fisherman and the other divers supported the conservation position.[71]

The MRWG met twenty-five times in twenty-two months to evaluate input from the Science Panel, the Socioeconomic Panel, and the general public and develop consensus. Members developed more than forty different designs for potential marine reserves and evaluated the ecological value and potential economic impact of each. By May 16, 2001, the CINMS and CDFG had received 9,161 public comments, and 94 percent favored a network of reserves that met the science panel's recommendations. A majority of the supporters agreed that at least 30 percent and up to 50 percent of the Sanctuary should be set aside. Six percent opposed any reserves or wanted smaller ones. Many comments supported restricting commercial fishing but not sportfishing or diving.[72]

On that day, the MRWG decided to end its work. As directed by the ground rules, it agreed to forward all areas of consensus and nonagreement to the Sanctuary Advisory Council. In the end, fifteen of the seventeen MRWG members supported the establishment of some marine reserves. The facilitators allowed opponents to block consideration of a second marine reserve in the Californian biogeographic zone. That left just the existing one north of Anacapa Island and an adjacent marine conservation area.[73] The SAC evaluated the records and recommendations and held its public meetings and forum to gather further input.[74] On June 19, 2001, based on its understanding of the areas of agreement and disagreement reached by the MRWG and the public comment on the issue, the SAC voted seventeen-to-one with one abstention to transmit the full public record of the MRWG and the SAC processes and to request that the staffs of the sanctuary manager and the CDFG craft a final recommendation to present to the CFGC in August 2001. It reported, "The SAC finds that the MRWG process was open, inclusive and community based."[75]

The Marine Sanctuary and CDFG staffs then produced a draft that gave substantial preference to commercial and recreational fishing interests over conservation interests. It had six alternatives for the system of reserves and two other options. Each alternative contained a proposed area for the state and a recommended area for state and federal territory combined. The preferred alternative offered ten marine reserves and two marine conservation areas totaling 19 percent of the state waters around the park islands, decidedly less than the 30 to 50 percent suggested by the MRWG Science Panel. The recommendation also suggested a potential "Federal waters phase" that would expand the reserve total to 25 percent of the sanctuary waters. Alternatives one and two limited the reserves to 12 percent of the state waters and 12 percent of the sanctuary waters. Alternative five sought 23 percent of the state waters and 34 percent of the sanctuary waters.

New Sanctuary manager Matt Pickett forwarded the modified design to the CFGC and it became the basis for public review over four more public meetings around the state after May 30, 2002. Comments were accepted until September 1, 2002. The commission and CDFG received 2,492 letters, emails, and oral comments. Of this total, 2,445 were form letters circulated by Environmental Defense that made identical comments. NPS regional director John J. Reynolds offered support for the project but contended that the recommended network of reserves was "too small to adequately sustain marine resources" and that "only Alternative 5 [was] sufficient to achieve conservation of biological diversity and fisheries at the Channel Islands."[76] The commission finally voted two-to-one to create the preferred option of 19 percent of the state waters. After the CFGC voted, the California Office of Administrative Law approved the Channel Islands MPA regulations, which took effect on April 9, 2003. Following the commission's decision, several recreational and commercial fishing interests collectively filed a suit in state court for an injunction to stay implementation of regulations making the reserves effective. The court denied the requested injunction and an appeals court affirmed that ruling.[77]

In 2004, the National Marine Sanctuary Program released a preliminary environmental document with a range of alternatives for establishing its own marine reserves to complement those of the state. In 2006, to provide protection to the seafloor and groundfish, the NMFS designated the federal

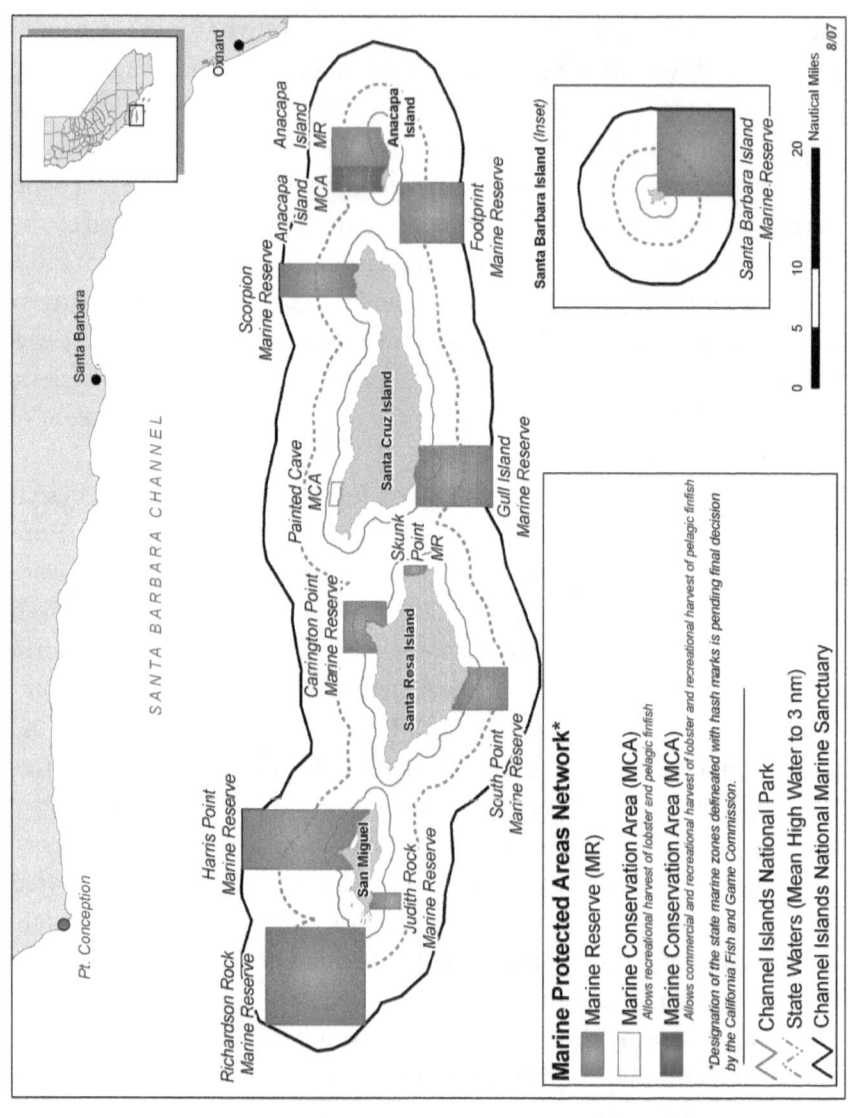

Map 14. Marine Protected Areas around Channel Islands National Park in 2020. Cartography by R. Rudolph, CINP.

water portions offshore of the state marine reserves as habitat areas of particular concern and prohibited bottom fishing under the Magnuson-Stevens Fishery Conservation and Management Act.[78] NOAA released a draft management plan and environmental impact statement (71 FR 29148) for public comment on May 19, 2006. It offered a no-action alternative, three alternatives that adhered closely to the spatial recommendations adopted by the SAC and CDFG, and one that greatly expanded the reserve area by adding eleven new ones and another marine conservation area. Of the three that matched the SAC and CDFG extent, oddly labeled 1a, 1b, and 1c, the first two applied federal rules to some or all of the state's waters. The state would have none of that, so option 1c became the preferred alternative. Some small gaps remained between state and federal marine zones that resulted from squaring off state marine zones in 2003 for enforcement and ease of recognition by boaters until the federal zones were established.[79] On May 24, 2007, the *Federal Register* announced the final rule to create the new federal marine reserves and noted that the state was busily amending any gaps where its sanctuaries' boundaries did not match those of the federal ones. The final rule took effect on July 29, 2007. The combined reserves prohibit fishing, oil exploration, ocean dumping, and other actions in 21 percent of the Channel Islands National Marine Sanctuary.[80]

Managing the Resources on Santa Rosa Island 7

The National Park Service has always had a difficult relationship with domestic animal grazing. The 1872 act establishing Yellowstone National Park forbade settlement or any commercial uses other than visitor services. The agency's Organic Act in 1916 allowed the secretary of the interior to permit grazing in any park other than Yellowstone as long as it did not conflict with protection of the resources. Secretary of the Interior Franklin Lane's instructions two years later reiterated this as a founding policy but banned sheep from all parks. At the same time, however, ranchers gained permission to graze some western national parks to benefit the World War I effort, in spite of opposition from officials on the ground. At Sequoia National Park, local officials had good reason to object. It wasn't until twelve years later that they could force out the grazers who complained that they would face economic ruin without access to the park's pastures. Cognizant of this, Secretary of the Interior Hubert Work wrote a policy letter in 1925 stating that grazing should be phased out of all parks and monuments as soon as possible. From that time forward, the prohibition on commercial grazing in parks has been the preferred policy of the NPS.[1]

Nevertheless, legislative exceptions to this ban on grazing exist in a number of the 424 units of the park system such as Point Reyes National Seashore and, of course, Grant Kohrs National Historical Site, dedicated as it is to telling the ranching story. Three conditions allow grazing to continue: (1) if it is specifically sanctioned in a park's enabling act, as it is at Point Reyes; (2) when a retained right of use (RUO) or leaseback is grandfathered in at the establishment of a new unit, such as City of

Rocks National Reserve, for a limited time; and (3) in a special use zone as described in the 1978 NPS management policy document. The Vail & Vickers families sold Santa Rosa Island to the National Park Service in 1986 and secured a special use permit (SUP) a year later, but the expectation of their continued operations past five years was not stated. They ignored the RUO and lease contract options. The Park Service has the right to terminate a special use permit without having to recompense the permittees, particularly if there is evidence of harm to natural resources. The prevailing attitude of some senior NPS officials was to avoid controversy with these politically well-connected families by ignoring the agency's own policies.[2]

Grazing and the Environment on Santa Rosa Island

During the first half of 1988, the park surveyed Santa Rosa Island vegetation to define the plant community types, map their distribution, and provide the baseline data necessary to allow future comparisons. University of California, Davis researchers collected vegetation data at 296 sites using a visual sampling method known as a relevé.[3] Principal investigator Ronilee Clark's report noted that most of the island consisted of grazed pasture with some vestigial coastal scrub and mixed chaparral. Other plant communities covered less than ten percent of the remaining land area. They noted a number of endemic species with diminished distributions, including three trees—the island oak (*Quercus tomentella*), the Santa Cruz Island pine (*Pinus remorata*), and the Santa Cruz Island ironwood (*Lyonothamnus floribundus* var. *asplenifolius*)—as well as low numbers of an endemic species of manzanita (*Arctostaphylos confertiflora*).

The Clark report stated that grazing by introduced livestock was having a negative impact on the island's natural ecosystems and would continue to cause resource damage as long as the animals remained. These assertions reflected the researchers' assessment of current conditions but were also based on evidence of past changes in the landscape derived from historical records. These sources corroborated the Clark report's claim that "the vegetation of the islands has undergone dramatic changes over the past century" with the introduction of ranching.[4]

HISTORICAL EVIDENCE

The first recorded description of the islands was made by Bartolomé Ferrelo, the pilot for Spanish explorer Juan Rodríguez Cabrillo, whose expedition spent nearly two months on Santa Rosa and San Miguel Islands during the winter of 1542–43. Ferrelo noted that the Spanish sailors were not able to gather firewood on either of the islands but instead had to sail to the mainland. If there were forests on Santa Rosa Island, they must not have been very accessible from the shore.[5]

Dr. J. T. Rothrock, a member of George Wheeler's western geographical survey in 1875, made a brief reconnaissance of the Northern Channel Islands. Although Rothrock visited only Santa Cruz Island, his observations are also relevant to Santa Rosa, which shares a similar history of sheep ranching during the nineteenth century. He wrote: "It is impossible to conceive [of] a more dreary waste than was here produced as the result of over-pasturage. The question may come up further on as to the reciprocal relations existing between vegetation and rain-fall. It would seem more than probable that ever since the discovery of the continent this and the adjacent islands had a more abundant supply of water than at present."[6] Rothrock's observations clearly described a landscape that had undergone a substantial transformation in relatively little time. Not only had it been denuded by overgrazing, it was also drier. Ronilee Clark and her associates believed that climate change may have been the cause for the retreat of the island forests from lower elevations. Later research in paleoclimatology has corroborated this conclusion. The only exception to this pattern of landscape change was the "fog forest," which survived within the elevation band influenced by the summer marine layer lying from one thousand to three thousand feet above sea level. Trees and other woody vegetation growing here subsidize their moisture requirements with fog condensation that drips from their leaves and twigs and is absorbed in the humus-rich soil beneath the forest canopy. Although Clark and her colleagues believed that the declining extent of the island forest was the result of a warming climate that occurred much earlier than the introduction of livestock, they posited that grazing had adversely affected new growth within these communities and threatened their longevity:

"The woodland communities on Santa Rosa Island are regularly visited by alien herbivores which forage and disturb the soil surface, causing the characteristic depauperate woody and herbaceous understory, little litter accumulation and surface soil erosion."[7]

The implications of such losses were far-reaching because the high-elevation woodlands and associated scrub capture a large amount of moisture. Indeed, early attempts to measure this fog drip were inconclusive because the gauges filled so quickly that they could not be read before they overflowed.[8] The condensed fog that drips to the ground is absorbed into the topsoil and gradually percolates downhill, radiating outward from the highlands to the plains and valleys below. This regular distribution of moisture from higher to lower elevations might have once kept the entire island well watered even during the seasons of extreme drought.

Although Clark believed that historic-era livestock grazing may not have been the initial cause of the reduced area of mature woodland, it had diminished woody scrub, which condenses fog at least as efficiently as trees. Even more important, unrestricted grazing had largely eliminated the herbaceous understory beneath woodland and scrub alike, allowing the humus-rich topsoil that once absorbed the falling moisture to erode away. The cumulative effects of these losses reduced the amount of moisture throughout the island by a significant amount. In order to preserve what remained of this ecologically vital phenomenon, the Clark report recommended the removal of all exotic grazing animals.

EARLY RELATIONS BETWEEN THE NPS AND VAIL & VICKERS

The relationship between the Park Service and the Vails on Santa Rosa Island remained mostly cordial for the duration of the Vail & Vickers Company's first special use permit, which expired in 1993. This was due in large part to the close relationship that had developed between the Vail family and Superintendent Bill Ehorn during the 1980s. Ehorn had worked closely with the Vails since 1979, first convincing them to support the park legislation, then negotiating over the sale of the island in 1986 and establishing the SUP agreement the following year. Ehorn had also become a personal friend of the family, spending about a week riding with the other cowboys, helping them gather the cattle.

Fig. 20. Fog frequently covers the higher portions of Santa Rosa Island. It condenses on the hilltops, providing a significant amount of water for vegetation. Photograph by L. Dilsaver, October 2017.

Fig. 21. A stand of Island live oak (*Quercus tomentella*) on Santa Rosa Island. Note the darker wet spots under the trees formed by the runoff of the condensing fog that sustains them. Photograph by L. Dilsaver, October 2017.

After Bill Ehorn left Channel Islands in 1989, this close relationship between the park and the Vail family deteriorated. The new superintendent, Mack Shaver, wanted the new SUP to emphasize that the NPS owned and controlled Santa Rosa Island. Setnicka, as operations chief for the park, would be on Santa Rosa Island most often, checking on staff and park resources located at the former military base at Johnsons Lee, on the southern coast of the island, far from the Vails' ranch. The Vails preferred the NPS to locate there. Shaver would be the face of negotiation, going to the island when he needed information for the agreement, as well as to look at ongoing resource projects.[9]

According to Nita Vail, Al Vail's daughter, her family came to believe that Superintendent Shaver rarely traveled to the islands or visited park neighbors directly, preferring to communicate by written correspondence and official memoranda. This seemed to alienate the Vails even though Shaver's policies remained essentially unchanged from Ehorn's. In reality, although Shaver's duties for the regional office took him out of the park for a week each month, he made it a practice to work on one island one day each week, partly to support the staff and partly to monitor issues. Tim Setnicka was left in charge during the superintendent's absences. However, some of the ranchers considered Setnicka dishonest.[10]

EARLY PARK PROJECTS

In January 1990, preliminary discussions on a development concept plan (DCP) for Santa Rosa Island began. Public scoping for the process started in February 1990 and produced an initial draft in 1991. The preferred alternative recommended a daily carrying capacity of about 230 visitors, with approximately three-quarters of these being overnight guests. The planners proposed visitor facilities through the adaptive use of existing ranch buildings at Bechers Bay, development of visitor contact stations and campgrounds there and at Johnsons Lee, concession-operated horseback trips, vehicle tours, and a small hotel or hostel for overnight accommodations.[11]

The DCP placed considerable emphasis on the restoration of natural systems over the remaining portions of the island in order to repair the effects of more than a century of livestock grazing. As such, the planners viewed ranching as causing a negative impact. They found only the historic ranch complex at Bechers Bay worthy of historic preservation. The final DCP for Santa Rosa Island was completed and approved in early 1995.[12] However, in the course of gathering the data for the DCP, and as a byproduct of the park's I&M program, park researchers collected more evidence that problems existed with the island's habitats. In 1991 park resource managers requested a survey by a team of scientists from the U.S. Forest Service (USFS) to assess water quality and associated habitats on Santa Rosa Island. The Forest Service team surveyed riparian habitats on Lobo and Arlington Creeks along the north side of the island. Once again, the scientists warned that these areas "continued to be highly impacted by cattle." Their conclusions supported the park's decision the following year to fence off the lower third of Lobo Canyon to keep cattle out of sensitive habitat that still supported native vegetation and ground-nesting birds. Al Vail tried to oppose that proposal, believing it would interfere with his cattle business, but failed.[13]

Another change that Vail & Vickers eventually had to accept—minor as far as ranching was concerned but significant for the future of natural resources on Santa Rosa Island—was construction of enclosures around the oak woodlands on Black Mountain and Soledad Peak. Vail family members insisted that the extent of woodland cover had not diminished over the course of the ranch's history, but it also had never increased.[14] This was because livestock grazing eliminated new young trees. Overcropping of the native groundcover had caused erosion of the topsoil from the steep slopes beneath these groves, making survival of new trees even less likely. Although few of the mature trees had actually died, as Vail family members observed, those remaining often suffered severe stress caused by the erosion of soil from around their roots. In some instances, individual oaks stood several feet above the present ground level.

Although most of the damage to Santa Rosa Island's oak woodland probably stemmed from the overstocking of sheep by the More family, the continued morbidity of these woodlands long after the Mores' departure weakened the Vail family's claim that they, by contrast, practiced wise and careful stewardship of the island's resources. Since the oak woodlands were not essential to beef cattle production, the Vails may not have noticed the impact that cattle were having on these trees and failed to appreciate that continued livestock grazing would eventually doom the groves. In March 1991, the NPS initiated one of the earliest tangible steps in the natural restoration of Santa Rosa Island with the eradication of feral pigs. This process lasted two years and killed nearly 1,200 animals. Vail & Vickers fully supported this action.[15]

THE SECOND PERMIT (1993)

The 1987 SUP allowed the ranchers to continue their operations but did not specifically elaborate what would happen if conflicts arose with park programs. As formally written, the special use permit was meant to allow "the purpose of operating a beef cattle ranch and a commercial hunting operation for feral elk, deer and domestic swine *compatible with the administration of the park and with the preservation of its resources*" (emphasis added).[16] This formula, which paraphrased the 1980 enabling act, stated that the park would have precedence over the ranch, and that the latter would be managed to accommodate park resource protection and related operations.[17] Critics of the agreement later referenced this passage, claiming that grazing as practiced under the SUP was not compatible with park values. Members of Congress had vociferously complimented the ranching activities on the island during hearings on the park bill and offered a RUO or a leaseback to allow it to continue. Even NPS director William Whalen had confirmed this understanding at the time, although he did not give approval to the hunting operation on NPS-owned land.[18] These statements led Superintendent Ehorn and other officials in the park and regional office to offer the 1987 SUP to allow for a phaseout of those practices over "five to ten years."

Many of the practical conditions written into the first SUP and reaffirmed in 1993 contradicted the "compatibility" phrase because they emphasized ranching as the principal activity on Santa Rosa Island. For example, the permit gave priority use of the pier at Becher's Bay, the most practical means of access to the island, for cattle operations. It also explicitly identified park-related activities as secondary to those of ranching, as suggested by the following clause: "The National Park Service will make every reasonable effort to refrain from exercising such right[s] or allowing such recreational or research use to the extent that such actions would unduly interfere or prevent the use of the land by the Permittee for the purposes intended under this permit."[19] The intended purposes were ranching and hunting. This bias was further supported by a Range Management Plan that was prepared by Dr. James Bartolome and W. James Clawson in anticipation of the renewal of the original SUP. This plan established a maximum stocking limit based on traditional rangeland management principles but had little to say about the preservation of natural resource values. It also failed to include exotic deer and elk in its calculations, resulting in a significant understatement of the grazing impact on the land.[20]

With such lenient restrictions placed on Vail & Vickers, critics of ranching on the island accused the NPS of bowing to private interests at the expense of publicly owned natural resources. But in the early years of the SUP agreement, some park administrators and many of the park's political supporters did not believe that there was any significant contradiction between ranch operations and fundamental park values, with the possible exception that visitation and public enjoyment of the park might have to be limited. Yet, P.L. 96–199 actually states, "Any right retained . . . shall be subject to such access and other provisions as may be required by the Secretary for visitor use and resources management." Key early park administrators nevertheless supported the continuation of traditional ranching even after limited park operations started on the island in 1987. In March of that year, during the early negotiations with Vail & Vickers, Bill Ehorn told the *Santa Barbara News-Press* that the ranchers would continue for "several years."[21] In 1994 he stressed that a twenty-five-year term was the expectation when the first SUP was signed: "There has been a long-term, good-faith process of negotiation which has always had ranch continuation as its cornerstone. The assumption has always been made that the Vails would continue their ranch operation as long as they had interest in doing so (up to some reasonable period of time which by standard NPS acquisition practices has generally been 25 years)."[22]

This statement, sent to like-minded Regional Director Stan Albright more than four years after Ehorn had left Channel Islands did not acknowledge the fact that an SUP lasts only five years and is not a "right." There was little in Ehorn's statement to suggest that the park might be compromising fundamental values by accommodating ranching. While he conceded that there might be some negative impacts to rare plants, he pointed out that the Park Service "has a long history of insisting on the coexistence of conflicting preservation and use objectives beginning with the organic act." He believed the park could resolve any potential problems through open-minded negotiation.[23] That confidence did not extend to Ehorn's successor, Mack Shaver. In a later interview, Shaver reported that the 1987 permit "sounded like the Vails had written the SUP to allow the Park Service on the island."[24]

Shaver decided that the renewal of the special use permit needed to be rewritten in order to give NPS the management authority over the island. He wanted it to: (1) get the Vails to stop off-road driving; (2) fence in riparian areas to keep stock and game animals out; (3) start planning to remove the deer and elk and reduce hunting; and (4) allow the NPS to establish housing away from Johnsons Lee.[25] He sent his proposed SUP to Regional Director Albright who rejected it out of hand and ordered the superintendent to keep the same conditions as the first permit and even lower the AUM (animal unit month) costs to the Vails. Later Shaver wrote:

> I always thought that we could solve all of those issues with a proper SUP. It would have cut the time way down and saved so much angst. The draft the staff and I wrote dealt with all the issues but the Vails called Stan and complained and Stan told me to put it back the way it had been in the first SUP. The only concession we really got was to move our island staff housing closer to the ranch from Johnson's [sic] Lee and an OK to use the pier and start planning a visitor campground. Once that got out, and it wasn't secret, the concerned agencies and organizations took off to force the issues via lawsuits. If Stan had had a backbone and approved the SUP as written, and supported us in enforcing it, it would have saved years of time and thousands of dollars because all those stipulations came to pass, but at large cost.[26]

Shaver and other park officials described Albright as extremely averse to controversy and anxious to let the Vails finish their twenty-five-year operations on Santa Rosa Island.[27] Chief of Resource Management Kate Faulkner later wrote: "The first permit indicated that a NEPA [National Environmental Policy Act] document (an EIS) [environmental impact statement] had been prepared. When it was clear that there was no EIS and there was nothing in the deed, Shaver tried to draft permits (we worked on separate permits for hunting and ranching) that reflected NPS legal responsibilities. This was shot down by the Vails and Albright."[28] Hence, the second SUP only differed from the first by reducing the grazing rate from $1.48 to $1.00 per animal unit month. This gave a significant financial benefit to the Vail & Vickers Company. Under the renewed agreement, the permittees were allowed approximately 5,000 head of cattle, 700 deer, and 1,100 elk. The deer and elk would continue to be hunted for recreation and profit.[29] At the same time, Tim Setnicka, as acting superintendent while Shaver traveled, nominated Vail & Vickers for the Governor's Environmental and Economic Leadership Award in 1993, the first year it was given. Governor Pete Wilson, who previously had supported the Vails, granted the award, considered to be California's most prestigious environmental honor, in recognition of Vail & Vickers' wise conservation of resources and their ability to maintain the continuing economic viability of the island cattle ranching operation.[30]

CRITICS OF RANCHING

In spite of the good relationship forged between Bill Ehorn and Vail & Vickers, as well as Stanley Albright's efforts to continue it, the park's scientific research led to growing criticism of ranching. The flurry of baseline studies and scientific investigations carried out by the park's I&M program revealed conditions that only had been suspected previously. Kate Faulkner wrote: "NPS managers attempted to modify grazing practices in order to mitigate damage to the most sensitive resources. NPS required that salt blocks be moved away from water courses in order to limit the numbers and duration that cattle spent in streams or nearby riparian habitats. V&V did not comply with this requirement. The NPS proposed to seasonally restrict grazing in Old Ranch Pasture to protect nesting Western Snowy Plovers and rare plants. V&V refused any modifications to their ranching operations."[31] In February 1993, the park summarized its position concerning the impacts of ranching on Santa Rosa Island in a briefing statement prepared for the 103rd Congress:

> Pressure exerted by grazing animals in combination with periods of drought has caused severe damage to insular communities, in some cases resulting in the possible loss of native plant and animal species and extensive soil erosion. . . . The soils on the island are eroding rapidly in a number of areas. Approximately 7 percent of the island is bare ground. An additional, unknown percentage of the island is bare ground between widely spaced plants. Loss of topsoil results in an expanding, and nearly impossible to reverse, situation where (1) vegetation cannot become established due to the lack of soil, and (2) additional erosion occurs due to the lack of vegetation.[32]

The briefing statement also reported that cattle grazing was negatively impacting sensitive riparian habitat on the island by forcing cattle to concentrate in those limited, well-watered areas during drought years. An NPS Water Resources Division research team corroborated those findings observing that "the current [1992 Bartolome and Clawson Range Management] plan is inadequate in its treatment of stocking levels, vegetation condition, and areas needing reduced or no grazing, [and] lacks sufficient restrictions to protect island resources."[33] The park found that cattle would have to be removed from Santa Rosa Island in order to restore the natural processes, a conclusion was incorporated into the 1995 DCP for Santa Rosa Island.[34]

As the ecological evidence mounted, Kate Faulkner became troubled with the legal position of the NPS and the unorthodox arrangement that allowed ranching to take precedence in management of the island under a special use permit. In 1992 she had queried NPS regional environmental compliance coordinator Jim Huddleston who had recommended an EA (environmental assessment) for the first SUP in 1988. This had not been done. He reviewed the current situation and concluded that a separate management plan and EA should be carried out to legally clarify policy. However, pressure from Regional Director Albright, forced him to reverse his statement and suggested that the SUP be handled through a categorical exclusion under NEPA.[35] Faulkner's frustration resulted not

Fig. 22. An endangered western snowy plover. Photographer and date unknown, CINP Digital Archives.

only from what the scientific data showed but also from what she saw as an operating premise that gave Vail & Vickers preference in designating when scientists and the public could go to various portions of the island. Hitherto, if cattle were present or a hunt was ongoing, the NPS had to change its schedule. She later wrote: "The Vails were adamant about resisting any changes to their operation. They saw it as a slippery slope. Before they knew it, the landowner might think they could tell the Vails what to do."[36]

The mounting evidence of damage from grazing collected by the park was supported by events occurring simultaneously outside the park. Foremost among these was the listing, on March 5, 1993, of the Pacific Coast population of the western snowy plover (*Charadrius alexandrinus nivosus*) as a threatened species under the Endangered Species Act (ESA).[37] Under pressure from the National Parks and Conservation Association (NPCA) to provide better protection for the plover, Channel Islands constructed a three-mile electrified fence to keep cattle off the dunes between Skunk Point and East Point. This stretch of native dunes represented one of the few remaining nesting habitats for the snowy plover on the California coast, and many scientists were worried that the cattle, which had unhindered access, might disturb or even crush the nesting birds. Trudy Ingram, a seabird biologist hired by the park, pointed out that cattle had an even greater indirect impact on the plover by creating conditions that supported predators such as ravens, which eat the plovers' eggs and chicks.[38]

Park administrators, represented by Superintendent Tim Setnicka after Mack Shaver's retirement, agreed to implement the proposal. Setnicka was sympathetic to the ranchers and critical of his own resource staff, but with the ESA involved, the park had to act to conserve a listed species. Park biologists wanted to seasonally restrict grazing, but neither Setnicka nor the Vails supported this more effective solution. Representative George Radanovich, who represented the distant Fresno area, protested the fence plan as an unnecessary expense to the taxpayer and a financial burden to the ranchers because it would limit their access to valuable grazing lands.[39] Congresswoman Andrea Seastrand, representing Santa Barbara, called it another overreach of the ESA on private property, blithely ignoring the fact that the NPS owned the island.[40] Workers completed the fence two years later, in June 1995, but it proved difficult to maintain and was generally ineffective at keeping the cattle off the dunes.[41]

Two years after the negotiation of the second SUP, the park encountered more serious challenge to existing management policies. In July 1995, the U.S. Fish and Wildlife Service (USFWS) proposed to list under the ESA nineteen plant species on the Channel Islands, sixteen of which lay within the park and eleven on Santa Rosa Island alone.[42] The USFWS biologists designated another seventy-four plants on Santa Rosa Island as "species of concern." They identified soil loss, habitat alteration, predation caused by cattle grazing, browsing by elk and deer, and competition with alien plant taxa as threats to the continued viability of these threatened plant species. Owing to a court-imposed moratorium, USFWS would not be able to do anything until after September 30, 1995, and a one-year review period would follow any decision to list. Nevertheless, this regulatory activity substantially increased pressure on the park to modify its permit with Vail & Vickers. In response to anticipated legal action, the Park Service, through its Water Resources Division (WRD), hosted an interagency team of specialists to make a field assessment of representative streams on Santa Rosa Island. The team included experts in vegetation ecology, fluvial geomorphology, hydrology, and riparian-wetland science. They conducted their fieldwork during the week of March 20, 1995.[43]

The NPCA and the California Native Plant Society (CNPS) were among the organizations carefully following this activity, and they had the enthusiastic support of some NPS natural resource officials who were also members of the organizations. Furthermore, Santa Rosa Island, as well as the other Channel Islands, represented a focal point of interest within the CNPS because of the high number of species, subspecies, and distinct varieties that only existed there. The Plant Society wanted to see the Vail & Vickers cattle and deer removed immediately, stating that the park could not afford to wait until the expiration of a sequence of SUPs in 2011 to ensure the continued survival of many of these rare plant species.[44]

Emily Roberson of CNPS pointed out that grazing privileges were permitted to Vail & Vickers on the condition that grazing and associated ranching activities were not "incompatible with the administration of the park or with the preservation of the resources therein." Any costs, in terms of environmental damage or added operational and management burdens on the Park Service, were borne by the taxpayer. Roberson and her colleagues believed that monitoring done by the Park Service already provided convincing proof that ranching activities were degrading native vegetation habitat and were therefore incompatible with the preservation of park resources.[45] Vail family members disagreed and publicly argued that there was no long-term monitoring data to support these assertions or the proposed listing. John Woolley, nephew of Al and Russ Vail, countered that the most significant ecological pressure on island vegetation had occurred prior to Vail & Vickers' arrival in 1902 when as many as one hundred thousand sheep were grazed on the island at a given time. Under Vail & Vickers' ownership, livestock grazing had been managed on a more sustainable basis and the survival of these endemics after nearly a century of continuous cattle ranching was proof of Vail & Vickers' wise stewardship of the land. Woolley believed that the listing of these species was unnecessary and that it would only contribute to the growing national criticism of the Endangered Species Act from private property owners. Like Representative Seastrand, he raised the threat to the environmental law despite the fact that the NPS owned the island.[46]

THE CLEANUP OR ABATEMENT ORDER

Events came to a head in the midst of this debate when, on May 17, 1995, the California Regional Water Quality Control Board (WQCB) issued a Cleanup or Abatement Order in response to high levels of coliform bacteria and suspended particulates that had been detected in the island's streams.[47] The order accused the Park Service of violating the water quality control plan for the Central Coast Basin by allowing excess amounts of nonpoint source pollution from grazing animals and road management practices to enter state waters. Threatening fines of up to $5,000 per day, the WQCB ordered the NPS to implement temporary mitigations by the beginning of the following year and to submit a complete report outlining a permanent mitigation plan to its Executive Office by June 1, 1996. The NPS appealed in order to gain more time while it prepared a management response.[48]

In June 1995, scientists from the Park Service's WRD team, who had conducted fieldwork on island streams three months earlier, published a technical report summarizing its findings. The scientists studied seven reaches subject to year-round cattle grazing and reported that six were "non-functional" based on a set of seventeen criteria that evaluated hydrology, vegetation, and stream geomorphological conditions. A seventh reach was rated "functional-at risk." They chose three other reaches as controls because they lay within areas that livestock could not access. Two of these, both in Lobo Canyon, were "properly functioning" but a third was "functional-at risk" largely due to upstream effects. Based on these assessments, the study team recommended stream corridor fencing, island-wide rotational grazing, and targeted seasonal grazing. None of these solutions would completely eliminate the negative environmental effects of cattle ranching, but the authors hoped that they might mitigate those effects to a tolerable level and allow the park to maintain its current stance on Vail & Vickers operations.[49]

Although the WRD report carefully maintained a cooperative tone and proposed solutions that were intended to allow commercial ranching to continue, it became clear that even its mildest recommendations would force the NPS to place more restrictions on the cattle operation. The Vails objected to the changes and appealed for more time.[50] Park natural resource managers suspected that the recommendations still would not be sufficient to restore the conditions sought by the Cleanup or Abatement Order. Many people who supported the Vails suspected that members of the park's natural resources staff had contacted the WQCB and convinced it to investigate.[51] Bill Ehorn suggested that it might have been University of California, Santa Barbara, graduate student John Cloud who became a self-proclaimed public clarion call for the cessation of ranching.[52]

Elden Hughes, a Sierra Club activist, called Shaver during the water quality debate, offering to accept records "over the transom," meaning unofficially and without attribution. Shaver did not agree to Hughes' suggestion. Instead, he arranged with the NPS and USFWS for a flight and press tour on Santa Rosa Island and asked the local USFWS chief to accompany him. Frank Clifford, the environmental reporter/editor with the *Los Angeles Times* met Shaver at the Camarillo Airfield for the flight to Santa Rosa Island. John Cloud, who then worked for the local USFWS office, also showed up instead of the local chief, to Shaver's consternation. In order to avoid a potential public relations problem, USFWS pulled Cloud off the flight within ten minutes of Shaver's call to Washington DC, replacing him with the local USFWS chief. The press tour demonstrated agency transparency, keeping the national press updated on a developing story where no conclusions had been made.[53]

Scientific reports, academic articles, and visiting experts had disseminated information about grazing's impact on the island's watercourses and denudation of extensive tracts of land for years. USFWS scientists had studied the conditions and proposed multiple plant species for endangered or threatened status based on their research. As these major challenges crystallized, more evidence of deficient ecological integrity surfaced.

National Biological Survey ecologist Kathryn McEachern reported the results of monitoring ten of the proposed endangered plants on Santa Rosa Island from 1994 to 1996. The study collected data on the demography and spatial patterns of individuals in selected populations. In the later surveys, most of the plants showed isolated distribution, encirclement by annual grasslands, poor seed production, and browsing damage by deer unless enclosure fences were in place.[54]

A report on the *Status of Resources on Santa Rosa Island* released by the natural resources staff listed twenty ecological and hydrologic problems in bleak terms. Among the findings were:

1. Four of the plant species that occurred on Santa Rosa Island in the recent past can no longer be located.
2. Deer heavily browse virtually all woody plants on the island and there are few young individuals of most woody species.
3. No regeneration of Santa Rosa Island Manzanita (*Arctostaphylos confertiflora*), a single-island endemic which is proposed for listing by USFWS, or of Island Manzanita (*Arctostaphylos tomentosa var. insulicola*), which occurs only on Santa Rosa and Santa Cruz Islands.
4. Several other unique Island Chaparral species are also being seriously impacted on Santa Rosa Island by the "trailing" and browsing of deer and elk.
5. A recent survey of [Indian paintbrush] *Castilleja mollis*, showed the percentage with broken stems to be 51%. Deer and cattle were observed to be the primary animals in the *Castilleja mollis* range.
6. A number of native plants only occur in scattered "refugia," usually cliffs, that cannot be easily reached by cattle, deer, or elk.[55]

At this point the NPCA became more actively involved. In August 1995, Brian Huse, the Pacific Coast regional director of the organization, retained the legal services of Santa Barbara's Environmental Defense Center (EDC), represented by Earthlaw attorney Neil Levine. The NPCA threatened to sue the Park Service for failing to comply with its legislatively mandated mission to protect the natural resources on Santa Rosa Island. This included the recently proposed plant species as well as the snowy plover. Levine wrote that "no written mandate exists that allows grazing to continue" and therefore, "the park is not legally responsible to Vail & Vickers."[56] The absence of any "written mandate" was the heart of the matter. Both Bill Ehorn and the Vails later stated that grazing was assured during their negotiations. Media outlets supporting the Vail & Vickers position reported that this arrangement, sealed with a handshake, was enough to satisfy the ranchers. However, Ehorn later denied that there was ever a handshake agreement. Former NPS solicitor Barbara Goodyear later confirmed that Latham and Watkins, the attorneys for Al and Russ Vail, certainly realized that the SUP in 1987 did not ensure the ranchers that they would be able to continue ranching for another twenty-five years as they always had.[57]

Park administrators continued to resist the pressure to change the condition of the SUP. Superintendent Tim Setnicka commented to the press, "There is very little evidence that the existing cattle ranch is forcing these [threatened plant] species into oblivion, yet this order has the force of law.... The order could force the Park Service to terminate ranching on the island."[58] But, having no choice in the matter, Setnicka agreed to develop a new resource management plan (RMP) specifically for Santa Rosa Island. Responsibility for writing the new RMP fell to the resource management division, the same biologists who had uncovered the evidence of damage by grazing. Naturally, they favored management practices that would end or at least ameliorate that damage.

In accordance with NEPA criteria, the proposed RMP required the concurrent preparation of an EIS in order to assess the potential consequences of any actions that the Park Service might take on the island. The EIS allowed a public review of the alternatives in order to determine if any significant opposition existed. The process officially started on September 15, 1995, when the NPS published a "Notice of Intent" in the *Federal Register*. One month after the notice, Representatives George Radanovich (R-Fresno), Andrea Seastrand (R-Santa Barbara), and Elton Gallegly (R-Simi Valley) wrote to the director of the Park Service urging an extension of the public scoping period on the RMP and requesting that the NPS "enter into 'careful and considered coordination, cooperation and consultation' with ranching interests."[59]

THE SANTA ROSA ISLAND RESOURCE MANAGEMENT PLAN (1997)

On May 6, 1996, the NPS released a draft of the Santa Rosa Island RMP.[60] It made the following proposals: (1) Remove the herd of approximately 600 mule deer within three years; (2) reduce the elk herd from 1,100 to 450, also within three years; (3) close the Old Ranch Pasture (7 percent of the island) completely; (4) require that more stubble be left in all pastures by the end of the season in order to reduce the erosional effect of winter rains; (5) divide another large pasture in half and require rotation of grazing between the two sides; (6) install exclusion fences along nine streams to protect riparian habitat. The ranchers blasted the plan for imposing unreasonable economic burdens and claimed that the plan represented an unlawful breach of contract because Congress had assured them a right to continue their cattle operation without significant interruption until 2011. This was false and again ignored the fact that Vail & Vickers did not have a contract.

The environmentalists, on the other hand, thought that the Park Service's proposed management plan was too conciliatory to the ranchers and would not adequately protect the island's natural resources. In response, the NPCA filed its long-threatened lawsuit against the NPS on October 22, 1996. Attorney Neil Levine filed a complaint that included thirteen causes of action that challenged the park's issuance of the 1993 SUP.[61] Much of NPCA's argument was summed up in its further accusation that the Park Service was in violation of its own Organic Act. By failing to protect the island's natural resources and by restricting public access in the interest of ranching, the Park Service was failing to manage Santa Rosa Island as a national park.[62] The NPCA asserted that this was not only a violation of the fundamental purpose of the Park Service, but that it directly contradicted Channel Islands National Park's own management policies. The environmental organization claimed that the park's general management plan had established a natural resource management goal of "lessening man's historic impact on the islands" and specifically directed the NPS to "discontinue ranching and other commercial operations" upon acquisition of Santa Rosa Island. NPCA recalled that during the year leading up to the first SUP, Superintendent Ehorn and Congressman Lagomarsino had supported Vail & Vickers' cattle operation for a five-to-ten-year phaseout period, but the NPS had allowed ranching to continue as before with no indication that it would conduct its duty henceforth.[63]

Of course, the conflicting claims of the scientists, park managers, and the ranchers drew intense media attention. Local people, allies of the parties involved, organizations of various constituencies, and even national newspapers argued, questioned authorities' qualifications, and hurled insults. Two virulent contingents volubly challenged each other—environmentalists and scientists seeking an end to nonnative animals versus ranching allies, historic preservation groups like the Santa Cruz Island Foundation, and a large number of locals who sympathized with the Vails and echoed their claim that the NPS had broken its word.

On April 17, 1997, the NPS published its final RMP and EIS for Santa Rosa Island. Representative George Radanovich, the Vails' political ally from Fresno County, introduced H.R. 1696 on May 21, 1997, "To honor agreements reached in the acquisition of Santa Rosa Island, California, by the National Park Service." This bill stated that, "notwithstanding any other provision of law, the National Park Service shall reissue Special Use Permit Number WRO-8120-2600-001 with an expiration date of 2011."[64] Representative Walter Capps (D-Santa Barbara), who actually represented Santa Rosa Island, opposed the bill and wrote to the House Resources Subcommittee on National Parks and Public Lands reminding its members that Vail &Vickers had refused an RUO for the cattle operation at the time of the initial sale in 1986.[65]

In a separate letter to Secretary of the Interior Bruce Babbitt, Capps urged that all parties come together to settle the dispute amicably.[66] But before any such reconciliation could be achieved, the attorneys for Vail & Vickers filed their own lawsuit against the Park Service in the U.S. Court for the Central District in Los Angeles.[67] The case was assigned to Judge William Rea. The lawsuit included a request for a preliminary injunction that would prevent the NPS from rescinding its 1993 special use permit prior to its scheduled expiration at the end of 1997. Specifically, the attorneys for Vail & Vickers cited four reasons why the injunction should be granted: (1) That weeds kept in check by grazing animals were a greater threat to the native plant species that the NPS and NPCA "purportedly seek to protect" than the cattle, deer, and elk were; (2) that without the injunction, Vail & Vickers would suffer the "irreparable injury of losing its ranching business"; (3) that the plaintiffs would also "be harmed by the intangible loss of a cultural livelihood"; and (4) the "balance of hardships" would favor the plaintiffs because the defendants would not be harmed to a degree that would "compel a contrary conclusion."[68]

On August 11, Judge William Rea issued a tentative ruling. It was intended to give the parties an understanding of the likely ruling that the judge would issue if the parties didn't settle the case.[69] It included the following statements:

> [1.] Even if Vail and Vickers had adopted one of the two methods [RUO and leaseback] detailed by CINPA [Channel Islands National Park Act] whereby they could retain the right to continue hunting and ranching on the Island—which Vail and Vickers did not do—CINPA makes explicitly clear that such a right would be terminable. Thus, the express language of CINPA—the statute under which the United States purchased the Island—is at odds with the Vail and Vickers argument that they were guaranteed the right to continue hunting and ranching no matter what.
>
> [2.] Of critical importance for this motion—the deeds and offers [of the sale to NPS] are absolutely silent as to Vail and Vickers' right to continue grazing and hunting on the Island. Accordingly, there is no indication at all in Vail and Vickers' offers or in the subsequent deeds that Vail and Vickers was to retain the right to hunt and ranch on the Island until the year 2011.
>
> [3.] A good deal of the legislative history for the CINPA indicates that even Congressional advocates for Vail and Vickers were not acting under the impression that the ranching and hunting operations would continue until the year 2011.
>
> [4.] Accordingly, plaintiffs really received the equivalent of over $7 million in exchange for not reserving the right to continue ranching and hunting on the Island. Thus, plaintiffs' claim that they stand to lose $4.4 million [under NPS restrictions] does not amount to any sort of true money loss.

[5.] If Vail and Vickers are truly concerned about losing the ability to maintain "cultural livelihood" that their families have practiced for the past century, then there is nothing that would prevent them from continuing to maintain such a lifestyle. Continuing their past ways may cost plaintiffs some money, but there is absolutely no impediment to the continuance of such a lifestyle.

[6.] In such a situation, where the harm to the plaintiffs will not be that substantial, and where the harm to the public interest may be very significant, the Court does not feel that it can conclude that the balance of hardships tips strongly in plaintiffs' favor.[70]

This was a tremendous blow to Vail & Vickers because it signaled that the Vails would likely lose their case, at which point the park could begin active measures and restrictions that the company held to be economically injurious.

A little more than a week before Judge Rea's decision, the USFWS published its final notice giving legal protection to thirteen plant species occurring within the Channel Islands, ten of which grew on Santa Rosa Island.[71] Formal listing under the Endangered Species Act raised the stakes in this controversy significantly by legally obligating the federal government to take active steps to mitigate known threats to the listed species. Since ranching had been identified as the principal source of impacts negatively affecting the viability of these plants, Section 7(a)(2) of the ESA now required the Park Service to implement appropriate modifications to ranching practices in order to protect the species. Now the protection of native plant species and water quality were the principal criteria and private agricultural economics simply did not matter.

This shift in the character of the relationship with Vail & Vickers understandably created a deep rift between the ranchers and the park and also intensified the ill feelings that existed between Superintendent Tim Setnicka and many of the staff within the natural resource division. Even the press began to notice. The *Los Angeles Times* quoted Kate Faulkner criticizing the agreement with the ranchers, while Superintendent Setnicka, in the same article, was quoted defending it. Former congressman Robert Lagomarsino, conveniently ignoring his 1987 declaration of a five-to-ten-year phaseout, commented: "My understanding was that [the Vails] would be able to stay there for at least 25 years to continue ranching. I am very sympathetic to the Vails. If I'd known how this would turn out, I probably would not have included them in the national park."[72]

THE SETTLEMENT AGREEMENT (1998)

By the end of 1997, Judge Rea's tentative ruling had been taken to heart and a mediated settlement was underway. A much-weakened Vail & Vickers sought to salvage what they could from their permit, and it was clear that financially it would be the hunting operation. The NPS, internally divided and under censorious attack by much of the media and public, wanted to calm the crisis. In December an agreement was reached among the three principal litigants—the Vail & Vickers Company, NPCA, and the Park Service. The USFWS and the California Regional Water Quality Control Board also were involved in the negotiations that resulted in a formal settlement agreement (SA). Announced on January 30, 1998, this agreement stipulated that ranching cease altogether on Santa Rosa Island, with all cattle to be removed by December 31 of that year. The agreement also stipulated that populations of exotic cervids (deer and elk) be closely regulated during an Adaptive Management Period that would extend through 2011. This stipulation could have been rejected by the NPS and NPCA but was allowed in an effort to conclude an amicable SA. Gone was the 1997 RMP's recommendation of three years to the end of their presence on the island.

In order to determine appropriate regulatory criteria, a three-member panel of reputable scientists would be appointed—one member selected by Vail & Vickers, another by the NPS, and a third to be selected by those two members. This panel would identify a small number of indicator plant species—canaries in the coal mine—that could be monitored to determine the potential effects of cervid grazing. The assumption was that a measurably negative impact on these species would indicate damage to the broader ecosystem and suggest that other species and vegetational assemblages were suffering as well. Management practices could then be adapted in response to these findings.

The SA required the science panel to submit two reports by December 31, 1998, one that identified the selected indicator species and described their baseline population numbers, distribution, and condition, and another that established standards and protocols for monitoring these species. Exactly one year after that, the panel had to submit a third report describing any significant changes in the status of the indicator species. On the basis of these reports, panel members would then submit individual recommendations to the superintendent and the NPS regional director concerning possible reductions in cervid populations. Any final decisions to this effect would be made by these officials with an explanation of any deviation from the individual recommendations issued in writing, so that Vail & Vickers could protest and ask for further mediation.[73] Barring any modifications required by the monitoring results, cervid population levels would be reduced according to an incremental schedule that was outlined in the Settlement Agreement. By 2011, all of the animals that could reasonably be culled without incurring "unusual cost" should be gone. Any remaining animals would subsequently be eliminated, but they would not be the responsibility of Vail & Vickers.[74]

The original appointees to the science panel were Michael Barbour, John Menke, and Ed Schreiner.[75] They identified two endemic species that they believed should be monitored as indicators of cervid impact—Santa Rosa Island manzanita (*Arctostaphylos confertiflora*) and a variety of Indian paintbrush (*Castilleja mollis*). Select populations of these species would be fenced off in small enclosures and compared with nearby unprotected populations. When the plants outside the protected zones showed no measurable diminishment in health, population or extent relative to those inside the enclosures, resource managers could assume that cervid impacts were negligible and they could allow existing numbers to persist without further reduction until the agreed-upon phaseout during the final years.[76]

Although the purpose of this science panel's preliminary report was to establish baseline conditions and determine appropriate monitoring protocols, the scientists already noted high levels of herbivore impact in certain areas, especially around Carrington Point. These observations led to an unusual recommendation—that future culling of cervids should be concentrated in these areas. This proposal appeared to contradict the purpose of monitoring the designated species as indicators of overall island conditions, as it would shift management toward a strategy that addressed only isolated populations rather than the entire island ecosystem. Another apparent problem in the design of the monitoring protocol was the selection of the indicator species themselves. Both *A. confertiflora* and *C. mollis* are rare island endemics and occur only within specific habitat types. They were chosen primarily because of their individual species value, prompted by their recent listing under the ESA, whereas their value as indicators of broader ecological conditions, though explicitly stated, was a secondary concern. Several interested parties claimed that this was a weakness in the research design during the public comment period on the proposed RMP. The park responded "*Arctostaphylos* and *Castilleja* were chosen as indicator species because they are two of the most heavily impacted species occurring on Santa Rosa Island, because those impacts have been unambiguously tied to deer and elk, [and] because they occur in habitats which are generally impacted."[77] However, the park also admitted that it would be too costly to monitor additional species, implying that the criteria for selecting these indicators had a financial constraint as well as a scientific goal.

Despite these problems, the park incorporated the recommendations of the science panel into an amendment to the final RMP/EIS. The preferred alternative called for adopting the terms of the settlement agreement, with the removal of cattle by the end of the year. It also called for the phased reduction of deer and elk beginning in 2000, with their numbers set by the NPS, based on input from the panel, and concluding with full elimination at the end of 2011. The hunting operation would continue to be directed by Vail & Vickers, though in principle its management would have to be vetted by NPS administrators in order to ensure the least adverse effect on park operations. How this vetting would occur was left ambiguous, and one public commentator's suspicion that it would not occur later proved accurate.[78]

Many other concerns relating to the management of the commercial hunt and the cervid populations on which it depended arose during the review process. Jayne Belnap, a research ecologist from the U.S. Geological Survey, noted that the cervids remained on the island because they were necessary to sustain the commercial hunting operation and benefitted only Vail & Vickers and their clients but not the public, represented by the National Park Service. The NPS explained that the cost of maintaining these herds would be shared between itself and the Vails. Belnap charged that this arrangement was unfair because the burden was subsidized by the public while the benefit was enjoyed entirely by the private owners and their clients.[79]

The End of Ranching on Santa Rosa Island

Although a bitter Vail & Vickers Company formally signed the SA, with the park's preferred alternative, its owners publicly claimed they did not agree with the terms of the resolution but only wanted to end the controversy. Vail & Vickers continued to insist that theirs was a legacy of good stewardship and that the preferred alternative and the SA itself went beyond what was necessary to protect the island environment. In their opinion, those steps exaggerated the problems associated with the deer, elk, and cattle. The company cited the opinion of Dr. John Menke, its selection for the three-member science panel, who observed that "at the present time, the native plant habitats are not threatened by grazing."[80] Vail & Vickers were recognized as responsible rangeland managers but were not managing the island for the same ends as those valued by park natural resource managers, botanists with the USFWS, or, ultimately, Judge Rea. Hunting, which had begun in 1978, was another matter. By the time of the settlement agreement, hunters were paying Multiple Use Management up to $7,500 for a four-day elk hunt, or $3,500 for a deer hunt.[81]

Circumstances surrounding the establishment of the park in 1980 have left some of the surviving principals rueful. Bill Ehorn claims that the park legislation was dependent on Vail & Vickers' cooperation. "I am convinced," he recalled several years later, "that had Congress not assured the Vails that the ranch would continue and had NPS not agreed that the park and the ranch could coexist, there would not be a park today that includes Santa Rosa Island."[82] He still believes this to be supported by the solicitude shown the Vails by many of the congressmen during the hearings on the proposed park bill.[83] Yet, Kate Faulkner showed that no written promise of a twenty-five-year duration for ranching was given when Vail & Vickers refused both the RUO and lease options.[84] Nothing

Fig. 23. Lobo Canyon showing the riparian recovery after the removal of cattle, deer, and elk. Photograph by L. Dilsaver, October 2017.

in the congressional deliberations or sales contract indicated that a five-year special use permit could be used and renewed for twenty-five years.

Removing cattle helped protect the natural resources, but this accomplishment had negative as well as positive consequences. On the positive side, the native habitat showed a clear improvement. This was especially evident in riparian ecosystems that had been directly impacted by cattle grazing. In 2004, a team of scientists returned to each of the ten stream sites that had been assessed in 1995. Using the same criteria for evaluation, the team found that all six of the assessment sites previously classified as "non-functional" were now in a "proper functional condition."[85] Exotic deer and elk continued to have an impact on island streams, primarily because they browsed the younger vegetation and inhibited the reproduction and spread of woody species in riparian corridors. Researchers also documented that grazing by these animals diminished vegetative cover on slopes above stream channels, contributing to erosion and excessive water turbidity after storm events. But these impacts were not as severe as the effects of year-round cattle grazing.[86]

The effects of this controversy extended beyond the park itself. One example was public opposition to the Gaviota National Seashore, which the NPS proposed for a seventy-six-mile stretch of coast on the mainland just north of the Channel Islands. Representative Lois Capps (D-Santa Barbara) requested that the Park Service conduct a feasibility study to determine whether this sparsely populated coastal area should be included within the national park system. Congress authorized the study in November 1999, just as President Clinton prepared to vacate the White House for George W. Bush. The NPS initiated the study early the following year and met angry resistance from local landowners, who opposed what many perceived as a threat to their private property rights by the federal government. Vail & Vickers' experience on Santa Rosa Island was repeatedly cited as an example of what could be expected if the proposal went forward. Mary Vail, one of Al Vail's two daughters, was a regular participant at the public scoping meetings and workshops that were held over the next few years. Her testimony helped galvanize opposition to the proposal among local private landowners, especially agriculturalists and ranchers. In response, the NPS abandoned the Gaviota National Seashore proposal at the end of the study period in early 2004.[87] Tim Setnicka commented to the press, "The Santa Rosa lawsuit was used by the opposition as a great example of the federal government breaking its promises. It was argued that, as a landowner, you can't trust the park service because, 'look what happened on Santa Rosa Island.'"[88]

New Owners on Santa Cruz Island

8

The two deeds signed by grantor Carey Stanton as director of the Santa Cruz Island Company and grantee the Nature Conservancy spelled out a framework for their relationship, but the two sides interpreted it differently in the years that followed. This led to a serious deterioration in relations between Stanton and TNC and controversy over resource management on the island.[1]

The sale specified that Stanton's rights on the island would expire in 2008 or when he died, whichever came first. The more significant conservation easement spelled out the details of their coexistence. It began with the following statement:

> It is the purpose of this Conservation Easement to preserve and protect in perpetuity and to enhance by restoration the natural ecological and aesthetic features and values of the Island. Specifically and without limitation of the general purposes, it is the purpose hereof to preserve, protect and enhance the soil composition, structure and productivity, the native flora and the native faunal habitat and the hydrologic and geologic features of the Island. In so doing it is the purpose of this Conservation Easement to foster the continuation of the agricultural and ranching practices as they are currently conducted in harmony with the ecological and aesthetic features and values of the Island and to allow other activities as are not inconsistent with the purposes and terms hereof.[2]

Thereafter, a number of detailed stipulations (1) reiterated the mandate to protect and enhance the natural environment; (2) established the rights of the conservancy to enter the island for scientific research, interpretation, and education as long as those activities were consistent with the use of the island by the grantor and would not "violate the privacy of the residential compounds on the Island"; (3) mandated that the company could continue "to pasture and graze livestock and to continue agricultural activity of the Island as those activities are currently practiced in a manner consistent with the maintenance of the natural flora and natural fauna and maintenance of soil composition, structure and productivity"; and (4) allowed for the continued use of "selective control techniques as heretofore conducted" to control feral animals.[3]

Although this arrangement appeared to leave little room for TNC, except as inheritor of the ranch after Carey Stanton's death, the agreement gave the organization considerable authority to manage the island's natural resources. TNC appointed Robert "Bob" Hansen to provide on-site stewardship of the new reserve. The relationship between Carey Stanton and the conservancy got off to a poor start when TNC declined to give him a seat on its California board of directors as he had expected. Nor did he anticipate the changes in his life on the island with the arrival of TNC. According to his assistant, Marla Daily: "For his part, he fully expected to be left alone, to enjoy his life and privacy for the rest of his years. He was completely unprepared for and astounded by their ambitious and aggressive nature. He didn't foresee the constant demand for his attention; the changes to his routine; and never expected to be sued by TNC."[4] The major management issue that TNC faced was the detrimental impacts of feral sheep and pigs, and that could only be solved by elimination of those animals. The conservancy focused on two questions: (1) What was the basic ecology and present status of the feral sheep population on Santa Cruz Island? and (2) What impacts were the sheep having upon the island's natural resources?

The ensuing research produced stark details about the impact of feral sheep on the Santa Cruz Island ecosystem. Wildlife biologist Dirk Van Vuren reported that (1) 36 percent of the island was heavily impacted by sheep; (2) densities in these areas averaged eighty-five animals per 100 acres, over twice the maximum stocking rate on a mainland sheep ranch; (3) the ovine population would probably recover from a massive,

Fig. 24. Sheep on Santa Cruz Island remained a source of income for Carey Stanton into the early 1980s and for the Gherinis into the 1990s, primarily through hunting concessions. Provided by John Gherini.

unsuccessful control attempt in just a few years; (4) endemic plants totaled only a fraction of one percent of available forage but comprised up to 17 percent of the sheep diet; and (5) an area disturbed by sheep supported less than one-half the number of birds and about one-half the number of bird species that existed in an adjacent undisturbed area. The endemic Santa Cruz Island scrub jay (*Aphelocoma coerulescens insularis*) had been reduced in numbers by 45 percent. Van Vuren recommended a combination of fencing, trapping, and hunting to eliminate the feral sheep.[5]

Other researchers were unanimous in calling for the removal of the sheep as soon as possible. Although this recommendation was consistent with the conservancy's goals for the reserve, it would cost considerably more money to implement than the organization had available. However, the Fleischmann Foundation was willing to offer $3 million for a well-justified grant proposal.[6] In order to secure the grant, TNC asked Carey Stanton, as the director of the SCIC, to sign an official letter of support for

New Owners 203

TNC's natural resource management. The formal letter Stanton wrote on March 28, 1980, was unequivocal in its support of eliminating feral animals:

> For many years the Santa Cruz Island Company has been active in attempting to control the feral sheep and pigs on the island, with the eventual goal being the total elimination of the entire feral population. We are certainly aware of the destruction caused by these animals. The environment does indeed suffer because of their presence, and there is virtually no economic gain derived from them. With the Conservancy's acquisition of an interest in the island, I am hopeful that a solution to this major problem can be found. I am pleased that the Conservancy is making a serious effort to learn more about the habits of these animals to be better prepared to cope with the situation. I will surely help all I can in any sensible effort to rid the island of these animals. Any effort to eliminate these animals will have to be massive. It will be expensive, involving much labor and equipment. This I know very well from the many years that my family and I have spent trying to solve the problem. It is a huge undertaking, but certainly worthwhile and essential to preserve the island ecology.[7]

However, this unqualified support for the mission of TNC overlooked two realities. First, the Santa Cruz Island Hunt Club did indeed provide a large and continuing income from its sheep hunts. It is uncertain why Stanton felt he needed to add the statement about "no economic gain" to the letter. The other mistake was in assuming that TNC would be unable to completely eliminate the sheep in a short time. Recreational hunters did not have a significant impact on a population estimated to be more than twenty thousand because of the fertility of the island's ewes. A systematic assault by professional hunters aiming at eradication was another story.

At that point, as in so many instances with the Channel Islands, different stories emerge about the letter. According to Marla Daily, Bob Hansen approached Stanton in 1980 asking for his agreement in a proposal to manage the feral sheep. Hansen and Carey Stanton were on friendly terms and reached what Daily recalls was a "gentleman's agreement"; although the formal proposal would call for the eradication of the sheep, in fact, management would continue at the same levels as before, controlling, but not eliminating, existing populations. This would assure the continued viability of the Santa Cruz Island Hunt Club. The two men shook hands, and then Stanton wrote the letter, as required before TNC could receive the Fleischmann grant.[8] However, Bob Hansen flatly denies that such an event and agreement ever happened: "Any agreement of that kind with Carey would have been above my pay grade. I was hired to manage TNC's project according to any approved and funded plan. Entering into agreements like what Marla described was not my charge."[9]

In 1981 TNC completed a comprehensive sheep management plan, incorporating Van Vuren's recommendations and addressing potential legal issues and anticipated public reactions. The conservancy allocated $240,000 and two full-time positions toward the project. Among the methodologies considered, trapping was soon abandoned after it was discovered that sale of the sheep off island was not economical, while the treatment itself would prove prohibitively time-consuming. Program managers decided instead to focus on fencing and hunting. In order to deflect public and media attention from the anticipated killings, TNC used the Santa Cruz Island Hunt Club as a shield and referred to its effort as a "Pasture Improvement Program" aimed at protecting forage for Stanton's cattle operation. Between 1981 and 1983, TNC workers installed or repaired more than one hundred miles of sheep-proof fencing, partitioning the Santa Cruz Island reserve into twenty-three separate pastures. Hunting began on December 17, 1981, using professional marksmen. Carey Stanton was away at that time, traveling in Europe, and was not present to monitor the scope or intensity of the operation. He continued to assume that the objective of the program was population maintenance rather than eradication.[10]

Once Stanton became aware of the full scale of the Nature Conservancy's project, he complained that he had been betrayed. Stanton directed most of his anger at Frank Boren who was the TNC representative on the board of the Santa Cruz Island Company. His relations with Boren were far less cordial than they had been with Hansen. By then TNC was well aware of Stanton's sensitivity to rebuke and outrage at usurpation of the island control he insisted was his alone. Hansen later wrote to his colleagues in TNC:

> Very early in the development of the Santa Cruz Island Project a pattern of diplomacy was established that required all TNC activity on the island be reviewed and "approved" by Dr. Stanton. Our lack of knowledge of day-to-day operations of the island, ambitious stewardship objectives (sheep) coupled with a desire to work cooperatively with a volatile land owner were reasons enough to choose this course. It is easy to recall the protracted discussions waged over construction of our cabins, boat, manager's residence, staff use of the island, not to mention the early days of our pasture/sheep eradication program. All along, Carey has been effective at keeping TNC on the defensive. The Conservancy has provided Carey with a steady stream of "infractions" which Carey has effectively seized upon and inflated to crisis level.[11]

TNC pondered ways to avoid further confrontation and accelerate its eradication of sheep. Its officers discussed options, including outright purchase of the Hunt Club, which would include the remaining sheep. Eventually, TNC filed suit on April 26, 1984, accusing the SCIC of not following Section 7 of the contract enjoining it to not allow "waste or depletion" of the island. This was because it "willfully and deliberately obstructed and prevented The Nature Conservancy's efforts to eliminate feral sheep."[12] Prior to the lawsuit, Frank Boren and Bob Hansen of TNC had met with Carey Stanton and his attorney David D. Watts at the lawyer's office. Stanton verbally forbid TNC from killing any more sheep. At that, Boren produced a copy of the letter Stanton wrote on March 28, 1980, as quoted above. Watts turned to Stanton and asked him if he had signed it. Stanton replied that he had but it didn't really mean anything. At that point, the lawyer slid the letter back to Boren and told him TNC could proceed as it saw fit. On July 27, an angry Stanton met Hansen on Santa Cruz Island and warned him that the press was going to get the story of the sheep slaughter. Hansen recalls that "five days later Carey flew to his 'vacation home' in Scotland and the *Los Angeles Times* and the rest of the media circus arrived at the TNC office in Santa Barbara."[13] A hunters' advocacy group called the California Wildlife Federation filed a suit against TNC that failed when the defendant showed the damage the sheep were doing to the environment.[14]

By this time Stanton's income had dwindled to a dangerously low level. He complained that TNC's eradication of sheep all but eliminated his primary source of funds. According to Marla Daily, Stanton negotiated with TNC's Frank Boren regarding compensation for the sheep and the loss of income from his hunt club. He initially valued the sheep at $100 per head, which would total $3,200,000 in lost assets, with TNC's killing of thirty-two thousand sheep. He later put a nominal base price of $20 per sheep as the figure and asked TNC to compensate him in the amount of $600,000.[15] TNC simply refused to pay anything for the sheep, arguing that their elimination was part of its charge to protect the island. TNC officials were well aware of the effect their program was having on the future of the hunt club but would not be lured into an onerous and continuing expense. Instead, they offered a ten-year program during which TNC would not veto use of the SCIC Director's Fund that went annually to Stanton for the operation of the company. This arrangement would begin once the population of sheep dropped to 250. The key stipulation was that Stanton could only use the money for the maintenance of historic buildings, furnishings, and other structures. Any amount unused in a given year for these purposes would go into an endowment for future maintenance.[16]

Ironically, the Santa Cruz Island Hunt Club went out of business in 1985. During the previous year, several accidents involving customers occurred, one of which left a woman paralyzed.[17] Mark Oberman, owner of Channel Islands Aviation, approached Stanton and offered to start a new hunting and recreation company on the island to be called Channel Islands Adventures. His flying service derived considerable income from transporting hunters to Santa Cruz Island and he was loath to lose it. The contract was similar to that with the defunct Santa Cruz Island Hunt Club. The major difference was that the hunt would have to focus on pigs. By late 1986 relatively few sheep remained.[18]

Over the next two years the abrasive relationship between Carey Stanton and TNC worsened. Bob Hansen divided restrictions placed on TNC into "great" and "petty" issues. In addition to his demand for payment for

Fig. 25. The Central Valley of Santa Cruz Island looking east. The trees nearly spanning the width of the valley in the distance are a mature eucalyptus grove that hide the Main Ranch from view. Photograph by L. Dilsaver, August 2018.

each sheep killed, Stanton insisted that no one could access the island without his personal permission; that he alone could be listed as owner of the island; and that his personal possessions would be maintained on the island as a museum. He also forbade publicity about the island rebuffing the Cousteau Society from making a documentary about the island.[19] Petty issues included a stream of complaints about TNC's base camp and its staff using the island for recreation. Stanton also refused to let TNC staff or researchers use the road through his Main Ranch in winter when the alternate route was impassable; to permit construction of a fence on his portion of the island to keep out trespassing sheep from the Gherini property; and to approve other restoration projects TNC sought to accomplish in a timely manner. Finally, he charged that if TNC wanted to hunt sheep in the Central Valley, it should do so with silencers so he and his guests would not hear it.[20]

Late in 1986 several events added to Carey Stanton's woes. He had turned to drinking and taking antidepressants to combat his frustration and periodic depression. His ranch manager and long-time friend, Henry Duffield, suffered a stroke that further incapacitated him. Faced with a bleak future, Duffield died by suicide on November 23, 1986. From that time forward Stanton's depression and drinking worsened. He had expected the arrangement with TNC to leave the island in a state of preservation that he proudly maintained was due to his care in managing its use. He also thought he would be left alone to continue directing its preservation unhindered until TNC would take over in 2008. By that time, he would be eighty-five years of age. Sometime during the night on December 8, 1987, he went to bed only to arise and go to the bathroom, probably feeling quite ill. There he died at the age of sixty-four. UC Research Station director Lyndal Laughrin found him the following morning. An autopsy later confirmed that a combination of tranquilizers, aspirin, and alcohol killed him. With that, TNC gained complete control of 90 percent of the Santa Cruz Island and the SCIC that ran it.[21]

MANAGEMENT OF WEST SANTA CRUZ ISLAND BY TNC

After Stanton's death, conflict arose between TNC and Channel Islands Adventures. Bob Hansen complained that customers and some of the guides of the company held loud beach parties, drove too fast, left gates in the fences open, shot birds, plundered archaeological sites and rare plants, trespassed on Gherini land, used mountain bikes, ignored state laws about hunting licenses, and behaved in a manner that reflected badly on TNC and its mission.[22] Mark Oberman countered that he never received notification of these complaints and that TNC wanted his company removed because the organization was concerned about its property tax exempt status.[23] The means by which TNC curtailed Channel Islands Adventures' hunting operation stemmed from a stipulation in its contract with Oberman. It held that Channel Islands Adventures would maintain an exclusive right to hunt pigs as long as it kept the population below 1,251. If not, it would receive a sixty-day notice to bring the numbers to within 110 percent of that target. After sixty days, if unremedied, the company would lose its exclusive right to hunt them. On March 7, 1989, TNC informed Oberman that he had ignored a notice of noncompliance and the grace period had passed, therefore his organization had lost its exclusive right. The conservancy announced that it would use a professional hunting company to kill the pigs and that Channel Islands Adventures would have to coordinate its activities around that operation.[24]

The Nature Conservancy's sheep eradication efforts continued up through 1989, with additional hunts in the so-called no-man's-land on the western slopes of the Montañon as late as 1997. By June of 1989, TNC's hunters had shot nearly thirty-two thousand sheep. Additionally, the Santa Cruz Island Hunt Club shot over five thousand animals up until its dissolution. That brought the total number killed to just over thirty-seven thousand, with fewer than five known to be still living west of the Montañon by the end of that year.

Bob Hansen continued as TNC's Southern California Field Representative until July 14, 1989. During the nineteen months following Carey Stanton's death, he acted as director of the Santa Cruz Island Company. His duties included removing the cattle from the island, completing the sheep eradication, dealing with Carey Stanton's possessions, and planning how to manage the large property TNC now owned. Questions of how many visitors to allow on the island, how to make the preserve a compelling example of restoration for potential donors, and how to deal with the biotic effects of removing the sheep from the ecosystem kept staff and volunteers busy. When Hansen left TNC, the Santa Cruz Island Company ceased to exist.

Reserve managers observed a marked increase in native species diversity and canopy cover following the conclusion of the sheep treatment. They found seedlings for three endemic woody species of Island oak (*Quercus tomentella*), Bush poppy (*Dendromecon rigida harfordii*), and Catalina ironwood (*Lyonothamnus floribundus asplenifolius*) within four years after the majority of sheep had been removed from northern enclosures. While mature individuals of these species remained relatively abundant, resource managers had observed few young seedlings in recent history, indicating a predictable failure of the species due to adverse grazing pressure. One endemic plant, silver bird's-foot trefoil (*Lotus argophyllus niveus*), that had dwindled to near extinction, made a dramatic comeback following the eradication of the sheep and became common in many areas.[25]

Newly appointed superintendent Mack Shaver negotiated a cooperative agreement with TNC to "coordinate all aspects of Park management relevant to their shared objectives [preserving natural and cultural resources with limited public access]." The agreement was signed in January 1991 and was effective for five years, with the possibility of renewal. It stipulated that the signatories would cooperate in developing a park-wide general management plan (GMP) to update the existing 1985 plan, a statement for management, and a development concept plan (DCP) for Santa Cruz Island. Both parties agreed to cooperate in research, including long-term resource inventory and monitoring, and in the development and implementation of feral animal and exotic plant management programs. They also agreed upon terms for cooperation in practical operations such as fire management, emergency response, communications, and facilities maintenance.[26]

Acquiring East Santa Cruz Island

The four children of Maria and Ambrose Gherini, brothers Pier and Francis and sisters Ilda McGinness and Marie Ringrose, owned equal shares of East Santa Cruz Island. The two sisters supported the sale of their island property to the NPS, and Pier Gherini became willing to sell his share as he neared the end of his life. When he died on June 29, 1989, his children faced an inheritance tax of more than $3 million. They agreed to sell their father's one-quarter share to the NPS. This had to be paid within nine months of Pier's death, so it was necessary to consummate the sale quickly. Fortunately for the Pier Gherini children, NPS regional director Stanley Albright sympathized with their concerns and worked hard to expedite the purchase of their fractional shares of the property. However, several challenges had to be overcome first. One was procedural. The federal government generally avoided buying fractional interests in real property. Subsequent events confirmed the wisdom of this policy, but circumstances at the time seemed to justify making an exception, and the Justice Department accordingly granted one.

The other challenges were primarily fiscal. The Park Service had originally offered $4,500,000 for each fractional interest in east Santa Cruz Island, but by 1989 it had only enough money available to buy one of these interests. Ilda McGinness and Marie Ringrose agreed to postpone negotiations with the Park Service so that Pier's estate could be settled first and the inheritance tax paid from the proceeds of the sale. But political considerations complicated the sale. Congress had not yet appropriated the funds and opposition within the House Appropriations Subcommittee prevented approval of the original offer. In the end, only $3,875,000 was available. Thomas Gherini, who was acting as executor of the estate, agreed to this sum, which was only slightly more than the amount of the inheritance tax. The sale took place on April 25, 1990. Pier Gherini's children made little money, but they reserved a right of use and occupancy (RUO) that allowed them to use three small parcels on East Santa Cruz Island for twenty-five years. The Park Service was then left in the awkward position of being a cotenant with the three remaining owners of East Santa Cruz Island.

In 1992 the NPS purchased the shares from Ilda McGinness and Marie Ringrose, leaving only the one-quarter interest held by Francis Gherini who opposed selling to the government. The hunting business was doing well, and Francis was earning a substantial profit from his contract with Jaret Owens. Rather than end this lucrative relationship, Francis decided to renew Island Adventure's contract. In December 1990, Francis signed a second three-year extension of Island Adventure Company's original operational agreement without consulting the other cotenants, including the National Park Service.

RELATIONS WITH ISLAND ADVENTURES

The new operational agreement authorized Jaret Owens to increase the hunt club's recreational offerings and to expand its infrastructure accordingly. One result of this was the construction of additional guest residences at Smugglers Ranch, close to the Conex shipping container that served as the island ranger station. The increased number of guests soon overwhelmed existing outhouse facilities, and many of the hunters began using the ranger's outhouse, leading to inevitable conflicts. The NPS eventually reacted to Island Adventures' growth by contacting county and state planning agencies that were responsible for regulating development within the coastal zone. As required by the California Coastal

Act of 1976, Santa Barbara County had certified a "Local Coastal Plan" in 1981 that required a conditional use permit for any commercial activities taking place on the islands. Knowing that Island Adventures lacked such a permit, the park began collecting evidence to document its activities.[27] However, the company obtained permission from the county to continue operating after Francis Gherini testified that the hunt club had existed prior to 1981. This was a lie. The Local Coastal Plan allowed businesses already in existence at the time it was implemented to continue operating.[28] Island Adventures began operating on East Santa Cruz Island late in 1983, but Gherini told county officials that the business was an extension of Pete Peterson's lease, which had been in effect since 1979. Peterson's lease was for raising sheep not killing them.[29]

Relations between the park and Island Adventures grew increasingly tense over the next few years, with periodic incidents exacerbating the situation. Most of these were minor when considered by themselves. For example, on one occasion in 1991, a ranger confronted Duane Owens, Jaret's father who helped manage the Scorpion site, and accused him of misusing Park Service property for commercial purposes related to Island Adventures. The property in question was the ATV that previous superintendent Bill Ehorn had allowed Owens to operate for patrol purposes on a volunteer basis. Duane Owens indignantly denied the accusation but agreed to stop using the vehicle.[30] Jaret Owens suspected that this confrontation was part of a pattern of harassment designed to drive Island Adventures out of business.

The younger Owens mysteriously obtained an internal park memorandum from Superintendent Mack Shaver that seemed to explicitly instruct park staff to "aggressively interfere" with Island Adventures. The memo actually consisted of answers to a formal questionnaire from the western regional budget officer that asked, "Have there been problems in holding an undivided interest in the property [East Santa Cruz Island]?" Shaver had written "yes" and listed various responsibilities that the Park Service would have to honor if it was to manage East Santa Cruz Island as a national park. They included removing feral animals, eliminating sport and commercial hunting, and providing accommodations and transportation only by a park-approved concessionaire. All of these items were well-established NPS management policies. Shaver concluded, "If unspecified interest ownership is to continue for a longer time, resource protection and visitor access can only be accomplished by the NPS taking a more aggressive role in exercising management responsibility, even if legal action by another cotenant is prompted." This was really a statement of fact rather than a call to arms.[31]

The issue was not with Island Adventures but with Francis Gherini, while Jaret and Duane Owens were simply caught in the middle.[32] The NPS suspected that Gherini would take the matter into the courts for resolution if the park insisted too strongly on its rights as cotenant. The agency was reluctant to do this, fearing that a judge would simply divide East Santa Cruz Island into four equal parts, much as the court had done with the heirs of Justinian Caire in 1925. This might resolve the immediate source of conflict, but it would leave Gherini and Island Adventures on the island.

This problematic cotenancy led to increasingly hostile interactions between park staff and Island Adventures. Late in 1991, Tim Setnicka visited East Santa Cruz Island with other staff members. On the second day of their tour, the group drove out to Smugglers where the hunting operation was based. On arriving there, Setnicka noticed a new outhouse not far from the NPS ranger station. Jaret Owens had purchased this structure and had it installed in response to the park's earlier complaints about his guests using the ranger's outhouse. For some reason, Setnicka assumed that the new structure was NPS property and that Owens had stolen it. Flying into a rage, he kicked the building over and filled the recently excavated pit underneath it.[33] He then arranged for a helicopter to airlift the building to Anacapa Island. Setnicka soon realized his error, and the park issued a formal apology to Island Adventures, but instead of returning the outhouse to East Santa Cruz Island, it was shipped to the mainland on a park boat, where Owens was told he could claim the now-infamous flying outhouse. This insulting response by Setnicka provided an ominous sign of the growing personalization of the conflict. Jaret Owens reacted to this and other recent frustrations by writing to Congressman Robert Lagomarsino and describing in detail the deterioration of affairs between himself and the park since the departure of Superintendent Bill

Ehorn. It was this letter that referenced the memorandum from Superintendent Shaver that Owens interpreted as harassment.[34]

A LEGISLATIVE TAKING

In 1992 Congress appropriated $12 million to purchase the remaining three fractional interests in East Santa Cruz Island, valuing each at $4 million based on a government appraisal made the previous year. Marie Ringrose and Ilda McGinness sold and, like the children of Pier Gherini, were allowed RUOs for a period of twenty-five years. Neither sister ever expressed an interest in using them. Francis Gherini rejected the government offer. The National Park Service now owned a majority three-quarter interest in East Santa Cruz Island. It seemed that this would improve the park's ability to manage the island, but in fact, little changed. Island Adventures continued to operate as before, while Francis Gherini remained intransigent in the face of every Park Service attempt to improve public access and resource protection. This may have stemmed from his desire to settle the estate through condemnation, because he believed he could obtain the greatest profit from this procedure.[35]

After four more years of mounting tension between the park and Island Adventures, this strategy began to seem like the only reasonable course of action. During the Senate hearing for the bill to create Channel Islands National Park, NPS director William Whalen had promised not to condemn the property of "all the landowners, with the exception of the Gherini property."[36] A condemnation, or legislative taking, would allow the federal government to seize the remaining private property and transfer it to the public domain with due compensation to the private landowner. Congress needed to implement the procedure through enactment of a bill, but condemnations were politically unpopular and rarely occurred.[37] Under the circumstances, however, a legislative taking seemed advantageous to all interested parties except Island Adventures. In 1996, Tim Setnicka approached Congresswoman Andrea Seastrand (R-Santa Barbara) to ask for her support. Setnicka invited the congresswoman to visit East Santa Cruz Island in order to convince her of the value of the property and the impossibility of continuing under the current cotenancy arrangement. Seastrand concurred on both points and agreed to sponsor the necessary bill. She introduced it to the House on September 11, 1996, as H.R. 4059.

There was not a little irony in Congresswoman Seastrand's role, given her reputation as a conservative supporter of private property rights, but Seastrand wanted the longstanding conflict resolved and believed that her bill would adequately preserve the value of Francis Gherini's interest. He retained attorney and former secretary of the interior William P. Clark to help him negotiate the terms of his compensation. This was to be based on fair market value, as determined by a mutually agreed appraisal. If no agreement could be reached after one year, the matter would be turned over to the courts for a judge to decide. Seastrand's bill would also ensure that Gherini retained a reserved right similar to those that his siblings had received.[38] Ordinarily, a reserved right could only be established through a negotiated settlement, as it had with the sale of Pier Gherini's interest, not through a legislative taking. By introducing this clause into her bill, Seastrand allowed an important exception to legal precedent on behalf of Francis Gherini. This additional concession was crucial to Seastrand's support of the legislation because it would allow Gherini to continue using the property on East Santa Cruz Island for another twenty-five years and appeared to preserve many of the privileges he already enjoyed for the duration of his life.

Congresswoman Seastrand's bill, H.R. 4059, successfully reported out of committee later that month. However, by the time it reached the House floor the RUO that Francis had insisted upon was gone. Gherini reacted to the deletion as soon as he discovered it by deeding an undivided 1 percent of his interest to the Santa Cruz Island Foundation (SCIF). This gift deed contained an unusual clause reserving to Francis Gherini and "his heirs a nonexclusive easement in gross, with the unrestricted right of use and occupancy for all recreational purposes over, under, through and across the entirety of said property." In other words, it contained the same reserved right that had been deleted from Seastrand's original bill. Gherini hoped that this maneuver would preserve his right by simply transferring it to another cotenant. It did not. Publicly, Gherini justified his action by claiming that the gift deed was made because he wanted SCIF to provide oversight over the Park Service, which he did not trust.[39]

Once H.R. 4059 reported out of committee, there was little chance that any further modifications would be made, because it was incorporated into the larger and more complex Omnibus Parks Bill, H.R. 4236. This bill contained numerous park-related proposals from around the country, many of which were high profile and hotly contested. In the frantic negotiations to reach a compromise, there was little opportunity to address less significant details, and the terms of the edited Seastrand bill remained unchanged.

Congress passed H.R. 4236 on October 3, 1996. President Bill Clinton signed it into law on November 12 as Public Law 104–333.[40] It amended section 202 of the Channel Islands Park Act to allow condemnation of the remaining private interest in East Santa Cruz Island, effective ninety days after Clinton's signature. That date occurred on February 10, 1997.[41] In effect, this legislatively "took" all rights, title, and interest to the Gherini Ranch except those reserved to the heirs of Pier Gherini. In addition to denying any reservation of use and occupancy to Francis Gherini, the condemnation also abolished the reserved rights of his sisters, Marie Ringrose and Ilda McGinness, though this appears to have been unintentional. It was not discovered until later when Francis Gherini attempted to reassert his sisters' rights in order to bolster his own claims.[42] The problem was legally resolved by compensating the two women the monetary value associated with their abrogated rights. This obviated the need to amend the legislation and possibly give Francis Gherini the opportunity to insert a reserved right for himself. This ended the debate over reserved rights, but the monetary compensation for Francis Gherini's interest still had to be determined and would depend on the appraised value of the property. The federal government was prevented by law from paying more than this amount, but Francis Gherini could still challenge the government's appraisal of $4 million.

Gherini continued to negotiate with the Park Service for monetary compensation for his quarter interest in East Santa Cruz Island. He countered with his own appraisal of $14 million, claiming that the property could support luxury housing. But he ignored the fact that the property's location within the coastal zone, regulated by the California Coastal Commission, prevented such a development. However, the matter was put to a jury, which decided on a compromise between the two appraisals, settling on $12,700,000. An additional $1,756,884 in interest was also awarded, raising the total to $14,456,884, which actually exceeded the amount that Francis had originally demanded. Ironically, Francis Gherini died less than a month after receiving this compensation. He was eighty-four at the time. His death brought the Gherini family's ranching legacy on East Santa Cruz Island to an end.[43]

During the negotiations, several other events and conflicts intensified the controversial acquisition of East Santa Cruz Island. A covert law enforcement investigation of Island Adventures began in 1995 after one of its former employees, Paul Starbard, contacted Julie Tumamait-Stenslie, an Ojai resident of Island Chumash descent. He told her about having seen a large collection of Native American artifacts, including skeletal remains, being shown to clients at Scorpion Ranch while he was working for Owens during the 1980s.[44] Alarmed by this information, Tumamait-Stenslie contacted Channel Islands chief ranger Jack Fitzgerald who initiated a formal investigation.[45] NPS special agents Todd Swain from Joshua Tree National Park and Jeff Sullivan from Yosemite National Park visited East Santa Cruz Island posing as clients of Island Adventures for a two-day hunting trip in August of that year. The two agents passed themselves off as wealthy "high-rollers" interested in hunting, spear-fishing, and collecting Native American artifacts to decorate their homes.

On September 29, 1996, NPS special agents Swain and Sullivan returned to East Santa Cruz Island again posing as clients. Island Adventures guide Brian Krantz excavated the site and offered the two agents several bone fragments. Swain and Sullivan secretly recorded the entire exchange. On December 16, the two rangers returned for a third visit but learned Brian Krantz had discovered he was under investigation and left the island just prior to their arrival.[46] With the undercover operation compromised, the Park Service acted quickly to get search and arrest warrants. Given the possibility of violence with armed hunters, the Park Service contacted the Santa Barbara County Sheriff's Department, which agreed to provide a special operations team. In order to maintain the element of surprise, the rangers used a U.S. Customs Service Blackhawk (H-60) helicopter to convey the officers to East Santa Cruz Island.

In the early morning of January 14, 1997, NPS rangers and county sheriff's department deputies from the special operations division flew to East Santa Cruz Island. At Smugglers, the Island Adventures staff were surprised when they encountered the group of officers dressed SWAT-style, wearing body armor and wielding AR-15 assault rifles. Guides Brian Krantz, Dave Mills, and Rick Berg were arrested on suspicion of disturbing Native American burial sites.[47] The charges were based on the Archaeological Resources Protection Act of 1979. The political and media responses to the conduct of these arrests were angrily critical. Congressmen Elton Gallegly of Simi Valley and Walter Capps of Santa Barbara both sent letters to NPS director Roger Kennedy expressing concern after hearing complaints from their constituents. Congressman Robert Lagomarsino also objected to the "commando-style" raid. Many locals suspected that the arrests were related to the condemnation proceedings against Francis Gherini. This was inevitable, given that the raid occurred only three weeks before the termination of Francis's tenure. The NPS pointed out that the undercover investigation had been initiated nearly two years before the condemnation was scheduled to take effect.[48] But this placed the beginning of the investigation after negotiations with Francis Gherini had already broken down. This coincidence fed the cynical assumptions of critics reflected in a *San Diego Daily Transcript* headline, "Calif. Island Raided, Seized for Use as National Park."[49]

On February 10, 1997, Gherini's share formally reverted to the NPS, which now became the sole owner of East Santa Cruz Island. Francis Gherini and Island Adventures had ninety days, until May 11, to vacate. Island Adventures chose to cease operations right away and hosted one final hunt over the remaining weekend before the effective date of the condemnation. The company invited approximately thirty hunters to come out to the island. By coincidence, the Nature Conservancy brought a team of professional hunters out that same weekend to continue the ongoing extermination of sheep from Carey Stanton's old lands. The TNC hunters happened to be working at that time on the isthmus that bordered the NPS property. This brought them into proximity with Island Adventures, whose guests were able to witness the conservancy hunters from a good vantage point. Although the Island Adventures people were also out to kill sheep, they were doing it for sport and were appalled at the business-like efficiency of their professional counterparts.

Island Adventures guest Jack Ku later described the grisly scene for the press, "I saw them just hitting the herd and shooting them. I saw the babies lying next to the [dead] moms . . . screaming 'baa, baa.'" His comments drew the attention of animal rights supporters who overlooked the fact that Ku was also shooting sheep that day.[50] In response to the publicity that these testimonials aroused, the director of the Ventura County Animal Regulation Department contacted the park and asked Superintendent Setnicka to intervene. Setnicka agreed to contact TNC and request that it halt the killing for the time being. But Diane Elfstrom Devine, the program manager for TNC's Santa Cruz Island Preserve, defended the sheep eradication plan and refused to curtail or modify the culling. Since TNC was a private organization killing privately owned domestic sheep on its own property, little could be done.

REMOVING FERAL SHEEP FROM EAST SANTA CRUZ ISLAND

The park already had eradicated feral pigs from Santa Rosa Island using lethal methods, and TNC was in the process of doing the same with feral sheep on the western side of Santa Cruz Island, with a clearly positive response from native vegetation. This seemed the obvious strategy to pursue on East Santa Cruz Island as well. Killing the animals was initially chosen as the most efficient and cost-effective means of mitigating this impact, but problems soon arose that caused the park more controversy. The most immediate problem was the negative publicity that killing the animals, especially the sheep, would attract. Under the present circumstances, however, with public attention already focused on the park for its handling of the Brian Krantz investigation and the Gherini property takings, the park expected to be scrutinized closely. This became apparent even before the arrest of the Island Adventures guides when Santa Barbara attorney Richard Tentler warned Setnicka in early December 1996 that the park's proposed sheep kill would elicit widespread popular opposition and might prove to be unacceptable on both environmental and cultural grounds. The attorney went on to demand that if the park chose to continue with the plan, it must comply with all applicable legislation, including the National Environmental Policy Act (NEPA), the National Historic Preservation Act, and eleven additional state and federal laws.[51]

Another indication that trouble could be expected was the response to TNC's eradication of sheep on the western side of Santa Cruz Island. This had been underway since 1980 with little public acknowledgement or criticism, though more than thirty thousand animals had been killed over the ensuing decade.[52] But when guests of Island Adventures brought TNC's practices to the attention of the media after their final sport hunting event on the weekend of February 8, 1997, the conservancy's relative invisibility ended. Two weeks later, former Island Adventures caretaker John Morgando returned to the isthmus with a video camera to document the grisly scene, where dead sheep had been left on the ground to rot. He shared his videotapes with local newspapers and television broadcasters and created a public sensation, stimulating numerous letters and calls to the park condemning the slaughter.

TNC at first ignored these complaints, though it eventually agreed to a moratorium on the killing. This was not much of a sacrifice for the conservancy, since the sheep were trespass animals that had escaped from Gherini lands to TNC's property to avoid Island Adventures hunters. The conservancy knew that the Park Service planned to remove the sheep from its side of the island as well, so it could afford to suspend its border patrols for the time being. The park, meanwhile, successfully deflected criticism by publicly distancing itself from TNC during this controversy and insisting that it shared no responsibility for the slaughter of the sheep on the isthmus.[53] Public outcry would be loud and long if the park were now to adopt its own eradication program. Since such an undertaking would require public comment through the NEPA review process, the negative publicity might actually prevent the park's proposal from going forward as attorney Richard Tentler had insinuated.

The final and most frustrating challenge to the park's proposal to eradicate the East Santa Cruz Island sheep, however, was Francis Gherini. The legislation that formally condemned the Gherini family's property allowed "the orderly termination of all current activities and the removal of any equipment, facilities, or personal property." This required the government to provide the necessary transportation to carry out this order or monetary compensation if private services were contracted. Francis Gherini used the stipulation to great effect by demanding extreme measures to protect his family's ranching property. Probably the most egregious example was his claim that about forty large tree stumps were actually furniture and therefore had to be transported off the island by the Park Service. Far more troublesome and costly, however, were his claims on behalf of the ranch animals, beginning with the approximately 1,500 sheep that remained on the open range.

Gherini insisted that these animals belonged exclusively to him and had to be removed according to his wishes. Of course, this was not true, because the other family members shared ownership. He first proposed that Island Adventures increase its per-hunter quota to allow paying sportsmen to eliminate the remaining animals.[54] At the rates currently being charged, this would have brought Francis a substantial profit, but it also would have prolonged the hunt club's presence on the island and continued to interfere with the park's management. The NPS rejected this proposal. Gherini then responded by veering to the opposite extreme and demanding inordinate measures to protect them. This gave a seemingly moral quality to his actions and allowed him to enlist the support of animal rights advocates. Insisting now that the sheep must be transported off the island, he demanded that they be helicoptered to Oregon, where a Christian organization, Discipleship Training International, operated a ranch for recovering alcoholics. He submitted a claim to the NPS for reimbursement of the cost to implement this plan.[55]

In the end, the NPS agreed to remove all sheep from East Santa Cruz Island at Francis Gherini's insistence rather than killing any of them, although Francis could claim ownership over only half of the herd, which had been divided equally, along with the rest of the estate, with the heirs of his deceased brother Pier. Francis donated his half of the sheep to Discipleship Training International, while the NPS sent the other half of the flock to Buellton to be auctioned at a stockyard in accordance with the wishes of Piers's heirs. Although the operation was expected to take one year, it ultimately required nearly two and cost the NPS more than $2 million, for a total of 9,278 sheep, or about $230 per head.[56]

THE HERITAGE HERD

Another issue that involved Francis Gherini was his support of the so-called heritage herd. Kirk Connelly, the husband of SCIF president Marla Daily, coined the name to describe the workhorses on East Santa Cruz Island that had been used by generations of sheep ranchers. At the time of the Gherini condemnation in early 1997, twelve horses in two discrete herds remained.[57] They had all been born in the wild and never ridden. Francis agreed to allow veterinarian Dr. Karen Blumenshine to inspect the East Santa Cruz Island herd. Blumenshine conjectured that they might be evolving into a unique breed.[58] Marla Daily supported this theory with enthusiasm. Francis Gherini also supported the idea and insisted that the horses were biologically and culturally significant and opposed the park's proposal to remove the horses along with the other introduced livestock. Francis turned the heritage herd over to Marla Daily and the SCIF to manage. Once again, Francis did not have the legal authority to do this. He only possessed a 50 percent share in the ownership of the horses, while the remaining 50 percent belonged to Pier Gherini's heirs. John Gherini has stated that he owned an interest in the horses and is still angry about this interference with his private property.[59]

Marla Daily took up the cause of the heritage herd with vigor. As soon as Francis Gherini gave her formal responsibility for the horses, she established Save the Heritage Herd, a project administered through her husband's nonprofit organization, Terra Marine Research & Education.[60] Subsequently, the Foundation for Horses and Other Animals (FHOA), incorporated under its own charter and registered on March 17, 1997, with Lynne Sherman as the first chair of its board of directors.[61] Later that year, the FHOA, represented by Santa Barbara attorney James R. Nichols Jr. filed a lawsuit against the NPS to protect the heritage herd and prevent the park from moving them off the island.[62] The NPS, supported by John Gherini, maintained that the horses did not represent a culturally significant legacy because they were descended from workhorses brought out to the island as recently as the 1970s. The NPS also asserted that the horses had an adverse impact on the island environment, were a danger to visitors, and a potential liability to the park. John Gherini noted that by the 1980s, the now-feral herd had grown to more than thirty individuals and had become a nuisance. The Gherinis culled nearly half of them at that time. John Gherini presented these facts to Marla Daily in a letter strongly criticizing her for supporting the idea of the heritage herd. He suggested that SCIF would be discredited by Daily's misrepresentation of the truth.[63]

Nevertheless, Marla Daily's perspective on the East Santa Cruz Island horses proved popular and was picked up by the local press. Newspaper columnist John Krist wrote that "they are living genetic heirlooms, preserving in their DNA the lineage of the horses brought here in the 1860s to herd cattle."[64] He offered no evidence to support this assertion. John Gherini replied that most of these claims were unfounded. However, attorney James Nichols insisted that the alleged genetic uniqueness was substantiated by DNA studies done by geneticist Dr. Ann Bowling, from the University of California, Davis, who was hired by FHOA. On January 13, 1998, Judge Kim Wardlaw of the U.S. District Court in Los Angeles ruled in favor of the NPS in the suit brought by FHOA the previous year, "on the grounds that the agency had been concerned since 1983 that grazing animals, including horses, would threaten the restoration of native plants on the island." The FHOA appealed Judge Wardlaw's decision, and in March of 1998 the NPS was enjoined from removing the horses until the appeal could be decided. The corralled horses were ordered released for the time being.[65] Ultimately, the U.S. Court of Appeals affirmed the district court's decision on grounds that the horses were private property, not wild, as FHOA now claimed, and therefore were not subject to conditions of NEPA, which would have required compliance through an environmental impact statement with public consultation.[66] On September 11, 1998, the Ninth Circuit Court of Appeals ruled that the park could remove the horses, which now numbered sixteen after an additional four colts had been born.[67] It also barred Dr. Blumenshine from any further participation.

From September 23 through 25, all visitors were restricted from East Santa Cruz Island while the capture and removal of the horses took place. Rangers awakened one group of campers early in the morning and told them to leave the island. Though the campers complied, this unexpected eviction, which came without warning or prior notice, elicited an angry and well-publicized response. The park's public information officer explained that the unusual action was done to protect people from a possibly dangerous situation. But Superintendent Setnicka later admitted that he had ordered the eviction in order to protect his staff and contractors from public scrutiny, especially after it became known that one of the campers was a young photographer, Tippy McKinsey, who was planning to make a documentary film of the horse removal for advocates of the heritage herd.[68] This led critics to accuse the park of attempting to conceal abusive treatment of the horses. While attempting to document alleged injuries to substantiate this claim, McKinsey and activist Andre Barclay were later caught trespassing at a quarantine facility on the mainland where the horses were confined for inspection. The horses proved to have been well treated and were eventually moved to a permanent home at Wild Horse Sanctuary in northern California.[69]

OTHER EXOTIC SPECIES ON SANTA CRUZ ISLAND

The removal of exotic livestock had its expected consequences. One was the explosive growth of some exotic plant populations such as fennel (*Foeniculum vulgare*). Fennel is a perennial herb that grows from a bulbous root to a height of five or six feet. It has a distinctive licorice odor and was originally imported from the Mediterranean region of southern Europe for culinary purposes. It has been present as a naturalized species on Santa Cruz Island since the late nineteenth century, when it may have been introduced with livestock brought over from the mainland.[70] As long as livestock were common, the fennel population was kept in check by their grazing, and mature plants remained relatively incidental in distribution and stand size. But as the livestock cropped the fennel and suppressed propagules, they also spread its seeds widely across the landscape and even helped to till them into the soil with their hooves. The effects of this activity did not become apparent until after the livestock were removed, first with the sheep that were eliminated between 1981 and 1987 on TNC's land, and then when approximately 1,500 cattle were removed from the same lands in 1988. At first there was little change in the fennel population, but in 1991, after substantial rains ended a five-year drought, the fennel began to grow at a rate far exceeding anyone's worst fears. Within only a couple of years, it increased its range to dominate approximately ten percent of the island. Mature plants formed nearly complete coverage over broad areas, growing so luxuriously and densely that a person could not easily walk through the infested zone.[71] The removal of the Gherini sheep from East Santa Cruz Island a few years later increased the scope of the problem. The faster-growing exotics suppressed or outcompeted native vegetation that had not yet recovered from years of overgrazing.

Some biologists criticized TNC for not doing enough to address the fennel problem and the related problem of feral pig population growth, which was also surging after the return of normal rainfall patterns.[72] The critics pointed out that there were five full-time TNC employees on Santa Cruz Island, but only one, ecologist Rob Klinger, worked directly for resource management. The others often spent their time maintaining the ranch facilities and hosting private donors at the Main Ranch in the Central Valley. Given the magnitude of the challenges TNC faced, these criticisms were not entirely justified. For one thing, little was known at that time about the growing cycle and effective treatment methodology for fennel, despite the plant's long association with humans as a culturally significant plant. The Santa Cruz Island Preserve became a laboratory for primary research on these questions. Rob Klinger established numerous enclosures in the Central Valley where visiting scientists studied fennel under controlled conditions and conducted experiments to learn how to effectively manage fennel populations and, if possible, to eradicate them.

Early research suggested that standard applications of glyphosate herbicides yielded limited results and concluded that the most effective treatment was digging the plants out of the ground. But this was hardly practical, given that the taproot could extend as much as ten feet into soil that, for much of the year, was as dry and hard as rock. Moreover, this treatment would have to be carried out over more than 3,000 acres of rugged landscape where fennel had become the dominant species. Eventually, Klinger opted for a strategy that combined both fire and herbicides. One of the factors that had inhibited the success of herbicide in early trials was the bulk of mature, above-ground biomass. Prescribed burns eliminated the majority of this material, allowing new, metabolically active growth to emerge in the cleared space where it could be sprayed more effectively with herbicides. Fire had the additional benefit of stimulating seed germination, forcing most of the accumulated seed bank to sprout all at once and be treated immediately. Otherwise, seed germination could be staggered intermittently over as much as seven years. TNC planned to implement this methodology on a large scale beginning in the Autumn of 1997, while the Park Service planned similar applications within its own boundaries. By that time, however, the island fox population was suffering a major collapse, and plans for treating the fennel were temporarily suspended out of concern that the foxes depended on the dense plant cover to escape predation by golden eagles. Another worry was the possibility of burning the foxes themselves when the fennel stands ignited.

Fennel was not the only invasive exotic plant on Santa Cruz Island. By the early 1990s, botanists had counted 154 invasive or potentially invasive species on the island along with approximately 480 native plant species.[73] Many of these exotics posed a threat to native diversity and habitat quality. Like fennel, many of these species were also encouraged by habitat modifications caused by exotic animals. The most obvious problem was rooting by pigs, which created ruderal soil conditions that favored species that had evolved with similar kinds of disturbance.[74]

One unexpected animal that assisted exotic plant invasion was the European honey bee (*Apis mellifera*). This species had been present on Santa Cruz Island for at least a century. Researchers comparing the habits of exotic honey bees with native bees discovered that the honey bee promotes the reproductive success of some introduced weeds. In one study, scientists found that the number of honey bees visiting the exotic yellow star thistle (*Centaurea solstitialis*) exceeded that of native bees by a ratio of thirty-three-to-one. The reverse was true with the native gumplant (*Grindelia camporum*), where native bee visits exceeded those by honey bees by a ratio of forty-six-to-one. Because plant reproduction depends on the activity of pollinators like bees, the scientists concluded that the honey bees' preference for yellow star thistle would increase the fecundity of this already aggressive invader. This gave it a competitive advantage over native species that were unaffected by the presence of the European honey bees.[75]

In a related study, researchers were able to derive more subtle conclusions. They found that the European honey bee exerted its greatest influence on exotic vegetation during periods of climatic stress. Honey bees store extensive quantities of food resources (honey on the comb) whereas most native bees do not. This enables them to remain active all year long and even to thrive during periods of environmental adversity, such as drought. While honey bees might prefer exotic plant species under normal conditions, under adverse conditions the researchers speculated that they would prefer native plants. This is because the native plant species are better adapted to California's extreme climatic variations and remain comparatively vigorous during a drought, while exotic plants, which are ill adapted to these events, do not. During these periods of relative stress, the exotic bees compete directly with native bees, threatening the survival of the latter. If this finding is combined with the results of the previous study that demonstrated a preferential advantage for exotic plant species during times of resource abundance, the net effect clearly favors exotic generalists like yellow star thistle over habitat specialists like the native gumplant.[76]

Convinced of the detrimental effects of the European honey bee on native habitat, University of California, Santa Barbara scientist Adrian Wenner, who had been involved in both research studies, decided to attempt the eradication of this exotic insect. At that time, the European honey bee was found only on Santa Cruz Island, though the threat of its potential migration to nearby Santa Rosa Island was a concern. Wenner admitted that his decision to eradicate the honey bee from Santa Cruz Island was connected to his learning of the recent crossover of the parasitic mite (*Varroa jacobsoni*) from the Asian honey bee (*Apis cerana*) to the European species. This evolution had already exterminated several domestic colonies in Florida and Wisconsin. Wenner realized that the mite could be used to eliminate similarly isolated populations, such as those on Santa Cruz Island. Rationalizing his idea on "the inevitability of invasion of Santa Cruz Island by varroa mites," Wenner "pre-empted that eventuality with a deliberate use of those mites as a biological control agent against the European honey bee, in line with our original goal to eliminate those exotic bees from the island."[77] The strategy proved successful, and by 1998, after eleven years of laborious field work, he eradicated the European bee from Santa Cruz Island. The project was too obscure to attract much public notice. During the final year, however, an apiary magazine learned of the project and included the following comment, made by two contributing biologists: "Such a program [to return the island to its natural state by eliminating introduced species such as the European honey bee] is ridiculous if not impossible. It is believed that Santa Cruz Island now contains the ONLY pure STRAIN of THIS BEE RACE in the world."[78] Apparently, the authors believed that mainland bees had hybridized subsequent to their introduction on Santa Cruz Island and were no longer pure strains, though what they meant by "pure" remains ambiguous. A similar argument had already been proposed by the FHOA in defense of the heritage herd, so the logic seemed to follow a pattern. As it happens, the writers' complaint fell on deaf ears, and nothing more came of the issue. As of December 2019, there are no exotic bees on any of the Northern Channel Islands.

THE LAST LAND ADDITION

Once the National Park Service gained possession of East Santa Cruz Island, it worked out a cooperative agreement with TNC that benefitted both. The conservancy donated to the Park Service 14 percent of the island stretching from the Montañon to Prisoners Harbor on November 2, 1999. The area, known as the "Isthmus," meant the NPS would now manage nearly a quarter of the island. This action angered some locals and members of the Santa Cruz Island Foundation, but TNC secured a number of concessions that dramatically eased its operations and costs. Principal among these was the transfer of the Prisoners Harbor Pier to the NPS. The pier provided the primary access to TNC's portion of the island and was used by them, their visitors, and the University of California's field station, as well as visitors coming with Island Packers. Historically, the U.S. Navy had been responsible for maintaining the pier, but it ignored the task as the structure deteriorated. By the time the NPS assumed ownership, it was no longer safe. Park officials contracted with Meek Construction to build a new pier for just under $500,000.[79]

Other benefits of the land transfer included an immediate NPS survey of the natural and cultural resources; NPS transportation of TNC staff, equipment, and supplies to the island and removal of trash to the mainland on park boats; NPS assumption of wildland fire management on the island that would include basing an engine at the Main Ranch;

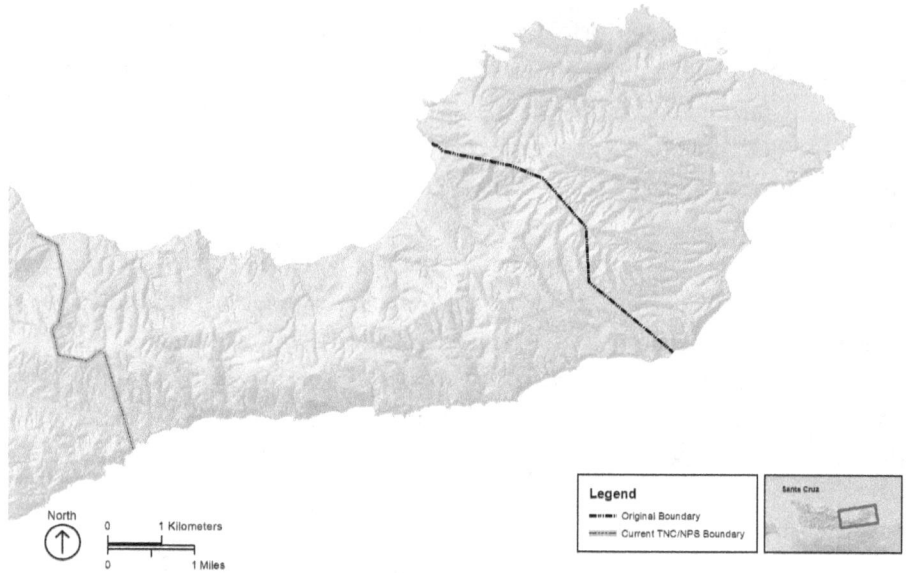

Map 15. The Nature Conservancy donated the Isthmus portion of Santa Cruz Island, 14 percent of the land, to the National Park Service in August 2000. Cartography by R. Rudolph, CINP.

development of fencing, signage, and interpretation to prevent visitors from accessing TNC property without a permit from that organization; assistance in maintaining roads and an airstrip on TNC land; and storage of conservancy supplies at the park headquarters in Ventura. The NPS officially took possession of the Isthmus on August 22, 2000, and opened it to the public.[80]

Two stipulations in the agreement required the NPS to design a plan for pig eradication and removal of fennel from the isthmus. TNC had already begun efforts there as well as on other parts of its holdings. On February 5, 2002, a third agreement committed both organizations to protecting the island fox. It promised to allow park biologists to capture foxes on TNC property and place them in protective cages near the Main Ranch. Critically beneficial for natural resource management, TNC agreed to provide advance funds for these operations should the NPS be unable to secure an immediate appropriation. This financial procedure later facilitated the effort to eliminate pigs on the island.[81]

Restoring Nature   9

The main story of Channel Islands National Park is restoration ecology. Exotic species have been recognized as a threat to island environments since the earliest days of the monument.[1] Excessive grazing by livestock, the trampling of soil by herds of ungulates at water sources, and rooting by feral pigs all created conditions to which many Eurasian weeds had adapted over millennia of coevolution with similar types of disturbance in their native environments. The same coevolution had not occurred on the California islands, where no ungulates existed after the endemic dwarf mammoth died out approximately twelve thousand years ago. As the National Park Service (NPS) evolved to emphasize science in its management policies, elimination of nonnative species became a priority. This is particularly so if man-made conditions threaten native species. Public resistance to the eradication of some exotics has become emotional and political. Yet, the agency follows a logic expressed by biologists around the world. Citing R. B. Primack's *Essentials of Conservation Biology*, Mark Rauzon writes:

> In the hierarchy of conservation, there are four levels of consideration: (1) survival of the species, (2) survival of the habitat of the species, (3) survival of the habitat crucial to a community of species, and (4) survival of an ecological unit critical to the evolutionary process. We hoped to operate at all levels, saving species with few available habitats over the vast Pacific. Some might say we were picking one species over another. Guilty as charged. Speciesism, as defined by *Merriam-Webster's Dictionary*, is prejudice or discrim-

ination based on a species; it is a human projection of values, the favorite son philosophy, and while lamentable, choices that favor the rarest with the greatest need must be made whenever possible.[2]

The Rats of Anacapa Island

The profound consequences of allowing these invasive exotic species to persist in the vulnerable island environments became increasingly clear as populations of native species began to perish.[3] Lowell Sumner provided the earliest documented account of exotic black rats (*Rattus rattus*) in 1939.[4] Domestic cats kept the rat population low, but they also preyed on the native deer mice (*Peromyscus maniculatus*). The latter were gone from East Anacapa Islet by 1979.[5] The cats did not survive, but the rats did, and over the years they became a significant nuisance. In response, the park's first chief of resources, Frank Ugolini, began control efforts by using snap traps and bait stations in 1983.[6] This was effective on top of the island, where administrative facilities and visitor use areas were developed, but did not eliminate them from cliffsides where several species of seabirds nested.

Eight species of nesting seabirds resided on Anacapa as of 2000.[7] The U.S. Fish and Wildlife Service (USFWS) listed one of these, the California brown pelican (*Pelicanus occidentalis*), under the Endangered Species Act (ESA). Both the USFWS and the California Department of Fish and Game (CDFG) listed the Scripps's murrelet (*Synthliboramphorus scrippsi*). It is one of the rarest seabirds, with a global population numbering between ten thousand and twenty thousand.[8] These elusive birds spend most of their life at sea, coming to land only to breed. They nest in as few as ten locations, all within the islands of Southern California and northern Mexico. Like the murrelet, the nesting population of brown pelicans is limited to the same islands. Both species are especially vulnerable because they are concentrated in small geographical areas during the breeding season.

Apart from the threat posed by an oil spill or industrial pollutants, the most serious impacts on these seabird populations were predation by cats and rats.[9] On Santa Barbara Island, feral cats reduced the nesting population of murrelets to zero by 1958. Following the eradication of the cats on Santa Barbara by 1978, the murrelets returned. Within ten years, their breeding population numbered approximately 1,500. On Anacapa attention focused on rats, since it was estimated that at least half of all murrelet nests were being destroyed by the rodents every year. Frank Ugolini's rat management program did not significantly decrease the predation, so Kate Faulkner, who replaced Ugolini in 1990, halted it. She realized that the rats would have to be exterminated.[10]

Several years after arriving at Channel Islands, Faulkner met Dr. Bernie Tershy, who was a specialist in the ecology and conservation of seabirds in Pacific Island ecosystems and was familiar with the threats posed by introduced predators. He had already participated in successful treatment programs in New Zealand and other countries. He told Faulkner that the eradication of rats from Anacapa Island was feasible. Working with Tershy's organization, Island Conservation and Ecology Group (ICEG), Faulkner developed a proposal for a study to gather data for a treatment plan that would completely eliminate the rats. Faulkner proposed an eradication program using Tershy's methodology to the Park Service's Natural Resources Advisory Committee on which NPS science advisor David Graber participated. Faulkner reported that in the process of dividing money for natural resource projects the fate of her proposal looked dim until Graber stated, "I think it's worth finding out if they can do it or not." The respect the others had for him swayed everyone at the table and the money came to the park.[11]

With NPS support for the proposal, Faulkner began working with ICEG and Gregg Howald, who had done rat eradication projects in Canada.[12] With his help, they started the field studies of all aspects of Anacapa's ecology that could be affected significantly by the eradication of rats. The NPS provided the money for the feasibility study. But the actual implementation of a meaningful project required significantly more funds. Fortuitously, these became available as a result of the *American Trader* settlement. The *American Trader* was an oil tanker owned by BP that had run over its anchor on February 17, 1990, off Huntington Beach, California. The resulting hull puncture released 416,598 gallons of crude oil and killed an estimated 3,400 seabirds. One result was the establishment of the American Trader Trustee Council (ATTC) to administer approximately $3 million in settlement funds.[13] The council was looking for restoration projects to mitigate injury to seabirds, because they had been directly harmed by the accident, and the Scripps's murrelet was specifically named in the mitigation proposal. That made Channel Islands an ideal location for restoration efforts because of its endemic population of this species. The ATTC accepted their proposal.

With the financial impediments overcome, the park next had to confront the practical challenges associated with implementation of the management plan itself. One problem was how to preserve the endemic island deer mice, which would be susceptible to any lethal treatment applied to the exotic black rats. During Ugolini's tenure, this challenge had been addressed mechanically, by placing poisoned bait within feeding stations that were accessible only to the black rats. They had to be entered through a vertical tube that could only be ascended by a mammal of sufficient size to press against both walls of the entrance pipe. The black rat was large enough to do this, but the island deer mouse was not.[14] This system worked tolerably well so long as the objective was management rather than eradication, but Faulkner could not realize her objectives through the same method. Dispersal of poisoned bait pellets across the island would work but would also kill the deer mice. The only apparent solution was to remove some deer mice prior to treatment, maintain them in a temporary holding facility, and return them to the island after the treatment was complete and the black rats were gone. Following the completion of an environmental impact statement (EIS) in October 2000, approximately one thousand deer mice, about half of the surviving population, were captured and held in cages in the Oil Building on East Anacapa, quickly dubbed the "Mouse House."[15]

The rat eradication plan consisted of two phases. In phase one, resource managers captured the mice on East Anacapa in October and November 2001. Resource managers distributed bait laced with the anticoagulant brodifacoum by helicopter along the plateau and later dispersed more by hand along the cliffs in order to ensure it covered the territory of every rat. They established a "buffer zone" on Middle Anacapa with rodenticide to prevent any rats from crossing to the eastern islet. After treatment of the islet, park officials released the mice during the following spring in order to maximize their chances of survival, because food resources were most abundant at this time. A year later, they carried out phase two, an identical sequence of steps, on the other islets. The timing of these applications was carefully planned, since rodent populations, both mice and rats, increase tremendously during the summer when food is abundant but suffer high mortality during the winter months when resources become scarce. They can lose as much as 75 percent of their population by the end of the winter. Biologists timed the treatment for the transition from summer to fall when populations remain high but food sources are rapidly declining. During this period of maximum resource stress, the rats were presumed to be most likely to take the bait, because they were beginning to starve.

After the treatments, intensive monitoring of the islands continued for another three years to make sure that no rats had survived. A single pregnant female could repopulate the islands in relatively little time, so it was crucial to ensure that the program's effect was thorough. Anything less than 100 percent effectiveness would constitute failure. Although the deer mice population remaining in the wild suffered massive mortality due to the poisonous bait, their population speedily recovered with the releases of the Mouse House inhabitants. The success of this program increased the overall resiliency of the species and demonstrated the restoration potential for native species and ecosystems. A 2010 survey of Scripps's murrelets on the island showed that hatching success had increased threefold to 85 percent.[16]

RESISTANCE AND RESULTS

From the perspective of resource managers at the park, the Anacapa Island rat eradication program was an unqualified success. Not only was the endemic deer mouse population protected and its historic range restored, but breeding populations of several threatened seabirds also were protected. The rats were not threatened as a species because they are widespread across much of the world. Nevertheless, animal rights advocates protested the park's treatment program, arguing that it constituted unjustifiable cruelty against the rats. Local animal rights activist Robert Puddicombe, a Santa Barbara bus driver and founder of the Channel Islands Animal Protection Association, undertook direct action in November of 2001. He and companion Robert Crawford traveled to East Anacapa Island in a small boat and surreptitiously scattered pellets of Vitamin K, an effective antidote to the anticoagulant that the park was using to poison the rats. A witness informed park rangers who arrested the two men as they attempted to return to the mainland.

Puddicombe's actions brought the park's restoration program to the attention of other animal rights activists, and, within days of his arrest, the Fund for Animals joined Channel Islands Animal Protection Association in filing a lawsuit against the National Park Service.[17] The plaintiffs claimed that the Anacapa Island Restoration Plan violated the Migratory Bird Treaty Act because the application of brodifacoum could kill some of the migratory ground-nesting birds that used Anacapa Island. In fact, some mortalities did occur in spite of the park's best efforts to limit the negative effects of the rodenticide.

The USFWS was a major supporter of the rat eradication project and were represented on the trustee board that funded the project. The agency initially had resisted giving the NPS the permit because they said it was not necessary and would establish a precedent that an unintentional take *required* a permit. Nevertheless, at the urging of the NPS, it issued one anyway and argued that the long-term benefits of the restoration plan outweighed its short-term negative impacts. After the agency issued its decision, the plaintiffs modified their suit to include the USFWS claiming that it violated the National Environmental Policy Act (NEPA) and the California Environmental Quality Act (CEQA) by issuing the permits to the NPS without due procedural compliance. The litigation delayed the program until the beginning of December 2001, when winter rains had begun and food resources on the island were beginning to rally. This threatened to reduce the efficacy of the poisoned bait by giving the rats an alternative source of sustenance.[18]

Court briefings concluded on November 26, and a hearing was held the following day. To the relief of the defendants, the court quickly denied the plaintiffs' initial claim that the USFWS had been in violation of law when it issued the NPS an incidental take permit. Judge Ellen Segal Huvelle concluded that the injunction sought by the plaintiffs would be detrimental to the public interest by endangering the existence of murrelets and other ground-nesting birds and wasting close to half a million dollars in *American Trader* funds. She also dismissed the related charge that Channel Islands National Park was violating the NPS Organic Act by implementing a treatment program that would adversely affect nontarget species, a consequence the plaintiffs claimed had not been adequately addressed by the defendant. Judge Huvelle observed that the plaintiffs' narrow interpretation of NPS management policies on this matter would prevent control of any pest species in the parks at all. She agreed with the federal agencies that the treatment program would have a long-term benefit for nontarget native species, even though it might adversely affect some individual animals in the short term.[19] As to the plaintiffs' allegation that the park had not adequately addressed the consequences of its plan, she pointed to the exhaustive work represented by the final EIS, which park resource managers had prepared and wrote, "Unlike many environmental impact statements that have been successfully challenged, the Park Service's EIS is a thoughtful, detailed document." On November 29, 2001, Judge Huvelle denied all of the plaintiffs' claims, including their request for an injunction to delay implementation of the Anacapa Island Restoration Plan.[20]

Robert Puddicombe and Robert Crawford were charged with a violation of federal law for attempting to feed wildlife and interfering with a National Park Service program. Crawford pled guilty to the charges and was sentenced to two years of probation, fined $200, and instructed to keep off the Channel Islands for two years. Puddicombe opted to plead not guilty and be tried by a judge. His trial occurred almost two years after the event, on July 10, 2003. He faced a potential penalty of a year in jail. The eyewitness testified that there were two individuals on Anacapa Island. He saw one person spreading pellets from a distance; he never saw both people spreading at the same time. Because Crawford had already pled guilty and there wasn't proof beyond a reasonable doubt that more than one person spread the bait, Puddicombe was found not guilty. Celebrating his acquittal, he commented, "As far as I'm concerned, this is like ethnic cleansing; it's a jihad against nonnative species."[21]

A portion of the *American Trader* funds the park had received were devoted to organizing a Scripps's Murrelet Monitoring Team in order to inventory baseline data on the bird's population size and breeding success prior to treatment of the rats and to monitor post-treatment conditions.[22] Following the eradication of the rats in 2002, the team recorded murrelet nesting attempts increased by 42 percent. Hatching success increased from 42 percent to 96 percent by 2005. By 2014 scientists estimated that the murrelet population on Anacapa had increased nearly 150 percent, from 450–600 breeding birds in 2001–3 to between 1,100 and 1,450 breeding birds in 2014. Early nests had all been located in sea caves while some new nests were on exposed cliffs or rocks outside of sea caves, suggesting that the birds felt less threatened and were able to colonize more open areas. Although growth in the murrelet population was slow, owing to the bird's natural reproductive habits, researchers estimated that sufficient nesting habitat existed on Anacapa Island to potentially support thousands of nesting pairs.[23] In 2003, seabird biologist Darrell Whitworth discovered two Cassin's auklet (*Ptychoramphus aleuticus*) nests on West Anacapa Island. Both nests successfully fledged at least one chick. This was the first time in more than seventy years that a Cassin's auklet had been known to nest on Anacapa Island. It had taken less than two years from the eradication of black rats for these birds to begin coming back.[24] He and other scientists were optimistic that nesting populations of pigeon guillemots and ashy storm-petrels would also become established or expand on Anacapa Island.[25]

The Pigs of Santa Rosa Island

The eradication of black rats on Anacapa Island was not the first exotic species program that Kate Faulkner managed after becoming chief of resources. As she entered duty in early 1990, the park had just received funding for the eradication of feral pigs from Santa Rosa Island. The Vails always considered the animals a nuisance and regularly hunted them to keep down the population. They claimed that the hogs ate the cattle's molasses blocks and dug up valuable soil, which caused erosion, encouraged weeds, and reduced pasture productivity. In 1949, N. R. Vail introduced hog cholera, which initially resulted in about 80 percent mortality, but later proved less effective. He abandoned the experiment in the mid-1950s. Thereafter, hunting remained the only artificial control on the pig population, and ranch vaqueros shot the animals on sight. However, this pressure had less effect on the pigs than seasonal variations in food and water.[26]

When the NPS acquired the island in 1986, park resource managers quickly recognized the gravity of the impact caused by the pigs. Far more than just a nuisance, the animals threatened many endemic natural resources on the island. Park scientists Gary Davis and Bill Halvorson made the following assessment: "Severe damage to native species and plant communities from pig activity is apparent over the entire island. Pig rooting, combined with prevailing winds, greatly accelerates soil erosion. This is most notable around the roots of endemic island oak. . . . Other signs of pig activity abound on the island, particularly rooting in search of native bulbs, tubers, and invertebrates in softer soils. Pigs also compete with native foxes for food, prey on native ground nesting birds, amphibians, and reptiles, and destroy herpetofaunal habitat."[27] In addition to impacts on natural resources, park officials also expressed concern over damage to archeological sites. Archaeologist Don Morris estimated that 90 percent were being adversely affected.

In August 1987 the park hosted a workshop to develop a treatment plan for Santa Rosa Island that brought land managers with experience in pig eradication from Hawaii and other parts of California. The proposal acquired greater urgency over the next few years in response to a drought that reduced the pig population from an estimated four thousand to fewer than two thousand. The remaining pigs were under stress as their food resources diminished, making this an ideal time to implement the proposed eradication program. By the end of the decade, the drought had persisted for three years and was not expected to last much longer, so it was imperative that action be taken quickly. Park scientists Davis and Halvorson prepared an environmental assessment with a Finding of No Significant Impact (FONSI) and a final treatment plan that was formally approved.[28]

The park then hired wildlife biologist Carmen Lombardo to survey the island and assess the size, distribution, and habits of the pig population. Lombardo divided the island into seven management zones, corresponding to natural features and existing cattle fencing. He then made aerial censuses over several weeks in January 1991 and supplemented them later with transect surveys of each zone. Based on these efforts, he estimated that the feral pig population numbered about 1,400. Park officials determined that eradication efforts could be implemented island wide, rather than first isolating each zone with fences and proceeding sequentially. Park advisors felt that with the pigs at low numbers and very hungry, hunters had a slightly better than even chance of being successful without fencing. Because fencing was estimated to cost $1 million, proceeding without it was the only option in the short term.

Wayne Long of Multiple Use Management (MUM), the same company that managed elk and deer hunts on Santa Rosa Island, secured the contract for $310,000.[29] Implementation of the actual treatment began on March 6, 1991. Over the next eleven months, MUM, park staff, and ranch hands killed a total of 1,175 pigs using a variety of methods, ranging from aerial gunning from helicopters to systematic ground hunts. No pig sign was detected after March 1993, and the population was presumed to be eliminated. The entire program had cost $780,000 over a period of three years.[30]

In April 1991, Superintendent Mack Shaver hosted a group of regional NPS scientists led by Associate Director for Natural Resources Dennis B. Fenn from the Washington DC, office, a soil scientist by training who knew a great deal about the challenges of soil erosion and restoration. The scientists were particularly impressed by the seriousness of the erosion problem resulting from overgrazing by introduced livestock and pigs.[31] Later that same month, the park hosted another site visit to Santa Rosa Island for members of the public, including many animal rights activists who were critical of the pig eradication program. The activists believed that the park's treatment program was both cruel and unnecessary, because they did not believe the pigs posed any serious threat to the island environment. If anything was to be done at all, the animal rights activists preferred that the Park Service use a nonlethal solution. They suggested capturing the pigs and transporting them off the island, neutering them, or restricting them with fences to a single "sacrificial" zone within the island itself. These proposals were not practical. The first had been considered but the U.S. Department of Agriculture opposed it, fearing that the pigs carried a contagious herpes virus that might be introduced to the mainland. Neutering and fencing were both too expensive, requiring expenditures that would continue indefinitely, and neither method was considered reliable. Later, Kate Faulkner recalled, "We were able to show the press significant damage by pigs. The press turned to the animal rights folks and said 'you know, the NPS does have a problem here. How do you propose to solve it?' The animal rights people had a lot of 'solutions' that would clearly not work (like fence off half the island and give that to the pigs and restore the other half). So, the animal rights people lost credibility in the eyes of the press."[32]

By this time, active elimination of the feral pigs was already underway, and the park continued with its original plan. Surprisingly, the animal rights community limited itself to these few public statements and made no formal protests. This relative silence contrasted markedly with their response to nearly every subsequent effort by the government to remove or eliminate exotic species from the Channel Islands.[33]

The Story of the Island Fox

Up to this time, key programs in the park's natural resource management had focused on the eradication of invasive exotic species, such as black rats and feral pigs. There had been little need to actively protect or restore native species, since these were generally able to recover on their own once the stress from exotic species was removed. This changed dramatically in the early 1990's when populations of the endemic island fox began plummeting on the three largest Northern Channel Islands. Although the immediate cause of this crisis would be linked to a mainland intruder preying on another exotic animal, management efforts had to focus first on protecting the foxes in order to preserve the species from almost certain extinction before anything could be done to remove the animals that threatened it. Moreover, removal proved to be far more complex in this case than it had been with black rats and feral pigs because this introduction was not directly anthropogenic. It was only one part of a long cascade of ecologically related events in which humans had played a crucial role but were no longer the principal agents. The story of the island fox illustrates the complexity of ecological relationships.

Fig. 26. An island fox. CINP Digital Archives, "Cultural Resources," photograph ESCI 2012.

The Channel Islands fox (*Urocyon littoralis*) is a distant relative of the more common grey fox (*U. cinereoargenteus*) found on the California mainland. Only about a third of the size of the mainland species, the island fox is about the size of the average house cat. Island foxes are found on the six largest of the eight Channel Islands. They are not present on Anacapa or Santa Barbara Islands. Mammalian carnivores do not usually occur on islands, so the presence of the fox is unusual.[34] Each island population represents a distinct subspecies. Joseph Grinnell described this distinction as early as the 1930s on the basis of subtle morphological differences that he and other biologists noticed among the foxes from each island, such as the number of tail vertebrae and, hence, the length of the tail. As a result, each island population has been given a distinct taxonomy: *Urocyon littoralis littoralis* for San Miguel Island; *U. l. santarosae* for Santa Rosa; *U. l. santacruzae* for Santa Cruz; *U. l. dickeyi* for San Nicolas; *U. l. catalinae* for Santa Catalina; and *U. l. clementae* for San Clemente Island. Genetic testing has since confirmed this classification of the island fox into six distinct subspecies.[35]

Genetic research has also provided clues as to the origins and distribution of the island fox. It is descended from a single colonization by a small number of mainland grey fox that migrated to the composite island of Santarosae when sea levels were lower, some sixteen thousand years ago.[36] The channel between Santarosae and the mainland coast was also much narrower. As the sea level rose, separating the four vestigial islands, the foxes adapted to their specific environments while growing smaller in size. They also became habitat generalists in order to take advantage of the limited resources of the islands. Foxes feed on native mice and ground-nesting birds, insects such as grasshoppers and Jerusalem crickets, and the fruits and berries of a wide variety of native plants. They also have relatively low reproductive rates. The females tend not to breed until older, and typical litter size ranges from two to three pups. The foxes are generally monogamous and breed, at most, once every year. Their relatively conservative reproduction means that preservation of a healthy population is strongly dependent on the survival of adults, which was not a problem until recent times, since the foxes have no native predators on the islands.[37] This absence of predators also has resulted in some notable behavioral idiosyncrasies in the island foxes, the most obvious being their general lack of wariness. The island foxes appear docile and inquisitive, often showing little fear of humans. They also remain active during much of the day instead of being primarily nocturnal like their mainland cousins. Genetic evidence strongly suggests that the Chumash brought the island fox from their original home in the northern islands to Santa Catalina, San Clemente, and San Nicolas Islands.[38]

Lyndal Laughrin conducted the earliest formal studies of the island fox from 1973 to 1977 for his doctoral dissertation at the University of California, Santa Barbara (UCSB).[39] The NPS began monitoring the island fox in 1993 after hiring biologist Timothy Coonan to develop the program. Resource managers believed that they were vulnerable to the same maladies as domestic dogs, but because of their isolation from the mainland, island foxes lack the natural resistance that mainland canid species have developed. Park managers worried about the risk of accidental introduction of a canid disease through pet dogs brought over by visiting boaters or from ranch dogs on Santa Rosa Island. While this was not perceived to be an immediate threat, it raised enough concern to justify monitoring the foxes.

Cathy Schwemm began monitoring fox populations on San Miguel Island in 1993 as part of the park's inventory and monitoring (I&M) program. Schwemm tagged captured foxes to facilitate identification and to distinguish between those she had counted and those she had not. Resource managers estimated the population density of the entire island by extrapolating from the numbers recorded in each area. This first census conducted on San Miguel Island resulted in an estimate of approximately 450 animals, considered a healthy population at or near the carrying capacity of the island.[40]

Also in 1993, Gary Roemer, a doctoral student at the University of California, Los Angeles, began researching the island fox population on Santa Cruz Island. He estimated just over 1,300 animals and opined that, as in the case of San Miguel Island, this was near the carrying capacity for the island.[41] He proposed doing research on Santa Rosa Island, but the Vails objected to his methods. They believed that trapping and tagging were inappropriate or cruel treatment of the island foxes. They also expressed concern that the scientists might introduce diseases by having so much contact with the animals.[42] The NPS owned Santa Rosa Island by this time. Superintendent Mack Shaver was in the midst of negotiations for a new special use permit and was not interested in pressing the issue. There seemed to be no compelling reason to risk exacerbating the park's difficult relationship with the Vails.

By 1994 researchers on Santa Cruz Island began to notice a sharp decline in the fox population. A year later, researchers monitored the foxes on San Miguel Island where the population fell alarmingly from an estimated 450 to about 40 over the next four years. The situation on Santa Cruz Island was less dramatic but still grave, and Gary Roemer quickly adjusted the focus of his research to address the new crisis. Although managers lacked baseline inventories for Santa Rosa Island, they suspected that the island fox population was declining there as well. Their fears proved correct when only fourteen surviving animals were found on the island at the beginning of the captive breeding program in 2000.[43] At the time, the only good fortune appeared to be that monitoring had begun prior to the beginning of the crisis. This alerted resource managers that the foxes were in trouble and provided them with precrisis baseline data that allowed them to make comparative assessments of the situation as the crisis developed. The value of this information was augmented by the fact that two precrisis data sets were available, one from the 1970s and another from the early 1990s. Because the island fox population had remained relatively stable over the intervening twenty-year period, it was possible to confirm that the crisis began in 1994 and not earlier.

At first the cause of the sudden decline in the park's fox population was unknown, and park resource managers suspected disease. Biologist Tim Coonan thought this could have been introduced by pet dogs that boaters had brought over. But he soon dismissed disease as the ultimate source of the crisis because only a few deaths could be attributed to it. Another potential factor that resource managers considered was malnutrition due to declining availability of food. They dismissed that idea after monitoring showed that most of the foxes had good body weight and obviously suffered from no shortage of resources. Managers also did studies on the food sources of the island foxes, such as the native deer mouse, but found that the rodents' population was not only healthy but actually increasing as the fox population declined.[44]

Scientists also suspected predation by avian raptors such as golden eagles or red-tailed hawks. They knew this was occurring, but few at that time believed predation alone could be responsible for such a rapid decline, though many thought it might be a contributing factor. Since further research was needed, the park applied for and received a $50,000 grant from Canon U.S.A. to initiate a more robust monitoring program. Using this money, resource managers were able to fit eight San Miguel Island foxes with radio collars in late 1998.[45] These collars were equipped with mortality sensors that broadcast an alarm if the fox ceased moving for a prescribed period of time. These allowed researchers to recover the fox carcasses as quickly as possible after death occurred in order to determine the cause of death more easily. Within several weeks of release, all but one of the radio-collared foxes were dead. Five of the seven carcasses showed unmistakable evidence of predation by a large raptor. Moreover, eagle feathers were discovered at two of the mortality sites on San Miguel

Island. Identification of the golden eagle (*Aquila chrysaetos*) as the source of the population decline seemed increasingly plausible.[46]

The relationship between golden eagle predation and the island fox crisis was largely confirmed the following year when scientists investigated an eagle's nest they located at Coche Point on Santa Cruz Island. They determined that it had been active since 1997 and that foxes represented a portion of the eagles' diet in addition to other small mammals, especially feral piglets. This discovery and similar subsequent finds allowed the researchers to begin piecing together the various parts of the complex story of the island fox and its decline. Gary Roemer proposed a "hyperpredation" model to interpret the evidence that had been collected up to that time. According to this model, the island foxes were not the primary target of eagle predation because they were neither sufficiently numerous nor fecund enough to attract and sustain a resident colony of golden eagles. Feral pigs (*Sus scrofa*), however, were. These exotic animals were remarkably fertile, able to produce up to three litters a year. Although mature pigs were too large and aggressive to be hunted by the golden eagles, the young piglets represented ideal prey, while the fecundity of the species allowed the local population to sustain considerable predation without serious impact on the population. The feral pig was, in short, the principal target of the golden eagle and the reason this otherwise alien raptor was able to colonize the Northern Channel Islands. The collapse of the island fox, according to Roemer's hyperpredation model, was simply an indirect consequence of a chain of events that had little to do with the fox itself.

Further investigation of golden eagle nest contents corroborated Roemer's model. Biologist Brian Latta of the Santa Cruz Predatory Bird Research Group began formal research in 2004 on golden eagle diet in the Northern Channel Islands. His work showed that piglets constituted approximately 60 percent of the nest detritus on Santa Cruz Island. On Santa Rosa, interestingly, Latta found that mule deer fawns constituted the largest percentage of detritus, totaling approximately 40 percent.[47] By the time of his investigation, feral pigs had been eradicated from the island, but deer and elk were common. Elk calves are too large for the eagles to hunt, but deer fawns are not. They represented Santa Rosa's analog for the Santa Cruz Island piglet. The lower natural fecundity of mule deer relative to the pig suggests that deer alone might not have been able to sustain the golden eagle, but the pig population on Santa Cruz Island, which persisted until 2006, was able to subsidize populations of golden eagles that nested on both Santa Rosa and Santa Cruz Islands. According to Roemer, the golden eagles were sustained by these relatively stable populations of exotic mammals and were thereby enabled to prey opportunistically on the island fox as well.[48]

RESPONSES TO THE CRISIS

As park resource managers began to appreciate the gravity of the threat to the island foxes, they drew wider attention to the problem and solicited help from professionals outside the park. Early in 1999, NPS managers organized a group of experts to evaluate the current status of the island fox and recommend appropriate recovery actions. This group became known as the Island Fox Conservation Working Group and comprised "a loose affiliation of public agency representatives, landowners, conservancies, zoological institutions, non-profits and academics."[49] The first meeting of the working group convened in Ventura on April 21 and 22 of that year and drew fourteen members. The participants were shocked by the urgency of the crisis. Many believed that the foxes were in imminent danger of going extinct if strong measures were not taken immediately. A few, such as Katherine Ralls of the Smithsonian Institution, thought it was already too late and castigated the Park Service for not acting sooner. Park biologist Tim Coonan responded that funding for fox research had been difficult to obtain, in part because the foxes were not yet listed under the Endangered Species Act, but clearly it was too late to be assigning blame.[50] The group eventually agreed to two strategies: protect the remaining foxes from further harm and remove the source of the threat.[51]

Both strategies needed more knowledge. Protecting the survivors, which by this time had diminished to as few as fifteen individuals on San Miguel and Santa Rosa Islands, would require raising the animals in a captive breeding program, where it was hoped their population could be increased to sustainable numbers. However, this had never been done with island foxes, and husbandry protocols would have to be developed from scratch. Removing the threat to the native fox populations was equally important for the animals' long-term survival, since the captured foxes would not be able to return to the wild until the conditions that precipitated the crisis were no longer present. But these conditions themselves were still not fully understood. Not until the underlying reasons for the arrival of the golden eagles were fully understood could practical measures be taken to mitigate the problem.[52]

The captive breeding program was a strategy of last resort. It required bringing all members of the wild population into captivity and raising them under artificial conditions. At the very least, it offered some assurance that the species would survive even if it was no longer able to exist in its natural habitat or without active human support. The decision to implement any captive breeding program is made only when the alternative is likely to be extinction of the species or, in the case of the island fox, of at least three distinct subspecies. Scientists cited two precedents for the proposed island fox captive breeding program—the California condor (*Gymnogyps californianus*) and the peregrine falcon (*Falco peregrinus*). The latter already showed signs of recovery in the wild. Both of these programs had been undertaken with the assistance of zoos, but the idea of locating captive breeding colonies of island foxes within existing mainland facilities, though compelling for its logistical advantages, was quickly rejected. The island foxes evolved within an isolated environment where few diseases were present, and managers feared that the animals would not be able to tolerate exposure to mainland diseases that they would inevitably encounter in zoos. Instead, the working group decided to build separate captive breeding facilities on each of the islands where the program would be implemented, despite the logistical challenges of maintaining these facilities in such isolated locations.[53]

Impelled by the urgency of the crisis, the park staff set about constructing pens for the island foxes on San Miguel Island almost immediately after the first meeting of the Island Fox Group. Park officials set aside $31,000 for this purpose, while the National Parks and Conservation Association started a fundraising campaign to assist the effort.[54] Channel Islands also received a base funding increase of $477,000 in 2005 through the NPS Natural Resources Challenge.[55] Park resource managers developed the original design for the pens based on structures used to house wolves, the closest available analogy. The pens consisted of chain-link fencing in an ell shape with sides approximately six feet tall and roofs. Each pen contained a wooden kennel-like box for shelter and privacy.[56]

Resource managers brought the first pair of island foxes into captivity on San Miguel Island in May of 1999, only one month after the decision to implement the captive breeding program.[57] By January 2000, fourteen island foxes had been captured, four males and ten females. Only one very scrappy female remained in the wild. Later that year, the park initiated a captive breeding program on Santa Rosa Island. Workers built the pens there in February and March and capturing began immediately thereafter. By May of the following year, fourteen foxes were housed there. This proved to be the entire surviving population on Santa Rosa Island.[58] When the Island Fox Group met again in 2001, its members decided to initiate a captive breeding program on Santa Cruz Island as well. At least four golden eagles were still present on the island and the wild fox population continued to decline. Despite ongoing losses to predation, however, island fox numbers on Santa Cruz Island remained higher than on Santa Rosa or San Miguel, totaling about fifty or sixty at this time. As a result, managers elected to hedge their bets and bring only a portion of the population into captivity. Ten pairs were captured by the end of the following year, and the remainder were left in the wild.[59]

The Santa Cruz Island program was managed cooperatively between NPS staff and the Nature Conservancy (TNC). The latter contracted this work out to the Institute for Wildlife Studies, a nonprofit organization that already had experience working with the island foxes on Santa Catalina Island.[60] Researchers believed that the lower population decline on Santa Cruz Island was due to the island having a denser vegetative cover than San Miguel or Santa Rosa had. This offered better protection from aerial predation.

The park completed the first captive breeding facility on Santa Cruz Island in 2002 and built a second facility in 2004. These new pens benefitted from the experience gained on San Miguel and Santa Rosa Islands. Workers separated the pens from one another and augmented their relative isolation with screening vegetation, which provided a degree of privacy for each breeding pair.[61] Another problem the new pens tried

Fig. 27. Island fox enclosures at the Windmill Site on Santa Rosa Island. Securing the foxes in these cages was a last-ditch effort to save them from predation by golden eagles. Photographer and date unknown, CINP Digital Archives, "Cultural Resources."

to address was male aggression toward females and pups. This may have resulted, in some instances, from an inaccurate pairing of mates by the biologists and been exacerbated by the stress of captivity. The new pens contained additional privacy structures, providing females a place to retreat from an aggressive male. A final problem that proved to be something of a surprise was caused by wild foxes approaching the pens and instigating fights through the fencing material with the foxes inside. This became a significant problem after 2003, when captive foxes began to be released, and biologists had to encircle most of the facilities with a perimeter of electrified wire to keep the wild foxes away.[62]

DEALING WITH THE THREAT

A 1999 investigation of a nest at Coche Point on Santa Cruz Island proved that golden eagles had been breeding on the Northern Channel Islands at least since 1997. Researchers believed breeding actually may have begun a few years earlier.[63] This timing correlated with the decline of the fox population, which became noticeable only after 1994. Removal of these birds from the Northern Channel Islands was therefore among the highest priorities of the working group, second only to protecting the foxes themselves. In 1999 the Park Service established a cooperative agreement with the Santa Cruz Predatory Bird Research Group in order to accomplish this task. The Institute for Wildlife Studies later took over the capture and relocation efforts. Removal of the birds began later that year and continued through 2004, with a total of forty-one golden eagles live captured on the islands and transported to Northern California.[64] At least eight remained that eluded capture despite the ingenious methods attempted by their human pursuers. The ultimate success of this program depended on better understanding why the golden eagles came to the islands in the first place in order to encourage the remaining birds to leave and to prevent future recolonization.[65]

The golden eagle is a year-round resident of western North America, where it is found primarily in hilly or mountainous terrain. It typically feeds on small terrestrial mammals, such as squirrels and rabbits.[66] Although native to the California mainland, golden eagles were not usually found on the Channel Islands before the 1990s. The mainland population of golden eagles had been growing steadily since 1962, when Congress passed the Bald and Golden Eagle Protection Act. By the 1980s, golden eagle populations in California had recovered to the point where juveniles were beginning to compete for territory. At the same time, the Northern Channel Islands offered an appealing opportunity for the young golden eagles because of an abundant supply of food that was available with the prodigious populations of feral pigs on Santa Cruz Island.[67] Also, the territorial niche had been left vacant for them by the extirpation of the bald eagle (*Haliaeetus leucocephalus*).

The bald eagle used to be common throughout the Channel Islands. In the 1940s, Grinnell referred to the islands as one of two "breeding metropolises" in California, the other being the northeast corner of the state. Historical data suggest there were at least twenty-four breeding pairs nesting on the islands at the beginning of the twentieth century, with possibly as many as nine pairs on Santa Rosa Island alone.[68] Park managers believed that a reestablished population of bald eagles would effectively prevent colonization of the Northern Channel Islands by golden eagles because the former competes for territory with other avian raptors. The key to the problem is that the bald eagle feeds primarily on fish, only occasionally hunting a terrestrial species. In the past, the fox and the bald eagle coexisted with little conflict, because they rarely interacted. Prior to the introduction of nonnative ungulates on the islands there was not an adequate food supply to support golden eagles. The disappearance of the bald eagles on the islands left a void and a plentiful food source for the golden eagles to move into the territory. The last confirmed bald eagle nest on the Channel Islands was reported in 1949.[69]

ORGANOCHLORINES AND CHRONIC ENVIRONMENTAL TOXICITY

The reason for this population collapse was a complex chain reaction caused by a group of organochlorine chemicals known as DDT and PCBs, both of which were produced in massive quantities in Southern California. The use of DDT against malaria-carrying mosquitoes proved extremely effective. By the beginning of 1960s, U.S. annual production of DDT reached eighty-five thousand tons.[70] Nevertheless, scientists and government resource managers were aware by the late 1940's that this pesticide might have undesirable effects. Subsequent research showed that egg shells thinned by as much as 19 percent among birds exposed to the pesticide, which caused failure during brooding because the parent crushed the more fragile egg. DDT and related organochlorines concentrate within species at the top of an ecosystem's trophic cycle.[71]

On July 9, 1970, congress established the Environmental Protection Agency (EPA) and the National Oceanic and Atmospheric Administration (NOAA), agencies that reflected a more ecology-based understanding of the environment.[72] Among the EPA's first actions after it became operational in early 1971 was to initiate cancelation proceedings against all DDT products and uses. This was a response to litigation brought against the EPA's federal predecessors by the Environmental Defense Fund, a nonprofit organization that had been recently established by a group of New York scientists specifically to challenge DDT use.[73] The EPA held hearings between August 1971 and March 1972. Registrants representing both industry and agriculture challenged fifteen of the canceled uses, mostly pertaining to agricultural applications.[74]

Among the witnesses called by the Environmental Defense Fund to challenge DDT during the EPA hearings was Dr. Robert W. Risebrough who had conducted research on the nesting colony of brown pelicans at Anacapa Island over the previous decade. He had estimated, as recently as 1964, that up to one thousand nests had produced successful fledglings. In 1969 he counted 298 nests on Anacapa Island but found only twelve eggs intact. A week later, all of those were crushed. The following year, Risebrough and his colleagues observed five hundred nests but only one successful fledgling. Examination of the failed nests revealed that the eggs with abnormally thin shells caused by DDT had been crushed.[75] Such detailed and conclusive evidence of the widespread impact of organochlorines convinced EPA director William Ruckelshaus to formally suspend DDT registration in the United States on December 31, 1972.[76]

While the negative environmental effect of DDT and related organochlorines was now well established, the reason why this effect appeared so highly pronounced in southern California had yet to be adequately explained. Between 1965 and 1966, a team of scientists led by Dr. Risebrough sampled anchovies from various locations off the coast of California. They found an average of 0.59 parts per million (ppm) DDT in San Francisco Bay, which drains California's vast Central Valley agricultural district, but 3.04 ppm off Port Hueneme near the Northern Channel Islands, and 14.0 ppm in San Pedro Bay near Los Angeles.[77] At the time of the EPA review in 1970, the Montrose Chemical Corporation was the sole U.S. manufacturer of the pesticide, producing more than twelve million pounds per year. Montrose had been dumping the chemical since at least 1953, when the Los Angeles County Sewer District issued a permit allowing the company to discharge its waste products through the county system.[78] During its thirty-five years of active production, Montrose is estimated to have discharged approximately 1,800 metric tons of DDT into the San Pedro Channel. In addition, between 350 and 700 metric tons of DDT were directly dumped from barges into the San Pedro Channel between 1947 and 1961. The sum of these discharges originating from a single manufacturer resulted in the Southern California Bight having the highest concentration of DDT of any marine ecosystem in the world.[79]

USA V. MONTROSE ET AL. (2001)

In 1980 Congress passed the Comprehensive Environmental Response, Compensation, and Liability Act, more commonly known as the Superfund Act. This act made industrial polluters liable for environmental damage caused by their activities, requiring them to assume financial responsibility for cleaning up hazardous waste or mitigating the damage caused by it.[80] On the basis of the Superfund Act, the United States and the state of California filed suit against Montrose Chemical Corporation, six other local private industries involved in the use or manufacture of organochlorines, the Los Angeles County Sanitation District, and more than 150 local government entities.[81]

The suit went to trial on October 17, 2000, and was settled in March of the following year. Settlement was achieved through a consent decree, whereby the defendants agreed to pay more than $140 million in damages. The portion allocated for restoration of natural resources was $63,950,000 and was to be administered by a group of Natural Resource Trustees, comprising both federal and state agencies with direct interests in the affected environment, including the NPS.[82] The court settlement defined the obligations and responsibilities of the Natural Resource Trustees in the following mandate: "The Trustees will use all damages to (1) reimburse past and future Damage Assessment Costs, and (2) restore, replace, or acquire the equivalent of the injured natural resources and/or the services provided by such resources. The Trustees will use the damages for restoration of injured natural resources, including bald eagles, peregrine falcons and other marine birds, fish and the habitats upon which they depend, as well as providing for implementation of restoration projects intended to compensate the public for lost use of natural resources."[83]

Examination of the hazardous waste deposits on the Palos Verdes Shelf convinced the court that cleanup would not be feasible and therefore damages would be addressed primarily through mitigation.[84] This decision had significant implications for the NPS, because it meant that fiscal resources that might have been exhausted by cleanup efforts within the southern Channel Islands were now available for restoration of resource values within the greater region. Channel Islands National Park represented one of the more desirable locations for mitigation efforts. The resources there were identical to those of the southern islands, but the greater distance from the immediate load of toxic waste on the Palos Verdes Shelf made it more likely that restoration efforts might succeed.

The trustees prepared a restoration plan in the fall of 2005 that identified four targets where restoration or mitigation efforts would be focused: the improvement of fisheries and associated habitat; the restoration of local bald eagle populations; the restoration of local peregrine falcon populations; and the restoration of local seabird populations.[85] The latter included brown pelicans, double-crested cormorants, Cassin's auklets, and Scripps's murrelets. The majority of settlement resources were devoted to fishery improvement and amounted to approximately $12 million. This money was divided between physical restoration of habitat, such as construction of artificial reefs, and public outreach to provide education about the risks of consuming contaminated fish.[86] The bulk of the remaining funds was divided between seabird restoration and bald eagle restoration. Peregrine falcon restoration only received about $300,000 because the peregrine had already demonstrated a strong recovery following the cessation of DDT discharges in 1970.

Many of the seabird populations were also rebounding on their own accord. Among the more notable examples was the California brown pelican. In 1970, only a single bird had successfully fledged on west Anacapa Island, the most significant breeding colony north of the Mexican border. By 1973 the colony supported an increasing number of fledglings. In recent years, brown pelicans have been so successful that their breeding colony has begun to expand to other islands and small islets within the Northern Channel Islands archipelago. In 2009 the USFWS removed the iconic bird from the endangered list.[87]

RESTORATION OF BALD EAGLE AND RETURN OF ISLAND FOX

As early as 1999, the Island Fox Group had recommended that bald eagles be reintroduced on the Northern Channel Islands in order to exclude golden eagles. Santa Cruz Island was identified as the preferred location. Within a year of the Montrose Settlement, the Institute for Wildlife Studies initiated a five-year feasibility study designed to assess bald eagle movements, survival and foraging habits.[88] In 2002, twelve young birds, equipped with radio and GPS transmitters, were successfully released from two hacking towers on Santa Cruz Island. Scientists hoped to release the same number of birds annually for the next five years.[89] By the end of the initial feasibility study, a total of fifty-nine juvenile bald eagles had been released on the Northern Channel Islands. Of these, thirty-four were known to have survived and still be present on the islands. In 2006, a healthy chick was hatched on Santa Cruz Island and subsequently fledged. This represented the first time that bald eagles had successfully bred on the Northern Channel Islands in more than fifty years.[90]

The reintroduction of bald eagles to the Northern Channel Islands boded well for the recovery of the island fox. If a permanent population could be reestablished, the chances of restoring the islands' ecological integrity seemed greatly increased. The bald eagles would once more occupy the niche that golden eagles had colonized within the hierarchy of island species, eventually displacing any remaining golden eagles and making the latter's future introduction unlikely. This would eliminate the immediate threat that caused the crisis in the island fox population, allowing the foxes to be released back into the wild once their populations had been restored to healthy levels through the captive breeding program. A demographic model developed by researchers concluded that each captive population needed to grow to at least forty breeding animals (twenty pairs) before the foxes could be released. They considered this the minimum number from which a viable wild population could be established.[91] By 2003 this target had been reached in the Santa Rosa Island and Santa Cruz Island facilities, and some members of the Island Fox Group recommended that releases begin at that time. Compelling reasons dictated that the foxes not be kept in captivity any longer than necessary. Reproductive success was substantially lower among captive foxes than wild ones, and the rate appeared to be declining. Researchers attributed this to the stress of captivity and to the relatively high incidence of mastitis, which affects the ability to nurse young.[92]

Fire and disease also posed a risk of a catastrophe. Fire was a very serious concern, because island staff had minimal fire-fighting capacity, and fire conditions could become extreme during the fall months when hot, dry winds blew from the mainland. Confined within their pens, the foxes would be unable to escape an approaching blaze, and an entire population or subspecies could potentially be eliminated in one devastating event. However, the risks of a premature release were also great. The group's original captive breeding plan that set the population target also stipulated that the threat from golden eagles must be eliminated before the foxes were released. Unfortunately, this goal had not been achieved by 2003, when an estimated thirteen golden eagles still remained in the northern islands despite continuing attempts to trap and relocate the birds.

These competing considerations led to disagreement among members of the Island Fox Group. Some suggested that the foxes be moved to long-term holding facilities on the mainland while others, including most NPS managers, recommended limited releases. In the end, the park released twelve foxes on Santa Rosa Island and nine on Santa Cruz Island during the fall and winter of 2003–4.[93] Initially, the worst fears of many group members were confirmed when more than half of the foxes released on Santa Cruz Island were killed by golden eagles within weeks. The remaining four animals were brought back into captivity. The foxes released on Santa Rosa Island did much better, with only one animal succumbing to predation. NPS managers chose to continue the release experiment despite the presence of some golden eagles.

Later that spring, the federal government listed the northern subspecies of island fox under the Endangered Species Act, making the U.S. Fish and Wildlife Service officially responsible for managing their recovery.[94] The wildlife agency allowed the NPS and the Institute for Wildlife Studies to remain lead authorities in the recovery efforts. USFWS staff reviewed the status of the conservation program and supported the continued reintroduction of foxes on Santa Rosa Island, despite the risk of predation. By the fall of that year, another thirteen animals were released on Santa Rosa Island, and reintroduction commenced on San Miguel Island with an initial ten animals released. These efforts continued over the next several years, with ten to twenty foxes released every year through 2007. Reintroduction also resumed on Santa Cruz Island in 2006. Once the island foxes were restored to the wild, their reproductive success increased substantially, and the population quickly rose. This recovery was most dramatic on San Miguel and Santa Rosa Islands, where the island fox population increased from lows of only fifteen at the nadir of the crisis to nearly four hundred by 2009. This was close to carrying capacity for San Miguel Island and almost half of the estimated capacity for Santa Rosa. Although golden eagles were still present on the Northern Channel Islands, their numbers had diminished, and the rate of predation on island foxes remained at a tolerable level. In August 2016, USFWS removed the island foxes from the endangered list, which signaled the fastest recovery of a mammal in the history of the Endangered Species Act.[95]

The Santa Cruz Island Restoration Plan

One of the final obstacles to successful recovery of the island fox populations was the elimination of feral pigs on Santa Cruz Island as a food source for golden eagles. The Nature Conservancy had always intended to eradicate all the pigs as well as the sheep. As early as 1987, TNC contractors studied the pig population with the aim of developing an eradication plan. However, a combination of factors delayed a TNC-sponsored hunt. First, the cost of the project would be prohibitive and too much money had been expended already on eliminating the sheep. Pigs are much harder to locate and kill than sheep and their ability to reproduce meant that it would take a much more intense effort. Second, it would only work if the entire island were rid of them. This meant that TNC had to wait for the Park Service to acquire the Gherini property and share in the cost of the program. Third, news of the sheep kill had come out and TNC wanted to avoid the inevitable reaction from animal rights people and others in the public. Sharing the spotlight with the NPS could ameliorate that negative attention.[96]

The NPS in cooperation with TNC began developing a "Santa Cruz Island Primary Restoration Plan" in 1998. It had two fundamental purposes: to eliminate the pigs on the island and control the dense stands of the invasive fennel (*Foeniculum vulgare*). A decision was made to totally eradicate the pigs rather than try to control the population, because the latter would prolong the destruction of natural and cultural resources and continually threaten all parts of the island. Control would also result in the killing of many more pigs and would be much more expensive than short-term eradication. As soon as killing of pigs slowed or stopped, the population would rebound. Fennel grew over approximately 1,800 acres of the island, in some places comprising nearly 100 percent cover. The removal of cattle and sheep during the 1980s relieved grazing pressure that had previously kept the species under control.[97]

In March 2001, the NPS released a draft EIS and held meetings at the Santa Barbara Museum of Natural History on March 5 and at the park headquarters the following day. Four alternatives were available: (1) no action; (2) simultaneous island-wide eradication of pigs after a burning and herbicide application to fennel; (3) elimination of pigs in the park portion of the island and control in other areas after the same fennel treatment; and (4) sequential island-wide eradication of pigs through "fenced zone hunting" after the fennel treatment. Public comments on this proposed plan were mostly positive. Many respondents preferred alternative two, which proposed initiating pig eradication without prior construction of the segmenting fences. This would allow treatment to begin sooner, but NPS and TNC managers realized that it could not be effectively implemented under existing budgetary constraints. They supported the park's preferred approach in Alternative Four. This established the same target, eradication of feral pigs, but over a longer period of time and with greater assurance of success.[98]

The draft drew sustained attention from animal rights people. Fifteen of the sixty-six substantive comments suggested that rather than killing the pigs, the agency should use Gonex, a sterilant, to halt or slow reproduction. Scientists from the park and TNC responded that all existing sterilization treatments had proven ineffective and would leave pigs on the island indefinitely, to the detriment of natural and cultural resources. Sterilization also would be cost prohibitive, and it probably would be impossible to treat all the wily sows on the rugged island. Live capture and transfer to the mainland would suffer from the same costs and USFWS, CDFG, and various other agencies rejected any transfer of the pigs for health reasons.[99] Despite these concerns, animal rights proponents continued to challenge what they called the "inhumane slaughter" of pigs. The NPS countered that the allegedly humane alternatives proposed by animal rights activists were not necessarily less cruel than the preferred strategy of lethal removal by a "well-placed bullet." Failure to do anything at all had ethical consequences as well, as biologist Adrian Wenner observed in the following account from his field experience on Santa Cruz Island:

> As a biologist, I have had extensive experience on the island and can report first-hand about the pig situation there. Feral pigs on the island number in the thousands. In good years, they reproduce to their full ability and soon exceed their food source. As they run out of easily obtainable food, such as acorns, they desperately plow up the ground in search of bulbs, roots and tubers, leaving the soil open to being washed away in future rains; and thereby exterminating native plants. They then eat non-nourishing grass as they starve. During the 1988 and 1989 droughts, for example, perhaps nine-tenths of the pigs died of starvation. But pigs don't starve immediately; as the weaker ones succumb, they get attacked and eaten by stronger pigs. At those times we could hear the squeals of pigs in such fights. By the end of 1989, nearly every pig I encountered was nothing more than a bag of bones that could hardly move. When they noticed us, they most often fell over as they tried to move. Even in good years feral pigs suffer. Last week we grabbed a piglet for examination. Dozens of black-legged ticks—vectors of Lyme disease—fleas and lice lived on its soft underside. Island feral pigs, when they overpopulate, cannot migrate to greener pastures; they starve. Is it more humane to let these feral pigs continue their overpopulation, starvation and cannibalism or eliminate a few thousand from the island now, before untold thousands die in the future during such cycles?[100]

These observations graphically described an ecosystem that had been disrupted. Wenner strongly insisted that restoring the integrity of the native ecosystem, rather than intervening to alleviate the pain or suffering of individual animals, represented the only effective and lasting solution. This message had little effect on animal rights activists. Michael Makarian, executive vice-president of Fund for Animals, commented publicly that the current NPS proposal was "an agency-wide vendetta against exotic animals."[101]

Regional Director Jon Jarvis signed the "Record of Decision" that approved alternative four in the final EIS on February 2, 2003. The following September, Channel Islands issued task agreements to build the fences and begin the hunt. Park workers built approximately forty-five miles of pig-resistant fence to segment the island into five distinct management districts, each comprising about 12,000 acres. In many cases, the new fences paralleled the remnants of the earlier sheep fences on TNC property. The island's Central Valley constituted a de facto sixth district in the middle of the treatment area enclosing about 3,000 acres. Professional hunters would then kill the pigs by working sequentially in each district as its respective fencing was completed. The final EIS had proposed a combination of fall burning followed by successive annual applications of herbicide by aerial spraying and mechanical means to remove most of the fennel.[102] Park biologists originally believed that this would assist hunters in locating their prey. When they learned that the pigs could be hunted effectively without first eliminating fennel, they dropped that part of the plan. Fennel subsequently became a lower priority for park vegetation managers, who focused instead on invasive plants that are not as dependent on disturbed soil conditions, including eucalyptus, olives, stone pines, and Harding grass (*Phalaris aquatica*).[103]

Both the NPS and TNC benefitted from cooperation in the removal of pigs. The Park Service paid for the planning procedure, but each organization paid half the cost of eliminating the pigs. Significantly, TNC could absorb the cost of the hunt immediately and wait for annual government appropriations to allow the agency to reimburse it.[104] TNC, being a private organization, could also take action much faster than a government agency bound by deliberate and time-consuming bureaucracy. Finally, in the legal challenges to follow, TNC could rely on Morrison & Foerster LLP, a San Francisco-based law firm that provided pro bono legal aid, to assist NPS solicitors in defending the action. In 2005, the NPS and TNC signed a two-year contract with the New Zealand-based company Pro Hunt. Its hunters began exterminating the pigs, unit-by-unit, in April of that year. Pro Hunt used a combination of techniques, including aerial gunning from helicopters and pursuit with trained dogs. By the following year, the hunters had killed more than two-thirds of the feral pigs.[105]

Unlike the pig hunt on Santa Rosa Island, the controversy over killing pigs on Santa Cruz Island did not abate. A storm of recrimination came almost daily from the *Santa Barbara News-Press*, national animal rights groups, and many local citizens who vilified the NPS. One unexpected source of severe criticism came in a three-article series by former superintendent Tim Setnicka who had been removed from that position two years earlier and who accused the NPS of lying, malfeasance, and a brutal disregard for the lives of animals. After seeing a slide show earlier that year at the park's twenty-fifth anniversary, he wrote that "it became apparent to all watching that a large portion of the park's history revolved around killing one species to save another."[106] He went on to summarize each of the major eradication efforts undertaken by the park over the preceding three decades, beginning with Superintendent Bill Ehorn's elimination of feral burros on San Miguel Island. He concluded that all of these projects had been undertaken surreptitiously in order to escape public oversight. Implicit in his conclusion was the suggestion that park staff knew they were doing something wrong and therefore had something to hide. Setnicka's article was couched as an exposé and designed to portray the park in the worst possible light. Not surprisingly, it was copied and vigorously distributed by animal rights groups, who took it as confirmation of their own suspicions. TNC also received a full dose of unwelcome attention. Lotus Vermeer, director of TNC's island operation during the process, recalls receiving hate mail, vandalism, and even death threats from unidentified sources. The park's biologists and other staff, already suffering some notoriety from the end of Vail & Vickers ranching and the acquisition of Francis Gherini's interest in East Santa Cruz Island, were branded as merciless killers.[107]

Despite the park's scrupulous adherence to the NEPA process, plaintiffs Richard Feldman, a local Santa Barbara businessman; Rob Puddicombe, fresh from acquittal over his attempt to defend Anacapa rats; and Elliott Katz, veterinarian and founder of *In Defense of Animals*, a California nonprofit advocating animal rights, filed a lawsuit. Represented by the Rubenstein Law Group of San Francisco, the plaintiffs alleged that the

NPS had disregarded appropriate NEPA process and insisted that the hunting be stopped and nonlethal management alternatives be considered. They also claimed the hunt harmed them by depriving the public of the opportunity to view wild pigs. Federal District Judge Dickran Tevrizian Jr. concluded that NEPA did not require the NPS to absolutely justify its decision to all parties, only that it had to consider other alternatives. He also claimed that the balance of harm would be to the park and TNC if the pigs stayed and not to people, who could see pigs at many other venues. He rejected their suit and denied all subsequent appeals.[108] By June of 2006, Pro Hunt had eliminated all of the nearly six thousand feral pigs on Santa Cruz Island. Initially, it was thought the hunt might take as much as six years to complete. The New Zealanders demonstrated their well-honed efficiency in ridding islands of nonnative species in only eighteen months at a cost of approximately $5 million.[109] TNC later hired another professional hunting contractor to begin eradication of exotic turkeys. The birds' population had increased following the removal of the pigs, raising fears that they might replace the pigs as prey for golden eagles. That action too was challenged by the same cadre of animal rights people to no avail. By 2007, nearly all of the approximately three hundred birds were dead.[110]

THE RETIREMENT OF TIM SETNICKA

While serving as assistant superintendent under Mack Shaver, Tim Setnicka objected to many natural resource management projects. His hostility to the program delayed conservation efforts for the island fox and nearly proved catastrophic. It began with his lack of support for the proposed monitoring in the early 1990s, before the population actually began to decline. Monitoring of the island fox was finally implemented in 1993, but only through the determined efforts of the natural resources staff, who prepared an environmental assessment to justify the proposal. NPS monitoring was limited to San Miguel Island, however, because Setnicka supported Vail & Vickers' opposition to monitoring on Santa Rosa Island and the NPS did not yet fully own any part of Santa Cruz Island. By 1999, when the island fox population had reached its nadir and only a handful of the animals remained in the wild, Setnicka, as superintendent, still failed to take any positive action. Only the combined authority of the Island Fox Conservation Working Group compelled him to support a captive breeding program.

Although Setnicka formally approved the breeding program, the park lacked adequate funds for its full implementation. In response, the park's resource staff appealed to the regional office in San Francisco. Officials there convened a panel of subject experts to investigate the situation.[111] They traveled to Channel Islands, met with park staff, and quickly concluded that the recovery program needed more resources in order to be effective. They prepared a written report strongly recommending a base funding increase to be used for this purpose, but the panel also prepared an *unwritten* report—delivered orally to the regional director that vigorously criticized Setnicka's opposition to the recovery program.[112] Soon thereafter, the NPS appropriated a base funding increase of $477,000 annually from the Natural Resource Challenge and the park was able to expand its captive breeding program to sustainable levels.[113]

Setnicka's management style and actions had become an issue by 2003. Acting regional director (and later NPS director) Jonathan Jarvis, when asked in an interview what significant actions he took regarding Channel Islands, responded, "I selected Russell Galipeau as superintendent, I removed Tim Setnicka as superintendent." The complaints from the natural resource management staff were not the only ones coming from the park staff. Finally, a member of the regional directorate and a department of the interior solicitor came to Ventura and interviewed park managers and staff for several days. By the end of that week Jarvis abruptly transferred Setnicka to a desk in the regional office.[114] The *Los Angeles Times* queried the regional office about the sudden move and reported on October 16, 2002: "The National Park Service official who removed Tim Setnicka as superintendent of Channel Islands National Park said Tuesday that his decision was based solely on the needs of the agency and not on any controversies kicked up during Setnicka's tenure. 'It would be an overstatement and an exaggeration to say anything else was going on here,' said Arthur Eck, deputy regional director in Oakland. 'Transferring managers is common in the park service,' he said."[115] Whether the *LA Times* reporter believed this innocuous explanation is suspect, however. On January 11, 2003, the same newspaper noted: "Tim Setnicka, who was recently reassigned from his job as superintendent of Channel Islands National Park, has retired. Setnicka, 57, headed the park from 1997 until last October, when he was abruptly removed from the job and given new duties at the National Park Service's Pacific West regional headquarters in Oakland. Setnicka, who spent 32 years with the park service, had a reputation for aggressiveness and blunt talk that some found intimidating."[116]

Channel Islands National Park in the New Century   10

As the centennial of the National Park Service (NPS) approached, issues old and new continued to challenge the staff at Channel Islands National Park. Russell Galipeau became superintendent of the park in May 2003. He managed Channel Islands for fifteen years, until June 2018, during which time some pernicious issues ended while new threats emerged to challenge the entire national park system.[1] Superintendent Galipeau brought considerable energy to the park as he faced the culmination of the Settlement Agreement (SA) and residential reservation of use and occupancy (RUO) with Vail & Vickers on Santa Rosa Island, production of a new general management plan (GMP), and a host of natural resource issues on both land and sea.

Managing Natural Resources on the Islands

After the pigs were gone from Santa Cruz Island and bald eagles returned to their island niche, the remaining exotic animals on the Northern Channel Islands included rats on the navy's San Miguel Island, Argentine ants on Santa Cruz Island, and the deer and elk on Santa Rosa Island. The NPS needed to solve the latter as soon as possible because the SA was approaching its end in 2011. Only then could the agency address water-quality issues, high erosion rates, endangered and threatened plants, and recovery of native plant communities.

The SA, signed in 1998, was supposed to calm the conflict between Vail & Vickers and the Park Service. Removing the cattle certainly improved the biological resources of Santa Rosa Island, but it did not quell the distrust of the Vail and Vickers families or the concern of resource managers

Fig. 28. The superintendents of Channel Islands National Park from 1974–2018. *From left to right:* Tim Setnicka, Mack Shaver, former congressman Robert Lagomarsino, Bill Ehorn, and Russell Galipeau. Photograph by Robert Schwemmer, March 2005, CINP Digital Image files.

for threatened native vegetation. The remaining elk and deer proved to be another source of intense debate and recriminations between the two parties. The SA imposed limits on the number of deer and elk that were allowed on the island each year. Beginning in 1999, Vail & Vickers were allowed no more than 425 deer and 740 elk on the island. Starting in 2000, the SA ordered an adaptive management approach to begin that would result in further reductions to deer and elk numbers based on the status of the two indicator species that the three-person scientific panel had chosen—soft-leaved paintbrush (*Castilleja mollis*) and Santa Rosa Island manzanita (*Arctostaphylos convertiflora*). If standards for their habitats and recovery were met, the cervid population sizes could continue through 2007. Thereafter the SA included a four-year "phase-out" period set to begin in 2008. Each year of the phaseout required a 25 percent annual reduction from the 2007 numbers, with final eradication in 2011. At the beginning of that final year, the island should have had no more than 106 deer and 185 elk. Three problems complicated this seemingly straightforward prescription: (1) a decision on how and by whom the animals would be counted each year, (2) continued evidence of ecological damage to endangered plant species, and (3) a late legislative attempt to repeal the SA and maintain the cervids on the island past 2011.[2]

On June 20, 2001, the U.S. Fish and Wildlife Service (USFWS) notified Park Superintendent Setnicka that data from his own scientists showed that the cervid management program was not working. This came after a meeting between the USFWS and the NPS.[3] The latter supplied data on the growth of the indicator species. USFWS officials investigated the scientific panel's collective and individual reports and drew their own conclusions. They warned that the manzanita situation on the island was tolerable in one area and poor in another (South Point); the deer population was much higher than the maximum allowed having reached nearly one thousand in 1999; and that the loss of seed bank and soil erosion were "alarming." The USFWS staff at the Ventura office recommended that the deer population be reduced to 350 individuals. They noted that Dr. Ed Schreiner of the scientific panel recommended cutting the number to 250 given the high birthrate of the animals, and Dr. Michael Barbour allowed 425 but recommended a focused cull in the South Point area. The letter did not cite what Dr. John Menke, the Vail & Vickers appointee to the panel, recommended.[4]

On May 15, 2002, Russ Vail contacted NPS regional director John Reynolds to ask what the Park Service would require so he and his family could form a new company—Vail Family LLC. Along with the Vickers LLC, it would manage the "Commercial Deer and Elk Operations" on the island. Notable in the terms was a stipulation that only the descendants of the original SUP holders could inherit those interests. The NPS began communicating with Timothy Vail, son of Russ; Nita Vail, daughter of Al; and Will Woolley, son of Margaret in the active management of Santa Rosa Island.[5] The new SUP specified that the permittee must not interfere with NPS research and management at any time or in any area. It also stated that the agency had the right to monitor and inspect the company's hunting operation whenever it saw fit.[6]

Superintendent Galipeau later recalled that counting elk on Santa Rosa Island was like counting cars in a parking lot—easy. However, counting deer on the island was like trying to count leaves in a parking lot on a windy day. They do not typically travel in herds, they move around a lot, and they hide well. The SA committed the NPS and Vail & Vickers to cooperatively count the animals each year. Most of the work was done by aerial survey with the cost split between the two parties. It did not take long for the park's resource managers to question the methodology of the annual December counts. Believing that the number of deer was significantly higher than what was being recorded, the park turned to professional ungulate biologist Dr. Peter Gogan of the U.S. Geological Survey for advice. He participated in the 2006 survey, studied the scientific literature on the subject, and made several recommendations to improve the validity of the count. Up to this point, Vail & Vickers had set the dates and most of the protocol for the annual surveys. Gogan made three suggestions: (1) adding ground surveys to find animals that were hidden by vegetation during daylight hours; (2) marking a number of deer so that if later counts showed only a fraction of the marked individuals, it could be assumed that an equal proportion of the unmarked ones might be hidden; and (3) having the NPS conduct and pay for a unilateral second count each year during August. Timothy Vail responded that a ground survey would be difficult, expensive, and cause a game drive of fast-moving deer that would inflate the count. He also forbade marking the animals, which remained his company's private property, and insisted that the SA mandated cooperative counts and that the Vails would sue the Park Service if it tried to conduct a unilateral one. Superintendent Galipeau defended Gogan and stated that the SUP did not restrict counts to one per year, that a planned ground survey would indeed take place, and that the next year would require the first 25 percent reduction in the cervid populations.[7]

In 2006 the park produced an internal report on the effects of deer and elk on the natural and cultural resources of Santa Rosa Island. It heaped criticism on the presence of the cervids and on the hunting operation that was their raison d'etre. Part of it was triggered by a December 19, 2005, discovery of a bald eagle suffering from eating fragments of a lead bullet fired by a hunter. That had triggered the report, which cited four categories of negative impacts. First, deer and elk threatened federally endangered plants, some of which occur only on Santa Rosa Island. *Castilleja mollis* seemed to be recovering, albeit slowly, but the Santa Rosa Island manzanita was not. Second, the presence of these cervids threatened the federally endangered island foxes. The unfolding island fox/golden eagle crisis led resource managers to discover that mule deer fawns had become the most important single food item for golden eagles. This allowed them to remain on the island and prey on island foxes. Third, the hunt threatened native wildlife and interfered with administration of the park. The bald eagle with lead poisoning was one problem. Another was the hunt itself, which closed over half the island to NPS staff, researchers, and visitors from August to September, a prime public visitation period. This made it extremely difficult for park staff to release and monitor island foxes. Finally, quoting statements by archaeologist Torben Rick, the report charged that deer and elk irreparably harmed archeological resources.[8] Timothy Vail vigorously disputed these claims.

In the midst of this controversy, another threat appeared, led by a congressman from a completely different area of California. Republican Duncan Hunter from San Diego County, who chaired the House Armed Services Committee, suddenly attached a rider to the 2007 defense authorization bill ordering that the deer and elk on Santa Rosa Island be protected and the island become a hunting refuge for disabled veterans (H.R. 5122). He claimed that while driving down the coast with two injured U.S. Marines he saw the island and they told him about the impending end of the cervids and hunting. He decided that shifting ownership of the island to the Department of Defense and preserving the deer and elk would be a proper way to honor the nation's disabled veterans. He added that it might also serve as a training center for special operations forces. A second part ordered the Settlement Agreement to be rescinded.

Hunter appealed to Paralyzed Veterans of America to send a member to the island to highlight the opportunity. The veterans' group did so, and the man flew to the island with Superintendent Galipeau and other park officials. Galipeau recalls that he was a pleasant, young man who seemed slightly bewildered about his task. Not long after, the organization abandoned support claiming that the island's steep hills and washes could not be traveled by its members. His amendment did not receive support during the conference committee between the House and Senate. In spite of this setback, Hunter added Section 1077 to the massive defense authorization bill that passed on October 17, 2006, as P.L. 109–364. It forbade the Park Service from destroying or removing the deer and elk from Santa Rosa Island. Hunter still hoped to make the island a veterans' hunting ground.[9] The Vails did not participate in drafting the legislation, but they were pleased that it would save the cervids and perhaps their hunting operation.

The department of the interior and local Representative Lois Capps, a democrat, were caught off guard. The prospect of losing the island after years of intense effort to restore its ecological integrity and millions of dollars spent appalled the Park Service, environmentalists, and most of the local mainland population. Capps had vigorously opposed Hunter's bill and testified to the full House:

> One might wonder why this provision is in a bill which deals with supporting our troops. The proposals and reasons behind it have evolved over time. At one point it was to establish a hunting preserve for the military's top brass and their guests. When that didn't fly, it was quickly changed to making Santa Rosa a place for disabled vets to hunt. But when the paralyzed veterans of America actually went to the island, they told Chairman Hunter, and I quote, "the Santa Rosa initiative is not viable."
>
> Then the provision morphed into saving the animals from extinction. That is right. The intention is that we are going to save the animals, though they continue to be hunted indefinitely and on the island. This provision is opposed by the Park Service, the PVA, the Humane Society, and many public lands groups. Even the U.S. Senate unanimously passed a resolution against this proposal.
>
> So why is it in the bill? Who knows.[?] What we do know is that taxpayers who paid $30 million for the island are now being told

by our chairman they can't visit it for nearly half the year. This is an insult to our constituents, to all taxpayers. It is also an insult to our troops whose service to this country is being used as a cover for this special interest boondoggle.[10]

Immediately Capps contacted California senators Dianne Feinstein and Barbara Boxer, both democrats. On April 25, 2007, the senators introduced S. 1209, entitled "Channel Islands National Park Management Act of 2007," and Representative Capps introduced H. R. 2029 to repeal Hunter's addition.[11]

This time there was a public hearing before the Senate Subcommittee on National Parks on May 15, 2007. All the interested parties spoke or submitted statements. Former congressman Robert Lagomarsino recalled the events surrounding the 1980 enabling legislation, including promises made to Vail & Vickers to let them ranch until 2011 [with an RUO or a lease]. He again urged that their operation not be ended before that date. Timothy Vail submitted an eleven-page statement reiterating the entire history of his company's relations with the NPS as the Vails & Vickers members saw it. He emphasized their current belief that it was a tragedy that the Park Service wanted to engage in an "unnecessary slaughter of healthy and magnificent elk and deer herds." He added the newspaper pieces by former superintendent Tim Setnicka who had suggested that the NPS had a secret vendetta against nonnative animals that led them to lie, obfuscate, and break laws in order to accomplish their program. The NPCA and the NPS naturally supported the bills. A group of pro-hunting organizations led by the National Rifle Association vehemently opposed them. Several republican senators also opposed the bill, notably Don Young (R-Alaska), who had hunted on Santa Rosa Island. Duncan Hunter later disingenuously claimed that the only purpose his law ever had was to prevent the slaughter of the deer and elk.[12]

Eventually S. 1209 became part of Public Law 110–161, the Fiscal Year 2007 Omnibus Appropriations law, signed on December 26, 2007. Entitled "Restoring Full Public Access to Santa Rosa Island," it ended the most serious political threat to the Park Service's program for ecosystem restoration. Vail & Vickers swallowed another bitter defeat that deprived them of an indefinite future on the island. Conflict over the populations of the deer and elk, how they were surveyed, unsuccessful efforts by the NPS to mount a second unilateral count in a given year, and more data on the status of the threatened species continued as 2011 approached. While most of the national media reported on the private hunting and how it restricted public access, a steady supply of articles sympathetic to the Vails told their side of the story. Ranching magazines, local newspapers, particularly the *Santa Barbara News Press*, and occasionally national venues aired the sad story about the end of a way of life that had been promised with a handshake. It became a fact in the minds of many locals and is still aired by long-time residents.[13]

On January 2, 2008, Timothy Vail wrote to Superintendent Galipeau again criticizing Peter Gogan for deer counts consistently higher than those Vail conducted with Wayne Long, owner of the hunt company Multiple Use Management. Vail pointed out that Gogan sat in the rear helicopter seat with the poorest view yet came up with a higher deer count. He also implied that by not turning in his count sheets immediately after the flights, he might be doctoring them later to present the higher figures. Galipeau responded by expressing concern that Vail thought Gogan might be "incompetent or cheating," and again rejected the implication. A month later, he reminded Vail that at the end of that year the cervid counts needed to be no more than 318 deer and 555 elk.[14] The claims and complaints in the correspondence from the Vails were so virulent and continuous that it led Galipeau to request clarification of "unresolved questions" connected to the SUP rights from the regional office even though the 2003 SUP appeared straightforward.[15]

The poisoned relationship between Vail & Vickers and the park's resource management severely curtailed communication. The question remained: What would the company do to remove its ungulate property from the island by December 31, 2011? Throughout the years of controversy, the NPS had never insisted that all the animals be killed. It simply wanted them off the island. During the 1990s, Vail & Vickers had moved some elk to a game reserve in Michigan. But adult mule deer do not typically survive transport, and no viable market existed for them. Fears of disease among the island's elk worried state and federal authorities, and testing all the elk on the island promised to be egregiously expensive and delay their removal by as much as two years. Studies also showed that the deer had a reproduction rate of 34 percent annually. This already threatened to prolong any form of removal. Before 2008, the park suggested that the hunts focus on female deer to counter this increase, but the former ranchers never implemented that procedure.[16]

Vail & Vickers faced a difficult decision. The company had the responsibility to remove any deer and elk on the island by the end of 2011 or they would have to share the cost of subsequent elimination with the NPS. Superintendent Galipeau offered to help with a deal to save them effort and money. He would simply state that the owners had done all they could and had maintained the herds under the maximum population numbers, which he did not believe they had done. That would trigger a clause in the last SUP that would let the NPS take over the animals and deal with them as it would. Timothy Vail initially rejected this transfer of assets to the park but, after reflection and consultation with the other owners, he called Galipeau and accepted the solution. The superintendent had one other stipulation for this to work. Members of the Vail and Vickers families had to stop berating the Park Service in the media. On April 10, 2011, three Vail heirs and three Vickers heirs signed the agreement.[17] Eight days later, the NPCA as a signatory to the 1998 Settlement Agreement added its approval. Multiple Use Management conducted a last commercial hunt in October 2011, and the Vails left the island at the end of the year. The Park Service used a professional hunt organization called White Buffalo to eliminate the rest of the ungulates. The hunters used a combination of ground hunting and helicopters. The elk presented no problem, but the deer were elusive, and it took until 2014 to be sure they were gone. White Buffalo's final report stated that they had eliminated approximately 479 deer during that period, a number that was substantially higher than the Settlement Agreement permitted Vail & Vickers to have on the island.[18]

THE NATURE CONSERVANCY ON SANTA CRUZ ISLAND

The Nature Conservancy (TNC) management of the western 76 percent of Santa Cruz Island matched the natural resource policies of the National

Park Service and coordinated with the government agency's programs. Removal of all the domestic and feral livestock allowed TNC to address the floral exotics and participate in wetland recovery at Prisoners Harbor with the NPS. It also expanded its outreach to potential donors and others interested in its core mission of restoration ecology. Among its restoration accomplishments with the NPS were protection of the island fox, the eradication of feral wild turkeys and honeybees, the reintroduction of bald eagles to the island, and progress toward the eradication of thirty-two species of nonnative, invasive plants. The experience gained from these actions led TNC to prepare an equivalent to an NPS general management plan entitled "Santa Cruz Island Ecological Management Strategy 2015–2025," released in August 2015.

The plan's authors noted that much of the conservation work conducted on Santa Cruz Island over the previous decades was reactive, addressed severe and urgent threats, and usually required the removal of invasive species. The new plan outlined a proactive management strategy with the following long-term goals:

1. The full suite of Santa Cruz Island's natural communities and the populations of native species constituting them are viable in the long term with a minimum of management action.
2. All major threats to island biota including invasive non-native species, novel diseases, climate change, human-ignited and natural wildfire, and disturbance by visitors and infrastructure built to serve them are eliminated, minimized, or mitigated.
3. Full native plant cover is rehabilitated to priority areas that were denuded by introduced animals or stripped of vegetation and soils by other anthropogenic activities.
4. Populations of native species deemed to have been extirpated from the island by anthropogenic activities are restored if deemed capable of long-term survival with minimal management following re-introduction and re-establishment.
5. Research results and lessons learned from conservation actions are systematically shared with the broader scientific and conservation management communities.

6. Legislation and policies which prevent, hinder, or unnecessarily slow conservation and restoration on Santa Cruz Island and the other California Islands are revised and policies that incorporate up-to-date information, ecological concepts, and best management and planning practices are adopted.[19]

The authors promised that the strategy would be revised every two years based on reviews of its success or failure.

ELIMINATION OF ARGENTINE ANTS

At the same time TNC released its plan, it coped with another invasive species that affected the island. This time the NPS and TNC cooperated to eradicate Argentine ants (*Linepithema humile*) from areas controlled by both organizations. Scientists believe the insects may have arrived on Santa Cruz Island as early as the 1960s but were not identified there until 1997. At that time, Adrian Wenner documented the Argentine ants at two dismantled navy facilities (the blue site near Valley Anchorage and the white site near the navy base). Materials were moved from the Valley Anchorage site to the University of California facility near the Main Ranch, which spread them to Cañada del Puerto, the outlet from the Main Ranch and the Central Valley. The ants then spread to the Cañada del Medio and were present in all four areas by 2010. Biologists dreaded the potential for the Cañada del Puerto invaders to wash down the stream, establish a new colony at Prisoners Harbor, and be picked up by visitors and spread all over the island. Valley Anchorage was by far the largest ant zone and the most rapidly expanding one. Argentine ants have a strong competitive ability and a diverse diet. They threaten numerous endemic insects and seventy species of island birds. They impact the native invertebrate community through direct predation, egg predation, and competition.[20]

Research on Argentine ants began on the mainland where they commonly inhabit urban areas. The queens do not fly, hence the spread overland is relatively slow. This allows easy delimitation of their colonies and focused treatment. TNC and NPS worked to find the appropriate concentration of toxicant to avoid killing the foragers and allow them to bring the bait back to the nest for the other ants, particularly the queen.

Field testing on Santa Cruz Island took place from 2010 through 2014. Resource managers planned to again delimit the infested areas with an extra buffer of 50 meters (164 feet) to account for wandering ants or cryptic nests outside the boundaries. Public scoping began on August 22, 2014, with a press release and establishment of a project website. Chief among the respondents were USFWS biologists who were concerned about the potential side effects on federally listed species, especially the recently recovered island fox. Eventually they agreed with program administrators that a fox is too large to be deleteriously affected by consuming the ants or the bait. Testing also showed that the impact of the treatment on water resources, flora, and other faunal species was very low. Helicopters deployed the bait over infestations at a rate of sixteen gallons per acre twelve times during the dry season from May through November 2015. If monitoring over the next ten years showed a new nest thereafter it would receive four hand-applied treatments to ensure eradication.[21] By August 2018, the 1,600-acre Valley Anchorage site and other infestation sites appeared to be completely free of Argentine ants.

AVIFAUNA ON THE ISLANDS

Many of the restorative actions taken by the NPS have been triggered by declines in avian species. The intense focus on protecting birdlife at Channel Islands is demanded by their rarity and diversity. Dr. Paul W. Collins of the Santa Barbara Museum of Natural History compiled a list of 387 species of birds found on or within 1.5 kilometers (0.9 mile) of the five park islands in 2011.[22] The majority are visitors that travel the Pacific Flyway as the seasons pass. The park's 2014 *Natural Resource Condition Assessment* listed forty-eight landbirds and thirteen seabirds that breed on the five park islands.[23] The Channel Islands National Marine Sanctuary's (CINMS) 2016 *Condition Report* reported that eight breeding seabird species are granted special protected status under federal or California state law. They include the ashy storm-petrel (*Oceanodroma homochroa*), black storm-petrel (*Oceanodroma melania*), California brown pelican (*Pelecanus occidentalis*), California least tern (*Sterna antillarum browni*), double-crested cormorant (*Phalacrocorax auritus*), rhinoceros auklet (*Cerorhinca monocerata*), Scripps's murrelet (*Synthliboramphus scrippsi*),

Fig. 29. NPS botanist Clark Cowan rolling up ice plant on East Anacapa Islet, demonstrating the hardiness of the nonnative species. Photographer and date unknown. CINP Photo Archives, photograph UAEM 11, DSCN4244.

and western snowy plover (*Charadrius alexandrinus nivosus*).[24] Eradication of nonnative ungulates has altered the habitats on the islands resulting in recovery of some species, but climate change worries ornithologists and park resource managers. Monitoring of landbirds began on several of the islands in the park in 1993. Each of the park's islands supports seabird colonies, with various species using different islands. However, the most important are San Miguel, including Prince Island and Castle Rock; Santa Barbara; and the islets of Anacapa. Efforts to improve East Anacapa habitat continue with the removal of exotic ice plant and replanting of native species. This effort has been supported by funds from the Montrose Settlements Restoration Program.[25]

After the Santa Barbara Island song sparrow became extinct, TNC took the lead in researching and monitoring the island scrub-jay (*Aphelocoma insularis*) that exists only on Santa Cruz Island. This has led park resource managers to ponder a solution that tests the agency's mission. The NPS is allowed to reestablish a species population if it can be shown that it once existed in a park area but disappeared due to human causes. If natural causes led to extirpation, the Park Service should not interfere. The island scrub-jay appears to have existed on Santarosae. Fossil evidence has been found on San Miguel and Santa Rosa Islands from the prehistoric human period. On the latter, the fossils appear to be ten thousand years old, but on San Miguel they date to within the last millennium. There are also notes of an ornithologist who visited Santa Rosa Island in 1982 and reported being told by the ranch foreman that scrub-jays occurred on the island.[26] This suggests that the birds were probably on Santa Rosa until at least that time. The policy issue was highlighted by TNC biologist Scott Morrison in 2014: "Managers need to understand when and why the jay population went extinct on Santa Rosa Island: did it go extinct 'naturally' in prehistoric time, or did it go extinct more recently due to anthropogenic factors? Depending on which it is, a reintroduction either would be consistent with a general interpretation of National Park Service (NPS) policy—i.e., restoring parks to their historic, natural condition—or it would be a more interventionist manipulation of the landscape, possibly even an 'impairment' of the park."[27]

If the birds inhabited Santa Rosa Island into the 1800s, the massive damage by sheep to its preferred woody habitat likely was the cause of its disappearance. Yet other considerations mandate extreme care in manipulating ecosystems. Ornithologists are uncertain about the impact of the birds on the recovering habitats of Santa Rosa Island. Island scrub-jays could have an adverse impact on other rare passerines by nest predation. Alternatively, restoration of the island scrub-jays could benefit native floral species, including island oaks and Torrey pines. The caching behavior of jays can accelerate restoration by disseminating seeds of the tree species and may have contributed already to native vegetation recovery on Santa Cruz Island following the removal of sheep. Resource managers at Channel Islands are still researching the broader environmental implications of transferring the island scrub-jays and searching for answers about the threat climate change poses for the birds' survival prospects with and without a second island home.[28]

FIRE MANAGEMENT

As the new millennium began, Channel Islands National Park gathered data for its next fire management plan. The need for a new plan was spurred by the removal of cattle from Santa Rosa Island and sheep from East Santa Cruz Island, as well as a directive from the NPS to plan for a "wildland urban interface initiative." Because non-NPS lands abutted park property, this type of plan was required. Citing the expected surge in the fuel load with post-grazing vegetative growth, the park requested $441,000 to complete GIS mapping of the five islands, especially the TNC portion of Santa Cruz; acquire new equipment; and hire a temporary employee to administer the planning process.[29] On June 26, 2001, an event occurred that reinforced the need for a new fire management plan. At 8:00 a.m., a less than two-acre fire known as the "Ford Point Fire" was reported on Santa Rosa Island. The grass fire grew to approximately 36 acres before it was contained the same day. It was not a dangerous fire, and it did not do significant damage, but the response highlighted a number of deficiencies in communications that could have resulted in a more serious conflagration. The park's fire specialist did not have a cell phone or pager and could not be reached, nor could anyone contact the fire management officer at Santa Monica Mountains National Recreation Area. Los Padres National Forest did supply a fire suppression plane before their normal 9:00 a.m. workday start, but even that frustrated Chief Ranger Jack Fitzgerald who had been required to purchase a ride from Aspen Helicopters to get to the site. A post-fire investigation reiterated the call for a new fire management plan. First, however, the park secured a cell phone for its own fire specialist.[30]

After the infamous Yellowstone Fire of 1988, the NPS underwent a rigorous review of its policies, and a new plan for all federal land agencies was promulgated in 1995. Six years later, a review of that fire plan upheld the basic policies of the NPS that stressed human safety; urban interface fire prevention; careful use of prescribed burns when appropriate; fire suppression when any threat to people, infrastructure, endangered species, or atmospheric conditions warrant it; a closely monitored "let burn" policy where none of these problems are present; and an absolute requirement for every park to have a fire management plan.³¹ In June 2006, the park released a more detailed and sophisticated fire management plan that included adaptations based on new research, wider partnerships with other fire control agencies, and a more extensive public review, but it did not significantly change the goals. Fire suppression remained paramount in any case of wildland fire, defined as "all fires that are not ignited by park managers for specific purposes." The issues of timely communication and rapid response were strongly emphasized as were education of the park staff and the public and planned removal of potential fire fuel around cultural sites. The latter, always expensive, is a frequent debate in parks where some scientists oppose the removal of potential nutrients from burned material that would enrich the soil after a fire.³²

RECLAMATION OF PRISONERS HARBOR WETLAND

The closest coastal access to the Main Ranch on Santa Cruz Island is the large, protected cove known as Prisoners Harbor. The area serves as the drainage for the Cañada del Puerto. Prisoners Harbor received its name in April 1830, when a ship carrying prisoners from Mexico dropped them off with provisions on Santa Cruz Island. When Justinian Caire took control of the island in 1880, he set to work improving the small ranch at Prisoners Harbor as the entryway to his island enterprises. A well-built pier already existed by the time Caire began his development projects in the ensuing decade. To maintain this valuable asset, Caire's workers planted nonnative eucalyptus groves in the Cañada del Puerto for use as pilings when the need arose.³³

The entire area at the mouth of the Cañada del Puerto was landscaped with grasses and trees planted in rows. Workers straightened the creek by building stone retaining walls and filled the wetland with cobble and gravel. This diminished the natural lagoon in the area. Laborers planted more eucalyptus trees in a row along the foot of the bluff behind the warehouse and sheep pens and added stone pines (*Pinus pinea*) near the foot of the pier.³⁴ In 1904 laborers planted thirty-nine pine trees on the west side of the pier, followed in 1908 by five hundred eucalyptus trees upstream from the harbor. In the 1950s, the Stantons constructed corrals on the former wetland for cattle.³⁵

After receiving the donation of the Isthmus from TNC, the NPS needed to investigate the physical and ecological status of the wetland at Prisoners Harbor. In May 2003, the NPS sent officials from the agency's Water Resources Division (WRD), led by wetland scientist Kevin Noon, to East Santa Cruz Island to delineate the wetland boundaries of the major creeks on the island, including Prisoners Harbor, and to identify restoration opportunities. Noon reported: "Historically, the Prisoners area was one of the largest back-barrier coastal wetlands on the Channel Islands. . . . To facilitate the island ranching operations and protect their investments at the harbor, ranchers channelized the creek and filled in the adjacent wetland with gravels from the surrounding hills and creek bed. This effectively eliminated the ecological value of the coastal wetland system, its floodplain functions, and much of its biological diversity."[36] He added that approximately 60 percent of the original wetland area had been filled or dredged and that the dredging had created a deep channel along the east bank stretching more than 1,500 feet (457 meters) from the beach to confine the creek. A 60-foot (18.3 meter) wide berm extended approximately 300 feet (91 meters) along the northwest side of the stream channel. Noon stated that "huge monocultures of nonnatives have replaced the more diverse native communities and reduced the functional values of the wetland areas, especially for birds and other wildlife." He suggested that the eucalyptus trees, in particular, needed to be studied to determine how much water they drew that would benefit native plants and wondered whether cultural resource managers would oppose their removal.[37]

After more study and testing by Noon, his colleagues, and park resource managers, the NPS held a meeting with various partners, including Island Packers, TNC, the Santa Cruz Island Foundation (SCIF), the Santa Barbara Museum of Natural History (SBMNH), Chumash representatives, the U.S. Geological Survey (USGS), and scientists from several University of California campuses. The purpose was to get input for a restoration plan. The options ranged from complete removal of the corrals with an attempt to restore the original hydrology and ecology to various lesser actions that would approach that goal. The responses to restoration were generally positive but predictably varied. Ecologists and natural resource people backed total restoration, others had caveats, and one opposed any action. Lotus Vermeer of TNC enthusiastically commended the project and promised to cooperate. Charles Drost of USGS and Paul Collins of SBMNH expressed concern about the fate of the western harvest mice that inhabited the existing wetland.

Chumash representatives Freddie Romero and Julie Tumamait-Stenslie approved the idea of restoring the pre-ranch environment but worried about archaeological resources that might be disturbed or destroyed by the process. Marla Daily and Tony Brown of the SCIF did not approve of the removal of the corrals, although Brown suggested keeping only a small portion on site. Finally, Lyndal Laughrin of the University of California Research Station cautioned that the NPS needed to balance preservation of historical resources with restoration of the ecosystem. He added that people today do not need to perpetuate the resource damage instigated by previous land owners. He noted that if the Caires and Stantons had been required to follow modern environmental protection laws, the structures at Prisoners Harbor would never have been built.[38]

The Park Service announced its intention to restore the wetland in the *Federal Register* on June 11, 2008. The notice mentioned the public outreach described above and explained that the corrals at the site were added by Carey Stanton in the 1950s and that they were a "small scale feature" that contributed to the Santa Cruz Island Ranching District, property that was potentially eligible for the National Register of Historic Places. The project would affect 59.7 acres (24 ha) of land, only 19 of which were owned by the NPS. The rest were TNC property, but the legal agreement between the two organizations allowed them to cooperate in such a project. The NPS promised to consult with the State Historic Preservation Officer (SHPO) in carrying out the proposed restoration.

The park released its draft EIS in May 2009, held an open house on June 23, and presented their "action" alternatives with a forty-five-day public scoping period. The EIS addressed four main components: (1) removing fill and controlling invasive species to restore the ecology, (2) restoring hydraulic function of the wetland by reconnecting the creek to the floodplain, (3) protecting sensitive archeological resources, and (4) improving the visitor experience. The NPS's preferred alternative was "B," which proposed: (1) removal of about 17,000 cubic yards of fill and eight cattle corrals, (2) relocation of a scale house, (3) removal of eucalyptus trees from 20 acres in the lower Cañada del Puerto, (4) control of invasive fennel and kikuyu grass (*Pennisetum clandestinum*), (5) removal of 250 feet of the berm to reconnect the creek with its floodplain, (6) construction of a protective barrier around a portion of the sensitive archeological site, and (7) improvements to the visitor experience. The draft EIS also offered a no-action alternative and an alternative "C" that would restore one-third of the wetland by removing 11,000 cubic yards of fill, retaining two corrals, and retaining the scale house in its current location. The Park sought reviews and written public comment on the draft EIS by July 15, 2009.[39]

The response from agencies, organizations, and the public was muted. After notifying seventy-three media outlets, and sending out 240 copies for review, the park only received eleven responses that offered anything more than a yes or no about the project. Considerable correspondence between Superintendent Russell Galipeau; archaeologist Susan K. Stratton, who represented the California SHPO; and the Santa Ynez Band of Mission Indians elicited adjustments to the plan to carefully cap the site of the former Chumash village. The Environmental Protection Agency expressed minor concern about the impact of runoff on the marine resources nearby. The USFWS approved after being assured that no endangered species, such as the island fox, would be threatened, and other state and federal agencies gave tentative approval with stipulations that various permits from them would be negotiated. In the meantime, project leader Paula Power led a team to quantify and measure the eucalyptus trees at the wetland and along the Cañada. They found more than 1,700 with diameters at breast height greater than six inches (15cm) including 304 with a girth greater than 24 inches (61cm).[40]

Mike Martin of the WRD staff did a hydrological study of the creek and found that channelizing the creek increased water velocity during flood stages and impacted the major archaeological site. Removing the berm would remove the threat. Park staff dismantled the corral system and removed old concrete piles and other debris from the filled area. They used lumber from the old corrals to build a smaller representative, one

Fig. 30. (*opposite top*) This oblique aerial photo shows Prisoners Harbor as designed by the Stantons during the 1950s. Corrals and nonnative vegetation covered the former wetland. Photographer unknown, August 2010, CINP Photo Archives, 5b_010810_151153_tag (2), NPgallery.nps.gov.

Fig. 31. (*opposite bottom*) Prisoners Harbor after reconfiguration and restoration of the wetland. Photographer unknown, June 2013, CINP Photo Archives, 5b-Prisoners Photomonitoring_6_7_2013[4](1), NPgallery.nps.gov.

Fig. 32. (*above*) This aerial photo shows eucalyptus along Cañada del Puerto on Santa Cruz Island near Prisoners Harbor. Provided by R. Rudolph, CINP.

Fig. 33. The area of Cañada del Puerto after Park Service removal of the eucalyptus grove. Provided by R. Rudolph, CINP.

next to the historic warehouse. Fennel, extensive mats of kikuyu grass, and thirty eucalyptus trees were removed prior to earthmoving activities. In September and October, the park staff removed 10,000 cubic yards (12,700 tons) of fill and deposited them on the east side of the creek. The material was graded to blend in with the existing topography. Discovery of the remnant of a historic stone wall under the berm during removal of the fill forced the park to reduce the amount of material it removed in order to protect it.

In a massive effort during November and December 2011, volunteers helped them plant fifteen thousand native wetland species of high wildlife value in their appropriate water-depth level. Native seed and acorns were planted in the fill disposal site. No plants were brought from other islands or the mainland because of a concern about transporting invasive organisms. They also created two open-water ponds, reconnected the creek with its floodplain, and exposed groundwater that had been buried for over one hundred years. The biological response was immediate. Endangered island fox, island scrub-jay, invertebrate fauna, waterfowl, along with many new resident and migratory birds soon appeared. Park officials installed a complex system of soil and atmosphere water instruments to monitor the ecosystem. A serious drought over the next few years inhibited growth and propagation of many of the new plants, but the federal standard for a wetland was met. Park officials reported, "With the installation of interpretive corrals, two trails, a viewing deck, and three interpretive signs, visitors now have many opportunities to view wildlife and experience the rich history at Prisoners Harbor."[41]

Managing Natural Resources in the Sea

Creation of the thirteen marine protected areas (MPAs) and the addition of more inventory and monitoring sites around the park islands brought a steep increase in data and a new understanding of marine ecology after 2003. Using money from the state of California and the NPS, biologists at Channel Islands added seventeen new monitoring sites to the existing sixteen in 2005. NPS marine biologists are assisted by and sometimes contract research out to the Partnership for Interdisciplinary Studies of Coastal Oceans (PISCO). The agency monitors 120 species plus water conditions including temperature, salinity, and acidity. Significantly, many of the new sites allow biologists to compare similar habitats within and outside the marine reserves. In addition, they allow monitoring in a marine environment under increasingly complex interactions of four major factors—environmental change, disease, fishing pressure, and invasive exotic species. The interplay of these factors has created highly variable conditions over both time and space.

Temperature is the most significant environmental factor. The distance from Santa Barbara Island in the warm southern area to San Miguel Island in the much cooler northern area of the park is only 50 miles (80 km). Yet, its contrast allows species from a transect of the mainland coast hundreds of miles in extent to exist in relative proximity. The temperature gradient changes seasonally as well as through ocean events that fluctuate over time, such as the El Niño-La Niña cycle. The inventory and monitoring program has tracked the dramatic variance in marine resource conditions that results from the cycle. During the decades from 1980 through 2000, it became more pronounced and included unusually strong El Niños in 1982–84 and 1997–98. These brought warmer waters with concomitant declines in kelp, spiny lobsters, and sea stars. Around Santa Barbara Island the kelp forest essentially vanished. Another milder El Niño in 2015–16 reinforced the pattern. But by that time another factor had altered the equation.[42]

Monitoring showed that after 2000 the cycle diminished, and measurements showed less annual variance but a gradual increase in water temperature. A marine heat wave was detected in the Gulf of Alaska in 2013 that soon expanded east and south, reaching the Pacific Northwest coast in late 2014. It became the largest and most widespread marine heat wave ever documented in the northeast Pacific Ocean. Climatologists branded it the "North Pacific Blob." It mixed with warm water in the Southern California Countercurrent shortly thereafter. In the Santa Barbara Channel region, it generated what is now called a "Warm Water Event" that coincided with the 2015–16 El Niño and placed great stress on the recovery of kelp forest habitats. Water temperatures warmed as much as 8°F (5°C) and caused major spatial shifts in food webs. Locally, productivity of nutrients was low, due to a reduction of coastal winds and the upwelling that brought them into the upper layers of the sea. The warm water event was linked in 2015 to a harmful algal bloom (*Pseudonitzschia*) along the West Coast that was unprecedented in size, duration, and toxicity. Seabird and marine mammal die-offs were documented during the warm water event due to shifts in the availability of prey and toxicity of the algal bloom. Northern anchovy (*Engraulis mordax*), Pacific sardine (*Sardinops sagax*), and market squid (*Doryteuthis opalescens*) are key prey for many predatory fishes, seabirds, and marine mammals in the pelagic food web around the Channel Islands. Reduction in the abundance and quality of these prey species available to breeding female sea lions at Channel Islands rookeries led to increased stranding of California sea lion pups starting in 2013. When the El Niño finally retreated, the kelp ecosystem began to rebound. Marine biologists speculate on whether climate change in the northern Pacific Ocean may intensify and produce more warm water events in the future.[43]

One resource that does not appear to suffer from an El Niño or a warm water event is Pacific eelgrass (*Zostera pacifica*). It too serves as a foraging, nursery, and biogenic habitat in subtidal and intertidal soft bottom regions. It is found off Santa Rosa, Santa Cruz, and Anacapa Islands. Data show that most eelgrass beds have been generally stable over time. While there is no evidence of a negative effect on eelgrass in most areas of the sanctuary, the beds in Frenchy's Cove continue to be disturbed from anchoring and lobster trap placements. Surveys of a 2003 experimental eelgrass transplant at Anacapa Island showed peak coverage in 2009 followed by a decline in areas open to fishing.[44]

The complexity of ecological relations between various components of the marine ecosystems around the Channel Islands is shown by the impact of disease on the population survival rates of the marine species. Sea urchins, the prime consumers of kelp, have been deeply affected by two strains—a "wasting disease" and a "black spot disease." Serious outbreaks have prevented sea urchins from colonizing an even larger proportion of kelp habitat. In areas with a low density of sea urchins, they lodge in cracks and crevasses in the sea floor and subsist on kelp fronds floating past. But when their population increases, they move from these limited sites, colonize the wider seafloor, and consume the "holdfasts" that anchor entire kelp plants to the bottom. The absence of most urchin predators in the 79 percent of the park waters outside the marine reserves means there are few checks on sea urchins other than the commercial fishery that takes them. Spiny lobsters (*Panulirus interruptus*), California sheephead (*Semicossyphus pulcher*), and sunflower sea stars (*Pycnopodia helianthoides*) prey upon them, but all are subject to human harvest. A booming market in Japan for red sea urchins (*Strongylocentrotus franciscanus*) offers a good substitute for the kelp industry's payments to divers who used to eradicate them. However, the diseases mean that most of the urchins lose the edible portions, which has caused annual commercial harvests to shrink from a high point of $25 million to $5 million over the last few years. Purple sea urchins (*Strongylocentrotus purpuratus*) apparently are less susceptible to the diseases but are small and undesirable to fishermen, and they are the culprits in most so-called urchin barrens.[45]

Sunflower sea stars eat sea urchins but the "warm water event" heavily impacted them. In water warmer than 65°F (18.3°C) they essentially dissolve in what is called a "sea star wasting syndrome." They inhabit a deep column of water, so after an El Niño event, the survivors from the colder submarine layer below 60 feet (18.3 meters) can quickly recruit the upper levels again. However, the warm water event has heavily impacted twenty species of sea stars at all depths. Marine biologists expected a major boom in sea urchin numbers, but at Johnsons Lee, where they carefully monitored the situation, it did not happen after the 2015–16 event. The scientists hypothesize that the sea urchin diseases prevented a rebound of their numbers.[46]

In August 2018, CINMS released the first volume of a new status report for the unit, including the waters of the national park.[47] The status of commercially important species such as black abalone (*H. cracherodii*), giant sea bass (*Stereolepis gigas*), and sea cucumber (*Parastichopus sp.*) remain depressed compared to historic levels. White abalone (*Haliotis sorenseni*) shows no signs of recovery, and most experts believe that it never will. David Kushner of the park staff disputes the common notion that white abalone were wiped out over a short period of time. He believes that they were taken previously but misidentified as pink abalone. He agrees that the species is probably doomed locally. Gary Davis, now retired from the park, states that an abalone species that declines to below 50 percent of its population is threatened, and below 20 percent is usually unrecoverable. Six other species of abalone inhabit the park—black, red (*H. rufescens*), green (*H. fulgens*), pink (*H. corrugata*), flat (*H. walallenssis*), and threaded (*H. assimilis*)—and all numbers are extremely low, except for black abalone at San Miguel Island. Threaded abalone, now sometimes called "pinto abalone," decreased at the same time as most of the others but was never harvested. However, it was at the extreme southern end of its range and may have decreased in number due to other factors.[48]

The California sea cucumber (*Parastichopus californicus*) and the warty sea cucumber (*P. parvimensis*) are recreationally and commercially harvested in Southern California. Surveys by the park from 1982 to 1999 found that average density peaked in 1990 at two sea cucumbers per square meter (3.3 feet) then gradually declined to an average density of 0.4 by 1999. Since 2005, warty sea cucumber density has been stable at San Miguel and Santa Rosa Islands but has decreased at Santa Barbara, Santa Cruz, and Anacapa Islands. Most of the improved density of warty sea cucumbers occurred within the marine reserves. Giant sea bass, an apex predatory fish, has been listed by the International Union for the Conservation of Nature (IUCN) as a critically endangered species. It too survives primarily in the MPAs.[49]

California spiny lobster and California sheephead that prey on sea urchins are far below historic levels due to harvest. However, lobsters have increased in number at Anacapa, Santa Cruz, and Santa Barbara islands since 2015. Sheephead have also increased since the 2009 assessment at some islands. Both Davis and Kushner attribute this to the establishment of the marine reserves and conservation areas. The 2018 sanctuary report notes that: "Average biomass of species targeted by fishing, such as rockfish, kelp bass, and lobster, has increased both inside and outside of MPAs since their implementation, but the rate of increase is much greater inside MPAs where fishing is not allowed. Increased biomass inside marine reserves, known as the 'reserve effect,' results from larger-sized individuals such as kelp bass and sheephead as well as higher densities inside the protected areas. The reserve effect is even more consistent for species subject to high fishing pressure including California spiny lobster, sea cucumber, and sheephead."[50] Interestingly, San Miguel Island is the coldest and the most distant from ports. Hence, it receives the fewest visits by fishing boats. It also showed the least variation in the biomass of popular species between no-fishing reserves and areas open to harvest. This supports the idea that fishing pressure is *the* major factor in recovery of those species that help the recovery of the kelp habitat.

David Kushner, Gary Davis, and other marine biologists are confident that the MPAs are working. As early as 2013, PISCO reported: "The Channel Islands MPAs appear to be fulfilling their role as refuges for many fish and invertebrate species. Heavily targeted species are bigger and more abundant inside these protected areas than in fished areas, and the increases are more pronounced and rapid inside MPAs compared to areas nearby."⁵¹ Kushner added that ten years of monitoring at Anacapa Island's reserves saw some recovery of sea cucumbers, kelp bass, and spiny lobsters. At Black Sea Bass Reef, a blanket of brittle stars (*Ophiuroide sp*) is rapidly disappearing due to the return of the lobsters.

At Santa Cruz Island, an El Niño episode devastated most of the kelp forest. A subsequent check of six monitoring sites checked showed kelp recovery in the three MPA sites and urchin barrens in the three sites outside them. An identical pattern of kelp or urchin domination occurred at six sites at Santa Rosa Island. In an August 2018 interview, Kushner stated that divers can easily tell when they are not in a marine reserve: "There's no fish. There's no lobster or not many. It's a bleak environment outside an MPA and inside the MPA there's a lush kelp forest full of fish and full of lobster. It's that obvious."⁵²

In its 2009 condition report, the CINMS found no problematic nonnative species but warned that invasive algae from mainland harbors and Santa Catalina Island could reach the Northern Channel Islands. According to the 2016 report, one of those species of concern, *Sargassum horneri*, is now present and expanding its range at three of the islands in the park. It is a fast-growing brown type of kelp from eastern Asia that can cause severe degradation to native kelp forest communities. It first appeared in Long Beach Harbor in 2003 and spread to Anacapa Island by 2009. By October 2016, it was established at multiple sites at Anacapa, Santa Barbara, and Santa Cruz islands. In addition, drift was observed at San Miguel and Santa Rosa islands, but monitoring had not detected established populations at these islands. In 2016, density increased substantially at Anacapa, Santa Barbara, and eastern Santa Cruz Islands, possibly due to the warm water event. Researchers also have found it in the rocky intertidal zone at Anacapa and Santa Barbara Islands. Marine biologists fear it may dominate available space and block light as it does within *Sargassum* thickets at Santa Catalina and San Clemente islands.⁵³

The Japanese brown alga (*Undaria pinnatifida*) is another exotic species of concern because it very quickly colonizes a new area and reaches high densities in intertidal and subtidal habitats. Although it has commercial value as the principal ingredient in miso soup, *U. pinnatifida* is listed as one of the world's one hundred worst invasive alien species by the IUCN.

It was first found growing in Los Angeles Harbor in 2000 and has now spread throughout Southern California harbors and as far north as San Francisco Bay. During surveys in June and July 2016, divers found many *U. pinnatifida* plants, ranging from juveniles to reproductive adults, at depths ranging from 30 to 50 feet (9.1 to 15.2 meters) at Keyhole, a monitoring site on the northern side of West Anacapa Island. It grows on all types of substrate, including rocky reef, bedrock, cobble, and sand. Marine biologists have urged that additional monitoring and ecological studies of this very new and aggressive invasive are needed.[54]

A third exotic species of eventual concern is *Watersipora spp.*, a Japanese bryozoan that colonizes both natural and manmade hard substrates. Bryozoans are a phylum of aquatic invertebrate animals that function as a colony. Individuals in these colonies are called zooids because they are not fully independent animals. Different component zooids are responsible for eating, hatching eggs, and defense. The latter also enable the colony to move. *Watersipora subtorquata*, commonly known as the red-rust bryozoan, is a species of colonial bryozoan in the family Watersiporidae. It is unclear from where it originated, but it has become invasive on the west coast of North America. It can reduce a kelp forest enough to impact fish and invertebrate species and is also a source of food for sea urchins. In 2011 *Watersipora* was observed for the first time in the sanctuary during kelp forest surveys by park divers. In 2017 researchers found it at two sites in the park, Cathedral Cove on Anacapa Island and Fry's Harbor on Santa Cruz Island. At that time, it existed in two distinct patches at Santa Cruz Island as well as on pier pilings. It had not yet seriously affected park ecosystems, but studies were underway to determine whether it could readily spread from oil platforms in the Santa Barbara Channel where it is more abundant.[55]

Research and discovery about the interplay of the four factors—environmental conditions, disease, fishing harvests, and nonnative species combined with unknowns such as climate change have demonstrated the worth of the marine monitoring program. The apparent recovery of native species, albeit slow, in the MPAs and their "spill-over effects" outside their boundaries justified their establishment in 2003 and enlargement thereafter. Whether the success of the reserves should encourage further enlargement to greater than 21 percent coverage remains highly controversial. As complex as resource management on the islands has proven to be, it is in the sea where the native habitats may undergo the greatest alteration.

Planning and the Wilderness Question

On October 1, 2001, the NPS announced that it would initiate a planning procedure for a new general management plan for Channel Islands National Park. During the sixteen years since the 1985 update to the original GMP, the Park Service had acquired new lands on Santa Rosa and Santa Cruz Islands, coped with a decline in the condition of marine life and some endemic terrestrial species, began eliminating nonnative species, and saw a 300 percent increase in park visitation. When Russell Galipeau arrived to superintend Channel Islands National Park in May 2003, the park was struggling with natural resource and land reclamation issues, so he slowed the planning process.[56]

On November 14, 2013, the park finally released a "Draft General Management Plan/Wilderness Study/Environmental Impact Statement." It identified six planning "issues/concerns." First, what should be done to enhance access for visitors to the islands? The primary question was whether airstrips for passenger airplanes should be improved to supplement concession and private boat access on East Santa Cruz Island and San Miguel Island. On the latter, planners sought a way to allow more visitors to see the pinniped rookery at Point Bennett. Because it requires a 16-mile (25.7km) round-trip hike to view the marine animals, time constraints made it sensible to reduce the access from more than four hours each way by boat to one hour each way by plane.[57]

Santa Rosa Island is the biggest single piece of conterminous property in the park, so road access on it formed a second planning issue. Over 150 years, Vail & Vickers and their predecessors had carved rough dirt roads all over the hilltops and into many canyons and beaches. In the interest of resource protection, the park staff wanted to close a number of roads and convert others to trails. The preferred alternative explained that 67 miles (108km) of roads on the island would be cut to 44 miles (71km) but did not specify which roads would be kept and which would be converted to trails or restored to natural conditions. The planners also considered and dropped the idea of horseback riding on this or any other park island.[58]

The third issue underpinned all the others—what type and balance of developments should be provided for visitors while continuing to protect park resources. Park planners had to decide where to add camping, other types of lodgings, more hiking trails, and recreational activities as well as the level of staffing and logistical support necessary to maintain them. During the comment period and in the public meetings, most of the past and potential visitors favored "keeping the islands as they are," while others wanted more recreation opportunities. Park planners favored adding forty-five "camper nights," to bring the total of individuals to 450, redesigning the campgrounds on Anacapa Island, Water Canyon on Santa Rosa Island, and Scorpion Valley on Santa Cruz Island and adding new ones at Smugglers Cove and Prisoners Harbor on Santa Cruz Island and at Bechers Bay and Johnsons Lee on Santa Rosa Island. Superintendent Galipeau also wanted some form of visitor lodgings at Bechers Bay by adapting the old Vail & Vickers ranch structures. He reasoned that preservation of the largest concentration of historic buildings in the park would be facilitated by their adaptive use. That facility would also become the center for enhanced visitor amenities, such as a food concession and vehicular tours of the island. It would also help sustain park administration in a more efficient manner, the fourth issue of the GMP process. On East Santa Cruz Island the park wanted a kayak concessioner at Scorpion Harbor and an education center at Prisoners Harbor.[59]

The fifth issue was the suitability of the islands for wilderness status. This had implications not only for the other issues listed above but also for myriad ongoing programs in the park. Initially Superintendent Galipeau had some reservations about including a wilderness proposal, but he agreed with Regional Director Jon Jarvis that status as a designated wilderness was the best way to minimize the development footprint. However, Galipeau and his staff raised questions and urged that more research be done before the NPS ask Congress to pass a Channel Islands wilderness bill. First, would wilderness prevent using mechanized vehicles and motorized equipment to carry out the inventory and monitoring (I&M) program? Would it halt the use of roads to implement ecological restoration? Would it apply to using radio-tracking equipment to research island fauna? If "one dirty fishing boat" wrecked on a wilderness coast and accidentally released a pregnant rat onto an island, would the NPS be able to act immediately or have to go through a detailed and lengthy review process to justify using the tools necessary to act in wilderness?

Galipeau later explained that a response to such an event would have to be carried out within forty-eight hours because beyond that time it becomes exponentially harder to find the rodent. In a year, one pregnant rat could become one hundred rats. How would the park respond to a future oil spill? All of these questions revolved around the potential legal ramifications of insistence by an environmental organization that the park must adhere strictly to the 1964 Wilderness Act. Despite these misgivings, both alternatives two and three proposed wilderness status for almost all of Santa Barbara Island, all of West and Middle Anacapa Islets, 99 percent of Santa Rosa Island, and 97 percent of the NPS property on East Santa Cruz Island. The total wilderness acreage would be 66,675 acres (26,982 ha) or 53 percent of the land within the park boundary. Although 98 percent of the NPS property would be in wilderness, ownership of western Santa Cruz Island by TNC and San Miguel Island by the U.S. Navy diminished the overall percentage.[60] The final issue that the GMP addressed was climate change. This was speculative but needed to be addressed in a plan that was projected to shape management policy for twenty years. The NPS promised that "the continued ecological restoration efforts on the islands will aid in ecosystem resilience against the impacts of climate change."[61]

During the comment period, the park received 1,091 written responses. Those, combined with the comments offered during December 2013 public meetings, allowed park planners to learn much about the public's reaction to its proposals. First, most people strongly indicated that they considered the boat trip to be part of the experience. On Santa Cruz Island, park planners also found that the number of visitors to this most popular portion of the park already had reached a level consistent with the stipulations of the enabling act for "limited visitor impact." The campground held 240 people, which the Island Packers boats could bring. In addition, the distance from the main development area at Scorpion Harbor to the old airfield at Smugglers was too far and would require extensive infrastructural upgrades and, possibly, a shuttle service. Use of the Smugglers airstrip had been terminated in the early 2000s because boat service to the island was sufficient for visitors' needs. Although private pilots and others disputed these findings, the park dropped the idea of an air service to East Santa Cruz Island. On the other hand, the reaction to the proposed air service to San Miguel Island was generally supportive.[62]

Second, the preponderance of public opinion opposed any expansion of the development footprint. In response, the NPS scaled back draft plans for concessioner accommodations on East Santa Cruz from eighteen to twelve, with most of them in seasonal tents. However, the planners broadened the area zoned as front country at Prisoners Harbor to accommodate more visitors to the isthmus section of the island. On Santa Rosa Island, changes from the draft plan included shifting the user capacity from five hundred people at Bechers Bay to that number for the entire island. Lodgings at the ranch area were changed to be only rustic accommodations. Park planners decided to convert the road system from one that circled the island to one that had three spokes reaching Torrey Pines, Lobo Canyon, and Johnsons Lee, with drop-off points along the way. Planners also suggested three possible locations for a proposed research center, including one at the ranch area where development already existed.[63]

The proposal for wilderness also changed dramatically. It had been opposed by many respondents as an unnecessary legal burden on visitors. Some among the public questioned whether islands used for grazing and military purposes qualified for wilderness designation. Others thought the islands were already like wilderness because of the difficulty of accessing them and the absence of any settlement. They wondered if giving it legal status was really necessary. Citing NPS policy, Galipeau answered that wilderness is not about the past, but is in fact a goal to reach.[64] The final plan proposed 66,576 (26,942ha) acres of wilderness and potential wilderness. The wilderness portions included 639 acres (259ha) of wilderness for Santa Barbara Island, 620 acres (251ha) on West and Middle Anacapa Islets, and 39 acres (16ha) of various offshore rocks. The 14,476 acres (5858ha) on East Santa Cruz Island and 50,802 acres (20,559ha) on Santa Rosa Island, remained potential wilderness due to "several continuing nonconforming uses" that would have to terminate before a recommendation could be tendered to congress. From a management standpoint, it did not matter because, in accordance with NPS wilderness policy, both areas would be protected from development as if they were already designated as wilderness.[65] On September 14, 2015, Acting Regional Director Martha J. Lee signed a final record of decision approving the final GMP/EIS and its preferred alternative.[66]

THE NAVY CLOSURE OF SAN MIGUEL ISLAND

The U.S. Navy bombed on and around San Miguel Island as late as the 1980s. Its 1976 agreement with the NPS had allowed rangers to shepherd limited numbers of visitors to Point Bennett along a trail that followed the World War II era road and to a few other locations near Nidever Canyon. During the 1980s, navy explosive ordnance disposal (EOD) teams investigated objects that looked threatening. In August 1982, an EOD team found a 250-pound general-purpose bomb near Hoffman Point and blew it up.[67] Then, in early 2014, a vegetation mapping crew came across a large, cylindrical metal object. The navy sent an EOD crew to investigate, and they determined the object was not a piece of ordnance. The find, however, disturbed Naval Base Ventura County commander Larry Vasquez who then closed San Miguel to both the public and Park Service personnel on April 7, 2014. He insisted that only rangers and researchers with unexploded ordnance (UXO) safety training be allowed back on the island.[68]

This stirred an angry reaction from the public, legislators, and the California Coastal Commission.[69] After months of inaction, in October 2014, a team of UXO technicians began conducting metal-detector surveys of the trails, airstrips, developed areas, and off-trail routes regularly used by researchers. Team members surveyed 182 miles of track line that covered less than 1 percent of the island's surface. They found no live ordnance but recovered several practice bombs. In general, all parties were relieved that so few items were found and that nothing explosive had been discovered. However, it took another eighteen months to complete a series of required studies and a new agreement between the NPS and the navy. By May 2016, the last of the required agreements were signed, and on May 17, 2016, San Miguel Island reopened to the public. By the end of that year, 211 people had received UXO safety training.[70] This was a stark example of how previous land activities can disrupt park purposes and preservation even decades after their occurrences.

In June 2018, Superintendent Russell Galipeau retired from the National Park Service. He was a few months short of the term of leadership served by Bill Ehorn. He oversaw the end of Vail & Vickers' hunting operation; completion of multiple new documents, including the 2015 GMP; and the final removal of nonnative domestic herbivores from all five islands. He retired somewhat earlier than he had projected. After a tour of Santa Rosa Island by new Secretary of the Interior Ryan Zinke and members of the Vail family, some park officials suspected that the NPS policies regarding livestock on the island might be suspended and that Zinke was looking for new leadership at the park.[71] Galipeau decided to retire before any such action could take place.

Status of Resources at Channel Islands National Park

In 2020 Channel Islands National Park and Channel Islands National Marine Sanctuary celebrated their fortieth birthdays. Including the years as a national monument, 82 years as a NPS unit had passed. During the middle years of the previous decade, the staffs of both federal units carefully studied the conditions of the natural resources under their care. The result for the park is called a Natural Resource Condition Assessment (NRCA), part of a program used to evaluate conditions in 270 national park units with significant natural resources. It reports trends in resource condition, identifies critical data gaps, and characterizes a general level of confidence for study results. The program is another outgrowth of the I&M program.[72] An NRCA provides a park with resource condition data to develop resource management plans, vulnerability assessments, special use permits, and GMPs. The credibility of NRCA results is derived from the data, methods, and reference values used in the project, which are designed for its stated purpose. The level of rigor can vary by resource or indicator, depending upon the amount and quality of existing data for and knowledge of each resource. For each current condition or trend reported, the assessment should identify critical data gaps and describe the level of confidence, at least qualitatively. "NPS staff and cooperating scientists select study indicators; recommend data sets, methods, and reference conditions; and help provide a multi-disciplinary review of draft study findings."[73]

For Channel Islands National Park, the NRCA team members focused on whether or not vegetation (primarily woody vegetation) was recovering on the five islands and how that was influencing recovery of the native terrestrial vertebrates. They evaluated the condition of vegetation and vertebrate communities on the islands using existing information from reports, theses, and journal articles as well as new analyses of recently available data collected on the islands by the I&M program. Although the final report is dated 2017, the data were collected by the end of 2014. The results were mixed but hopeful. Four of the five islands—Anacapa, Santa Cruz, San Miguel, and Santa Rosa—exhibited some native vegetation recovery. However, Santa Barbara Island showed very little recovery.

Anacapa Island's three islets have experienced varied recovery since the removal of sheep in 1938. The western and middle islets now support native perennial grasslands, live-forever communities, and a teeming population of brown pelicans. The two islets benefit from closure to visitation that also inhibits importation of exotic vegetation. East Anacapa Islet, however, has not recovered as much due to the dense infestation of ice plant and relatively heavy visitor use. Active eradication of ice plant and other nonnative plants by the NPS continues and may eventually enable the eastern islet to match the recovery of its neighbors. Nevertheless, woodland and chaparral vegetation lag behind native grasses and only occur in small stands on the islet. The eradication of rats led to recovery of most native birds, although a few landbird species are troubled by the native deer mice that prey upon their eggs. The NRCA characterized Anacapa Island as being in moderate condition but having a high probability of eventual recovery provided that the agency continues active restoration on the eastern islet.[74]

Removal of domestic sheep and feral pigs from Santa Cruz Island has allowed a rapid ecological change that varies across the landscape depending on terrain, maritime exposure, and climate. Coastal sage scrub and riparian vegetation are recovering most rapidly, while pine and oak woodland recovery is promising but spatially uneven. Scientists believe that the likeliest scenario is the establishment of a mosaic of native woody vegetation with an understory of nonnative and herbaceous vegetation. This process is slower on the warmer south side of the island. Steep slopes remain threatened by erosion and dense stands of fennel still occupy areas of the Central Valley and Christy Ranch regions. Some endemic species that suffered dramatic losses are rebounding while others are not. Although it is early in the restoration phase, Santa Cruz Island appears to be evolving into a landscape dominated by native scrub, chaparral, and woodland that retains annual grassland openings and nonnative understory. Populations of terrestrial vertebrates on the island have benefited tremendously from the removal of nonnative animals. Recovery of the island fox has led to adjustment of the bird, mice, and spotted skunk populations, and most species have seen increases in recent years. Authors of the NRCA rated Santa Cruz Island as being in a moderate condition with positive trends in recovery although uneven for some floral species.[75]

Santa Rosa Island is in an early but accelerating stage of native vegetation recovery since removal of the last ungulates. When the data were collected, it had been sixteen years since cattle left the island but only two years since the last deer were eliminated. However, scientists reported that the potential for natural recovery was high for most of the island. Santa Rosa is not as topographically rugged as Santa Cruz, and this has more evenly spread the benefits of eradicating nonnative ungulates. Riparian areas have regained herbaceous vegetation but still lack trees. Woody plants have begun to recruit in woodland, chaparral, and coastal sage scrub since release from deer browsing. Researchers identified some factors that hinder their recovery, including competition from dense brome grasses, lack of soil and litter to form seedbeds in upland areas, inability to capture and retain water from fog, and continued erosion and sedimentation. Drought years also have slowed recovery, and climate change is threatening as well. Habitat recovery for animals has been generally good, although species dependent on standing and downed woodlands have lagged behind others. As on Santa Cruz Island, the restoration of the island fox has rippled through the vertebrate populations and achieved ecological integrity. The "Condition Assessment" for Santa Rosa Island rated its recovery as moderate for vegetation and good for animals.[76]

Sheep grazing and the continuity of strong winds damaged San Miguel Island more than any of the other islands. Its denuding led to extensive sand dunes that covered much of the surface and eliminated most of the native vegetation. During the late twentieth century, a mix of native and nonnative plants slowly began to stabilize the coastal dunes leading to low scrub in some areas. Island vegetation has recovered, somewhat, from the impacts of sheep prior to World War II, but areas of exotic grassland persist, and the chaparral present before settlement has not reappeared on the island. The NRCA scientists reported that active restoration is needed to find native seed sources, grow plants for seed increase, and develop chaparral habitat on the island. Vertebrate populations are healthy and at relatively high densities, probably due to the limits on visitor access imposed by the navy. Island foxes have recovered from the precipitous decline of the mid-1990s and may number more than before the crisis. Landbirds also exist at fairly high densities. Scientists opine that while there may not be the same composition of native vegetation communities that existed prior to the introduction of nonnative grazing animals, this may not be as important as on other islands. They believe that similarities among the scrub and even the grassland habitats on San Miguel, the relaxed niches exhibited by island species, and the generalist nature of island foxes indicate some recovery from the desert-like landscape described by observers throughout the preceding century. The NRCA rates San Miguel's condition as moderate, except for native chaparral, and good for animals with high potential for greater recovery.[77]

Finally, there is Santa Barbara Island and here the picture darkens. The "Condition Assessment" notes that the island

> is still dominated by exotic annual vegetation more than 30 years after rabbits were removed, in what appears to be a new stable state for the island. Vegetation cover and composition fluctuate with the precipitation rather than trending toward a more native shrubby condition over most of the island. Upland native shrub recovery has not occurred naturally, and is insufficient to provide habitat for the

nesting seabirds that used the island before ranching.... Factors limiting recovery appear to be aridity, the lack of native soil seed banks, widespread crystalline iceplant seed bank, and plowing of the uplands that destroyed soil structure and native seed banks. The potential for natural recovery of SBI [Santa Barbara Island] vegetation to a condition like pre-ranching is low. Island vegetation needs active recovery to move it out of its current annual-dominated state towards a landscape dominated by native scrub.

The lack of native scrub has inhibited animal recovery and the populations of birds, reptiles, and mammals remain low. Although the Santa Barbara song sparrow went extinct in 1958, none of the other vertebrate species are similarly threatened, but scientists worry that climate change could endanger some of them in the future. The report rates the vegetative condition of Santa Barbara Island as poor, the animal condition as moderate, and the recovery potential of both as low. The cessation of visitation due to the collapse of the landing facility may give the island a welcome respite, but significant and expensive proactive steps will be required by the NPS to bring the island to the level of improvement seen on the other four islands.[78]

Channel Islands National Marine Sanctuary also conducts and publishes "Condition Assessments" for the resources in its protected area. This includes a much larger portion of the ocean than the area within the park boundary. Nevertheless, it still provides a good idea of what is happening in the one-mile sections around the park islands. The report's 2016 summary offered a guarded analysis of the resources:

The abundance and diversity of wildlife seen around the northern Channel Islands is remarkable compared to many parts of the world and was a main reason for its sanctuary designation. Although the 2016 status and trends are quite variable across the range of species in the sanctuary, overall, the data indicate that many of the sanctuary's living resources are showing relative stability or improvement since 2009. For example, most kelp forest and seafloor-associated fishes are stable or increasing, especially inside no-take zones [the marine reserves and marine conservation areas]. Additionally, the

Fig. 34. Managing five islands requires the use of expensive technology. Photographer and date unknown, CINP Digital Archives, DSCF 2136.

number of native species in sanctuary habitats, which is one measure of biodiversity, appears to be stable with no known recent local extinctions; however, the island-wide drastic declines in sea stars, a keystone species in rocky shore and shallow reef habitats, coupled with the establishment of a few non-indigenous species at some island monitoring sites, contributed to worsening trends in the status of nearshore communities and raises concerns about future impacts to ecological integrity and biodiversity.[79]

The "Condition Assessment" insisted that monitoring living resources in sanctuary habitats needs to continue to determine whether key species and community assemblages will return to past patterns or if new patterns are emerging in response to changing climate and other human pressures. The effects of the warm water event that began in 2013 and lasted until 2016 were troubling. Failure to establish larger no-fishing reserves around the islands certainly continues to stress the various near-shore species. The inclusion of 21 percent of the island coastlines shows that recovery is possible. But, the continuing decline of all species of abalone, the arrival and spread of exotic organisms such as *Sargassum horneri* and *Undaria pinnatifida*, ongoing climate change, and the pressure of overfishing in the larger region present threats that will be difficult to measure, let alone to control.

Conclusion

The history of natural resource management in Channel Islands National Park consists of two stories that illustrate the issues faced by the National Park Service in America and by other land management and preservation agencies in this and other countries. They are (1) the acquisition of land and sea for preservation and (2) restoration of the ecological integrity in those habitats. Channel Islands has had extraordinary, in some cases groundbreaking, experiences with both processes.

Following removal of the original inhabitants in the early nineteenth century, all eight of the Channel Islands underwent use by ranchers, fishermen, sea mammal hunters, the military, and sporadic residents. The federal government owned the five smallest islands, while Santa Cruz, Santa Rosa, and Santa Catalina became private domains. The establishment of Channel Islands National Monument in 1938 incorporated the two smallest islands, Anacapa and Santa Barbara. The U.S. Navy took over the remaining three, including the westernmost of the Northern Channel Islands, San Miguel. The National Park Service (NPS) always wanted to include the two biggest islands of the northern group, Santa Cruz and Santa Rosa, in a park, but either faced unwillingness by the owners to sell or lacked the funds necessary to meet their demands.

When the lion's share of the biggest island, Santa Cruz, finally did sell, it was to the Nature Conservancy (TNC), rather than the NPS, in 1978. Establishment of the national park on March 5, 1980, included all the northern islands within its new boundary but forbade the NPS from acquiring TNC land unless there was a threatened change in land use that would not be in conformance with NPS purposes. From the standpoint of ecological management, this was readily acceptable, but 90 percent of the island remained off limits to national park visitor access. The NPS plays a long game in land acquisition, however, and has not given up. The eastern portion of Santa Cruz Island came to the agency in 1997, and two years later TNC donated 14 percent of the land adjacent to East Santa Cruz Island to the NPS, giving the agency control of 24 percent of the island and the important Prisoners Harbor access to the island.

Santa Rosa Island proved to be the most controversial of all the land acquisitions by the NPS in the park. The Vail & Vickers Company and some range management consultants claimed that raising cattle improved or at least stabilized the island's forage after decades of destruction by sheep prior to 1901. As the largest land area available for a proposed Channel Islands National Park, the agency desperately wanted the island. Initially, the company sought to remain outside the park boundary. Friendship with Superintendent Bill Ehorn and praise for their stewardship from legislators during the congressional hearings led the Vails to agree to have their island included in the park but only if purchase of their land preceded all other land sales. Congressman Robert Lagomarsino, as author of the bill to create the park, other legislators, and NPS director William Whalen offered the company a reservation of use and occupancy (RUO) for twenty-five years to continue its cattle and hunting operations. The company chose only a 7.6-acre RUO for its residence and operations center.

After the bill passed in 1980, it took six years for the government to allocate the funds to purchase the island and another year for the ranchers and the NPS to agree to a special use permit for a five- or possibly ten-year phaseout. Yet, Lagomarsino, Ehorn, and a number of later park and regional NPS officials came to believe that the company could continue its operations on all the island as before until 2011, when their limited residential RUO expired. Problems started when the NPS and various scientists began realizing the actual condition of the natural resources. Vail & Vickers believed that their operations would take spatial and temporal precedence over those of the park. The ecological damage exposed by the inventory and monitoring program and frustration with restrictions on activities of the NPS—the rightful owners of the island—split the park staff and led to a lawsuit that ended with a 1998 court-established settlement agreement. Cattle ranching on the island ceased and hunting of deer and elk became constrained. The park enjoyed great support from scientists, environmentalists, other state and federal government agencies, and eventually, courts of law. However, some members of the local public and media accused the NPS of reneging on a deal established in good faith if not by strictly legal means. That reputation for the agency still resonates among some locals. The deer and elk hunting continued for the rest of the twenty-five years, to 2011, although it was bitterly contested to the end. Acquisition of San Miguel Island remains a fond hope of the National Park Service. The U.S. Navy still owns the island and, after years of post-World War II bombing and missile strikes, it is loath to relinquish it to the NPS. Because the NPS does not own TNC and navy land, any considerations of wilderness status or, conversely, significant visitor infrastructural development are unavailable.

The "ownership" of the sea adjacent to the islands has had a complicated history as well. When the monument was established, the boundary was the high-tide line and the state of California owned the waters out to three miles from the coast. Following a 1947 Supreme Court case and a 1949 proclamation by President Harry Truman, the monument gained control out to the one-mile line for the two small islands. However, four years later, Congress allocated control out to three miles to the states. In 1978 the Supreme Court verified that state jurisdiction. Establishment of the Channel Islands National Park and Channel Islands National Marine Sanctuary in 1980 led to complex overlapping of the Park Service's one-mile boundary, the state's three-mile boundary, and the Sanctuary's six-mile boundary. When it came time to establish marine reserves, the California Department of Fish and Game was responsible for the first three miles from the islands, the sanctuary for the next three miles, and the NPS, as the instigator of the campaign for the reserves and the producer of most of the monitoring data, officially remained a cooperating law enforcement agency.

The Organic Act of 1916 defines the purposes of the national park system and the agency that runs it: "to conserve the scenery and the natural and historic objects and the wildlife therein and to provide for the enjoyment of the same in such manner and by such means as will leave them unimpaired for the enjoyment of future generations." The key word is *unimpaired*. The NPS has operated with the assumption that the word means unchanged from natural ecological integrity. Federal and state courts, in hundreds of cases, have agreed.

Gary Davis's inventory and monitoring program identified the compelling need for ecological restoration. The data exposed have led management to focus on the removal or eradication of exotic fauna, such as feral pigs, sheep, and cattle, and invasive plants, such as sweet fennel. The park has also implemented habitat restoration. It maintains plant nurseries on Anacapa, Santa Barbara, Santa Rosa, and East Santa Cruz Islands, where native species are cultivated for revegetating disturbed areas. The reestablishment of the bald eagle is another, highly publicized example of the restoration of an element of the environment to the islands. Establishment of marine protected areas has helped preserve many species as well as entire habitats in the sea. The relatively minor physical development that occurred within the historic period on the Channel Islands, compared with the remainder of Southern California, has left much of its natural environment substantially intact. The opportunity to restore ecological integrity to the islands is enhanced by their isolation. The sea forms a natural barrier against further invasion of exotic species. Isolation makes it feasible to maintain and manage any progress made in the restoration of the islands' ecological integrity, unlike mainland landscapes of comparable size.

An obvious question pertaining to any restoration program is implied in the term itself—restoration *to what*? For many years, the National Park Service was guided, directly or indirectly, by the principles expressed in the 1963 Leopold Report, which stated: "As a primary goal, we would recommend that the biotic associations within each park be maintained, or where necessary recreated, as nearly as possible in the condition that prevailed when the area was first visited by the white man. A national park should represent a vignette of primitive America."[1] In accordance with these principles, Channel Islands should be restored to conditions that existed at or just prior to the early nineteenth century, when Mexican colonists first introduced significant changes to the native landscape.

Resource managers now look at a variety of factors that contribute to the health of a naturally functioning ecosystem but consider practical limitations. In practice, the objective is often still defined by the pre-European environment, to the extent this is known. But it does not have to be. On the Channel Islands, much of the environment has been so greatly altered by human activities within the historic period and even the precontact millennia that it would be impossible to restore the environment to a purely natural condition. Restoration efforts have therefore concentrated on improving the integrity of ecological systems to the point where they can become self-sustaining and resilient. Resource managers have attempted to accomplish this by removing or eliminating invasive exotic species that have impaired the integrity of these systems and by otherwise improving habitat conditions that will allow native populations to recover and survive future challenges. Protecting 21 percent of the islands' coastal waters through marine reserves has been successful, but a much larger percentage is sought by marine biologists.[2]

The park has been lauded for the restoration efforts of its resource management program, especially among professional conservation biologists and resource managers, but it has also been challenged. The most vocal criticism has come from animal rights activists, who continue to condemn any efforts to eliminate exotic species. In siding with the park, the courts have explicitly supported the principle that eliminating a population of introduced animals is a justifiable price for improving an entire ecosystem and preserving native species. Resource managers have attributed a higher biological priority to the preservation of a species or the habitats that support assemblages of species than to the preservation of a handful of exotic individuals that threaten those species. But this important distinction is lost on many animal rights activists, some of whom reject the very concept of a species as a meaningless abstraction.[3]

In the end, the Northern Channel Islands have benefitted from the committed efforts of park natural resource managers, despite cacophonous criticism of their restoration objectives and occasionally of their ethics by animal rights people and some local media sources. The bald eagle has been successfully reintroduced. Other seabirds, such as the brown pelican, Scripps's murrelet, and the double-crested cormorant, are increasing in numbers. The island fox has made a remarkable recovery and now exists in numbers approaching its precrisis population on all of the affected islands. Invasive sweet fennel remains a problem on Santa Cruz Island, as do other exotic plant species, but the principal sources of disturbance that led to its establishment and subsequent dispersal have been removed, and the infestation is at least contained. Santa Barbara Island has had the least successful ecological restoration, but with concerted effort by the NPS and volunteers it may still be returned to ecological integrity.

In 2012 a natural resources panel reviewed the original Leopold Report and offered recommendations for the centennial of the NPS. The members took into account the advances in science and the dynamism of natural processes. They also tried to balance their recommendations with the allied mission of providing education and recreation to the public. Their report stated:

> The overarching goal of NPS resource management should be to steward NPS resources for continuous change that is not yet fully understood, in order to preserve ecological integrity and cultural and historical authenticity, provide visitors with transformative experiences, and form the core of a national conservation land- and seascape.
>
> *Continuous change* is not merely constant or seasonal change; it is also the unrelenting and dynamic nature of the changes facing park systems expressed as extreme, volatile swings in conditions (such as unexpected, severe wet seasons) within long-term trends of change (such as decadal droughts). It is an essential finding of this committee that given the dynamic and complex nature of this change, the manager and decision maker must rely on science for guidance.
>
> *Ecological integrity* describes the quality of ecosystems that are largely self-sustaining and self-regulating. Such ecosystems may possess complete food webs, a full complement of native animal and plant species maintaining their populations, and naturally functioning ecological processes such as predation, nutrient cycling, disturbance and recovery, succession, and energy flow.[4]

Channel Islands National Park may never eliminate all the unwanted floral exotics from the islands and some species such as the Santa Barbara song sparrow are gone for good, but elimination of exotic animals, continued suppression of aggressive exotic plants, and enforcement of no-fishing marine reserves offer hope that ecological integrity is being restored.

Channel Islands National Park's evolution has been an occasionally tumultuous progression testing these laws and policies. In 2020 the park began advertising for a concessioner to operate on Santa Rosa Island within the grounds of the former Vail & Vickers residential complex. This will happen in order to satisfy the Organic Act's stipulation about the enjoyment of current and future generations. But, in spite of recent threats from political forces, they must still preserve the ecosystems "unimpaired." In the face of climate change, increasing visitation, and relentless efforts by some to turn back time to exploitative practices, preservation will remain the mantra for the National Park Service, the Nature Conservancy, and the overwhelming majority of people who actually visit the five islands and their surrounding waters.

NOTES

Introduction

1. National Park System Advisory Board, "Revisiting Leopold," 450.
2. Dilsaver and Babalis, *Oceanic Park*.

1. The Channel Islands

1. CINP, "Geologic Formations," accessed June 29, 2018, https://www.nps.gov/chis/learn/nature/geologicformations.htm; McEachern et al., "Managed Island Ecosystems," 755–78.
2. CINP, "Geologic Formations," 2018; McEachern et al., "Managed Island Ecosystems," 755–78.
3. McEachern et al., "Managed Island Ecosystems," 755–78.
4. Acreage and distance to the mainland figures for the park islands were provided by CINP GIS specialist Rockne Rudolph, December 13, 2018.
5. Schoenherr, Feldmeth, and Emerson, *Natural History*, 285–91; Davidson, A. et al., *Natural Resource Condition Assessment*, 124.
6. Schoenherr, Feldmeth, and Emerson, *Natural History*, 274–76; Davidson, A. et al., *Natural Resource Condition Assessment*, 154.
7. Davidson, A. et al., *Natural Resource Condition Assessment*, 191.
8. CINP, "Geologic Formations."
9. Schoenherr, Feldmeth, and Emerson, *Natural History*, 304–5; Davidson, A. et al., *Natural Resource Condition Assessment*, 97.
10. Davidson, A. et al., *Natural Resource Condition Assessment*, 64; Schoenherr, Feldmeth, and Emerson, *Natural History*, 349.
11. CINMS, *Channel Islands National Marine Sanctuary*, 8–11.
12. CINMS, *Channel Islands National Marine Sanctuary*, 8–11.
13. Davidson, A. et al., *Natural Resource Condition Assessment*, 22–23.
14. Davidson, A. et al., *Natural Resource Condition Assessment*, 22–23.

15. NOAA, "What are El Niño and La Niña?," accessed May 9, 2018, https://www.climate.gov/news-features/understanding-climate/el-ni%C3%B1o-and-la-ni%C3%B1a-frequently-asked-questions; Gary Davis email comments to Lary Dilsaver, February 20, 2019.
16. McEachern et al., "Managed Island Ecosystems," 755–78.
17. Junak et al., *Checklist of Vascular Plants*.
18. Davidson, A. et al., *Natural Resource Condition Assessment*, 30.
19. Davidson, A. et al., *Natural Resource Condition Assessment*, 29–42; NPS, *Anacapa Island Restoration Plan: Final Environmental Impact Statement*, CINP, October 2000.
20. Davidson, A. et al., *Natural Resource Condition Assessment*, 35–42.
21. Davidson, A. et al., *Natural Resource Condition Assessment*, 35–42.
22. Davidson, A. et al., *Natural Resource Condition Assessment*, 35–42.
23. Davidson, A. et al., *Natural Resource Condition Assessment*, 41–42.
24. CINMS, *Channel Islands National Marine Sanctuary*, 32–35.
25. Glassow, *Channel Islands Archaeological Overview*, 11–17; Livingston, *Island Legacies*, 9–11.
26. Kennett, *Island Chumash*; Glassow et al., "Prehistory of the Northern California Bight," 191–213; Erlandson, "Search for Early Shell Middens," 1; Gamble, "Archaeological Evidence," 301–15.
27. Rick, Erlandson, and Vellanoweth, "Paleocoastal Marine Fishing," 595–613; Erlandson, "Search for Early Shell Middens," 1.
28. Livingston, *Island Legacies*, 9–11.
29. Livingston, *Island Legacies*, 11–13.
30. Ogden, *California Sea Otter Trade*, 8.
31. Livingston, *Island Legacies*, 19–20.
32. Livingston, *Island Legacies*, 20–22.
33. CINP, "Chinese Abalone Fishermen," accessed October 17, 2018, https://www.nps.gov/chis/learn/historyculture/abalone-fishing.htm; Gary Davis comments to Lary Dilsaver, February 20, 2019.
34. Scofield, "History of Kelp Harvesting," 135–57.
35. The Treaty of Guadalupe-Hidalgo signed on February 2, 1848, cost Mexico more than 525,000 square miles of territory including the state of California.
36. Wellman, *Trampling Herd*, 13–58; Livingston, *Island Legacies*, 25–27.
37. Roberts, *Historic Resource Study*, 92–99.
38. Livingston, *Island Legacies*, 787.
39. Livingston, *Island Legacies*, 797–807.
40. Livingston, *Island Legacies*, 787–93; Public Law 74-351 (49 Stat. 885).

41. Livingston, *Island Legacies*, 793–97.
42. Livingston, *Island Legacies*, 841–43.
43. Livingston, *Island Legacies*, 852.
44. Ellison, *Life and Adventures*, 32, 43.
45. Livingston, *Island Legacies*, 54–55.
46. Livingston, *Island Legacies*, 69–81.
47. Livingston, *Island Legacies*, 81–82.
48. The island was managed by Dr. James Barron Shaw, who was the first to introduce sheep to the island.
49. Livingston, *Island Legacies*, 408, 438–50; Chiles, *California's Channel Islands*, 103–57; Gherini, *Santa Cruz Island*, 38–62.
50. Gherini, *Santa Cruz Island*, 63–115.
51. Gherini, *Santa Cruz Island*, 117–60; Livingston, *Island Legacies*, 557–73.
52. Gherini, *Santa Cruz Island*, 187.
53. Gherini, *Santa Cruz Island*, 181–91.
54. Gherini, *Santa Cruz Island* 161–64.
55. Livingston, *Island Legacies*, 146–54.
56. Livingston, *Island Legacies*, 152–59.
57. Livingston, *Island Legacies*, 179–89.
58. Livingston, *Island Legacies*, 213.
59. Handley et al., "Exploring Long-Term Trends," 275.
60. Davidson, A. et al., *Natural Resource Condition Assessment*, 29–32.
61. Davidson, A. et al., *Natural Resource Condition Assessment*, 29–32.
62. Philbrick, "Plants of Santa Barbara Island," 329, 353.

2. A Monumental Task

1. Toll, "Proposed Channel Islands National Park," March 21, 1933, National Archives San Bruno Branch (hereafter NASB), Record Group (RG) 79, National Archives, College Park, Maryland (hereafter CHIS) Collection, box 14, folder 201, 68. Toll does not provide any further context or cite sources for this proposal.
2. Frederick Law Olmsted Jr., "Report of the State Parks Survey of California," December 29, 1928, www.parks.ca.gov/pages/795/files/Olmsted_Report_SP_Survey_1928.pdf, 57.
3. G. R. Putnam, Commissioner of Lighthouses, to Horace Albright, June 14, 1932, (attachment in Roger Toll report); Superintendent of Lighthouses to Chief Landscape Architect Thomas C. Vint, July 15, 1932, NASB, RG79, CHIS Collection, box 14, folder 201.

4. Director Albright to William Colby, Chairman, California State Conservation Commission. October n.d., 1932, NASB, RG79, CHIS Collection, box 14, folder 201.
5. Albright to Colby, 1932, NASB, RG79, CHIS Collection, box 14, folder 201; Toll, "Proposed Channel Islands National Park."
6. Thomas Vint to Dr. W. A. Setchell, February 7, 1933, NARA, RG 79, entry 20, Roger Toll Records, box 2, folder CHIS.
7. Dr. Edward L. Greene, whom Setchell replaced in 1895, also researched the Channel Islands. W. A. Setchell to Thomas Vint, February 9, 1933, NARA, RG 79, entry 20, Roger Toll Records, box 2, folder CHIS; R. L. Moe and D. Browne, "W. A. Setchell (1864–1943) and N. L. Gardner (1864–1937)," accessed April 12, 2019, http://ucjeps.berkeley.edu/history/biog/setchell.html.
8. Cockerell, "San Miguel Island," 181; Schoenherr, Feldmeth, and Emerson, *Natural History*, 8.
9. Moe and Browne, "W. A. Setchell and N. L. Gardner."
10. Joseph Grinnell was director of UCB's Museum of Vertebrate Zoology from 1908 until 1939. See also H. C. Bryant to Regional Director, October 21, 1937, wherein he notes Grinnell and Loye Miller's urging protection of the Channel Islands for their biological resources, NASB, RG79, CHIS Collection, box 14, folder 201.
11. Joseph Grinnell to Thomas Vint, February 10, 1933, NASB, RG79, CHIS Collection, box 14, folder 201.
12. David Banks Rogers to Roger Toll, February 3, 1933, (attachment to Roger Toll Report, 1933), NASB, RG79, CHIS Collection, box 14, folder 201.
13. Roger Toll to Wayland T. Vaughn, Scripps Institute of Oceanography, February 18, 1933, NASB, RG79, CHIS Collection, box 14, folder 201.
14. Roger Toll to Wayland T. Vaughn, NASB, RG79, CHIS Collection, box 14, folder 201.
15. Harold C. Bryant, "Report on Proposed Channel Islands National Monument," September 20, 1937, NASB, RG 79, CHIS Collection, box 14, folder 201.
16. Bryant, "Report on Proposed"; Lawrence F. Cook, deputy chief forester (NPS), to Director NPS, Oct. 20, 1937, describing the trip with Bryant and Bernard F. Manbey; both in NASB, RG 79, CHIS Collection, box 14, folder 201.
17. Dr. Theo. D. A. Cockerell to Bryant, with manuscript of article on San Miguel Island enclosed, Oct. 28, 1937, NASB, RG79, CHIS Collection, box 14, folder 201; Cockerell's manuscript was later published as Cockerell, "San Miguel Island," 180–87; and "Botany of the California Islands," 117–23.

18. Harold Bryant to the Regional Director, October 21, 1937, NASB, RG 79, CHIS Collection, box 14, folder 201.
19. Bryant, "Report on Proposed."
20. Penciled note on letter of January 14, 1938, by Bernard Manbey comments that he, Cook, and Bryant toured islands, but only Bryant recommended inclusion in monument, NASB, RG 79, CHIS Collection, box 14, folder 201.
21. Bryant, "Report on Proposed."
22. Rothman, *America's National Monuments*.
23. Director Arno Cammerer, "Memorandum for the Secretary," February 7, 1938, NASB, RG 79, CHIS Collection, box 14, folder 201. This observation was taken directly from Harold Bryant's report.
24. Arno Cammerer, "Memorandum for the Secretary," February 7, 1938; and Acting Asst. Dir. Fred T. Johnston to Moskey, December 14, 1937; both in NASB, RG 79. CHIS Collection, box 14, folder 201.
25. Presidential Proclamation No. 2281, April 26, 1938.
26. Acting Secretary of the Navy Leahy to the Secretary of the Interior, September 12, 1938; and Acting Secretary of the Interior Harry Slattery, to Secretary of the Navy, December 2, 1938; both in NASB, RG 79, CHIS Collection, box 14, folder 201.The source of the Interior's information about grazing on San Miguel Island was an article in the *Oakland Tribune* from October 6, 1938.
27. Harry Slattery to Secretary of the Navy, December 2, 1938, NASB, RG 79, CHIS Collection, box 14, folder 201.
28. U.S. Navy to Department of the Interior (hereafter DOI), December 12, 1938, NASB, RG 79, CHIS Collection, box 14, folder 201.
29. Arno Cammerer to Regional Director, Region IV, January 5, 1939, NASB, RG 79, CHIS Collection, box 14, folder 201.
30. Various correspondence between NPS and U.S. Coast Guard, April 1939, NASB, RG 79, CHIS Collection, box 14, folder 201.
31. In Lowell Sumner's time, the bird was known as the Santa Barbara song sparrow.
32. Sumner was quoting from Townsend, "Birds from the Coast," 131–42.
33. Lowell Sumner to the Director, July 15, 1939; and Lowell Sumner, "Wildlife Studies on the Channel Islands National Monument," transmitted Feb. 27, 1940, by the regional director to Superintendent Scoyen; both in NASB, RG 79, CHIS Collection, box 14, folder 201.
34. Lowell Sumner, "Wildlife Studies on the Channel Islands National Monument," transmitted Feb. 27, 1940, by the regional director to Superintendent Scoyen; both in NASB, RG 79, CHIS Collection, box 14, folder 201.

35. Summarized by Roberts, *Historic Resource Study*, 166.
36. Sumner, "Wildlife Studies," NASB, RG 79, CHIS Collection, box 14, folder 201, 68.
37. Sumner, "Wildlife Studies," NASB, RG 79, CHIS Collection, box 14, folder 201, 69. Herbert Lester worked for Robert Brooks, who held the lease from the navy.
38. Acting Chief, Wildlife Division Victor Cahalane memo, August 14, 1939, NASB, RG 79, CHIS Collection, box 14, folder 201.
39. NPS Assistant Director to All Field Offices, "Guidelines for Resources Management in the Areas in the Natural Category of the National Park System," October 14, 1965, Pinnacles National Park, Museum Collection 3658, box 25, folder 4.
40. John White to Sequoia National Park, August 26, 1939, NASB, RG 79, CHIS Collection, box 14, folder 201; note that Colonel White was Scoyen's predecessor at Sequoia. Eivind Scoyen came to Sequoia in 1939. In 1941 he was transferred to Kings Canyon, and John R. White became superintendent of Sequoia and CINM. Administration of Sequoia and Kings Canyon were merged in 1943, and E. T. Scoyen became superintendent of both units from 1947 until 1956. He also served as superintendent of CINM from 1947 until 1955.
41. Brinkley, *Rightful Heritage*, 421.
42. Regional Director Frank Kittredge memorandum for the Director, September 15, 1939, noted that $515 would be applied to fiscal year (FY) 41; and Kittredge to Superintendent Scoyen, November 29, 1939, reported that no funds would be available for FY 40; both in NASB, RG 79, CHIS Collection, box 14, folder 201.
43. *California Fish and Game*, vol. 25 (1939) 246.
44. Frank Kittredge to Herbert C. Davis, California Department of Fish and Game (CDFG), June 29, 1939; and Davis to Kittredge, July 6, 1939; both in NASB, RG 79, CHIS Collection, box 14, folder 201.
45. Lowell Sumner, "Memorandum for the Regional Director," August 24, 1939, NASB, RG 79, CHIS Collection, box 14, folder 201.
46. Acting Associate Director to Acting Regional Director, September 25, 1939; and Sumner, "Memorandum for the Regional Director," August 24, 1939; both in NASB, RG 79, CHIS Collection, box 14, folder 201.
47. Director Cammerer to Rear Admiral Russell R. Waesche, Commandant, USCG, March 7, 1940, formally requested for patrol of islands, minimum of one visit each island per month from April 15 to August 15, less during other

months; Sumner, "Memorandum for the Regional Director," August 24, 1939; both in NASB, RG 79, CHIS Collection, box 14, folder 201.
48. Regional Director to Commander Parker, USCG, March 21, 1940; and Sumner, "Memorandum for the Regional Director," August 24, 1939; both in NASB, RG 79, CHIS Collection, box 14, folder 201.
49. Regional Biologist to Regional Director, February 28, 1941; E. T. Scoyen to A. Brazier Howell, Council for the Conservation of Whales, April 1, 1941; both in NASB, RG 79, CHIS Collection, box 14, folder 201.
50. Roberts, *Historic Resource Study*, 96.
51. Roberts, *Historic Resource Study*, 80–88.
52. Jack C. von Bloeker Jr., Los Angeles County Museum of History, Science and Art, to Perry R. Gage, acting regional director, January 2, 1940, NASB, RG 79, CHIS Collection, box 14, folder 201.
53. Victor Cahalane memorandum, August 14, 1939, NASB, RG 79, CHIS Collection, box 14, folder 201.
54. Sumner, "Memorandum for the Regional Director," November 13, 1939, NASB, RG 79, CHIS Collection, box 14, folder 201.
55. Sumner, "An Investigation of Santa Barbara, Anacapa, and San Miguel Islands," June 28, 1939, CINP Archives, Acc. 250, Cat. 4016, Series 3, folder 2, 18.
56. Frank Kittredge to Superintendent Scoyen, October 25, 1939; Kittredge to Scoyen, November 29, 1939; both in NASB, RG 79, CHIS Collection, box 14, folder 201.
57. Bonnot, "Sea Lions," 371–89.
58. Eivind Scoyen, memorandum for the Director, May 20, 1940, NASB, RG 79, CHIS Collection, box 14, folder 201.
59. Clarence Fry to Eivind Scoyen, July 10 and May 29, 1941, NASB, RG 79, CHIS Collection, box 14, folder 201.
60. Clarence Fry to Eivind Scoyen, July 10 and May 29, 1941, NASB, RG 79, CHIS Collection, box 14, folder 201.
61. Colonel White had been superintendent of Sequoia from 1920 through 1938, NASB, RG 79, CHIS Collection, box 14, folder 201.
62. Roberts, *Historic Resource Study*, 168.
63. Roberts, *Historic Resource Study*, 127–38.
64. Livingston, *Island Legacies*, 865–68; Halvorson and Davis, *Science and Ecosystem Management*; Lowell Sumner to Superintendent, December 9, 1954, NASB, RG 79, CHIS, Central Coded Subject Files (1953–), box 30.
65. Roark et al., *American Promise*, 995–1004.

66. Sumner, "Air Inspection," May 1948, CINP Archives, Acc. 00298, Cat. 6835, folder 62.
67. Sumner, "Air Inspection," CINP Archives, Acc. 00298, Cat. 6835, folder 62, 2.
68. Sumner, "Air Inspection," CINP Archives, Acc. 00298, Cat. 6835, folder 62, 11.
69. Lowell Sumner attributed this to the attitude of the island's private owners, claiming that "very little appears to be known about the area because the private owners have been inhospitable to visiting scientists." Sumner, "Air Inspection," CINP Archives, Acc. 00298, Cat. 6835, folder 62, 14–15.
70. Acting Regional Director Maier to Director, May 14, 1948, NASB, RG 79, CHIS Collection, box 14, folder 201.
71. Acting Director Hillory Tolson to the Regional Director, July 6, 1948, NASB, RG 79, CHIS Collection, box 14, folder 201.
72. Secretary of the Interior J. A. Krug to Secretary of the Navy John L. Sullivan, July 29, 1948, NASB, RG 79, CHIS Collection, box 14, folder 201.
73. Roberts, *Historic Resource Study*, 146.
74. Superintendent John White to the Regional Director, August 15, 1946, NASB, RG 79, CHIS Collection, box 14, folder 201.
75. Eivind Scoyen to the Regional Director, June 7, 1951; and H. L. Crowley to Asst. Regional Director Hill, February 28, 1952; both in NASB, RG 79, CHIS Collection, box 14, folder 201.
76. Dorr Yeager to Regional Director, May 16, 1950, NASB, RG 79, CHIS Collection, box 14, folder 201.
77. J. W. Sefton to Herbert Maier, March 1, 1949, NASB, RG 79, CHIS Collection, box 14, folder 201.
78. Raymond E. Hoyt memo for Dorr Yeager and Lowell Sumner, March 3, 1947, NASB, RG 79, CHIS Collection, box 14, folder 201.
79. Sumner, "Memorandum for the Regional Director," March 24, 1947, NASB, RG 79, CHIS Collection, box 14, folder 201.
80. Superintendent John White, memo for the Regional Director, April 21, 1947, NASB, RG 79, CHIS Collection, box 14, folder 201.
81. Owen A. Tomlinson to Director Newton Drury, May 13, 1947, NASB, RG 79, CHIS Collection, box 14, folder 201.
82. Eivind Scoyen to Director Arno Cammerer, May 29, 1940, NASB, RG 79, CHIS Collection, box 14, folder 201.
83. NPS Chief Counsel G. A. Moskey to Asst. Director Conrad Wirth, January 17, 1941, NASB, RG 79, CHIS Collection, box 14, folder 201.

84. Newton Drury to the Director of the BLM, June 12, 1947; and the BLM director's response to Drury, July 11, 1947; both in NASB, RG 79, CHIS Collection, box 14, folder 201.
85. Regional Director Tomlinson to Director Drury, October 28, 1947, NASB, RG 79, CHIS Collection, box 14, folder 201; Roberts, *Historic Resource Study*, 139–42.
86. Lowell Sumner to the Regional Director, November 18, 1947; and Director Drury to the Regional Director, December 22, 1947; both in NASB, RG 79, CHIS Collection, box 14, folder 201.
87. NPS, "Revised Boundary Status Report," January 16, 1948, NASB, RG 79, CHIS Collection, box 14, folder 201.
88. Radigan et al., *Jurisdiction over Submerged Lands*; 79th Cong., S. committee hearings on S.J. Res. 83 and S.J. Res. 92, March 27–30, 1939; Shalowitz, "Boundary Problems," 1021–48; Shalowitz and Reed, "Legal Background," 3–14.
89. Proclamation No. 2825 (63 Stat. 1258) February 9, 1949; Secretary of the Interior J. A. Krug to President Harry Truman, July 2, 1948, NASB, RG 79, CHIS Collection, box 14, folder 201.
90. Public Law 31 (67 Stat. 29); The U.S. Department of the Navy did not object to the proposed boundary extension provided it would not interfere with guided missile test programs or access rights at Anacapa, November 9, 1948.
91. Shalowitz and Reed, "Submerged Lands Act," 115–81.
92. Breeden, "Federalism and the Development," 1112.
93. U.S. Supreme Court, United States v. California, Third Supplemental Decree, 436 U.S. 32 (1978); and Shalowitz and Reed, "Tidelands Litigation," 33–35.
94. Dorr Yeager and Volney Westley, "Master Plan Development Outline, Channel Islands National Monument, California," NPS, Region Four, San Francisco, March 31, 1952, Denver Service Center, Technical Information Center, and CHIS is the NPS code for Channel Islands National Park (hereafter DSC, TIC, CHIS), 159_2000.
95. "Rabbit Kingdom 'Bombed' by Plane," *San Diego Union*, October 22, 1955; Bill Thomas, "Santa Barbara Isle Almost Hareless," *Evening Tribune* (San Diego), October 28, 1963.
96. Edwin L. Stanton to Newton Drury, September 9, 1940, NASB, RG 79, CHIS Collection, box 14, folder 201.

97. Arthur Demaray to Edwin Stanton, September 16, 1940, NASB, RG 79, CHIS Collection, box 14, folder 201.
98. Newton Drury to Regional Director, June 16, 1950, NASB, RG 79, CHIS Collection, box 14, folder 900.
99. Herbert Maier to Newton Drury, Chief, California Department of Beaches and Parks, April 23, 1951, recalling a letter of previous year (when Drury was still NPS director) and wondering whether California might be able to purchase Santa Cruz Island because NPS could not, NASB, RG 79, CHIS Collection, box 14, folder 201.
100. Edwin L. Stanton to Newton Drury, September 9, 1940, NASB, RG 79, CHIS Collection, box 14, folder 201.
101. Among the most influential critiques of the national park crisis were a couple of popular articles written by historian Bernard DeVoto, "Shall We Let Them Ruin Our National Parks?" 17–19, 42–46, and "Let's Close the National Parks," 49–52.
102. Histories of Mission 66 include Carr, *Mission 66: Modernism*; Everhart, *National Park Service*; and Conrad Wirth's insider version in his autobiography, *Parks, Politics, and the People*.
103. Unrau and Williss, *Expansion of the National Park Service*, 155–60.
104. Wirth, *Parks, Politics, and the People*, 192–200; Sadin, *Managing a Land in Motion*, 46–48.
105. George L. Collins and Lowell Sumner, *Report on San Miguel Island of the Channel Islands, California*, 1957, CINP Archives, Cat. 6835, folder 18.
106. Secretary of the Interior, Proposed Channel Islands National Park, Calif., 95th Cong., 1st Sess., H.R. 95–264, Part 21 (1977).
107. NPS, *Pacific Coast Recreation Area Survey* (Washington DC: DOI, 1959).
108. NPS, *Pacific Coast Recreation*, 10.
109. NPS, *Pacific Coast Recreation*, 11.
110. Sadin, *Land in Motion*, 86.
111. President John F. Kennedy, "Special Message to Congress on Natural Resources," February 23, 1961, http://www.presidency.ucsb.edu/ws/index; Sadin, *Land in Motion*, 86–87.
112. Roberts, *Historic Resource Study*, 180–81.
113. Gherini, *Santa Cruz Island*, 217.
114. Sadin, *Land in Motion*, 84–93; Roberts, *Historic Resource Study*, 181–82.
115. NPS, *Sea-Dominated National Park*, CINP, DOI, 1963.
116. NPS, *Sea-Dominated National Park*.

117. Secretary DOI, "Proposed Channel Islands National Park, California" 1977, CINP Central Files, 1.A.2, Cultural/Natural Resource Management Program/Planning, "Proposed Legislation," 3.
118. Secretary DOI, "Proposed Channel Islands National Park," 4.
119. NPS, *Anacapa Island Light Station, Channel Islands National Park: Cultural Landscape Inventory*, (San Francisco: Pacific West Regional Office, 2005).
120. License and Agreement [Cooperative Agreement], U.S. DOI, NPS, and U.S. Department of Transportation, U.S. Coast Guard (License No. DOT CG11-3075, Agreement No. 11 CGD RL02-70, January 9, 1975); NPS, *Draft General Management Plan, 1980*, 136.
121. "Memorandum of Agreement between the Department of the Navy and the Department or the Interior relating to Protection of Natural Values and Historic and Scientific Objects on San Miguel and Prince Islands, California," May 7, 1963, CINP Superintendent's files.
122. "Superintendent's Annual Report 1967 Fiscal Year, Cabrillo and Channel Islands National Monuments," May 29, 1967, CINP Archives, Cat. 13117, box 1, folder 7; Chris Horton interviewed by Timothy Babalis on August 15, 2009, and by Ann Huston on March 30, 2019. Comments by Chris Horton and Craig Johnson to Laura Kirn and Ann Huston, November 5, 2019.
123. Roger Rudolph (CINM ranger 1969–71), telephone interviewed by Ann Huston, June 9, 2019.
124. George Bowen (CINM ranger 1967–69), "Channel Islands National Monument: As I Remember," manuscript on file at CINP Archives. Roger Rudolph (CINM ranger 1969–71), telephone interviewed by Ann Huston, June 19, 2019.
125. Secretary DOI, "Proposed Channel Islands," 5.
126. Secretary DOI, "Proposed Channel Islands," 6, CINP Central Files, 1.A.2, Cultural/Natural Resource Management Program/Planning, "Proposed Legislation."
127. Gherini, *Santa Cruz Island*, 202–6.
128. This was changing. Stewart Udall, who had become Secretary of the Interior in 1961, criticized the development priorities of Conrad Wirth.
129. Gherini, *Santa Cruz Island*, 202–6.
130. U.S. Bureau of Outdoor Recreation, "Channel Islands, California: Island Study," DOI, February 1968, Pacific West Regional Office Library, San Francisco; Secretary DOI, "Proposed Channel Islands," 6, CINP Central Files, 1.A.2, Cultural/Natural Resource Management Program/Planning, "Proposed Legislation."

131. Jeff Robinson (son of Don) personal communication to Ann Huston, July 10, 2019.
132. Chris Horton interviewed by Timothy Babalis, August 15, 2009, transcript on file at CINP Archives; Chris Horton comments to Laura Kirn and Ann Huston on November 5, 2019.
133. The comment, which was reported in the press, was resented by the landowners and sternly rebuked by Carey Stanton and Pier Gherini. Gherini, *Santa Cruz Island*, 217–19.
134. Amendment to H.R. 3645, 93rd Cong. (1973–74), introduced by Congressman Moss; Secretary NPS, "Proposed Channel Islands," 8, CINP Central Files, 1.A.2, Cultural/Natural Resource Management Program/Planning, "Proposed Legislation."
135. Secretary DOI, "Proposed Channel Islands," 8, CINP Central Files, 1.A.2, Cultural/Natural Resource Management Program/Planning, "Proposed Legislation."
136. Livingston, "Island Legacies," 39; comments from Chris Horton to Laura Kirn and Ann Huston on November 5, 2019; Chris Horton, interviewed by Timothy Babalis, August 15, 2009, transcript in CINP Archives.

3. Legislative Protection

1. General sources on WWII and postwar urban development in California include Lotchin, *Fortress California*; Abbott, *Metropolitan Frontier*; and Verge, "Impact of the Second World War," 289–314.
2. Gurish, *Overview of California Ocean*; Paterson, "Great Fresh Water Panacea," 307–22.
3. Pub. L. No. 89–454, enacted by Congress on June 17, 1966.
4. U.S. Commission on Marine Science, *Our Nation and the Sea*.
5. U.S. Commission on Marine Science, *Our Nation and the Sea*, 57.
6. A barrel of oil contains 42 U.S. gallons; Santa Barbara Maritime Museum exhibit, "Santa Barbara Oil Spill," accessed October 10, 2018; County of Santa Barbara Planning and Development, "Brief Oil and Gas History of Santa Barbara County," accessed September 9, 2009, http://www.countyofsb.org/energy/information/history.asp.
7. "Santa Barbara Oil Spill 1969," *Los Angeles Times*, February 22, 2016; County of Santa Barbara, "Brief Oil and Gas." More recently, the 1989 Exxon Valdez and 2010 BP/Deepwater Horizon spills have surpassed the volume of oil released in the Santa Barbara event; George Bowen, "Channel Islands

National Monument: As I Remember," unpublished manuscript in CINP Archives, Cat. 9948.
8. Bowen, "Channel Islands National Monument," unpublished manuscript in CINP Archives, Cat. 9948.
9. U.S. Stat. 1280, enacted Oct. 27, 1972 (16 U.S.C.).
10. U.S. Commission on Ocean Policy, "Evolution of Ocean Governance," appendix 6, 17ff.
11. 16 U.S.C. § 1458 ©-(d).
12. U.S. Commission on Ocean Policy, "Evolution of Ocean Governance," appendix 6, 21–22. The susceptibility of OCS leases to consistency review was later challenged in court.
13. However, some species identified by the Marine Mammal Protection Act, such as walruses, polar bears, and sea otters, were administered by the U.S. Fish and Wildlife Service.
14. Pub. Res. Code §§30000 *et seq.*; Gurish, *Overview of California Ocean*, 20–29.
15. Gurish, *Overview of California Ocean*, 21–22.
16. Santa Barbara County, "Coastal Land Use Plan 1982."
17. See Senator Wallop's statement in the *Hearing Before the Subcommittee on Parks, Recreation, and Renewable Resource of the Committee on Energy and Natural Resources*, S. 1104, 96th Cong., 1st Sess., (1979), 87–88.
18. Santa Barbara County, "Coastal Land Use Plan 1982"; California Coastal Commission, Technical Services Division, "LCP Status, South Central Coast Area as of July 1, 2011," accessed May 4, 2014, www.coastal.ca.gov.
19. Coastal Zone Management Act, Pub. L. No. 92-583, (1972); U.S. Commission on Marine Science, *Our Nation and the Sea*, 86–97.
20. Fishery Conservation and Management Act of 1976. Pub. L. No. 94-265, (1976).
21. NMFS is a successor to the Bureau of Commercial Fisheries. Its new identity dates from 1970 when it was absorbed by the newly established National Oceanic and Atmospheric Administration (NOAA).
22. NPS, *Draft General Management Plan 1984*, CINP, 1984, 9; NPS, *Resource Protection Case Study (Land Protection Study)* (Washington DC: DOI, June 1982). The prohibition on oil and gas development was enacted in 1955 with the Cunningham-Shell Act. It was later extended to include nearly all of California's coastal waters with the Coastal Sanctuary Act of 1994.
23. NPS, *Resource Protection Case Study*.

24. This and much of the following is based on Bill Ehorn's own account, supplemented by the oral histories of staff who worked with him. See especially, William Ehorn, "Establishment of Channel Islands National Park," undated typescript, not earlier than 1995, CINP Museum Collection, Acc. 00298, Cat. 6835, folder 39; CINP Superintendent's Annual Reports, March 11, 1976, and March 23, 1978, CINP Archives, Cat. 13117, box 1, folder 7.
25. Bill Ehorn, comments to Laura Kirn and Ann Huston on November 5, 2019.
26. Superintendent's Annual Reports for 1974 and 1976 (February 10, 1975, and March 21, 1977), CINP Archives, Cat. 13117, box 1, folder 7.
27. Carey Stanton was also ideologically opposed to government management, according to Marla Daily who was interviewed by Timothy Babalis, August 19, 2009, transcript in CINP Archives, Cat. 35818.
28. National Marine Fisheries Service is also called NOAA Fisheries.
29. The plural is a reference to Prince Island as well as San Miguel Island. The former is really a large rock just outside Cuyler Harbor. Williams et al., "Administrative History of San Miguel Island," 1.
30. NPS, *Statement for Management for San Miguel and Prince Islands*, CINM, December 1, 1978.
31. "Channel Islands National Monument Annual Aquatic Resources Report for 1972," CINP Archives, Cat. 13117, box 8, folder 7; "Special Regulations, Areas of the National Park System; Channel Islands National Monument, California; Submerged Features, Wrecks, and Fishing," *Federal Register* 37.53, March 17, 1972; Bill Ehorn comments to Laura Kirn and Ann Huston, November 5, 2019.
32. Wohnus, "Kelp Resources of Southern California," 199–205; Scofield, "History of Kelp Harvesting," 199–205.
33. "The Statement of Kelco to the Sub-Committee on Parks, Recreation, and Renewable Resources of the Senate Energy and Natural Resources Committee, Commenting on Legislation to Establish a Channel Islands National Park," submitted August 2, 1979, in the *Hearing Before the Subcommittee on Parks, Recreation, and Renewable Resource of the Committee on Energy and Natural Resources*, S. 1104, 96th Cong., 1st Sess., (1979), 109–41.
34. Gary Davis interviewed by David Louter, June 11, 2007, transcript on file in CINP Archives, Cat. 30177, 25; this interpretation is derived from actual accounts of Bill Ehorn's behavior at that time, described by close associates like Gary Davis, and from descriptions of his character by others who knew him.
35. Ehorn, "Establishment of Channel Islands National Park," undated typescript, 6, CINP Archives Acc. 00298, Cat. 6835, folder 39.

36. "To Establish Channel Islands National Park," H.R.380, 94th Congress (1976).
37. "To Establish Santa Monica Mountains and Seashore Urban National Park California," H.R. 7264, 95th Congress (1977).
38. "To Establish Channel Islands National Park," H.R. 2975, 96th Congress (1979). For text of original bill see CINP, Central Files, Santa Rosa Island (hereafter SRI) Binder 1, Section B.1.b.
39. H.R. 2975, CINP, Central Files, SRI Binder 1, Section B.1.b.
40. Lagomarsino to Senate, July n.d., 1979, CINP, Central Files, SRI Binder 1, B.4.a.
41. Lagomarsino to Senate, July 12, 1979, CINP Central Files, SRI Binder 1, B.1.c.
42. *Hearing Before the Subcommittee on Parks, Recreation, and Renewable Resource of the Committee on Energy and Natural Resources*, S. 1104, 96th Cong., 1st Sess., (1979), 90.
43. *Hearing Before the Subcommittee on Parks, Recreation, and Renewable Resource of the Committee on Energy and Natural Resources*, S. 1104, 96th Cong., 1st Sess., (1979), 90.
44. "Amending the National Parks and Recreation Act of 1978," H.R, 3757, 96th Congress (1979): "No provision of this title [concerning the right of the Secretary of the Interior to enter into cooperative agreements with the State of California] shall be deemed to affect the rights and jurisdiction of the State of California within the park, including, but not limited to, authority over submerged lands and waters within the park boundaries, and the marine resources therein."
45. Kelco to the Senate, CINP Central Files, SRI Binder 1, B.4.c.
46. CINP Central Files, SRI Binder 1, B.4.c.
47. Daniel Tobin Jr. to Dale Bumpers, February 15, 1980; and Bur Low to Dale Bumpers, November 13, 1979; both reproduced in *Congressional Record*, Senate, February 18, 1980, 1420–21.
48. Al Vail to Senator Wallop, November 7, 1979, in *Congressional Record*, Senate, February 18, 1980, 2887; Nita Vail interviewed by Timothy Babalis, September 25, 2009.
49. "Presentation by Bill Ehorn and Robert Lagomarsino at California State University, Channel Islands Library Archives Dedication," January 2003, CINP Archives, Cat. 35833; Bill Ehorn telephone interview with Lary Dilsaver, May 30, 2019.
50. "House Report 96–119," May 4, 1979.
51. The Vails were well aware of the impact inheritance taxes had on Carey Stanton's decision to sell most of Santa Cruz Island.

52. Livingston, *Island Legacies*, 297–98.
53. Bill Ehorn, comments to Laura Kirn and Ann Huston, November 5, 2019.
54. Sec. 202(c) of the enacted law (Pub. L. No. 96–199).
55. Rep. Keith Sebelius, Congressional Record, House, 3344, CINP Central Files, SRI Binder No. 1, B.3.c.
56. Both of these stipulations appear in Lagomarsino's original version of the bill, H.R. 2975.
57. Pub. L. No. 96–199, 94 Stat. 74.
58. NPS, *Draft General Management Plan 1984*, 9; NPS, *Resource Protection Case Study*, June 1982. The prohibition on oil and gas development was enacted in 1955 with the Cunningham-Shell Act. It was later extended to include nearly all of California's coastal waters with the Coastal Sanctuary Act of 1994.
59. Testimony of Jack Gehringer, National Marine Fisheries Service, before the House Merchant Marine and Fisheries Committee, Subcommittee on Fisheries and Wildlife Conservation and the Environment, June 5, 1979, CINP Central Files, SRI Binder No. 1, B.4.d. The other three national marine sanctuaries designated in California were Gulf of the Farallones, established in 1981; Cordell Bank, established in 1989; and Monterey Bay, established in 1992.
60. The six-mile extension of the sanctuary included OCS lands within the Santa Barbara Channel. Essentially, all submerged lands beyond the three-mile state territorial limit from any shoreline (including the shores of coastal islands) were OCS and within the jurisdiction of the Minerals Management Service. Secretary of the Interior Ken Salazar issued a secretarial order on May 19, 2010, splitting MMS into three new federal agencies: the Bureau of Ocean Energy Management, the Bureau of Safety and Environmental Enforcement, and the Office of Natural Resources Revenue.
61. The agreement also addressed the mutual responsibilities of Point Reyes National Seashore and the Gulf of the Farallones National Marine Sanctuary, which had been established earlier that year; NOAA, "National Marine Sanctuary Timeline," accessed April 28, 2009, http://sanctuaries.noaa.gov/about/history/welcome.html.

4. Resource Management

1. The immediate cause of Secretary Udall's investigation was a report about criticism of NPS wildlife policy in Yellowstone. Carr, *Mission 66*, 307–8.
2. Leopold, "Wildlife Management."
3. Leopold, "Wildlife Management."

4. Assistant Director to All Field Offices, "Guidelines for Resources Management in the Areas in the Natural Category of the National Park System," October 14, 1965, Babalis, *Heart of the Gabilans*, 199, note 32.
5. Although this principle was assumed at the time Deputy Director William Briggle explicitly stated: "No new science/research projects may be undertaken unless identified as a need in an approved Resource Management Plan," Babalis, *Heart of the Gabilans*, 199n33.
6. George Bowen (Santa Barbara Island ranger), "Channel Islands National Monument as I Remember," CINP Archives, Cat. 9948; NPS, "Channel Islands National Monument, Resource Management Plan: Anacapa Island," n.d., CINP Archives, Acc. 00298, Cat. 6835, folder 4.
7. Superintendent's Annual Research Reports for 1968–75, CINP Archives, Cat. 13117, box 8, folders 6 and 7.
8. General management plans were stipulated under Section 203 of National Parks and Recreation Act of 1978, Pub. L. No. 95–625, (1978). The legislation also required parks to revise existing plans in a timely manner, which was understood to mean every fifteen to twenty years.
9. Unless otherwise noted, the following is from Gary Davis, interviewed by David Louter, June 11–12 and August 28, 2007. Transcript on file in CINP Archives, Cat. 30177; Gary Davis telephone interviewed by Lary Dilsaver, June 7, 2018.
10. In the 1970s, the superintendent of Everglades also managed Fort Jefferson National Monument (now Dry Tortugas National Park), Biscayne National Monument (now National Park), and Big Cypress National Preserve. Gary Davis had experience with all four units. Gary Davis interview with Lary Dilsaver, September 3, 2018.
11. Norton, "B. Robertson Jr.," 111–12.
12. H.R. 2975, "To establish Channel Islands National Park," March 26, 1979. For text of original bill see CINP, Central Files, SRI Binder No. 1, Section B.1.b.
13. This concern was also expressed, for example, by Rep. Keith Sebelius, during House concurrence hearings on final revision, CINP, Central Files, SRI Binder No. 1, Section B.3.c.
14. NPS, *Channel Islands National Park: Biennial Natural Resources Study Report, October 1982* (Ventura CA: NPS, 1982), 10, CINP Archives, Cat. 13117, box 9.
15. NPS, *Channel Islands National Park: Biennial Natural Resources Study Report*.
16. Gary Davis interviewed by David Louter, August 28, 2007.
17. CINP, Superintendent's Annual Report for 1983 (February 29, 1984), CINP Archives, Cat. 13117, box 1, folder 5.

18. CINP, Superintendent's Annual Report for 1984 (March 14, 1985), CINP Archives, Cat. 13117, box 1, folder 5; Davis and Halvorson, "Resource Issues Addressed."
19. The resource categories represented by the ten monitoring handbooks completed in 1988 were: pinnipeds, intertidal communities, sea birds, kelp forests, landbirds, terrestrial vegetation, terrestrial vertebrates, visitors, weather, and fisheries.
20. Davis and Halvorson, *Channel Islands National Park*, 12.
21. Gary Davis interviewed by Lary Dilsaver, September 3, 2018.
22. Livingston, *Island Legacies*, 103.
23. Dr. Charles L. Douglas of University of Nevada, Las Vegas, conducted an aerial survey of feral burros in December 13–14, 1976. He submitted his report with recommendations on February 10, 1977, to superintendent Ehorn. CINP Archives, Cat. 13117, box 8, folder 6.
24. Superintendent's Annual Report for 1978, CINP Archives, Cat. 13117, box 8, folder 7; Bill Ehorn, "Establishment of Channel Islands National Park," n.d., CINP Archives, Acc.00298, Cat. 6835, folder 39; Bill Ehorn and Robert Lagomarsino oral history, January 16, 2003. Recording and transcript on file in CINP Archives, Cat. 35833; Bill Ehorn comments to Laura Kirn and Ann Huston, November 5, 2019.
25. Livingston, *Island Legacies*, 865–68; Lowell Sumner to Superintendent, December 9, 1954, NASB, RG 79, CHIS, Central Coded Subject Files (1953–), box 30.
26. Lowell Sumner to Jack von Bloeker, October 31, 1955, NASB, RG 79, CHIS, Central Coded Subject Files (1953–), box 30.
27. Jack C. von Bloeker to Dr. Lowell Sumner, October 19, 1955; Lowell Sumner to Jack von Bloeker, October 31, 1955; Phil C. Orr to Dorr Yeager, September 5, 1957; Dorr G. Yeager to Phil C. Orr, September 9, 1957; all in NASB, RG 79, CHIS, Central Coded Subject Files (1953–), box 30; Livingston, *Island Legacies*, 865–68.
28. Superintendent's Annual Reports, 1975–1980, CINP Archives, Cat. 13117, box 8, folders 6 and 7.
29. Ehorn public talk, January 16, 2003. Transcript in CINP Archives, Cat. 35833.
30. Wohnus, "Kelp Resources of Southern California," 199–205; and Scofield, "History of Kelp Harvesting."
31. CINM, "Annual Fisheries Resources Report," CINP Archives, Cat. 13117, box 8, folder 7.

32. 36 Code of Federal Regulations (hereafter CFR) 7.84 "Channel Islands National Monument"; NPS, "Annual Aquatic Resources Report for 1972," January 18, 1973; and NPS, "Annual Aquatic Resources Report for 1974: CINM," December 24, 1974; both in CINP Archives, Cat. 13117, box 8, folder 7.
33. Power et al., *Natural Resources*.
34. Littler, "Overview of Rocky Intertidal Systems"; Superintendent's Annual Research Report, 1977–1982, CINP Archives, Cat. 13117, box 8, folder 5, and box 9, folder 2.
35. NPS, "Annual Aquatic Resources Report for 1975: Channel Islands National Monument," December 17, 1975, CINP Archives, Cat. 13117, box 8, folder 7; Superintendent's Annual Report for 1975 (March 11, 1976), CINP Archives, Cat. 13117, box 1, folder 7.
36. NPS, "Annual Aquatic Resources Report for 1966: Channel Islands National Monument," January 10, 1967, CINP Archives, Cat. 13117, box 8, folder 7.
37. NPS, "Annual Aquatic Resources Report for 1982: Channel Islands National Park," December 16, 1982, CINP Archives, Cat. 13117, box 8, folder 4.
38. Regional Director Tomlinson to a prospective concessioner, October 5, 1945, NASB, CHIS, box 14, folder 900.
39. NPS Regional Biologist to Regional Director, February 28, 1941, NASB, CHIS, box 14, folder 201.
40. George Miller, June 15, 1942, and Lowell Sumner, July 8, 1942, NASB, CHIS, box 14, folder 700, "Wildlife."
41. Scammon, *Marine Mammals*.
42. Scammon, *Marine Mammals*, 169.
43. Ogden, "Russian Sea-Otter and Seal Hunting," 217–39.
44. Bolin, "Reappearance of the Southern Sea Otter," 301–3; Bonnot, "Sea Lions, Seals and Sea Otter," 371–89.
45. An Act to Improve the Operation of Certain Fish and Wildlife Programs, Pub. L. No. 99-625 (H.R. 4531), (1986); USFWS, *Translocation of Southern Sea Otter*, 2005; Rathbun, Hatfield, and Murphey, "Status of Translocated Sea Otters," 322–75.
46. Booth, "Reintroducing a Political Animal," 156–58; Jim Primrose (letter), "Transplanting Sea Otters to San Nicolas Island," *Los Angeles Times*, July 18, 1987; Joanna M. Miller, "Scientists Call Otter Project Unrealistic," *Los Angeles Times* (Ventura County Edition), October 19, 1992; NPS, "Restoration of Southern Sea Otters within the Channel Islands National Park: Briefing Statement," February 1993, CINP Archives, Cat. 13117, box 1, folder 10.

47. Bonnot, "Sea Lions, Seals and Sea Otter," 371–89; Peterson, LeBoeuf, and DeLong, "Fur Seals," 899–901. According to George (Bud) Antonelis, the North Pacific Fur Seal Convention became a nexus for the National Marine Fisheries Service research station on San Miguel Island as well as other breeding rookeries.
48. Ogden, "Russian Sea-Otter and Seal Hunting."
49. Scammon, *Marine Mammals*, 115–23.
50. Bonnot, "Sea Lions, Seals and Sea Otter," 371–89; Bonnot claimed they were already extinct in California waters by 1870, but this conflicts with Scammon's observations.
51. Bonnot, "Sea Lions, Seals and Sea Otter," 371–89.
52. Bonnot, "Sea Lions, Seals and Sea Otter," 371–89.
53. Schoenherr, Feldmeth, and Emerson, *Natural History*, 124–26; Allen, Mortenson, and Webb, *Field Guide to Marine Mammals*, 431–42.
54. Ogden, "Russian Sea-Otter and Seal Hunting," 217–39.
55. Cronise, *Natural Wealth of California*, 440.
56. Bonnot, *Fish Bulletin No. 14*.
57. Bonnot, *Fish Bulletin No. 14*, 1–16; Bonnot, "California Sea Lion Census for 1936," 108–12; and Bonnot and Ripley, "California Sea Lion Census for 1947," 89–92.
58. DeLong and Melin, "Thirty Years of Pinniped Research," 401–6.
59. Cliff Fiscus, Robert DeLong, and George Antonelis, "Investigator's Annual Report," January 4, 1979, CINP Archives Cat.13117, box 8, folder 5; Superintendent's Annual Research Report, 1968, CINP Archives Cat.13117, box 8, folder 7; U.S. Department of Commerce, "National Marine Fisheries Service, Marine Mammal Protection Act Fact Sheet," accessed January 12, 2010, http://www.nmfs.noaa.gov/pr/laws/mmpa/.
60. Superintendent's Annual Report for 1975 (March 11, 1976), CINP Archives, Cat. 13117, box 1, folder 7; Ehorn, "Establishment of Channel Islands National Park," undated typescript, CINP Archives, Acc. 298, Cat. 6835, folder 39; Bill Ehorn, "Recollection of Dr. Leopold and His Influence on Management of San Miguel Island," undated typescript, CINP Archives, Acc. 298, Cat. 6835, folder 39.

5. Building the New Park

1. NPS, *General Management Plan 1985*, CINP, 1985.
2. Pub. L. No. 96-199, Section 202(a).

3. NPS, *Resource Protection Case Study*; Superintendent's Annual Report for 1983 (Feb. 29, 1984), CINP Archives, Cat. 13117, box 1, folder 5.
4. Greg Gress telephone conversation with Timothy Babalis, June 25, 2012, and lands documents provided by Gress; Jack Fitzgerald comments to Ann Huston, March 10, 2020.
5. Power, *California Islands*, 1980.
6. Only Carey Stanton vigorously supported research on his land by allowing the University of California to establish a research center near the Main Ranch.
7. Pub. L. No. 96–199, Section 204(a).
8. NPS, *General Management Plan 1985*, 10–11.
9. Greg Gress conversation with Timothy Babalis, July 30, 2010.
10. U.S. General Accounting Office, *Federal Land Acquisition and Management Practices*, 81–135.
11. For example, the Land and Water Conservation Fund Act of 1965 (78 Stat. 897), which forbids interstate land exchanges. These would have included OCS areas, which lie outside state boundaries. The Land and Water Conservation Fund Act would have to be amended to classify OCS areas as part of the state they adjoin for the purposes of making such an exchange. NPS, *Resource Protection Case Study*, 1982, 22.
12. Dilsaver, *Preserving the Desert*, 187.
13. NPS, *General Management Plan 1985*, 11; Superintendent's Annual Report for 1982 (May 25, 1983), CINP Archives, Cat. 13117, box 1, folder 6.
14. NPS, *Channel Islands National Park: Land Protection Plan 1984*, CINP, February 1984.
15. Superintendent's Annual Report for 1984 (March 14, 1985), CINP Archives, Cat. 13117, box 1, folder 5.
16. Superintendent's Annual Report for 1983 (February 29, 1984), CINP Archives, Cat. 13117, box 1, folder 5.; William C. Kelly Jr. to William H. Ehorn, June 21, 1983, CINP Superintendent's Files, folder "SRI."
17. NPS, *General Management Plan 1985*, 15; San Miguel Island is ineligible because the navy owns it.
18. Technically the "Vickers Company Ltd., James Vail Wilkinson, Nathan Russell Vail, Margaret Vail Woolley, and Alexander Lennox Vail" owned the island and Vail & Vickers Company managed the ranch and other operations. NPS solicitor Barbara Goodyear communication to Lary Dilsaver, November 13, 2019.
19. NPS, *Management Policies 1978*, DOI (U.S. General Printing Office, 0-721-256/720, 1978), U.S. Department of the Interior, 9–4.

20. Jack MacDonald, chief appraiser, Western Region, to Chief, Division of Land Resources, Western Region, May 29, 1986, CINP, Central Files, SRI Binder No. 1, Section C.4.d; Bill Ehorn telephone interview with Lary Dilsaver, May 30, 2019.
21. Ticor Title Insurance Company, "Warranty Deed," recorded December 30, 1986, in "Santa Rosa Island Administrative History," CINP, Central Files, SRI Binder No. 1, C.1. a.
22. William C. Kelly Jr., Latham and Watkins, to Edward R. Haberlin, Chief of Land Resources, Western Regional Office, December 11, 1986; and Edward R. Haberlin to Jill Slater, Latham and Watkins, December 18, 1986; both in CINP Central Files, SRI Binder 2, C.4.g.
23. Bill Ehorn telephone interview with Lary Dilsaver, May 30, 2019.
24. William M. White, Chief Appraiser, NPS, "National Park Service Appraisal Review: Estimated Fair Market Rental, Tract 102–01 (Vail & Vickers), Santa Rosa Island, Channel Islands National Park, Santa Barbara County, California," July 16, 1986, CINP Central Files, SRI Binder 2, C.5.c. The cost of transportation between Santa Rosa Island and the mainland was estimated at $120,000 per year, or about $2.22 per AUM. This was deducted from the rental calculations to arrive at the figures quoted above.
25. Latham and Watkins, attorneys, to Ed Haberlin, December 11, 1986, CINP Central Files, SRI Binder 2, C4g; Faulkner, "Bringing Santa Rosa Island," 930–41.
26. Senator Pete Wilson to Secretary of the Interior Donald P. Hodel, January 28, 1987, CINP, Central Files, SRI Binder 1, C.6.b.
27. William Ehorn to *Santa Barbara News-Press*, March 15, 1987; William Ehorn to Stanley Albright, January 25, 1994, copy courtesy of Marla Daily, Santa Cruz Island Foundation.
28. Robert J. Lagomarsino, "Notes of presentation at February 10, 1987, media event announcing the acquisition of Santa Rosa Island by the NPS." Robert J. Lagomarsino Collection: Federal Collection, 1974–1992. Collection Number: 1/92. Broome Library, California State University Channel Islands; Faulkner, "Bringing Santa Rosa Island," 937.
29. Barbara Goodyear email to Lary Dilsaver, November 20, 2019.
30. Bill Ehorn telephone interview, May 30, 2019; Bill Ehorn interviewed by Laura Kirn and Ann Huston, November 6 and 7, 2019.
31. Bill Ehorn telephone interview with Lary Dilsaver, May 30, 2019.
32. Jack D. MacDonald to Edward Haberlin, Chief, Division of Land Resources, Western Regional Office, September 9, 1987, CINP, Central Files SRI Binder 3, D.2.a.

33. Superintendent's Annual Report for 1987, May 9, 1988, CINP Archives, Cat. 13117, box 1, folder 8; "Memo," Chief of Operations to the Superintendent, CINP, March 2, 1993, CINP, Central Files, SRI Binder 3, Sec. D.1.c.
34. Wuerthner, "Gone Astray," 23–25.
35. DOI, NPS, "Special Use Permit No. WRO-8120-2600-001," December 29, 1987, CINP, Central Files, SRI Binder 3, Sec. D.1.a.
36. Bill Ehorn, comments to Laura Kirn and Ann Huston, November 5, 2019; Faulkner, "Bringing Santa Rosa Island," 930–41.
37. Later, Chief of Resources Kate Faulkner told *Los Angeles Times* reporter Hilary MacGregor, "We are aware of no agreement between Vail & Vickers and the Park Service regarding continued use of the land." In the same article, Superintendent Tim Setnicka disagreed with Faulkner, claiming that there was an understanding that the cattle operation would continue until 2011. Hilary MacGregor, "Island Squeeze," *Los Angeles Times*, May 25, 1997.
38. Nita Vail, interviewed by Timothy Babalis, September 25, 2009.
39. Terry Young, "Santa Rosa Island a Rare California Adventure," *Chicago Tribune*, October 25, 1987.
40. Kate Faulkner comments to Lary Dilsaver, May 20, 2019.
41. Kate Faulkner comments, May 20, 2019.
42. Chief of Operations to the Superintendent, Channel Island National Park, March 2, 1993, CINP, Central Files, SRI Binder No. 3, D.1.c.
43. Lynn Brittan, Soil Conservation Service, to Edward Haberlin, Chief, Western Regional Office, NPS, April 15, 1987, CINP, Superintendent's Files, folder SRI.
44. Bartolome and Clawson, *Range Management Plan*.
45. Bartolome and Clawson, *Range Management Plan*; Superintendent's Annual Report for 1993, April 19, 1994, CINP Archives, Cat. No. 13117, folder 8. The water quality monitoring program was set up with technical assistance from the Park Service's Water Resources Division, the state's Regional Water Quality Control Board, and the U.S. Forest Service.
46. Superintendent's Annual Report, May 9, 1988, CINP Archives, Cat. 13117, box 1, folder 8.
47. Superintendent's Annual Report, May 9, 1988, CINP Archives, Cat. 13117, box 1, folder 8.
48. Edwin L. Stanton to Newton Drury, September 9, 1940, NASB, RG79, CHIS Collection, box 14, folder 201.
49. Schuyler, "Control of Feral Sheep," 443–52; Livingston, *Island Legacies*, 639–44.

50. Henry Duffield was an experienced cowboy but had contracted polio and could no longer work. He met Carey Stanton in Mexico. Later Edwin Stanton offered him a job as ranch manager. Marla Daily interviewed by Timothy Babalis, August 19, 2009, recording on file at CINP Archives, Cat. 35818.
51. Marla Daily interview with Timothy Babalis, August 19, 2009, CINP Archives, Cat. 35818.
52. Marla Daily interview with Timothy Babalis.
53. Marla Daily interview with Timothy Babalis.
54. Gherini, *Santa Cruz Island*, 169.
55. Marla Daily interview with Timothy Babalis.
56. Marla Daily interview with Timothy Babalis.
57. William Ehorn, "The Establishment of Channel Islands National Park," undated typescript, not earlier than 1995, CINP Archives, Acc. 00298, Cat. 6835, folder 39; Marla Daily interview.
58. The Nature Conservancy, accessed June 19, 2012, http://www.nature.org.
59. Marla Daily interview with Timothy Babalis.
60. Gherini, *Santa Cruz Island*, 171–72; John Gherini comments to Lary Dilsaver on April 14, 2019.
61. See chapter 1; except where otherwise noted, Caire and Gherini family histories are drawn from Gherini, *Santa Cruz Island*, 1997.
62. Gherini, *Santa Cruz Island*, 217; "A Master Plan for the Gherini Ranch Development, Santa Cruz Island," prepared by George Vernon Russell, Fellow of the American Institute of Architects, Engineers, Planners, June 1965. CINP Library; John Gherini comments to Lary Dilsaver, 2019.
63. Stanley Albright to Robert Lagomarsino, December 9, 1992. CINP Archives, Cat. 6494, box 7B.
64. Peterson, *Once Upon an Island*, 163–64; John Gherini comments to Lary Dilsaver, 2019.
65. Duane Owens to Francis Gherini, Dec. 30, 1990, CINP Archives, Cat. 6494, box 7B.
66. The government's appraisal of East Santa Cruz Island was completed in 1985 and negotiations with the Gherini family for the purchase of their property began shortly thereafter.
67. Mark Senning, conversation with Timothy Babalis, August 12, 2009; John Gherini comments to Lary Dilsaver, 2019. Both letters are in the possession of John Gherini.

68. Duane Owens and Jaret Owens to Congressman Robert Lagomarsino, November 13, 1992, CINP Archives, Cat. 6494, box 7B.

6. Growth of Resource Management

1. NPS, *Resource Protection Case Study*, June 1982; Superintendent's Annual Report for 1981 (May 19, 1982), CINP Archives, Cat. 13117, box 1, folder 6.
2. Superintendent's Annual Report for 1980, CINP Archives, Cat. 13117, box 1, folder 6.
3. Kate Faulkner interviewed by Timothy Babalis, August 5, 2009; NPS, *Resource Management Plan*, CINP, 1984.
4. Gary Davis interviewed by David Louter, June 12, 2007, CINP Archives, Cat. 30177; Gary Davis email to Lary Dilsaver, May 31, 2019.
5. Gary Davis comment to Lary Dilsaver, February 20, 2019.
6. Gary Davis interviewed by David Louter, August 28, 2007, CINP Archives, Cat. 30177.
7. Lyle, *Proceedings of the Ocean Studies Symposium*, 1983.
8. Gary Davis to Superintendent, CINP, January 31, 1984, with Superintendent's Annual Report for 1983 (February 29, 1984), CINP Archives, Cat. 13117, box 1, folder 5.
9. The workshop was held October 28–30, 1986.
10. Public Law 93–378, "Forest and Rangeland Renewable Resources Planning Act of 1974," approved August 17, 1974, Sec. 5 (16 U.S.C. 1603).
11. NPS, *State of the Parks: A Report to Congress*, Office of Science and Technology, May 1980; from $44 million to $93 million between 1980 and 1984.
12. U.S. General Accounting Office, *Parks and Recreation*, 1987; NPS, *Natural Resources Inventory and Monitoring Initiative* (Washington DC: DOI, 1987), 3.
13. NPS, *Standards and Guidelines for Natural Resources Inventorying and Monitoring*, 1987 [draft].
14. Associate Director for Natural Resources Gene Hester to the Senior Scientist, July 25, 1988, Pacific West Regional Office (hereafter PWRO) Library, Natural Resource Files, CHIS, San Francisco; NPS, *Standards and Guidelines for Natural Resources Inventorying and Monitoring* (Washington DC: NPS, 1987 [draft]), PWRO Library, Natural Resource Files, CHIS, San Francisco.
15. The workshop was held September 6–8, 1989.
16. Bruce Kilgore to Regional Director, September 15, 1989, PWRO Library, Natural Resources Files, CHIS, San Francisco.

17. Section 204, "An Act to Provide for Improved Management and Increased Accountability for Certain National Park Service Programs, and for Other Purposes," National Parks Omnibus Act, Pub. L. No. 105–391, 112 Stat. 3497 (1998).
18. Related by Mark Senning, conversation with Timothy Babalis, August 12, 2009; Chris Horton interviewed by Timothy Babalis, August 15, 2009. Transcripts on file at CINP Archives.
19. Chris Horton interviewed by Timothy Babalis, August 15, 2009. Transcripts on file at CINP Archives.
20. Mack Shaver and Holly Bundock to Lary Dilsaver, October 28, 2019, text of their comments held by Chief of Cultural Resources Laura Kirn at CINP.
21. Mack Shaver and Holly Bundock to Lary Dilsaver, October 28, 2019.
22. Mack Shaver and Holly Bundock to Lary Dilsaver, October 28, 2019; the National Biological Survey was merged into the existing U.S. Geological Survey on October 1, 1996.
23. Conversation between Ray Sauvajot and Timothy Babalis, August 1, 2009; Gary Davis interviewed by David Louter, June 11, 2007, CINP Archives, Cat. 30177.
24. Halvorson was replaced by Kathryn McEachern in January 1993.
25. Superintendent's Annual Report, March 10, 1993, CINP Archives, Cat. 13117, box 1, folder 8; NPS, *Channel Islands National Park: Resources Management Plan*, DOI, 1994.
26. Pigati et al., "Evidence of Repeated Wildfires," 35–47.
27. CINP, "Wildland Fire Management Plan 1989 Season," January 26, 1989, CINP Central Files, 1.A.2., Cultural/Natural Resource Management Program/Planning, folder "Wildlife Fire Management ('89-'82)," A1.
28. Robert Arnberger acting for William Ehorn to Carey Stanton, October 12, 1982; and William Ehorn to Al and Russ Vail, November 23, 1982; both in January 26, 1989, CINP Central Files, 1.A.2., Cultural/Natural Resource Management Program/Planning, folder "Wildlife Fire Management ('89-'82)," A1.
29. CINP, "Interagency Agreement between the National Park Service and United States Forest Service Los Padres National Forest," June 11, 1993, CINP Archives, Cat. 13117, Acc. 00401, box 3, folder 5.
30. Fire Management Specialists to Chief, Branch of Fire Management, July 20, 1989, CINP Archives, Cat. 13117, Acc. 00401, box 3, folder 5.
31. NPS, *Fire Management Plan*, November 1991, CINP Library.

32. CINP, "Superintendents Annual Reports"; all in CINP Archives, Cat. No. 13117.
33. Tim Setnicka to Vail & Vickers, March 7, 1997, CINP Central Files, 1.A.2 Fire Management Range, "Cultural/Natural Resource Management Program/Planning"; Acting Field Supervisor, USFWS Ventura Office to Superintendent, Channel Islands National Park, June 16, 1997, CINP Central Files, 1.A.2. folder "Wildland Fire Management '06–89"; John J. Reynolds to Superintendent, Channel Islands National Park, June 16, 1997, CINP Archives, Acc. 304.4, Cat. 10145, folder 79.
34. Gary Davis telephone interview with Lary Dilsaver, June 21, 2018.
35. E. C. Fullerton to Mack Shaver, July 1, 1991, CINP Archives, Cat. 10145, Acc. 00304, box 1, folder 3.
36. Ecological integrity is defined in this volume's introduction and is drawn from National Park System Advisory Board Science Committee, "Revisiting Leopold," 450.
37. Schoenherr, Feldmeth, and Emerson, *Natural History*, 104–5.
38. Shaw, "Spiny Lobster."
39. White abalone occur at depths as great as 60 meters (197 feet), where the majority of the surviving population is presently found. Historically, they may have occurred in water as shallow as 5 meters (16.4 feet), but these populations would have been the first to suffer from overharvesting.
40. U.S. Department of Commerce, *Recovery Plan for White Abalone*, 2008.
41. Scientists also monitored other species that occupy the same habitat and share a close ecological relationship to the abalone, such as sea stars (*Pycnopodia helianthoides*), which prey on them; sea urchins (*Strongylocentrotus purpuratus* et al.), which compete with them for food; and kelp, the abalone's principal food source.
42. Data provided by Gary Davis to Lary Dilsaver by email June 13, 2018.
43. Davis et al., "Abalone Population Declines," pt. 5.
44. Davis et al., "Abalone Population Declines," pt. 5.
45. U.S. Department of Commerce, *Recovery Plan for White Abalone*, 2008.
46. Davis et al., "Abalone Population Declines," pt. 5.
47. Gary E. Davis and Jenifer E. Dugan, "Biosphere Reserves as Marine Harvest Refugia," Channel Islands National Park and Biosphere Reserve, April 27, 1990; and Bruce Kilgore to Stanley Albright, n.d.; both in PWRO, Natural Resource Files, CHIS, "Marine Refugia," San Francisco.

48. Both CINP and the surrounding National Marine Reserve became a unified Biosphere Reserve in 1986 with approval by the U.S. State Department and United Nations Educational, Scientific and Cultural Organization.
49. Dan Richards comments to Lary Dilsaver, October 17, 2019; the pathogen is a Rickettsiales-like prokaryote that infects gastrointestinal epithelia. It was tentatively named *Xenohaliotis californiensis*. Friedman et al., "*Candidatus* Xenohaliotis californiensis," 847–55.
50. Parker, Haaker, and Togstad, "Case Histories for Three Species," pt. 7; Moore et al., "Withering Syndrome," 112–17.
51. U.S. Dept. of Commerce, NOAA, "Endangered Status for Black Abalone," *Federal Register* 74 (9) January 14, 2009, 1937–1946.
52. Gary Davis, "Science and Society: Marine Reserve Design for the California Channel Islands," Report to the NPS, n.d., provided by Davis to Lary Dilsaver, September 3, 2018; U.S. Department of Commerce, *Recovery Plan for White Abalone*, 2008; CFR 7.84, 1973.
53. The four institutions are Oregon State University; University of California, Santa Barbara; University of California, Santa Cruz; and Stanford University. Partnership for Interdisciplinary Studies of Coastal Oceans , "The Science of Marine Reserves," 2002, http://www.pisco.org, 7.
54. CINMS, *Final 2002 Environmental Document Marine Protected Areas in the National Oceanic and Atmospheric Administration's Channel Islands National Marine Sanctuary, Volume 1,* NOAA, DOC, October 2002, 1–5.
55. Notable among them were Jim Donlon, patriarch of Ventura County's founding agribusiness family; lawyer Steve Roberson; and businessman and national railroad labor negotiator Evans Hughes.
56. Gary Davis interviewed by Lary Dilsaver, September 3, 2018.
57. The ten government seats on the SAC were held by National Marine Fisheries Service, NPS, Minerals Management Service, U.S. Navy, U.S. Coast Guard, CDFG, California Resources Agency, California Coastal Commission, and the counties of Santa Barbara and Ventura. The ten community seats included tourism, business, recreation, fishing, education, research, conservation, and three members at large.
58. California Fish and Game Code, Marine Life Protection Act [2850–2863] (Chapter 10.5 added by Stats. 1999, Ch. 1015, Sec. 1).
59. For a list of the members of the Marine Reserves Working Group see Dilsaver and Babalis, *Oceanic Park,* 309–10, note 739.
60. Davis, "Science and Society," 1745–51.

61. CINMS, *Final 2002 Environmental Document*, segments 1,3 to 1,4.
62. CINMS, *Final 2002 Environmental Document*, appendix 3.
63. Partnership for Interdisciplinary Studies of Coastal Oceans, "Science of Marine Reserves," 18.
64. Gary Davis to Park Marine Reserve Players, October 10, 2000, Gary Davis files provided to Lary Dilsaver, folder "Reserves Maps."
65. Science Advisory Panel, Marine Reserve Working Group (MRWG), "Estimating Reserve Size for Conservation and Fisheries Management," January 17, 2001, Gary Davis files provided to Lary Dilsaver, folder "Alts for Marine Reserves."
66. Melinda Burns, "Channel Sanctuary Talks Turn to What's In, Out," *Santa Barbara News-Press*, September 28, 2000.
67. Vernon R. Leeworthy and Peter C. Wiley, "Proposed Marine Reserve Channel Islands National Marine Sanctuary Socioeconomic Team," January 10, 2000, Gary Davis files, folder "Alts for Marine Reserves."
68. Jacob P. Kritzer, Tira Foran, and Rodney M. Fujita, "An Economic Overview of Santa Barbara and Ventura Counties and Their Marine Resource-Based Industries," Environmental Defense, n.d., Gary Davis files, folder "Alts for Marine Reserves."
69. Leeworthy, Wiley, and Stone, "Socioeconomic Impact Analysis," 104.
70. Davis, "Science and Society," 1745–50.
71. Gary Davis telephone interviewed by Lary Dilsaver, October 4, 2018.
72. Gary Davis telephone interviewed by Lary Dilsaver, October 4, 2018; CINMS, *Final 2002 Environmental Document*, appendix 3; *Federal Register*, Vol. 72, May 24, 2007, 29210.
73. A marine conservation area is less restrictive allowing some lobster and finfish takes.
74. CINMS, *Final 2002 Environmental Document*, appendix 3.
75. CINMS, *Final 2002 Environmental Document*, appendix 3.
76. CINMS, *Final 2002 Environmental Document*, segment 8,4.
77. Davis, "Science and Society," 2005.
78. *Federal Register*, Vol. 72, May 24, 2007, 29210; NOAA, "Marine Zones Now in Federal Waters of NOAA's Channel Islands National Marine Sanctuary," https://channelislands.noaa.gov/marineres/archive.html.
79. The term "Marine Protected Area" (MPA) is now the state's preferred term.
80. *Federal Register*, Vol. 72, May 24, 2007, 29210 and August 14, 2007, 45320.

7. Managing the Resources

1. Dilsaver, *America's National Park System*, 20–21, 34–39, 48–51; Tweed and Dilsaver, *Challenge of the Big Trees*, 140–41.
2. William Ehorn to Stanley Albright, January 25, 1994, copy courtesy of Santa Cruz Island Foundation; NPS, *Management Policies 1978*, DOI (U.S. General Printing Office, 0-721-256/720, 1978), II-4.
3. Clark et al., *Plant Communities*; relevé is a visual estimation of different species' coverage along one or more transects.
4. Clark et al. did not consult these primary documents directly but instead relied on published secondary sources, including Philbrick, *Proceedings: Symposium on the Biology*, and Halvorson, Fenn, and Allardice, "Soils and Vegetation," 109–18.
5. Cabrillo National Monument Foundation, *Account of the Voyage*, 80.
6. Rothrock, "Report Upon the Operations," 203.
7. Clark et al., *Plant Communities*, 47.
8. Sarah Chaney, park botanist, personal communication with Timothy Babalis, August 8, 2009; Fischer and Still, "Evaluating Patterns of Fog Water," 1–13.
9. Mack Shaver and Holly Bundock to Lary Dilsaver, October 28, 2019.
10. This opinion of Setnicka and the ranching community's negative assessment of Superintendent Shaver, were expressed by Nita Vail, Al Vail's daughter, in conversation with Timothy Babalis, September 25, 2009.
11. NPS, *General Management Plan 1985*; Mack Shaver and Holly Bundock to Lary Dilsaver, October 28, 2019; Kate Faulkner comment to Lary Dilsaver, January 14, 2019.
12. NPS, *Development Concept Plan and* Environmental Impact Statement Santa Rosa Island, Channel Islands National Park, CINP, *Santa Rosa Island*, September 1995.
13. Bill Ehorn taped ranch visit, December 6, 2001. Recording and transcript on file CINP Archives, Cat. 35833.
14. Margaret Vail Woolley, interview by Ann Eggers Jones, March 10, 1994. Transcript on file at Santa Cruz Island Foundation.
15. See chapter 9.
16. See chapter 9.
17. Pub. L. No. 96–199, Section. 202 (d)(2).
18. Whalen responded to a question from Senator Bumpers, "Mr. Chairman, on the land that will be ours and under our control, we would have no hunting. On the privately retained property, hunting could still occur but we would

hope to work with the landowner on the whole hunting program." *Hearings Before the Subcommittee on Parks, Recreation, and Renewable Resources, of the Committee on Energy and Natural Resources*, U.S. Senate, 96th Cong., 1st. Sess., (1979).

19. NPS, "Special Use Permit," 1987.
20. Bartolome and Clawson, *Range Management Plan*; Kate Faulkner commented on January 14, 2019, "The U.S. Fish & Wildlife Service wrote a 12-page letter to CHIS describing the shortfalls of the Range Management Plan in protection of the island ecosystem and individual species."
21. William Ehorn to *Santa Barbara News-Press*, March 15, 1987.
22. William Ehorn to Stanley Albright, January 25, 1994, copy courtesy of Marla Daily, Santa Cruz Island Foundation.
23. William Ehorn to Stanley Albright, January 25, 1994, copy courtesy of Marla Daily, Santa Cruz Island Foundation.
24. Mack Shaver interviewed by Ann Huston, March 29, 2019. Recording on file in CINP Archives.
25. Mack Shaver interviewed by Ann Huston, March 29, 2019. Recording on file in CINP Archives.
26. Mack Shaver and Holly Bundock to Lary Dilsaver, October 28, 2019.
27. Mack Shaver and Holly Bundock to Lary Dilsaver, October 28, 2019.
28. Kate Faulkner communication to Lary Dilsaver, May 20, 2019.
29. See chapter 5; NPS, "Special Use Permit No. WRO-8120-2600-001," December 29, 1987, CINP Central Files, SRI Binder No. 3, D.1.a.
30. Mack Shaver interviewed by Ann Huston, March 29, 2019. Recording on file in CINP Archives.
31. Kate Faulkner communication to Lary Dilsaver, May 20, 2019.
32. NPS, Western Region, "103rd Congress Briefing Statement: Loss of Soils and Vegetation due to Grazing on Santa Rosa Island," February 1993, History Program Collection, PWRO, San Francisco.
33. NPS, Western Region, "103rd Congress Briefing Statement."
34. NPS, Western Region, "103rd Congress Briefing Statement"; Cece Sellgren, "Fall 1995 Forage Monitoring Program Santa Rosa Island," February 5, 1996, CINP Archives, Cat. 06843, Acc. 00304.5, Series 1, folder 057.
35. Kate Faulkner communication, May 20, 2019.
36. Kate Faulkner comment on the Babalis draft of this manuscript, September 15, 2014, CINP Archives.
37. Karen J. Miller, "Determination of Threatened Status," 864–74.

38. Independent studies cited in the Fish and Wildlife Service's final rule had found that these predators accounted for 67 to 69 percent of nest failures in monitored populations.
39. Although Radanovich did not represent Santa Barbara County, he was a personal friend of the Vails and provided additional legislative support for them later.
40. Kate Faulkner comments to Lary Dilsaver, May 20, 2019.
41. Joanna Miller, "Cattle Battle Heats Up on Santa Rosa Island Habitat," *Los Angeles Times*, July 5, 1995.
42. U.S. Fish and Wildlife Service, "Proposed Rule to List Three Plants," 37,987–93 and "Proposed Rule for 16 Plant Taxa," 37,993–8011; Joanna Miller, "Survival List: 16 Plants Found Only on Channel Islands Nominated as Endangered Species," *Los Angeles Times*, August 3, 1995.
43. Rosenlieb et al, *Federal Interagency Riparian Assessment*.
44. Joanna Miller, "Biologists Working on Plan to Protect Park's Rare Species Conservation," *Los Angeles Times*, July 11, 1994.
45. Emily Roberson, "Cattle Degrading Island Ecosystems," *Los Angeles Times*, September 19, 1995.
46. John J. Woolley, "Endangered Status for Plants Could Harm Island," *Los Angeles Times*, August 9, 1995.
47. Roger W. Briggs to C. Mack Shaver, May 17, 1995, with attached "Cleanup or Abatement Order No. 95–064," CINP Archives, Cat. 6843, Acc. 00304.5, box 7, folder 258.
48. Roger W. Briggs to Tim J. Setnicka, October 17, 1996, CINP Central Files, 2.A.1., "NPCA v. NPS, SRI," folder 1; Kathryn McEachern, "Summary of Proposed Endangered Plant Data Collected on Santa Rosa Island by National Biological Service Staff and Collaborators, 1994–1996," CINP, Central Files, 1.A.2. Management of Natural Resources, folder "Plant Life, NPS & USFWS."
49. Rosenlieb et al., *Federal Interagency Riparian Assessment*.
50. Al Vail to Roger Briggs, June 16, 1995, CINP Archives, Cat. 06843, Acc. 00304.5, box 7 of 9, folder 258.
51. Nita Vail, conversation with Timothy Babalis, September 25, 2009.
52. William Ehorn email to Lary Dilsaver, February 27, 2018. John Cloud was a graduate student in the Geography Department at the University of California, Santa Barbara. He received his doctorate in 2000 and later worked for NOAA.

53. Mack Shaver interviewed by Ann Huston, March 29, 2019. Recording on file in CINP Archives; Mack Shaver and Holly Bundock to Lary Dilsaver, October 28, 2019.
54. Kathryn McEachern, "Summary of Proposed Endangered Plant Data Collected on Santa Rosa," CINP Central files, 1.A.2. Management of Natural Resources, folder "Plant Life, NPS & USFWS."
55. CINP, "Status of Resources on Santa Rosa Island," n.d., CINP Archives, Kate Faulkner files, folder 2.
56. Keith Hamm, "A Conflict over Endangered Humans and Other Species," *Independent* (Santa Barbara), September 5, 1996.
57. Barbara Goodyear email to Lary Dilsaver, November 13, 2019.
58. Kenneth Weiss, "Park Service Moves to Limit Grazing on Santa Rosa," *Los Angeles Times*, October 15, 1995. The "order" Setnicka referred to would come from the U.S. Fish and Wildlife Service executing the Endangered Species Act.
59. Representatives George Radanovich, Andrea Seastrand, and Elton Gallegly to Director Roger Kennedy, October 25, 1995, CINP Archives, Cat. 6494, box 10, "Santa Rosa Island Lawsuits 1996–98."
60. NPS, *Draft Resources Management Plan* and Environmental Impact Statement for Improvement of Water Quality and Conservation of Rare Species and Their Habitats on Santa Rosa Island, CINP, 1996; Kenneth R. Weiss, "Plan Would Limit Deer, Grazing on Island," *Los Angeles Times*, May 7, 1996.
61. National Parks and Conservation Association (NPCA) v. Roger Kennedy, Director of the National Park Service et al., CV 96-7412, Complaint for Declaratory and Injunctive Relief, E.1.a (CD Cal. 1995); Mack Reed, "Suit Alleges Damage to Santa Rosa Island," *Los Angeles Times*, October 23, 1996. The NPCA also sued the U.S. Fish and Wildlife Service for failing to list threatened rare plant species.
62. NPCA v. Roger Kennedy, CV 96-7412 WJR (RNBX) (CD Cal.1995).
63. NPCA v. Roger Kennedy, CV 96-7412 WJR (RNBX) (CD Cal. 1995); Robert J. Lagomarsino, "Notes of presentation at February 10, 1987, media event announcing the acquisition of Santa Rosa Island by the NPS," California State University Channel Islands, Broome Library, Robert J. Lagomarsino Collection: Federal Collection, 1974–1992, collection no. 1/92.
64. "To Honor Agreements Reached in the Acquisition of Santa Rosa Island, California, by the National Park Service." See CINP Archives, Cat. 6494, box 10, "Santa Rosa Island Lawsuits 1996–98."

65. Melinda Burns, "Range War," *Santa Barbara News-Press*, n.d. Capps had recently replaced republican Representative Andrea Seastrand in the House.
66. Walter Capps to Bruce Babbitt, May 21, 1997, CINP Archives, Cat. 6494, box 10, "Santa Rosa Island Lawsuits 1996–98."
67. Alexander Lennox Vail et al., v. Galvin et al., CV 97-4098 WJR (RNBX) (CD Cal. 1997).
68. "Vail & Vickers' Reply to Oppositions to Motion for Preliminary Injunction," Consolidated Case No. 96-7412, July 29, 1997, CINP Central files, 2.A.1., "Vail & Vickers Civil Litigation," folder 1.
69. NPS Solicitor Barbara Goodyear email to Lary Dilsaver, November 13, 2019.
70. Judge Rea Tentative Ruling, Alexander Lennox Vail et al. v. Denny Galvin et al., August 11, 1997, CINP Archives, Cat. 40739, Series 6 and 7, box 4.
71. U.S. Fish and Wildlife Service, "Final Rule for 13 Plant Taxa," 40954–74. This rule became effective on September 2, 1997.
72. Hilary MacGregor, "Island Squeeze," *Los Angeles Times*, May 25, 1997.
73. Section 4 of the Endangered Species Act requires the identification and protection of critical habitat needed to recover a listed species. If monitoring revealed that cervids continued to degrade critical habitat for any of the endangered plants or animals on Santa Rosa Island, even if they did not *directly* affect those species, the Fish and Wildlife Service would be obligated to insist on further management action.
74. "Settlement Agreement," draft press release, December 31, 1997; and Environmental Defense Center, "News Release," January 30, 1998; both in CINP Archives, Cat. 6494, box 10, "Santa Rosa Island Lawsuits 1996–98."
75. Dr. Michael Barbour was a botanist in the Department of Plant Sciences at University of California, Davis; Dr. John W. Menke was a range ecologist in the Department of Agronomy and Range Science also at UC Davis; and Ed Schreiner was a research biologist with the USGS.
76. Michael Barbour, John Menke, and Ed Schreiner, "Progress Report on the Monitoring and Status of Two Indicator Plant Species, *Arctostaphylos confertiflora* and *Castilleja mollis*, and Their Habitats on Santa Rosa Islands, Channel Islands National Park," December 30, 1998, CINP digital files, file:///D:/Documents/1b.%20CHIS%20Main%20Files/Santa%20Rosa/1998%20Panel%20Report.PDF.
77. NPS, *Draft Resources Management Plan* and Environmental Impact Statement. These questions were raised most directly by the California Native Plant Society.

78. John Cloud in NPS, *Draft Resources Management Plan* and Environmental Impact Statement.
79. Jayne Belnap in NPS, *Draft Resources Management Plan* and Environmental Impact Statement.
80. This view was implicit in all of the statements.
81. Anderson and Leal, *Enviro-Capitalists*, 73–75.
82. Ehorn to Regional Director Stanley Albright, January 25, 1994, copy courtesy of Marla Daily, Santa Cruz Island Foundation.
83. Kate Faulkner comments to Lary Dilsaver April 29, 2019; Ehorn to Regional Director Stanley Albright, January 25, 1994, copy courtesy of Marla Daily, Santa Cruz Island Foundation.
84. Faulkner, "Bringing Santa Rosa Island," 930–941.
85. Wagner et al., *Riparian System Recovery*.
86. Wagner et al., *Riparian System Recovery*.
87. Kenneth Weiss, "National Seashore Washing Out With Bush Administration," *Los Angeles Times*, August 20, 2002; NPS, *Gaviota Coast: Draft Feasibility Study* and Environmental Assessment, *April 2003* (San Francisco: NPS, Pacific Great Basin Support Office, 2003); NPS, *Gaviota Coast: Feasibility Study, February* and Environmental Assessment; Errata and Summary of Public Comments and Responses, February 2004 (San Francisco: NPS, Pacific Great Basin Support Office, 2004); Kenneth Weiss, "Status as National Seashore Rejected for Gaviota Coast," *Los Angeles Times*, March 10, 2004; Martha Crusius and Ray Murray, Planning Division, NPS, PWRO conversation with Timothy Babalis, notes in CINP Archives.
88. Tim Setnicka, "Santa Rosa Saga, Part Two: Bureaucracy Abounds as the Battle Over Santa Rosa Island Continues," *Santa Barbara News-Press*, October 15, 2006.

8. New Owners

1. Key officials for the Nature Conservancy's Santa Cruz Island Preserve program included California State director Peter Seligmann, California land steward Steven Johnson, Robert "Bob" Hansen as the first SCI preserve manager, and later, SCI project director Peter Schuyler as Hansen's replacement as SCI preserve manager, and Frank Boren as the Conservancy's representative on the Santa Cruz Island Company Board of Directors. Most of the communication between Carey Stanton and TNC was with Bob Hansen, whom Stanton liked, and Boren, whom he did not trust.

2. A copy of the official real estate purchase deed is located in CINP Archives, Cat. 10145, Acc. 00304.4, L1425, folder 12; The conservation easement deed is in CINP Archives, Cat. 10145, Acc. 00304.4, L1425, box 1, folder 2.
3. "Conservation Easement," CINP Archives, Cat. 10145, Acc. 00304.4, L1425, box 1, folder 2.
4. Marla Daily email to CINP, October 19, 2019.
5. Dirk Van Vuren, "Abstract," 1981, Santa Barbara Museum of Natural History Archives (hereafter SBMNH Archives), Bob Hansen Collection, box 78, folder 4032; Carey Stanton later blamed his problems with TNC's hunt on this study and forbade any research later conducted on the island from including management recommendations. This became an issue after TNC and SBMNH established a program to administer funds for scientific research on the island. Stanton insisted that he review all the proposals to make sure they did not have offending recommendations.
6. Schuyler, "Control of Feral Sheep," 443–52.
7. Carey Stanton to Patrick F. Noonan, March 28, 1980, provided to Lary Dilsaver by Bob Hansen.
8. Marla Daily interviewed by Timothy Babalis, August 19, 2009. Transcript on file in CINP Archives. Marla was not actually present during these negotiations. Her account reflects what Carey Stanton told her after the events took place; Marla Daily email to CINP, October 19, 2019.
9. Bob Hansen personal communication to Lary Dilsaver, September 19, 2018.
10. Bob Hansen telephone interview with Lary Dilsaver, September 1, 2018; Marla Daily later noted, "The hunting that began on December 17, 1981, was strategically planned by TNC to take place when Carey would be at his house in Eriskay, Scotland. He was given no notice of the marksmen in helicopters that would be swarming Santa Cruz Island in his absence, killing thousands of sheep. He felt extremely violated and betrayed by TNC and their stealth operation. He felt TNC was trying to bankrupt him by putting the Hunt Club, a significant part of the island's income, out of business." Marla Daily comments to CINP, October 19, 2019.
11. Bob Hansen to Frank Boren, Steve Johnson, Steve McCormick, September 16, 1986, SBMNH Archives, Bob Hansen Collection, box 78, folder 4034.
12. Lawsuit materials in SBMNH Archives, Bob Hansen Collection, box 79, folder 4036.
13. Bob Hansen telephone interview with Lary Dilsaver, September 1, 2018; Bob Hansen email to Lary Dilsaver, September 19, 1986.
14. Schuyler, "Control of Feral Sheep," 450.

15. Marla Daily reported that Frank Boren agreed to provide the funds at a rate of twenty dollars per sheep but then refused to return Stanton's phone calls and claimed he was not authorized to make such a deal. This led to Stanton's mistrust of and conflict with Boren. Marla Daily comments to CINP, October 19, 2019.
16. Steve Johnson and Bob Hansen to Laurel Mayer, September 11, 1984, SBMNH Archives, Bob Hansen Collection, box 78, folder 4026; Bob Hansen interview with Lary Dilsaver, September 1, 2018.
17. According to Marla Daily, "there was a lawsuit, a woman fell off a cliff, allegedly on drugs, out at the Christy Ranch out on the cliffs and they sued, the insurance wasn't renewed." Marla Daily comments October 19, 2019.
18. Mark Oberman email to Lary Dilsaver, June 2, 2019.
19. Marla Daily recalled: "I was witness to Carey's call from Jacques Cousteau when he denied him access to film *Cousteau's Rediscovery of the World* (1986) on Santa Cruz Island." Marla Daily comments, October 19, 2019.
20. Bob Hansen to Frank Boren et al., September 16, 1986, SBMNH Archives, Bob Hansen Collection, box 78, folder 4026.
21. Lyndal Laughrin interviewed by Lary Dilsaver, August 29, 2018.
22. Bob Hansen interviewed by Lary Dilsaver, September 1, 2018.
23. Mark Oberman email to Lary Dilsaver, June 2, 2019.
24. Mark Oberman email to Lary Dilsaver, June 2, 2019; Steve Johnson to Mark Oberman, March 7, 1989; Bob Hansen to Steve McCormick and Steve Johnson, October 27, 1988; and Memorandum: Bob Hansen to the Files, November 7, 1986; all in SBMNH Archives, Bob Hansen Collection, box 78, folder 4024; E. Lewis Reid to Steve Johnson, February 23, 1989, SBMNH Archives, Bob Hansen Collection, box 78, folder 4025.
25. Schuyler, "Control of Feral Sheep," 450.
26. "Cooperative Agreement between the National Park Service and the Nature Conservancy," finalized January 8, 1991, History Program Files, PWRO Archives, San Francisco.
27. This occurred between 1991 and 1992 while John Morgando was acting as Island Adventures' resident caretaker at Smugglers Ranch. John Morgando to CINP, January 28, 1997, CINP Archives, Cat. 6494, box 7B.
28. "The existing hunt clubs and landing permit systems which are operated by the property owners [on the Channel Islands] shall be allowed to continue at their current levels without permit requirements." Santa Barbara County, *Coastal Land Use Plan*, 215.

29. John Gherini to Rep. Walter Capps, April 7, 1997, CINP Archives, Cat. 6494, box 7B.
30. Duane Owens and Jaret Owens to Rep. Robert Lagomarsino, November 13, 1992, CINP Archives, Cat. 6494, box 7B.
31. Superintendent of CINP to Budget Officer, NPS Western Region, March 26, 1991, CINP Archives, Cat. 6494, box 7B.
32. NPS Regional Director Stanley Albright to Representative Robert Lagomarsino, December 9, 1992, CINP Archives, Cat. 6494, box 7B.
33. Don Morris interviewed by Timothy Babalis, August 8, 2009. Transcript on file in CINP Archives.
34. Owens to Rep. Robert Lagomarsino, November 13, 1992, CINP Archives, Acc. 265, Cat. No. 6494, box 7B; Earl Whetsell interviewed by Timothy Babalis, August 10, 2009. Transcript on file in CINP Archives.
35. John Gherini to Walter Capps, April 7, 1997, CINP Archives, Cat. No. 6494, box 7B.
36. *Hearing Before the Subcommittee on Parks, Recreation, and Renewable Resource of the Committee on Energy and Natural Resources*, U.S. Senate, 96th Cong., 1st Sess., on S.1104, (1979).
37. The most recent had taken place in 1988, when the government seized a private inholding within Manassas National Historic Battlefield, where the owner was proposing to develop a shopping mall.
38. William Clark was an old friend of Francis Gherini. Clark had served as Secretary of the Interior under President Reagan from 1983 to 1985.
39. "Gherini, Park Service Still Feuding," *Santa Barbara News-Press*, March 20, 1997.
40. Gebe Martinez, "A Park Bill That Was No Walk in the Park," *Los Angeles Times*, October 4, 1996.
41. Pub. L. No. 104–333 also named the park's visitor center in Ventura after Congressman Robert J. Lagomarsino. The bill was introduced by Rep. Elton W. Gallegly (R-Simi Valley).
42. John Gherini to Walter Capps, April 7, 1997, CINP Archives, Cat. No. 6494, box 7B.
43. "Santa Cruz Land Baron Dies," *Ventura Star*, April 30, 1999; the final sale figure with interest was provided by Greg Gress, Pacific West Regional Office Lands Division.
44. Starbard's acquaintance was eventually prosecuted by the Ventura County District Attorney's Office. *Santa Barbara News-Press*, January 22, 1997.

45. Nick Welsh, "The Taking of Santa Cruz Island," *Independent* (Santa Barbara), April 17, 1997.
46. Ian Williams, conversation with Timothy Babalis, August 4, 2009; Jack Fitzgerald, conversation with Timothy Babalis, August 5, 2009; Jack Fitzgerald, interview with Ann Huston, October 9, 2019.
47. Tim Setnicka to Friends of Channel Islands National Park, February 11, 1997, CINP Archives, Cat. 6494, box 7A; Michael Parrish, "This Is the Park Service: Come Out with Your Hands Up," *Outside*, May 1997, 27–28.
48. Jack Fitzgerald interview, October 9, 2019.
49. Don Morris interviewed by Timothy Babalis, August 8, 2009. Transcript in CINP Archives; "Calif. Island Raided, Seized for Use as National Park," *San Diego Daily Transcript*, February 11, 1997; Krantz was found guilty on September 5, 1997, and sentenced to three years of probation and 250 hours of community service. Nick Welsh, "Hunting Guide Krantz Digs His Own Grave," *Independent*, Sept. 11, 1997.
50. T. J. Sullivan, "Sheep Killing on Island Upsets Last Bow Hunters," *Ventura County Star*, February 11, 1997.
51. Richard W. Tentler to Superintendent Tim Setnicka, December 5, 1996, CINP Archives, Cat. 6494, box 7B. According to his own statement, Tentler's law office was a member of the Environmental Law Action Coalition, "a group of attorneys who have agreed to selectively intervene in cases involving severe environmental impact." The letter—which claimed to represent the interests of numerous animal rights advocates, preservationists, and environmentalists—was copied to members of Congress, the DOI, and the White House.
52. Schuyler, "Control of Feral Sheep."
53. Carol Spears, Public Information Officer, Channel Islands National Park, February 12, 1997, CINP Archives, Cat. 6494, box 7A.
54. Francis Gherini to NPS, February 5, 1997, CINP Archives, Cat. 6494, box 7B.
55. John Costello, Western Regional Office Lands Division, to CHIS, March 25, 1997; and John Gherini to Representative Walter Capps, April 7, 1997; both in CINP Archives, Cat. 6494, box 7B.
56. Melinda Burns, "A Ewe Turn," *Santa Barbara News Press*, December 6, 1999; Jack Fitzgerald, interview with Ann Huston on October 10, 2019.
57. Karen M. Blumenshine, Suzanne V. Benech, Ann T. Bowling, and Ned K. Waters, "Preliminary Survey of Physical, Genetic, Physiological and Behavioral Traits of Feral Horses (*Equus caballus*) on Santa Cruz Island," n.d., CINP Archives, Ephemera Coll., CHIS 0265, box 9.

58. Blumenshine et al., "Preliminary Survey," CINP Archives, Ephemera Coll., CHIS 0265, box 9.
59. Marla Daily comment to CINP, October 19, 2019; John Gherini interviewed by Lary Dilsaver, September 3, 2018.
60. Terra Marine Research & Education (TMRE) evolved from the educational programs organized by Kirk's father, Bill Connally, who had founded Island Packers in 1968. TMRE was incorporated in 1986 for the purpose of conducting "research and education in the marine sciences and related fields." Accessed July 3, 2010, http://www.tmre.org.
61. Lynne Sherman to the Save the Heritage Herd Project, April 14, 1997. Memo notes that Foundation for Horses and Other Animals will adopt the Save the Heritage Herd project once FHOA obtains tax-exempt status. Until then, the project remains with TMRE. Material relating to Heritage Herd in CINP Archives, Cat. 6494, box 9; Marla Daily comment to CINP, October 19, 2019.
62. Barbara Werger was the president of FHOA. Karen Blumenshine continued to work with the organization as a professional advocate for the herd.
63. John Gherini to Marla Daily, December 9, 1996, CINP Archives, Cat. 6494, box 9.
64. John Krist, "Wild Beauty," *Santa Barbara Magazine*, Spring 1997, 60–66.
65. "Wild Horses' Removal Blocked," *Santa Barbara News-Press*, March 21, 1998; NPS, *Channel Islands National Park: Land Protection Plan 1984*, CINP, February 1984.
66. The land protection plan had been prepared as prerequisite to the park's general management plan, which was completed later that year with a Finding of No Significant Impact (FONSI). The FONSI obviated the need for a full Environmental Impact Statement. It was this decision that FHOA challenged.
67. Foundation for Horses and Other Animals v. Babbitt, U.S.C.A. 9th, No. 98-55148, (1998).
68. Gary Polakovic, "Island Evacuated for Wild Horse Removal," *Los Angeles Times*, September 24, 1998.
69. "Horses Removed from Channel Island," *Ventura County Star*, September 24, 1998.
70. Bossard, Randall, and Hoshovsky, eds., *Invasive Plants of California's Wildlands*.
71. Colvin and Gliessman, "Fennel (*Foeniculum vulgare*) Management," 184–89; Brenton and Klinger, "Modeling the Expansion of Fennel," 97–504; and Beatty and Licari, "Invasion of Fennel," 54–66.

72. Melinda Burns, "Island Faces New Natural Challenges," *Santa Barbara News-Press*, April 28, 1997.
73. Junak et al., *Flora of Santa Cruz Island* (1995).
74. Ruderal is defined as a badly disturbed condition or a "wasteland."
75. Barthell et al., "Yellow Star-Thistle,," 269–73.
76. Wenner, Thorp, and Barthell, "Removal of European Honey Bees," 256–60.
77. Wenner, Thorp, and Barthell, "Removal of European Honey Bees," 256–60.
78. Kate Faulkner email to Tim Setnicka, "New Heritage Herd—Honey Bees on SCI," August 26, 1997, CINP Archives, Cat. 6494, box 9.
79. "Cooperative Agreement between the National Park Service and the Nature Conservancy," November 2, 1999, CINP Archives, Cat. No. 40496, Series 1, folder 63; Project Management Information System, 06226, NPS electronic database.
80. Kent Bullard, personal communication with Ann Huston on September 20, 2019.
81. Kent Bullard, personal communication with Ann Huston on September 20, 2019.

9. Restoring Nature

1. See for example Wright, Dixon, and Thompson, *Fauna of the National Parks*.
2. Primack, *Essentials of Conservation Biology*, 601; Rauzon, *Isles of Amnesia*, 70–71.
3. By 1896, cats were observed to be extremely abundant. Schoenherr, Feldmeth, and Emerson, *Natural History*, 348.
4. Lowell Sumner and Richard M. Bond, "An Investigation of Santa Barbara, Anacapa, and San Miguel Islands," June 28, 1939, CINP Archives, Acc. 250, Cat. 4016, Series 3, folder 2, 27.
5. Steve Chawkins, "Rat Patrol," *Los Angeles Times*, October 1, 1987.
6. "Rat Eradication Project, 1983–1992," CINP Archives, Cat. 6842, folder 3; Superintendent's Annual Reports for 1983 and 1984 (February 29, 1984, and March 14, 1985), CINP Archives, Cat. No. 13117, box 1, folder 5.
7. The eight species are the Scripps's murrelet (*Synthliboramphorus hypoleuca*), which was known at that time as Xantus's murrelet; double-crested cormorant (*Phalacrocorax auritus*); Brandt's cormorant (*Phalacrocorax penicillatus*); Pelagic cormorant (*Phalacrocorax pelagicus*); pigeon guillemot (*Cepphus columba*); black oystercatcher (*Haematopus bachmani*); brown pelican (*Pelecanus occidentalis*); and the western gull (*Larus occidentalis*). The Cassin's auk-

let (*Ptychoramphus aleuticus*) was believed to have nested on Anacapa Island as recently as the early twentieth century, but no nests have been observed for more than eighty years. NPS, *Anacapa Island Restoration Plan: Final Environmental Impact Statement*, CINP, October 2000, 39 ff. and 127–136.

8. Bird Life International (2009) Species factsheet: *Synthliboramphus hypoleucus*, accessed September 19, 2009, http://www.birdlife.org; Carter et al., "Biology and Conservation," 81–87; Karnovsky et al., "At-Sea Distribution," 89–104.

9. On the impact of introduced mammals, especially rats, see McChesney and Tershy, "History and Status," 335–47.

10. Kate Faulkner later noted that Ugolini's efforts focused on removing rats only from areas where humans could place poison bait boxes. Rats on the cliffs in the bird-nesting areas were unaffected. Kate Faulkner interviewed by Timothy Babalis, August 5, 2009. Transcript on file at CINP Archives.

11. Kate Faulkner interviewed by Timothy Babalis, August 5, 2009. The actual amount allocated for the plan was $35,000.

12. Island Conservation is a charitable organization that was first established as a network of conservationists in 1994, accessed October 25, 2010, http://www.islandconservation.org.

13. The Trustee Council comprised representatives from the CDFG, the National Oceanic and Atmospheric Administration (NOAA), and the U.S. Fish and Wildlife Service (USFWS).

14. "A Roof Rat Bait Station That Excludes Deer Mice," 1989, CINP Archives, Cat. 6842, "Rat Eradication Project, 1983–1992," folder 3.

15. The Record of Decision was signed in November of 2000.

16. Darrell L. Whitworth and Harry R. Carter, "Measuring the Response of Scripps's Murrelets (*Synthliboramphus scrippsi*) 12 Years after the Eradication of Black Rats (*Rattus rattus*) at Anacapa Island, California: Nocturnal Spotlight Surveys and Nest Monitoring," (unpublished report, California Institute of Environmental Studies, Davis, California, 2015).

17. The Fund for Animals was founded in 1967 by author and animal rights advocate Cleveland Amory, who was directly involved with issues related to the Channel Islands.

18. Kate Faulkner interviewed by Timothy Babalis, August 5, 2009.

19. United States District Court for the District of Columbia, "The Fund for Animals et al. v. Fran Mainella et al.," Civil Action No. 01-2288-ESH, November 29, 2001.

20. U.S. District Court, "The Fund v. Mainella."
21. Daryl Kelley, "Activist Not Guilty of Impeding Rat Killings," *Los Angeles Times*, July 11, 2003.
22. The team included researchers from the Channels Islands National Marine Sanctuary, California Institute of Environmental Studies, Humboldt State University, and Hamer Environmental. Hamer, Schuster, and Meekins, "Radar as a Tool," 81–87.
23. Whitworth et al., "Initial Recovery of Xantus's Murrelets," 131–37.
24. Jenifer Ragland, "Rare Bird Hatches a Comeback," *Los Angeles Times*, June 2, 2003; Chuck Graham, "The Xantus's Murrelet of Anacapa Island," *Birding*, May/June 2007, 46–51.
25. Whitworth et al., "Initial Recovery of Xantus's Murrelets, 2005."
26. Livingston, *Island Legacies*, 295–97.
27. Gary E. Davis and William H. Halvorson, "A Resource Management Proposal to Remove Feral Pigs from Santa Rosa Island, Channel Islands National Park, California," April 11, 1990, PWRO Library Natural Resources File Cabinet, N1615, "CHIS Feral Pig Removal."
28. Davis and Halvorson, "A Resource Management Proposal."
29. On multiple-use management, see the business' own website, http://www.mumwildlife.com; Anderson and Leal, *Enviro-Capitalists*, 73–75.
30. CINP Superintendent to Western Regional Director, October 1, 1991, PWRO Library Natural Resources File Cabinet, N1615, "CHIS Feral Pig Removal"; Lombardo and Faulkner, "Eradication of Feral Pigs."
31. Joanna Miller, "Scientists Tour Islands to Assess Damage to Nature," *Los Angeles Times*, April 8, 1991.
32. Kate Faulkner comment to Timothy Babalis, September 15, 2014.
33. Kenneth Weiss, "Santa Rosa Island Wild Swine Gathers Momentum," *Los Angeles Times*, April 24, 1991; Melinda Burns, "Island Faces New Natural Challenges," *Santa Barbara News-Press*, April 28, 1997; Kate Faulkner interview by Timothy Babalis, August 5, 2009.
34. Crooks, "Demography and Status of the Island Fox," 257–62.
35. Fahey and Vissman, "Endangered and Threatened Wildlife and Plants," 10,335–53.
36. Fahey and Vissman, "Endangered and Threatened Wildlife and Plants," 10,335.
37. Fahey and Vissman, "Endangered and Threatened Wildlife and Plants," 10,336.

38. Fahey and Vissman, "Endangered and Threatened Wildlife and Plants," 10,335–36; Coonan Schwemm, and Garcelon, *Decline and Recovery of the Island Fox*.
39. Laughrin, "Island Fox"; Laughrin, "Populations and Status."
40. Coonan et al., "Decline of an Island Fox Subspecies," 32–41.
41. Roemer, "Ecology and Conservation of the Island Fox"; Fahey and Vissman, "Endangered and Threatened Wildlife and Plants,"10,338.
42. This explanation was offered by Nita Vail in conversation with Timothy Babalis, September 25, 2009.
43. Hilary MacGregor, "Rare Island Foxes Dying," *Los Angeles Times*, August 16, 1998.
44. Coonan et al., "Decline of an Island Fox Subspecies," 49, 74–80. A meeting of experts, convened by the Institute for Wildlife Studies in early 1999, concluded that disease or parasitism were probably not responsible.
45. Hilary MacGregor, "Rare Island Foxes Dying," *Los Angeles Times*, August 16, 1998; Coonan, Schwemm, and Garcelon, *Decline and Recovery of the Island Fox*, 50.
46. Gary Polakovic, "Mystery of Vanishing Foxes Ends," *Los Angeles Times*, April 3, 1999; Coonan, Schwemm, and Garcelon, *Decline and Recovery of the Island Fox*, 48.
47. Collins and Latta, "Nesting Season Diet of Golden Eagles on Santa Cruz and Santa Rosa Islands."
48. Roemer et al., "Golden Eagles, Feral Pigs, and Insular Carnivores," 791–796.
49. Members of the working group are listed in Dilsaver and Babalis, *The Oceanic Park*, 440, note 718.
50. Gary Polakovic, "Island Foxes May Soon Die Out, Scientists Warn," *Los Angeles Times*, April 24, 1999.
51. Coonan, "Findings and Recommendations," 58.
52. Coonan, Schwemm, and Garcelon, *Decline and Recovery of the Island Fox*, 72ff.
53. Coonan, Schwemm, and Garcelon, *Decline and Recovery of the Island Fox*, 82.
54. Gary Polakovic, "Capture Program Launched to Save Threatened Foxes," *Los Angeles Times*, May 20, 1999.
55. Jack Fitzgerald interview with Ann Huston, October 9, 2019. NPS, Statement "Recover Endangered Foxes at Channel Islands National Park," NPS electronic database.

56. Coonan, Schwemm, and Garcelon, *Decline and Recovery of the Island Fox*, 82ff.
57. Coonan, Schwemm, and Garcelon, *Decline and Recovery of the Island Fox*, 83.
58. Coonan, Schwemm, and Garcelon, *Decline and Recovery of the Island Fox*, 84.
59. Coonan, Schwemm, and Garcelon, *Decline and Recovery of the Island Fox*, 85.
60. The Institute for Wildlife Studies was also involved in efforts to relocate golden eagles off island; Coonan, Schwemm, and Garcelon, *Decline and Recovery of the Island Fox*, 73.
61. Coonan, Schwemm, and Garcelon, *Decline and Recovery of the Island Fox*, 85.
62. Coonan, Schwemm, and Garcelon, *Decline and Recovery of the Island Fox*, 91.
63. Latta et al., "Capture and Translocation of Golden Eagles," 2005.
64. Latta, *Channel Islands Golden Eagle*.
65. Coonan, Schwemm, and Garcelon, "Decline of an Island Fox Subspecies."
66. Sibley, *Sibley Field Guide to Birds*.
67. As noted above, feral pigs were eradicated from Santa Rosa Island in 1992.
68. Kiff, "Historical Changes in Resident Populations," 651–73 and Dooley, Sharpe, and Garcelon, "Movements, Foraging, and Survival of Bald Eagles," 313–21.
69. NOAA, "Restore Bald Eagles to the Channel Islands," in *Montrose Settlements Restoration Program*, appendix B.
70. NOAA, "Executive Summary," in *Montrose Settlements Restoration Program*.
71. Dunlap, *DDT*, 274–75.
72. 116 Cong. Rec. H6523 (H.Doc. Nos. 91-364, 91-365, and 91-366); Ruckelshaus, "Consolidated DDT Hearings," 13,369–76.
73. Dunlap, *DDT*, 281–82; "Our Story: How EDF Got Started," Environmental Defense Fund, last modified 2022, www.edf.org.
74. Environmental Defense Fund v. Ruckelshaus, 439 F. 2d 584 (DC Cir. 1971); Ruckelshaus, "Consolidated DDT Hearings."
75. Gress, *Reproductive Status of the California Brown Pelican*; "Pesticides Peril Bird Life," *Santa Barbara News-Press*, April 22, 1969; Schreiber and Risebrough, "Studies of the Brown Pelican," 119–35.
76. Ruckelshaus, "Consolidated DDT Hearings."
77. Irving S. Bengelsdorf, "Scientific Sleuths Have Nailed Another Global Lifetaker," *Los Angeles Times*, March 20, 1969; Risebrough et al., "DDT Residues in Pacific Sea Birds," 589–91.
78. NOAA, *Montrose Settlements Restoration Program*.
79. U.S. Environmental Protection Agency, *Ecological Risk Assessment*.

80. U.S. Environmental Protection Agency, accessed October 25, 2009, http://www.epa.gov/superfund/policy/cercla.htm.
81. The Los Angeles County Sanitation District No. 2 (LACSD) operates the Joint Water Pollution Control Plant (JWPCP), located just south of Torrance. The JWPCP releases waste effluent through discharge pipes located at White's Point on the southeast corner of the Palos Verdes Peninsula.
82. The other trustees were NOAA; the U.S. Fish and Wildlife Service; the California Department of Fish and Game; the California State Lands Commission; and the California Department of Parks and Recreation.
83. United States and State of California v. Montrose Chemical Corp. of California, et al. Partial Consent Decree 2001, http://www.justice.gov/enrd/consent-decree/file/1359886/download
84. The EPA ultimately decided to focus its investigations on the no action, institutional controls and in-place alternatives. The EPA is also continuing to evaluate capping as a potential response action for the Palos Verdes shelf. No action was taken on the capping proposal. Instead, emphasis was placed on protecting the public from pollution and restoring affected resources in places where the immediate effects of organochlorine discharges were less substantial, including the Northern Channel Islands.
85. NOAA, *Montrose Settlements Restoration Program.*
86. For example, the educational comic book, *There's Something Fishy Going on Here*, produced jointly by Montrose Settlements Restoration Program and Cabrillo Marine Aquarium.
87. U.S. Fish and Wildlife Service, "Brown Pelican Populations Recovered Removed from Endangered Species List," accessed April 22, 2019, https://www.fws.gov/southeast/news/2009/11/brown-pelican-populations-recovered-removed-from-endangered-species-list/.
88. U.S. Department of Commerce, *Feasibility Study*, http://www.darrp.noaa.gov/southwest/montrose/pdf/mon02-2.pdf.
89. Dooley, Sharpe, and Garcelon, "Movements, Foraging, and Survival of Bald Eagles."
90. Gabrielle Dorr, "Bald Eagles on the Northern Channel Islands," Montrose Settlements Restoration Program Fact Sheet, January 2008, CINP Library; David Kelly, "Four Bald Eagles Returned to the Channel Islands," *Los Angeles Times*, May 21, 2002; Barbara Whitaker, "On Wings of Eagles," *New York Times*, July 29, 2002; Jenifer Ragland, "Twelve Eagles to Land in Channel Islands Park," *Los Angeles Times*, July 20, 2003.
91. Latta et al., "Capture and Translocation of Golden Eagles," 341–50.

92. Coonan, Schwemm, and Garcelon, *Decline and Recovery of the Island Fox*, 94; Mastitis is defined as inflammation of the breast or udder tissue.
93. Coonan, Schwemm, and Garcelon, *Decline and Recovery of the Island Fox*, 107.
94. U.S. Fish and Wildlife Service, "Listing of the San Miguel Island Fox," 10,335–53; Margaret Talev, "Island Foxes Proposed for Endangered Status," *Los Angeles Times*, December 11, 2001; Holly Wolcott, "Islands' Foxes Are Now Protected," *Los Angeles Times*, March 5, 2004.
95. Coonan, Schwemm, and Garcelon, *Decline and Recovery of the Island Fox*, 107–14; Catalina Island Conservancy, "Foxes," accessed October 10, 2012, http://www.catalinaconservancy.org/index.php?s=support&p=foxes.
96. Lotus Vermeer interviewed by Lary Dilsaver, March 12, 2018.
97. Tim Setnicka to Mr. Reg Barrett, December 2, 1998, CINP Central Files, Drawer 6, folder "Pig Litigation 3."
98. NPS, *Santa Cruz Island Primary Restoration Plan: Final Environmental Impact Statement*, CINP, June 2002.
99. NPS, *Santa Cruz Island Primary Restoration Plan: Final Environmental Impact Statemen*, CINP, June 2002, 147–86.
100. Quote from Dr. Adrian W. Wenner in *Santa Cruz Island Primary Restoration Plan: Final Environmental Impact Statement*, 181–82.
101. Jenifer Ragland, "Hunters to Trap and Shoot Pigs on Santa Cruz Island," *Los Angeles Times*, September 17, 2002.
102. NPS, *Santa Cruz Island Primary Restoration Plan: Final Environmental Impact Statement*, CINP, June 2002, 13–14.
103. NPS, *Santa Cruz Island Primary Restoration Plan: Final Environmental Impact Statement*, CINP, June 2002, 13–14; Kate Faulkner, email to Timothy Babalis, July 8, 2010.
104. CINP received a base funding increase of $498,000 in 2002 from the Natural Resource Challenge for the Santa Cruz Island restoration project, which included the pig eradication. NPS, OFS electronic database 5224.
105. Lotus Vermeer interview with Lary Dilsaver, 2018.
106. Timothy J. Setnicka, "Ex-Park Chief Calls for Moratorium on Island 'Hunt,'" *Santa Barbara News-Press*, March 25, 2005.
107. Timothy J. Setnicka, "Ex-Park Chief Calls for Moratorium on Island 'Hunt,'" *Santa Barbara News-Press*, March 25, 2005; between 2004 and 2006, more than forty articles and opinions appeared in the *Santa Barbara News-Press* decrying the pig hunt, including those by Setnicka; Lotus Vermeer interview with Lary Dilsaver, 2018.

108. Gregory W. Griggs, "Suit Filed to Halt Pig Eradication on Santa Cruz Island," *Los Angeles Times*, May 20, 2005; Catherine Saillant, "Activists Seek Halt of Feral Pig Hunt," *Los Angeles Times*, July 8, 2005; Gregory W. Griggs, "New Court Fight Looms in Pig Killing," *Los Angeles Times*, July 15, 2005; Gregory W. Griggs, "Activists Seek Injunction against Wild Pig Hunt," *Los Angeles Times*, August 23, 2005; Gregory W. Griggs, "2nd Bid to Stop Pig Eradication Is Denied," *Los Angeles Times*, September 27, 2005.
109. Gregory W. Griggs, "Camping Ban on Santa Cruz Island Is Lifted," *Los Angeles Times*, March 21, 2006; Gregory W. Griggs, "Suit to Stop Wild Pig Eradication Is Dismissed," *Los Angeles Times*, March 30, 2006; and Coonan, Schwemm, and Garcelon, *Decline and Recovery of the Island Fox*, 67.
110. "Feral Pigs Become Scapegoats—In the U.S. and Around the World," *Animal People News*, January/February 2007, http://www.animalpeoplenews.org/07/1/feralpigsscapegoats1_07.html.
111. Panel members included Jim Shevock, the Cooperative Ecosystem Studies Unit coordinator from the University of California, Berkeley; Peter Dratch from the Park Service's natural resources directorate in Fort Collins, Colorado; and Natalie Gates, wildlife biologist from Point Reyes National Seashore.
112. Natalie Gates, telephone conversation with Timothy Babalis, September 23, 2009.
113. "Recover Endangered Foxes at Channel Islands National Park," OFS electronic database; Jack Fitzgerald interview with Ann Huston, October 9, 2019.
114. Jon Jarvis interviewed by Dan Wakelee, December 17, 2007. Transcript in California State University, Channel Islands Archives. Interviews with many former employees of the park while Tim Setnicka was superintendent testify to the resentment he caused.
115. "Park Chief's Transfer Routine, Official Says," *Los Angeles Times*, October 16, 2002.
116. "Blunt-Spoken Ex-Leader of National Park Retires," *Los Angeles Times*, January 11, 2003.

10. The New Century

1. Cheri Carlson, "Galipeau Retires from Leading Channel Islands National Park after 40-Year Career," *Ventura County Star*, June 2, 2018, https://www.vcstar.com/story/news/special-reports/outdoors/2018/06/02/galipeau-retires-leading-channel-islands-national-park-after-40-year-career/641477002/.
2. NPS, *Resources Management Plan for Improvement of Water Quality*, 1998.

3. The meeting included Ray Bransfield and Bridget Fahey of the USFWS and Kate Faulkner, Tim Coonan, Dirk Rodriguez, and Sarah Chaney of the NPS.
4. Acting Field Supervisor, Ventura Office of USFWS, to Superintendent CINP, June 20, 2001, CINP Central Files, 2.A.1, "Vail & Vickers," folder 5.
5. Barbara Goodyear to Russell Vail, March 27, 2003; and "Draft Vail & Vickers SUP Renewal," June 16, 2003; both in CINP Superintendent's files, folder "SRI V&V Correspondence."
6. "Special Use Permit for Commercial Deer and Elk Hunting Operation on Santa Rosa Island, October 1, 2003, to December 31, 2008," CINP digital archives, March 3, 2004.
7. Timothy B. Vail to Russell E. Galipeau, July 6, 2007, CINP Superintendent's files, "SRI V&V Correspondence 2007"; Russell Galipeau to Vail & Vickers, July 24, 2007, CINP Central files, 2.A.1, "Vail & Vickers," folder 6.
8. Russell Galipeau to Vail & Vickers, July 24, 2007, CINP Central files, 2.A.1, "Vail & Vickers," folder 6.
9. Pub. L. No. 109–364, Stat. 2083, Section 1077, "To authorize appropriations for fiscal year 2007 for military activities of the Department of Defense."
10. Congressional Record, House of Representatives, Volume 152, Number 125, September 29, 2006, 7972–76.
11. Channel Islands National Park Management Act of 2007, S. 1209, 110th Cong. (2007).
12. *Legislative Hearing on S. 1209 Before the Subcommittee on National Parks of the Committee on Energy and Natural Resources*, 110th Cong. (2007).
13. "End of an Era on Santa Rosa Island," *Ventura County Star*, November 12, 2011.
14. Russell Galipeau interviewed by Lary Dilsaver, March 19, 2018; Timothy Vail to Russell Galipeau, July 6, 2007, CINP Superintendent's files, folder "SRI V&V Correspondence 2007"; Russell Galipeau to Timothy Vail, July 24, 2007, Timothy Vail to Russell Galipeau, January 2, 2008, Russell Galipeau to Dr. Vail, January 25, 2008, and Russell Galipeau to Permittees, February 26, 2008; all in CINP Central files, 2.A.1, "Vail & Vickers," folder 6.
15. Russell Galipeau to the Files, "Unresolved Questions (legal or policy citations required for answers)," 2008, CINP Superintendent's files, folder "V&V Correspondence 2008."
16. Russell Galipeau interview, March 19, 2018; Kate Faulkner email to Lary Dilsaver, November 16, 2018.
17. Nita Vail, Timothy Vail, Susan M. Woolley, Sandra Vickers Naftzger, Henry Vickers Eggers, and Ann Vickers Crawford-Hall, "Supplement to Special

Use Permit PWR-CHIS-2600-09-01"; and Susan F. Petrovich to Russell Galipeau, April 21, 2011; both in CINP Superintendent's files, folder "SRI SUP Supplement."

18. Susan F. Petrovich to Russell Galipeau, April 21, 2011; "Pro Hunters Hit Santa Rosa Island," *Santa Barbara Independent*, October 15, 2011; a note written on the printed copy of this article indicates that White Buffalo was the contractor used in the hunt. That information was conveyed to Russell Galipeau by Greg Gress of the regional office; Kate Faulkner email to Lary Dilsaver, November 16, 2018.
19. John J. Knapp et al., "Santa Cruz Island"; TNC, August 2015.
20. NPS, "Management of Non-native Argentine Ants; Santa Cruz Island," January 15, 2015, 5–14, 29–36, file:///D:/Documents/Writing%20CHIS/Argentine%20Ants/Management%20of%20Argentine%20Ants%20on%20Santa%20Cruz%201-15-15.pdf.
21. Lyndal Laughrin interviewed by Lary Dilsaver, August 30, 2018.
22. Paul W. Collins, "Channel Islands National Park Bird Checklist," November 4, 2011, https://www.nps.gov/chis/learn/nature/birds.htm.
23. NPS, *Channel Islands National Park Natural Resource Condition Assessment*, CINP, 2014, 35–38.
24. CINMS, *Channel Islands National Marine Sanctuary Condition Report 2016*, Volume 1, NOAA, DOC, 2018, 36.
25. NPS, *Channel Islands National Park Natural Resource Condition Assessment*, CINP, 2014, 35–38.
26. Kate Faulkner comment to CINP, May 4, 2020.
27. Morrison, "A Bird in Our Hand," 77–93.
28. Morrison, "A Bird in Our Hand," 77–93.
29. NPS, "Planning for Community Wildland Urban Interface Fire Management Response," 2000, CINP Central Files, 1.A. 2, folder "Wildland Fire Management '06–89."
30. Robert Taylor personal communication to Lary Dilsaver, December 19, 2018; Patricia Neubacher to Superintendents Santa Monica Mountains National Recreation Area and Channel Islands National Park, October 12, 2001, CINP Central Files, Case Incidents 2B, folder "Ford Point Fire 2001."
31. NPS, "1995 Federal Wildland Fire Management Policy," 418–22.
32. NPS, *Channel Islands National Park Wildlife Fire Management Plan*, CINP, June 2006, 10–19.
33. Livingston, *Island Legacies*, 406–07, 416.

34. Livingston, *Island Legacies*, 406, 424, 439–46, 450–63; Gherini. *Santa Cruz Island*, 82–94.
35. Santa Cruz Island Company Ledger, 295–96, 337, Santa Cruz Island Foundation; Livingston, *Island Legacies*, 450–63.
36. Kevin Noon, "Report for Travel to Channel Islands National Park during May 11–16, 2003," CINP digital files, 5–6, 9–11.
37. Kevin Noon, "Report for Travel to Channel Islands National Park during May 11–16, 2003," CINP digital files, 5–6, 9–11.
38. CINP, "Notes from Meeting between NPS and Partners Regarding Potential Wetlands Restoration at Prisoners Harbor, Santa Cruz Island, Channel Islands National Park, 5 April 2007," CINP digital files; NPS, *Cultural Landscape Inventory, Santa Cruz Island Ranching District*, CINP, May 2009, 17.
39. *Federal Register*, 73 (113), June 11, 2008, 33,109–11; NPS, *Prisoners Harbor Coastal Wetland Restoration Plan Final Environmental Impact Statement, Channel Islands National Park, Santa Cruz Island, Santa Barbara County*, CINP, February 2010, i–ix.
40. NPS, *Prisoners Harbor Coastal Wetland Restoration Plan*; Paula J. Power et al., "Restoration of a Coastal Wetland," 442–54, https://doi.org/10.3398/042.007.0134.
41. Paula Power et al., "Restoration of a Coastal Wetland" 442–54, https://doi.org/10.3398/042.007.0134; CINP, "A Call to Action: Prisoners Harbor Coastal Wetland Restoration," CINP Briefing Statement, n.d., http://www.nature.nps.gov/water/crystalclear/assets/docs/CHIS_Crystal_Clear_Brief.pdf; Paula Power interviewed by Lary Dilsaver, November 2, 2018.
42. David Kushner interviewed by Lary Dilsaver, August 16, 2018; Gary Davis interviewed by Lary Dilsaver, September 2, 2018.
43. David Kushner interview, August 16, 2018; CINMS, "*Condition Report 2016*," 94–96.
44. CINMS, "*Condition Report 2016*," 101.
45. David Kushner interview, August 16, 2018.
46. David Kushner interview, August 16, 2018; Multi-Agency Rocky Intertidal Network, "Sea Star Wasting Syndrome," November 5, 2018, https://www.eeb.ucsc.edu/pacificrockyintertidal/data-products/sea-star-wasting/.
47. CINMS, *Condition Report 2016*.
48. CINMS, *Condition Report 2016*, 115–16; David Kushner interview, August 16, 2018; Gary Davis interview, September 2, 2018.
49. CINMS, *Condition Report 2016*, 117.

50. CINMS, *Condition Report 2016*, 121–22.
51. Partnership for Interdisciplinary Studies of Coastal Oceans, "A Decade of Protection, 10 Years of Change at the Channel Islands," 2013, file:///D:/Documents/Writing%20CHIS/Channel%20islands%2010-Yr%20MPAS%20Brochure.pdf.
52. David Kushner interview, August 16, 2018.
53. CINMS, *Condition Report 2016*, 121–22.
54. CINMS, *Condition Report 2016*, 123; CINP, "Invasive Kelp Spreads into New Territory," accessed June 21, 2018, https://www.nps.gov/articles/invasive-kelp-spreads-into-new-territory.htm.
55. CINMS, *Condition Report 2016*, 123.
56. Russell Galipeau interviewed by Lary Dilsaver, March 9, 2018.
57. NPS, *Draft General Management Plan 2013*, 131; NPS, "Environmental Assessment for Regulation of Airstrips on San Miguel Island Channel Islands National Park," December 1983; Rodney McInnes to William Ehorn, April 6, 1984; and James W. Burns to William Ehorn, April 17, 1984; all in CINP, Central Files, GMP Files, folder "GMP-in park reference materials."
58. CINP, *Draft General Management Plan 2013*, 131–32.
59. CINP, *Draft General Management Plan 2013*, 129, 132–37.
60. NPS, *Draft General Management Plan 2013*; Galipeau interview, March 9, 2018.
61. NPS, *Final General Management Plan 2015*, ix–x.
62. NPS, *Record of Decision for CINP* Final General Management Plan 2015, *CINP*, 2015.
63. NPS, *Record of Decision for CINP*; Russell Galipeau interview, March 9, 2018.
64. Russell Galipeau interview, March 9, 2018.
65. NPS, *Final General Management Plan/Wilderness Study/Environmental Impact Statement 2015*, CINP, April 2015, 48–54, 137; at the end of 2021, no official wilderness proposal has been submitted to Congress.
66. NPS, *Record of Decision for CINP*.
67. Williams et al., "Administrative History of San Miguel Island," 1–20.
68. Williams et al., "Administrative History of San Miguel Island," 1–20.
69. Charles F. Lester to C. L. Stathos, September 5, 2014, CINP, Superintendent's File, folder "Navy."
70. Williams et al., "Administrative History of San Miguel Island"; NPS, "National Park Service Report to the Navy, San Miguel Island 2016," CINP Digital files.
71. Suspicion individually expressed to Lary Dilsaver by Laura Kirn, Ken Convery, and Russell Galipeau, September 2019.

72. Davidson et al., *Natural Resource Condition Assessment 2014*, 14–18, 124; NPS, "Natural Resource Condition Assessment Program," https://www.nps.gov/orgs/1439/nrca.htm. Accessed October 24, 2018.
73. NPS, "Natural Resource Condition Assessment Program." The NPS Natural Resource Stewardship and Science Office in Fort Collins, Colorado began publishing these reports in 2008.
74. Davidson et al., *Natural Resource Condition Assessment 2014*, 117–18.
75. "Natural Resource Condition Assessment Program," 143–44.
76. Davidson et al., *Natural Resource Condition Assessment 2014*, 182–83.
77. Davidson et al., *Natural Resource Condition Assessment 2014*, 216–17.
78. Davidson et al., *Natural Resource Condition Assessment 2014*, 91–92.
79. CINMS, *Marine Sanctuary Condition Report 2016, Volume I*, 10.

Conclusion

1. Leopold, "Wildlife Management in the National Parks."
2. This management strategy is consistent with goals that have been recommended by the Science Committee of the National Park Service Advisory Board in a recent reevaluation of the 1963 Leopold Report, "Revisiting Leopold: Resource Stewardship in the National Parks," (2012). This committee has proposed that the overarching goal of NPS natural resource management should be the preservation of ecological integrity within a context of continuous change. See Dilsaver, ed., *America's National Park System*, 450.
3. Robert Puddicombe's comment: "To me the idea of species is just an abstract concept.... These animals are here and alive now. Their lives have value."
4. Dilsaver, ed., *America's National Park System*, 450.

BIBLIOGRAPHY

Archives and Manuscript Materials

CINM. Channel Islands National Monument.
CINMS. Channel Islands National Marine Sanctuary.
CINP. Channel Islands National Park.
DOI. Department of the Interior.
    Proceedings of the Fifth California Islands Symposium. Washington DC: Minerals Management Service, 1999.
NOAA. National Oceanic and Atmospheric Administration.
    Montrose Settlements Restoration Program, Final Restoration Plan/EIS/EIR, Natural Resource Trustees, October 2005.
NPS. National Park Service.
U.S. Bureau of Outdoor Recreation. "Channel Islands, California: Island Study." DOI, February 1968.

Published Works

Abbott, Carl. *The Metropolitan Frontier: Cities in the Modern American West*. Tucson: University of Arizona Press, 1993.
Allen, Sarah G., Joe Mortenson, and Sophie Webb. *Field Guide to Marine Mammals of the Pacific Coast*. Berkeley: University of California Press, 2011.
Anderson, Terry Lee, and Donald Leal. *Enviro-Capitalists: Doing Good While Doing Well*. Lanham MD: Rowman & Littlefield, 1997.
Babalis, Timothy. *Heart of the Gabilans: An Administrative History of Pinnacles National Monument*. San Francisco: NPS, Pacific West Regional Office, 2009.
Barthell, John F., Robbin W. Thorp, Adrian M. Wenner, and John M. Randall. "Yellow Star-Thistle, Gumplant, and Feral Honey Bees on Santa Cruz Island: A Case of Invaders Assisting Invaders." In *Proceedings of the Fifth California Islands Symposium*, 1999, 269–73.

Bartolome, James W., and W. James Clawson. *Range Management Plan, Santa Rosa Island*. Ventura CA: CINP, 1992.

Beatty, S., and D. Licari. "Invasion of Fennel (*Foeniculum vulgare*) into Shrub Communities on Santa Cruz Island CA." *Madroño* 39 (1992): 54–66.

Bolin, Rolf L. "Reappearance of the Southern Sea Otter along the California Coast." *Journal of Mammalogy* 19, no. 3 (1938): 301–3.

Bonnot, Paul. "California Sea Lion Census for 1936." *California Fish and Game* 23 (1937): 108–12.

———. *Fish Bulletin No. 14: Report on the Seals and Sea Lions of California*. Sacramento CA: California Division of Fish and Game, 1928.

———. "The Sea Lions, Seals and Sea Otter of the California Coast." *California Fish and Game* 37, no. 4 (Oct. 1951): 371–89.

Bonnot, Paul, and W. E. Ripley. "The California Sea Lion Census for 1947." *California Fish and Game* 34 (1948): 89–92.

Booth, William. "Reintroducing a Political Animal." *Science* 241, no. 4862 (1988): 156–58.

Bossard, Carla, John M. Randall, and Marc C. Hoshovsky, eds. *Invasive Plants of California's Wildlands*. Berkeley: University of California Press, 2000.

Breeden, Richard. "Federalism and the Development of Outer Continental Shelf Mineral Resources." *Stanford Law Review* 28, no. 6 (1976): 1112.

Brenton, Bob, and Rob Klinger. "Modeling the Expansion of Fennel (*Foeniculum vulgare*) on the Channel Islands." In *The Fourth Channel Islands Symposium: Update on the Status of Resources*, edited by W. Halvorson and G. Maender, 497–504. Santa Barbara CA: Santa Barbara Museum of Natural History, 1994.

Brinkley, Douglas. *Rightful Heritage: The Renewal of America*. New York: Harper Collins, 2016.

Cabrillo National Monument Foundation. *An Account of the Voyage of Juan Rodriguez Cabrillo*. San Diego CA: Cabrillo National Monument Foundation, 1999.

Carr, Ethan. *Mission 66: Modernism and the National Park Dilemma*. Amherst: University of Massachusetts Press, 2007.

Carter, Harry R., Spencer G. Sealy, Esther E. Burkett, and John F. Piatt. "Biology and Conservation of Xantus's Murrelet: Discovery, Taxonomy and Distribution." *Marine Ornithology* 33, no. 2 (2005): 81–87.

Chiles, Frederick C. *California's Channel Islands: A History*. Norman: University of Oklahoma Press, 2015.

Clark, Ronilee A., William L. Halvorson, Andell A. Sawdo, and Karen C. Danielsen. *Plant Communities of Santa Rosa Island, Channel Islands National Park,*

Cooperative Park Studies Unit Technical Report No. 42. Davis: University of California, 1990.

Cockerell, T. D. A. "The Botany of the California Islands." *Torreya* 37 (November-December, 1937): 117–23.

———. "San Miguel Island." *Scientific Monthly* 46 (February 1938): 181.

Collins, Paul W., and Brian C. Latta. "Nesting Season Diet of Golden Eagles on Santa Cruz and Santa Rosa Islands, Santa Barbara County, California." Santa Barbara Museum of Natural History Technical Reports, No. 3, 2006.

Colvin, Wesley I., III, and Stephen R. Gliessman. "Fennel (*Foeniculum vulgare*) Management and Native Species Enhancement on Santa Cruz Island, California." In *Proceedings of the Fifth California Islands Symposium*, 1999, 184–89.

Coonan, Timothy J. "Findings and Recommendations from the Island Fox Working Group; Convened in Ventura, California April 21–22, 1999." In *Recovery Strategy for Island Foxes (Urocyon littoralis) on the Northern Channel Islands*, 58. Ventura CA: NPS, CINP, 2003.

Coonan, Timothy J., Robert C. Klinger, and Linda C. Dye. "Trends in Landbird Abundance at Channel Islands National Park, 1993–2009." Natural Resource Technical Report NPS/CHIS/NRTR—2011/507.

Coonan, Timothy J., Catherin A. Schwemm, and David K. Garcelon. *Decline and Recovery of the Island Fox*. New York: Cambridge University Press, 2010.

Coonan, Timothy J., Catherin A. Schwemm, Gary W. Roemer, David K. Garcelon, and Linda Munson. "Decline of an Island Fox Subspecies to Near Extinction." *Southwestern Naturalist* 50, no. 1 (March 2005): 32–41.

Cronise, Titus Fey. *The Natural Wealth of California*. San Francisco: H. H. Bancroft, 1868.

Crooks, Kevin. "Demography and Status of the Island Fox and the Island Spotted Skunk on Santa Cruz Island, California." *Southwestern Naturalist* 39, no. 3 (1994): 257–62.

Davidson, Ana, Kathryn McEachern, Tim Coonan, Tim Bean, Amon Armstrong, and Brian Hudgens. *Channel Islands National Park: Natural Resource Condition Assessment 2014*. Fort Collins CO: NPS, 2017.

Davidson, George. *Directory for the Pacific Coast of the United States, Reported to the Superintendent of the U.S. Coast Survey*. Washington DC: U.S. Coast Survey, 1862.

Davis, Gary. "Science and Society: Marine Reserve Design for the California Channel Islands." *Conservation Biology* 19, no. 6 (December 2005): 1745–51.

Davis, Gary E., and William L. Halvorson. *Channel Islands National Park Natural Resources Monitoring Program: 1990 Status Report*. Davis: University of California, Cooperative Parks Study Unit, 1990, 12.

———. "Resource Issues Addressed by Case Studies of Sustained Research in National Parks." In *Science and Ecosystem Management in the National Parks*, edited by William L. Halvorson and Gary E. Davis, 321–33. Tucson: University of Arizona Press, 1996.

Davis, Gary E., Daniel V. Richards, Peter L. Haaker, and David O. Parker. "Abalone Population Declines and Fishery Management in Southern California." In *Abalone of the World: Biology, Fisheries and Culture*, edited by S. A. Shepherd, Mia J. Tegner, and S. A. Guzman del Proo. Part 5. Cambridge MA: Blackwell Scientific, 1992.

DeLong, Robert L., and Sharon R. Melin, "Thirty Years of Pinniped Research at San Miguel Island." In *Proceedings of the Fifth California Islands Symposium*. Washington DC: DOI, Minerals Management Service, 1999.

DeVoto, Bernard. "Let's Close the National Parks." *Harper's Magazine* 207, no. 1241 (October 1953): 49–52.

———. "Shall We Let Them Ruin Our National Parks?" *Saturday Evening Post* 223, no. 4 (July 1950): 17–19, 42–46.

Dilsaver, Lary M., ed. *America's National Park System: The Critical Documents*. 2nd ed. Lanham MD: Rowman & Littlefield, 2016.

———. *Preserving the Desert: A History of Joshua Tree National Park*. Staunton VA: George F. Thompson, 2016.

Dilsaver, Lary M., and Timothy Babalis. *The Oceanic Park: An Administrative History of Channel Islands National Park*. Report to the NPS, DOI, April 2021.

Dooley, Jessica A., Peter B. Sharpe, and David K. Garcelon. "Movements, Foraging, and Survival of Bald Eagles Reintroduced on the Northern Channel Islands, California." In *Proceedings of the Sixth California Islands Symposium*, edited by David K. Garcelon and Catherin A. Schwemm, 313–21. Arcata CA: Institute for Wildlife Studies, 2005.

Dunlap, Thomas R. *DDT: Scientists, Citizens, and Public Policy*. Princeton NJ: Princeton University Press, 1981.

Ellison, William Henry, ed. *The Life and Adventures of George Nidever [1802–1883]*. Tucson: Southwest Parks and Monuments Association, 1984.

Erlandson, Jon M. "The Search for Early Shell Middens on San Miguel Island, California." Research Report submitted to the Foundation for the Exploration and Research on Cultural Origins and National Park Service/Channel Islands National Park, September 15, 2001.

Everhart, William. *The National Park Service*. Boulder CO: Westview, 1983.

Fahey, Bridget, and Sandy Vissman. "Endangered and Threatened Wildlife and Plants: Listing the San Miguel Island Fox, Santa Rosa Island Fox, Santa Cruz

Island Fox, and Santa Catalina Island Fox As Endangered." *Federal Register* 69, no. 44 (2004): 10335–53.

Faulkner, Kate Roney. "Bringing Santa Rosa Island into Channel Islands National Park: The Written Documents 1979–1987." *Western North American Naturalist* 78, no. 4 (2018): 930–41.

Fischer, Douglas T., and Christopher J. Still. "Evaluating Patterns of Fog Water Deposition and Isotropic Composition on the California Channel Islands." *Water Resources Research* 43 (2007): 1–13.

Friedman, C. S., K. B. Andree, K. A. Beauchamp, J. D. Moore, T. T. Robbins, J. D. Shields, and R. P. Hedrick. "*Candidatus* Xenohaliotis californiensis gen. nov., sp. nov., A Pathogen of Abalone, *Haliotis* spp., Along the West Coast of North America." *International Journal of Systematic Evolutionary Microbiology* 50 (2000): 847–55.

Gamble, Lynn H. "Archaeological Evidence for the Origin of the Plank Canoe in North America." *American Antiquity* 67, no. 2 (2002): 301–15.

Garcelon David K., and Catherin A. Schwemm, eds. *Proceedings of the Sixth California Islands Symposium*. Arcata CA: Institute for Wildlife Studies, 2005.

Gherini. John. *Santa Cruz Island: A History of Conflict and Diversity*. Spokane WA: Arthur H. Clarke, 1997.

Glassow, Michael A., ed. *Channel Islands Archaeological Overview and Assessment*. NPS, December 2010.

Glassow, Michael A., Lynn H. Gamble, Jennifer E. Perry, and Glenn S. Russell. "Prehistory of the Northern California Bight and the Adjacent Transverse Ranges." In *California Prehistory: Colonization, Culture, and Complexity*, edited by Terry L. Jones and Kathryn A. Klar, 191–213. Lanham MD: AltaMira, 2007.

Graham, Chuck. "The Xantus's Murrelet of Anacapa Island." *Birding* (May-June 2007): 46–51.

Gress, Franklin. *Reproductive Status of the California Brown Pelican in 1970, with Notes on Breeding and Natural History; Report 70–6*. Sacramento: California Department of Fish and Game, Wildlife Management Administration, 1970.

Gurish, Jonathon. *Overview of California Ocean and Coastal Laws*. Oakland: California Ocean Protection Council, 2007.

Halvorson, William L., and Gary E. Davis, eds. *Science and Ecosystem Management in the National Parks*. Tucson: University of Arizona Press, 1996.

Halvorson, William L., Dennis B. Fenn, and William R. Allardice. "Soils and Vegetation of Santa Barbara Island, Channel Islands National Park, California, USA." *Environmental Management* 12 (1988): 109–18.

Halvorson, William L., and G. Maender, eds. *The Fourth Channel Islands Symposium: Update on the Status of Resources*. Santa Barbara CA: Santa Barbara Museum of Natural History, 1994.

Hamer, Thomas E., Sarah M. Schuster, and Douglas Meekins. "Radar as a Tool for Monitoring Xantus's Murrelet Populations." *Marine Ornithology* 33, no. 2 (2005): 81–87.

Handley, T., D. Rodriguez, J. Yee, and A. K. McEachern. "Draft: Exploring Long-Term Trends in Vegetation of Santa Barbara and Santa Rosa Islands, Channel Islands National Park." Unpublished technical report, U.S. Geological Survey, Channel Islands Field Station, Ventura CA, 2013.

Hochberg, F. G., ed. *Third California Islands Symposium: Recent Advances in Research on the California Islands*. Santa Barbara CA: Santa Barbara Museum of Natural History, 1993.

Jackson, William L. "Preliminary Hydrologic and Geomorphic Analysis, Scorpion Flood '97, Channel Islands National Park." In NPS, *Damage Assessment Report: Scorpion Flood 97, Channel Islands N.P.* Ventura CA: CINP, 1998.

Junak, Steve, Tina Ayers, Randy Scott, Dieter Wilken, and David Young. *A Flora of Santa Cruz Island*. Santa Barbara CA: Santa Barbara Botanical Garden, 1995.

Junak, Steve, S. Chaney, R. Philbrick, and R. Clark. *A Checklist of Vascular Plants of Channel Islands National Park*. Tucson AZ: Southwest Parks and Monuments Association, 1997.

Karnovsky, Nina J., et al. "At-Sea Distribution, Abundance and Habitat Affinities of Xantus's Murrelets." *Marine Ornithology* 33, no. 2 (2005): 89–104.

Kennett, Douglas J. *The Island Chumash: Behavioral Ecology of a Maritime Society*. Berkeley: University of California Press, 2005.

Kiff, Lloyd F. "Historical Changes in Resident Populations of California Island Raptors." In *The California Islands, Proceedings of a Multidisciplinary Symposium*, edited by D. M. Power, 651–73. Santa Barbara CA: Santa Barbara Museum of Natural History, 1980.

Kilgore, Bruce M. "Fire Management in Parks and Protected Areas: Introduction and Summary." *George Wright Forum* 22, no. 4 (2005): 8–11.

Knapp, John J., John M. Randall, Christina L. Boser, and Scott A. Morrison. "Santa Cruz Island Ecological Management Strategy 2015–2025." The Nature Conservancy, August 2015.

Latta, Brian C. *Channel Islands Golden Eagle Translocation Program: Summary Report, 1999–2004*. Report submitted to the Nature Conservancy and the NPS. Santa Cruz CA: University of California, Santa Cruz Predatory Bird Research Group, 2005.

Latta, Brian C., Daniel E. Driscoll, Janet L. Linthicum, Ronald E. Jackman, and Gregg Doney. "Capture and Translocation of Golden Eagles from the California Channel Islands to Mitigate Depredations of Endemic Island Foxes." In *Proceedings of the Sixth California Islands Symposium*, edited by David K. Garcelon and Catherin A. Schwemm, 341–50. Arcata CA: Institute for Wildlife Studies, 2005.

Laughrin, Lyndal L. "The Island Fox: A Field Study of its Behavior and Ecology." PhD diss., University of California, Santa Barbara, 1977.

———. "Populations and Status of the Island Fox." In *The California Islands: Proceedings of a Multidisciplinary Symposium*, edited by D. M. Powers, 745–49. Santa Barbara CA: Santa Barbara Museum of Natural History, 1980.

Leeworthy, Vernon R., Peter C. Wiley, and Edward A. Stone. "Socioeconomic Impact Analysis of Marine Reserve Alternatives for the Channel Islands National Marine Sanctuary." NOAA, National Ocean Service, October 7, 2005.

Leopold, A. Starker. "Wildlife Management in the National Parks." In *America's National Park System: The Critical Documents*, edited by Lary Dilsaver, 210–24. Lanham MD: Rowman & Littlefield, 2016.

Littler, M. M. "Overview of Rocky Intertidal Systems in Southern California." In *The California Islands: Proceedings of a Multidisciplinary Symposium*, edited by D. M. Powers, 265–306. Santa Barbara CA: Santa Barbara Museum of Natural History, 1980.

Livingston, Dewey. *Island Legacies: A History of the Islands Within Channel Islands National Park*. NPS Historic Resource Study, 2016.

Lombardo Carmen, and Kate Faulkner. "Eradication of Feral Pigs (Sus scrofa) from Santa Rosa Island, Channel Islands National Park, California." In *Proceedings of the Fifth California Islands Symposium, March 29–April 1, 1999*. Santa Barbara CA: DOI, Minerals Management Service, 1999.

Lotchin, Roger W. *Fortress California, 1910–1961: From Warfare to Welfare*. Oxford, UK: Oxford University Press, 1992.

Lyle, Virginia, ed. *Proceedings of the Ocean Studies Symposium, November 1982*. San Francisco: California Coastal Commission, 1983.

MacGregor, J. S. "Changes in the Amount and Proportions of DDT and Its Metabolites, DDE and DDD, in the Marine Environment Off Southern California, 1949–72." *Fishery Bulletin* 72, no. 2 (1974): 275–93.

McChesney, Gerard J., and Bernie R. Tershy. "History and Status of Introduced Mammals and Impacts to Breeding Seabirds on the California Channel and Northwestern Baja California Islands." *Colonial Waterbirds* 21, no. 3 (1998): 335–47.

McEachern, K. T., T. Atwater, P. W. Collins, K. Faulkner, and D. Richards. "Managed Island Ecosystems." In *Ecosystems of California*, edited by H. Mooney and E. Zavaleta, 755–78. Oakland: University of California Press, 2016.

Miller, Karen J. "Determination of Threatened Status for the Pacific Coast Population of the Western Snowy Plover." *Federal Register* 58, no. 42 (March 5, 1993): 12864–74.

Mooney, H., and E. Zavaleta, eds. *Ecosystems of California*. Oakland: University of California Press, 2016.

Moore, James D. Carl A. Finley, Thea T. Robbins, and Carolyn Friedman. "Withering Syndrome and Restoration of Southern California Abalone Populations." *CalCOFI Reports* 43 (2002): 112–17.

Morrison, Scott A. "A Bird in Our Hand: Weighing Uncertainty about the Past against Uncertainty about the Future in Channel Islands National Park." *George Wright Forum* 31, no. 1 (2014): 77–93.

National Park Service (NPS). "Review and Update of the 1995 Federal Wildland Fire Management Policy." In *America's National Park System: The Critical Documents*, 2nd ed., edited by Lary M. Dilsaver, 418–22. Lanham MD: Rowman & Littlefield, 2016.

National Park System Advisory Board Science Committee. "Revisiting Leopold: Resource Stewardship in the National Parks." DOI, August 25, 2012. In *America's National Park System: The Critical Documents*, 2nd ed., edited by Lary M. Dilsaver. Lanham MD: Rowman & Littlefield, 2016.

Norton, Robert L. "B. Robertson Jr., August 22, 1924–January 28, 2000." *North American Birds* 54, no. 1 (2000): 111–12.

Ogden, Adele. *The California Sea Otter Trade 1784–1848*. Berkeley: University of California Press, 1941.

——. "Russian Sea-Otter and Seal Hunting on the California Coast, 1803–1841." *California Historical Society Quarterly* 12, no. 3 (1933): 217–39.

Parker, David O., Peter L. Haaker, and Heidi A. Togstad. "Case Histories for Three Species of California Abalone, Haliotis corrugata, H. fulgens and H. cracherodii." In *Abalone of the World: Biology, Fisheries and Culture*, edited by S. A. Shepherd, Mia J. Tegner, and S. A. Guzman del Proo. Part 7. Cambridge MA: Blackwell Scientific, 1992.

Paterson, Alan M. "The Great Fresh Water Panacea: Salt Water Barrier Proposals for San Francisco Bay." *Arizona and the West* 22, no. 4 (1980): 307–22.

Peterson, Michel. *Once Upon an Island: A Love Affair with Santa Cruz Island*. Santa Barbara CA: Santa Cruz Island Foundation, 1998.

Peterson, Richard S., Burney J. LeBoeuf, and Robert L. DeLong. "Fur Seals from the Bering Sea Breeding in California." *Nature* 219, (1968): 899–901.

Philbrick, Ralph N., ed. "The Plants of Santa Barbara Island." *Madroño* 21, no. 5 pt. 2 (1972): 329, 353.

———. *Proceedings: Symposium on the Biology of the California Islands*. Santa Barbara CA: Santa Barbara Botanic Garden, 1967.

Pigati, Jeffrey S., John P. McGeehin, Gary L. Skipp, and Daniel R. Muhs. "Evidence of Repeated Wildfires Prior to Human Occupation on San Nicolas Island, California." *Monographs of the Western North American Naturalist* 7 (2014): 35–47.

Power, Dennis M. *The California Islands: Proceedings of a Multidisciplinary Symposium*. Santa Barbara CA: Santa Barbara Museum of Natural History, 1980.

———. *Natural Resources of the Channel Islands National Monument, California*. Santa Barbara CA: Santa Barbara Museum of Natural History, 1979.

Power, Paula J., Joel Wagner, Mike Martin, and Marie Denn. "Restoration of a Coastal Wetland at Prisoners Harbor, Santa Cruz Island, Channel Islands National Park, California." *Monographs of the Western North American Naturalist* 7, no. 1 (2014): 442–54.

Primack, R. B. *Essentials of Conservation Biology*. Sunderland MA: Sinauer Associates, 2010.

Rathbun, Galen B., Brian B. Hatfield, and Thomas G Murphey. "Status of Translocated Sea Otters at San Nicolas Island, California." *Southwestern Naturalist* 45, no. 3 (2000): 322–75.

Rauzon, Mark J. *Isles of Amnesia: The History, Geography, and Restoration of America's Forgotten Pacific Islands*. Honolulu: University of Hawaii Press, 2016.

Rick, Torben C., Jon M. Erlandson and René L. Vellanoweth, "Paleocoastal Marine Fishing on the Pacific Coast of the Americas: Perspectives from Daisy Cave, California." *American Antiquity* 66, no. 4 (2001): 595–613.

Risebrough, Robert W. "Studies of the Brown Pelican." *Wilson Bulletin* 84 no. 2 (1972): 119–35.

Risebrough, Robert W., D. B. Menzel, D. J. Martin, and H. S. Olcott. "DDT Residues in Pacific Sea Birds: A Persistent Insecticide in Marine Food Chains." *Nature* 216, no. 5115 (1967): 589–91.

Roark, James L., Michael P. Johnson, Patricia Cline Cohen, Sarah Stage, and Susan M. Hartmann. *The American Promise: A History of the United States*. 3rd ed. Boston: Bedford/St. Martins, 2005.

Roberts, Lois Weinman. *Historic Resource Study Channel Islands National Monument and San Miguel Island California*. NPS Contract No. CX-2000-7-0065, May 1979.

Roemer, Gary W. "The Ecology and Conservation of the Island Fox." PhD diss., University of California, Los Angeles, 1999.

Roemer, Gary W., C. Josh Donlan, and Frank Courchamp, "Golden Eagles, Feral Pigs, and Insular Carnivores: How Exotic Species Turn Native Predators into Prey." *Proceedings of the National Academy of Sciences* 99, no. 2 (2002): 791–96.

Roemer, Gary W., David K. Garcelon, Timothy Coonan, and Catherine Schwemm, "The Use of Capture-Recapture Methods for Estimating, Monitoring and Conserving Island Fox Populations." In *The Fourth California Island Symposium: Update on the Status of Resources*, edited by W. L. Halvorson and G. J. Maender. Santa Barbara CA: Santa Barbara Museum of Natural History, 1994.

Rosenlieb, Gary, Bill Jackson, Cece Sellgren, Jim Wolf, Joel Wagner, Jeff Reiner, Kathryn McEachern, and Don Pritchard. *Federal Interagency Riparian Assessment and Recommendations for Achieving Water Quality Management Goals, Santa Rosa Island, Channel Islands National Park*, Technical Report NPS/NRWRD/NRTR-98/202. Fort Collins CO: NPS, Water Resources Division, 1995.

Rothman, Hal. *America's National Monuments: The Politics of Preservation*. Lawrence: University Press of Kansas, 1994.

Rothrock, J. T. Acting Asst. Surgeon, U.S. Army, "Report Upon the Operations of a Special Natural-History Party and Main Field-Party No. 1, California Section, Field-Season of 1875, Being the Results of Observations Upon the Economic Botany and Agriculture of Portions of Southern California." In Lt. George M. Wheeler, Corps of Engineers, "Annual Report Upon the Geographical Surveys West of the One Hundredth Meridian in California, Nevada, Utah, Colorado, Wyoming, New Mexico, Arizona, and Montana: Appendix JJ of the Annual Report of the Chief of Engineers for 1876," H. Exec. Doc. 1, pt. 2, v. 11, 44th Cong., 2nd. Sess., 1876.

Ruckelshaus, William D. "Consolidated DDT Hearings: Opinion and Order of the Administrator [Environmental Protection Agency]." *Federal Register* 37, no. 131 (July 7, 1972): 13,369–76.

Sadin, Paul. *Managing a Land in Motion: An Administrative History of Point Reyes National Seashore*. Seattle WA: Historical Research Associates, 2007.

Santa Barbara County. *Coastal Land Use Plan*, 1982; republished 2009, 2014, and 2019.

Scammon, Charles M. *The Marine Mammals of the North-Western Coast of North America*. San Francisco: John H. Carmany, 1874.

Schoenherr, Allan A., C. Robert Feldmeth, and Michael J. Emerson. *Natural History of the Islands of California*. Berkeley: University of California Press, 1999.

Schreiber, Ralph W., and Robert W. Risebrough. "Studies of the Brown Pelican." *Wilson Bulletin* 84, no. 2 (1972): 119–35.

Schumacher, Paul. "Some Remains of a Former People." *Overland Monthly* 15, no. 4 (1875).

Schuyler, Peter. "Control of Feral Sheep (*Ovis aries*) on Santa Cruz Island, California." In *Third California Islands Symposium*, edited by F. G. Hochberg, 443–52. Santa Barbara Museum of Natural History, 1993.

Scofield, W. L. "History of Kelp Harvesting in California." *California Fish and Game* 45, no. 3 (July 1959): 135–57.

Scott, Stanley, ed. *Coastal Conservation: Essays on Experiments in Governance*. Berkeley: Institute of Governmental Studies, University of California, 1981.

Sellars, Richard West. *Preserving Nature in the National Parks: A History*. New Haven CT: Yale University Press, 1997.

Shalowitz, Aaron L. "Boundary Problems Raised by the Submerged Lands Act." *Columbia Law Review* 54, no. 7 (1954): 1,021–48.

Shalowitz, Aaron L., and Michael W. Reed. "Legal Background." In *Shore and Sea Boundaries*, Vol. 1, Pt. 2, 3–14. Washington DC: U.S. Coast and Geodetic Survey, 1962.

———. "Submerged Lands Act (Public Law 31)." In *Shore and Sea Boundaries* 1, pt. 2, 115–81. Washington DC: U.S. Coast and Geodetic Survey, 1962.

———. "The Tidelands Litigation." In *Shore and Sea Boundaries* 3, pt. 1, 33–35. Washington DC: U.S. Coast and Geodetic Survey, 2000.

Shaw, William N. "Spiny Lobster." U.S. Fish and Wildlife Service Biological Report 82 (11.47), April 1986.

Sibley, David Allen. *The Sibley Field Guide to Birds of Western North America*. New York: Alfred Knopf, 2003.

Stewart, Brent S., Pamela K. Yochem, Robert L. DeLong, and George A. Antonelis, "Trends in Abundance and Status of Pinnipeds on the Southern California Channel Islands." In *Third California Islands Symposium: Recent Advances in Research on the California Islands*, edited by F. G. Hochberg. Santa Barbara CA: Santa Barbara Museum of Natural History, 1993.

Trefethen, James B., ed. *Transactions of the Twenty-Eighth North American Wildlife and Natural Resources Conference*. Washington DC: Wildlife Management Institute, 1963.

Toll, Roger W. "Proposed Channel Islands National Park, California: Report to Horace M. Albright, Director, National Park Service." March 21, 1933.

Townsend, C. H. "Birds from the Coast of Western North America and Adjacent Islands, Collected in 1888–'89, with Descriptions of New Species." *Proceedings of the United States National Museum* 13 (1890): 131–42.

Tweed, William C., and Lary M. Dilsaver. *Challenge of the Big Trees: A Resource History of Sequoia and Kings Canyon National Parks*. 2nd ed. Staunton VA: George F. Thompson, 2016, 140–41.

Ulanski, Stan. *The California Current: A Pacific Ecosystem and Its Fliers, Divers, and Swimmers*. Chapel Hill: University of North Carolina Press, 2016.

U.S. Commission on Marine Science, Engineering, and Resources. *Our Nation and the Sea: A Plan for National Action*. Washington DC: Government Printing Office, 1969.

U.S. Commission on Ocean Policy. "The Evolution of Ocean Governance Over Three Decades." In *An Ocean Blueprint for the 21st Century*, appendix 6. Washington DC: Government Printing Office, 2004.

U.S. Department of Commerce. *Recovery Plan for White Abalone (Haliotis sorenseni)*. Long Beach CA: National Marine Fisheries Service, 2008.

———. Montrose Settlements Restoration Program. *Feasibility Study for Reestablishment of Bald Eagles on the Northern Channel Islands (NCI), California*. Washington DC: U.S. Department of Commerce, National Oceanic and Atmospheric Administration, 2002.

U.S. Environmental Protection Agency. *Ecological Risk Assessment for the Palos Verdes Shelf*. San Francisco: Environmental Protection Agency, Region 9, 2003.

U.S. Fish and Wildlife Service. "Final Rule for 13 Plant Taxa from the Northern Channel Islands, California." *Federal Register* 62, no. 147 (July 31, 1997): 40954–74.

———. "Listing of the San Miguel Island Fox, Santa Rosa Island Fox, Santa Cruz Island Fox, and Santa Catalina Island Fox as Endangered: Final Rule." *Federal Register* 69, no. 44 (2004): 10335–53.

———. "Proposed Rule to List Three Plants From the Channel Islands of Southern California as Endangered," *Federal Register* 60, no. 142 (July 25, 1995): 37987–93.

———. "Proposed Rule for 16 Plant Taxa From the Northern Channel Islands, California," *Federal Register* 60.142 (July 25, 1995): 37993–8011.

———. *Translocation of Southern Sea Otters: Draft Supplemental Environmental Impact Statement*. DOI, 2005.

U. S. General Accounting Office. *Federal Land Acquisition and Management Practices: Report to Senator Ted Stevens*. Washington DC: General Accounting Office, 1981.

——. *Parks and Recreation: Limited Progress Made in Documenting and Mitigating Threats to the Parks; Report to the Chairman, Subcommittee on National Parks and Recreation, Committee on Interior and Insular Affairs, House of Representatives*. Washington DC: General Accounting Office, 1987.

U.S. Minerals Management Service, *Proceedings of the Fifth California Islands Symposium*. Washington DC: DOI, 1999.

U.S. Senate. "Hearing before the Subcommittee on Parks, Recreation, and Renewable Resource of the Committee on Energy and Natural Resources." U.S. Senate, 96th Congress, 1st Session, on S.1104, July 19, 1979.

——. "Legislative Hearing on S. 1209 before the Subcommittee on National Parks of the Committee on Energy and Natural Resources." 110th Congress, May 15, 2007.

Unrau, Harlan D., and G. Frank Williss. *Administrative History: Expansion of the National Park Service in the 1930s*. Denver CO: NPS, Denver Service Center, 1983.

Van Vuren, Dirk. *The Feral Sheep of Santa Cruz Island: Status, Impacts and Management Recommendations*. Santa Barbara CA: Nature Conservancy, 1981.

Verge, Arthur C. "The Impact of the Second World War on Los Angeles." *Pacific Historical Review* 6, no. 3 (1994): 289–314.

Wagner, Joel, Michael Martin, Kate Roney Faulkner, Sarah Chaney, Kevin Noon, Marie Denn, and Jeff Reiner. *Riparian System Recovery after Removal of Livestock from Santa Rosa Island, Channel Islands National Park, California*, Technical Report NPS/NRWRD/NRTR-2004/324. Fort Collins CO: NPS, Water Resources Division, 2004.

Wellman, Paul I. *The Trampling Herd*. Philadelphia: J. B. Lippincott, 1939, 13–58.

Wenner, Adrian M., Robbin W. Thorp, and John F. Barthell. "Removal of European Honey Bees from the Santa Cruz Island Ecosystem." In *Proceedings of the Fifth California Islands Symposium*, 1999, 256–60.

Whitworth, Darrell L., Harry R. Carter, and Franklin Gress. "Recovery of a Threatened Seabird after Eradication of an Introduced Predator: Eight Years of Progress for Scripps's Murrelet at Anacapa Island, California." *Biological Conservation* 162 (2013): 52–59.

Whitworth, Darrell L., H. R. Carter, R. J. Young, J. S. Koepke, F. Gress, and S. Fangman. "Initial Recovery of Xantus's Murrelets Following Rat Eradication on Anacapa Island, California." *Marine Ornithology* 33, no. 2 (January 2005): 131–37.

Williams, Ian, Mike Hill, Rob Danno, Reed McCluskey, Mike Maki, Bill Ehorn, and Ann Huston. "The Administrative History of San Miguel Island: The National Park Service on San Miguel from 1963 to 2016." *Western North American Naturalist* 78, no. 4 (2018): 1.

Wirth, Conrad. *Parks, Politics, and the People.* Norman: University of Oklahoma Press, 1980.

Wohnus, J. F. "The Kelp Resources of Southern California." *California Fish and Game* 28, no. 4 (1942): 199–205.

Wright, George M., Joseph S. Dixon, and Ben H. Thompson. *Fauna of the National Parks of the United States: A Preliminary Survey of Faunal Relations in National Parks.* Washington DC: Government Printing Office, 1933.

Wuerthner, George. "Gone Astray." *National Parks* (November-December 1997): 23–25.

INDEX

Page numbers in italics indicate illustrations.

abalone, 19, 20, 77, 154–59, 292, 307
air transport services, 207, 296, 299. *See also specific companies*
Alaska, 18, 104, 110–13, 290
Albright, Horace, 29
Albright, Stan, 147, 179, 180–81, 211
Aleuts, 18, 111
algae, 9, 12, 15, 154, 156, 294
algal bloom (*Pseudonitzschia*), 290
algin, 78
alien species. *See* nonnative species
American Sports Fishing Association, 165
American Trader settlement funds, 233, 235, 237
American Trader Trustee Council (ATTC), 233–34
Anacapa Island : about, 1, 7, *8*, 13, 17, *54, 55*; bird species on, 38, 45, 253, 255, 279; development plan for, 53–56; land use history of, 20–21, 47; naval missile testing at, 325n90; park history of, xiv, 29, 34, 117–18, 309; rat eradication at, 232–38; status of natural resources on, 302; structures on, 61, 74. *See also* Channel Islands
Anacapa Island Light Station, 61
animal grazing. *See* ranching
animal rights activism, 313; on burro eradication, 102–3; for horses, 223–25; on pig eradication, 240–41, 258–61, 262–63; on rat eradication, 235–36; on sheep eradication, 220, 221–22. See also species eradication; *and specific organizations*
Antiquities Act (1906), 35–36
archaeological evidence: aerial surveys of, 119; of humans, 16–17, 33, 284, 285; and theft of human remains, 218–19; underwater, 5
Archaeological Resources Protection Act (1979), 219
Argentine ants (*Linepithema humile*), 277–78
Arlington Man, 16
arthropods, 13

385

ashy storm-petrel (*Oceanodroma homochroa*), 14, 238, 278
Asian honey bee (*Apis cerana*), 228
Assessment of Visitor Impact on Anacapa Island Tidepools project, 109
Avalon Foundation, 58

Babbitt, Bruce, 146, 191
Baker, James K., 62, 92
Bald and Golden Eagle Protection Act (1962), 251
bald eagles (*Haliaeetus leucocephalus*), 14, 41, 251–52, 255–56, 271
Barbour, Michael, 195, 269, 350n75
Barclay, Andre, 225
barley (*Hordeum*), 27, 28
Barron, William E., 23
Bartholomew, George, 115
Bartolome, James, 179
basketry, 17
bats, 14
Bay Conservation and Development Commission, 67
bees, 227–29, 276
Beilenson, Anthony, 79, 80
Belgian hares, 22, 40, 43. *See also* rabbits
Belnap, Jayne, 196–97
Berg, Rick, 219
Bermuda grass (*Cynodon dactylon*), 27
birds, 13–14, 278–80. *See also* landbirds; seabirds; *and specific species*
Biscayne National Park, 94, 333n10
black abalone (*Haliotis cracherodii*), 154–55, 157, 158–59, 292. *See also* abalone
black mustard (*Brassica nigra*), 27
black oystercatcher (*Haematopus bachmani*), 357n7
black rats (*Rattus rattus*), 232–38, 358n10
black storm-petrel (*Oceanodroma melania*), 278
bluefin tuna, 95
Blumenshine, Karen, 223, 224, 356n62
boats: Island Chumash technology of, 16, 17, 18; kelp damage from, 78, 79, 152; NPS use of, 44, 62, 65, 76, 138, 214, 229; as private transport services, 130, 298–99. *See also* U.S. Coast Guard
bombing on San Miguel Island, 1, 23, 48–49, 51, 52, 62, 88, 152, 300, 311, 325n90
Bond, Richard M., 38, 40, 44
Bonnot, Paul, 112, 113–14, 336n50
Boren, Frank, 205, 207, 353n15
Boundary Status Report for Channel Islands (1946), 49–50, 52
Bowling, Ann, 224
Boxer, Barbara, 273
Brandt's cormorant (*Phalacrocrax penicillatus*), 14, 357n7
Brittan, Lynn, 128
brittle stars (*Ophiuroide sp*), 294
brome (*Bromus*), 27, 303
Brooks, Robert L., 23, 49, 62
Brown, Locky, 166
Brown, Tony, 284
Bryant, Harold C., 32, 34
Bryant Report, 34–35, 36
bryozoan, 295
Bullard, Kent, 137

bull thistle (*Cirsium vulgare*), 27
Bureau of Commercial Fisheries, 115
Bureau of Land Management (BLM), 51, 121
Burlew, E. K., 37
Burns, Melinda, 163–64
burros (feral), 101–3, 262, 334n23
Burton, Philip, 81
Bush poppy (*Dendromecon rigida harfordii*), 210

Cabrillo, Juan Rodríguez, 16, 17–18, 173
Cabrillo National Monument, 53, 62, 92
Cahalane, Victor, 40, 43
Caire, Justinian, 214, 282
Caire family, 23–25, 30, 54
caliche, 6–7, 7
California Abalone Association, 158
California brown pelican (*Pelecanus occidentalis californicus*), 14, 38, 45, 93, 232, 255, 278, 313, 357n7
California Coastal Act (1976), 212–13
California Coastal Commission, 69–70, 217, 300
California condor (*Gymnogyps californianus*), 248
California Current, 8–9, 12
California Department of Fish and Game (CDFG): as ally to fishermen, 77; CINMS and, 311; cooperation with SAC and MRWG, 166–69; oil spill monitoring by, 107; species monitoring and management by, 41, 42, 115, 155, 159; state ecological reserves by, 71
California Environmental Quality Act (CEQA), 68, 236

California Fish and Game Commission (CFGC), 159–61, 167
California least tern (*Sterna antillarum browni*), 278
California Marine Life Protection Act (1999), 161
California myotis (*Myotis californicus caurinus*), 14
California Native Plant Society (CNPS), 185, 350n77
California Office of Administrative Law, 167
California Regional Water Quality Control Board (WQCB), 186, 194
California seablite (*Suaeda californica*), 28
California sea cucumber (*Parastichopus californicus*), 292
California sea lion (*Zalophus californianus*), 15, 111, 112–14, 290
California sheephead (*Semicossyphus pulcher*), 291, 293
California State Lands Commission, 71
California Wildlife Federation, 207
Cammerer, Arno, 35, 38
camping and campgrounds, 45, 176, 180, 297, 298
Canon U.S.A., 245
capital gains tax, 124
Capps, Lois, 199, 272–73
Capps, Walter, 191, 219
captive breeding program, 247–50, 264
Carrillo, Carlos, 25
Carrillo, Jose Antonio, 25
Carter, Jimmy, 87
Cassano, Edward, 161

Cassin's auklet (*Ptychoramphus aleuticus*), 14, 43, 238, 255, 357n7
Castillero, Andrés, 23
Catalina ironwood (*Lyonothamnus floribundus asplenifolius*), 210
cats (feral), 14, 22, 40, 43–44, 105, 232
cattle ranching: effects on habitat by, 177, 181–86; on San Miguel Island, 22; on Santa Cruz Island, 24, 25, 131; on Santa Rosa Island, 26, 124–29, 131, 190, 194. *See also* Vail & Vickers Company
CDFG. *See* California Department of Fish and Game (CDFG)
cervid monitoring and eradication, 194–96, 198, 267–75. *See also* deer; elk
cetaceans, 110
Channel Islands: about, xiii, 1–15; Euro-American exploitation of, xiii, 17–20; field survey and report of, 30–33; flora and fauna overview, 12–14; human arrival on, xiii, 16–17; LCP on, 69–71; marine species overview, 14–15, 18–19; oceanic features of, 8–10; physiography of, 2–5; pre-park development of, 20–21. *See also individual islands*
Channel Islands Adventures, 207, 209, 210
Channel Islands Animal Protection Association, 235–36
Channel Islands Aviation, 207
Channel Islands deer mouse (*Peromyscus maniculatus ssp.*), 13, 14, 234–35, 245
Channel Islands fox (*Urocyon littoralis ssp.*), xiii, 13, 14, 227, 230, 241–58, 289, 314

Channel Islands Marine Resource Restoration Committee (CIMRRC), 160–61
Channel Islands National Marine Sanctuary (CINMS), 10; *Condition Report* (2009), 294; *Condition Report* (2016), 278, 305–6; description of, 87–89; establishment of, 87, 157–69, 311; monitoring of, 152; *Status Report* (2018), 292, 293
Channel Islands National Monument: community relations and, 72–77, 80–81; development plans for, 53–56, 62–65; establishment of, 33–37, 109, 309; management of, 37–38, 44–49, 61–62, 107; Mission 66 and, 56–58; natural resource management plan for, 40, 92–93; plan for national seashore or marine park designation, 58–61; seaward boundary extension of, 49–53, 109; *Sumner Report*, 38–44
Channel Islands National Park: about, xiii–xv, 1, 2, 5, 309–15; establishment of, 79–87, 117, 217, 309; fire management at, 13–14, 148–51, 226–27, 229, 257, 281–82; general management plan for, 118–22, 130, 139–40, 296–300; interagency cooperative management of, 153–59; inventory and monitoring in, 93–101, 139–45, 147, 153–59, 244–46, 289–90; leadership transitions of, 65, 145–47, 184, 265, 301; managing ocean habitats and resources of, 107–16; NRMP for, 40, 91, 108, 128, 139, 150, 189–94; proposals for, 62–65, 70; resource manage-

ment division of, 147–48; status of natural resources at, 301–7. *See also* National Park Service (NPS); *and specific islands*
Channel Islands National Park Act (1980), 77–87, 117, 217, 310
Channel Islands National Park Management Act (2007), 273
Channel Islands National Seashore, 59–61
Channel Islands song sparrow (*Melospiza melodia graminea*), 13–14, 38–39, 305, 315, 321n31
chaparral, 12, 27, 172, 188, 302–4
Chapman, Howard, 73, 77, 106, 133
Chinese abalone hunting and fishing, 19, 20
Chinese trade markets, 18, 19, 113
Chittle, Jake, 135
Christy Ranch, 151
Chumash, xiii, 16–17, 18, 218, 243, 283–85
CINMS. *See* Channel Islands National Marine Sanctuary (CINMS)
City of Rocks National Reserve, 171–72
Clark, Ronilee, 172, 173–74
Clark, William P., 216, 354n38
Clark Report, 172, 173–74
Clawson, W. James, 179
Cleanup or Abatement Order (1995), 186–89
Clifford, Frank, 187
climate, 10–12, 22. *See also* drought; El Niño
climate change, 12, 173, 279, 280, 290–91, 298, 303, 305, 307, 315
Clinton, Bill, 217

Cloud, John, 187, 348n52
Coastal Sanctuary Act (1994), 329n22, 332n58
Coastal Zone Conservation Act (1972) 69–70
Coastal Zone Management Act (CZMA), 69, 71
coastal zones: seaward boundary of CINM, 49–53, 109; state management of, 67, 69–70, 153, 156–57, 159–69, 311; surveys and reports of, 57–58. *See also* Channel Islands National Marine Sanctuary (CINMS); marine reserves, state
Cockerell, Theodore D. A., 34–35
Colby, William, 30
Collins, Paul W., 278, 284
commercial fishing. *See* fishing
Committee on Interior and Insular Affairs, 81
Comprehensive Environmental Response, Compensation, and Liability Act (1980), 254
Comprehensive Ocean Area Plan (1972), 69
Connelly, Kirk, 223
Cook, John O., 65
Cook, Lawrence F., 34
Coonan, Timothy, 243, 245, 247
Cordell Bank, 332n59
cotenancy, 212–16
Cousteau Society, 208, 353n19
Cowan, Clark, 279
Cranston, Alan, 64, 72, 82
Crawford, Robert, 236, 237
Creamcups (*Platystemon californicus*), 28
Cunningham-Shell Act (1955), 329n22, 332n58

Daily, Marla, 132, 133, 135, 202, 204–5, 207, 223–24, 284
Daisy Cave, San Miguel Island, 16, 17
Dana, William Goodwin, 19
Davis, Gary, 73; coastal monitoring by, 79, 88, 109; on fishing advocacy studies, 157, 165; I&M program by, 94–100, 139–47, 155, 159–60, 163, 165, 312; on NBS, 146; park experience of, 333n10; pig eradication and, 239; on sea life, 292, 293
Davis, Herbert C., 42
DDT, 96, 252–53, 255
Death Valley National Monument, 101
deer: eradication of, 180, 188, 190, 197, 198, 267–75; golden eagle diet of, 246–47; introduction of, 85; monitoring of, 194, 196, 198, 269–72, 274–75; sport hunting of, 128, 178, 179, 180, 240
deer mice (*Peromyscus maniculatus*), 232, 234, 302
DeLong, Robert, 74, 76, 115
denudation, 20, 37, 38, 104, 173, 187, 276, 304. *See also* erosion
development concept plan (DCP), 176–77
Devine, Diane Elfstrom, 220
Diederich, Leo, 64
Discipleship Training International, 222
diving clubs, 166
double-crested cormorant (*Phalacrocorax auritus*), 255, 278, 313, 357n7
Douglas, Charles, 101–2
Douglas fir (*Pseudotsuga menziesii*), 35
Drost, Charles, 284
drought, 20, 174, 182, 228, 239, 289. *See also* climate

Drury, Newton, 50, 51, 54
Duffield, Henry, 73, 131, 209, 340n50
dwarf mammoth, xiii, 231

eagles: bald, 14, 41, 251–52, 254–56, 271; golden, 227, 245–47, 248, 249, 250–52, 256, 257–58, 271
East Santa Cruz Island, 24, 25, 62, 121, 136–38, 211–25, 229–30, 296–97, 310. *See also* Santa Cruz Island
Eck, Arthur, 264
ecological integrity, as concept, xv
ecological reserves, 71–72, 87
ecological restoration: about, xiv–xv, 231–32, 313–15; cervids and, 194–96, 198, 267–75; fire management and, 150, 226–27, 229; island fox and, 241–58; NRCA on, 301–7; pig eradication and, 238–41; rat eradication and, 232–38; sheep eradication and, 202–6, *203*, 210, 220–22, 258; *Sumner Report*, 39–40; Superfund Act and monies for, 254–55; wetland at Prisoners Harbor, 276, 282–84. *See also* The Nature Conservancy (TNC); species eradication
Ecological Society of America, 135
The Economic Effects of Sportsfishing Closures in Marine Protected Areas (Southwick), 165
economic impacts of state marine reserves, 163–65
education center, 297
egg harvesting, 20–21, 41, 46
Ehorn, William H., *268*; burros and, 101–3, 262; Gherini family and, 79, 137–38, 213; management style of,

145–46; as park superintendent, 65, 72–77, 80, 84–85, 94, 105–6; on resource protections, 79; Vail & Vickers Co. and, 74, 174–76, 178, 189, 197, 310
Eisenhower, Dwight, 57
elk: eradication of, 180–81, 190, 198, 267–75; introduction of, 85; monitoring of, 179, 194; sport hunting of, 128, 197
El Niño, 10–12, 156, 157, 289–92, 294. *See also* climate
Endangered Species Act (1973), 69, 110, 159, 183–86, 193, 232, 247, 257, 258, 349n58, 350n73
Engle, Claire, 60
Environmental Defense Center (EDC), 188
Environmental Defense Fund, 252–53
environmental impact statement (EIS): on Anacapa Island, 234, 237; on Prisoners Harbor, 284–85; for Santa Cruz Island, 259, 261, 300; for Santa Rosa Island, 181, 189, 191, 196
Environmental Protection Agency (EPA), 252–53, 285, 362n84
Erlandson, Jon, 17
erosion, 20, 38–39, 53, 177, 182. *See also* denudation
Essentials of Conservation Biology (Primack), 231–32
Estimating Reserve Size for Conservation and Fisheries Management (2001), 163–64
eucalyptus trees, *208*, 261, 282, 283, 285, *287*, 288
European honey bee (*Apis mellifera*), 227–29

Everglades National Park, 94, 95, 333n10
Everhardt, Gary, 73, 74
Evison, Boyd, 140, 142–43
Evison Report, 141, 143
exotic species. *See* nonnative species
explosive ordnance disposal (EOD), 300
explosives, 300–301. *See also* bombing on San Miguel Island
extinct species, 13–14, 28, 39, 279–80

Farallon Islands, 112
Farallon Plate, 2
Faulkner, Kate, 148, 181, 182–83, 193, 197, 233–34, 238, 241
Federal Land Acquisition and Management Practices (GAO), 119–20
Federal Register, 87, 169, 189, 284
Feinstein, Dianne, 273
Feldman, Richard, 262
Fenn, Dennis B., 240
fennel (*Foeniculum vulgare*), 27, 225–27, 230, 258–59, 261, 288, 303, 314
Ferrelo, Bartolomé, 173
fescue (*Vulpia*), 27
Finding of No Significant Impact (FONSI), 102, 151, 239, 356n66
fires and fire management, 14, 148–51, 226–27, 229, 257, 281–82
fish, 15, 77–78
Fishery Conservation and Management Act (1976), 71, 169
fishing: advocacy for, 163–66; of bluefin tuna, 95; by Chinese, 19; by Chumash, 16, 17; federal management of, 71, National Park Service management of, 77, overharvesting, 95, 107, 114, 154–55, 165, 307,

fishing *(cont.)*
343n39; pinniped culling and, 41, 109–10, 111, 114; state management of, 153, 156–57, 159–61. *See also* marine species
Fitzgerald, Jack, 218, 281
flat abalone (*Haliotis walallenssis*), 292. *See also* abalone
Fleischmann Foundation, 203
flora and fauna, overview, 12–14, 26–28
Flournoy, Frank, 30
fog, 173–74, *175*
Forest and Rangeland Renewable Resources Planning Act (1974), 141
Foster, W. A. S., 30–31
Foster Report, 31
Foundation for Horses and Other Animals (FHOA), 223, 224, 356n61
Franciscan missionaries, 17
Fry, Clarence, 46
Fund for Animals, 236, 260, 358n17
Fur Seal Act (1966), 111
fur seals, 14, 18–19, 44, 111–12
fur trade, 18

Galipeau, Russell, *268*; cervid population control and, 270–75; as park superintendent, 264, 267; planning process and, 296–99; retirement of, 301
Gallegly, Elton, 189, 219, 354n41
gas leases. *See* oil and gas development
Gaviota National Seashore (proposed), 199
General Accounting Office (GAO), 119, 121, 141–42

general management plan (GMP), 93, 118–22, 130, 139–40, 211, 267, 296–300, 333n8. *See also* natural resource management plan (NRMP)
Get Oil Out (GOO), 68
Gherini, Francis, 65, 136–37, 138, 212, 213, 214, 215–19, 221–22, 223
Gherini, John, *75,* 223–24
Gherini, Pier, 24, 62–65, *63, 75,* 136, 137, 211
Gherini family, 24–25, 63–65, 122, 136–38, 211–18
giant bladder kelp (*Macrocystis pyrifera*), 78, 107, 152. *See also* kelp forests
giant coreopsis (*Coreopsis gigantea*), 28, 43, 104
giant sea bass (*Stereolepis gigas*), 292, 293
Gingrich, Newt, 146
Gogan, Peter, 270, 274
gold, 21
golden eagle (*Aquila chrysaetos*), 227, 245–47, 248, 249, 250–52, 256, 257, 271
Gonex, 259
Goodyear, Barbara, 125, 189
Gowen cypress (*Cupressus goveniana*), 35
Graber, David, 233
Grand Canyon National Park, 101
Grant Kohrs National Historic Site, 171
grasses, 27, 28, 38–39
grazing. *See* ranching
Green, Ted, 73
green abalone (*Haliotis fulgens*), 154, 292. *See also* abalone
grey fox (*Urocyon cinereoargenteus*), 242

Grinnell, Joseph, 32, 242, 251, 320n10
Guadalupe fur seal (*Arctocephalus townsendi*), 14–15, 111, 112, 115
Guadalupe Island, 112
Gulf of the Farallones National Marine Sanctuary, 332n59, 332n61
Gull Island, 49–50, 51

Haaker, Peter, 155
Halvorson, William "Bill," 98, 100, 127, 140, 142–43, 239
Hansen, Robert "Bob," 202, 204–10, 351n1
harbor seal (*Phoca vitulina*), 15, 111, 113
Harding grass (*Phalaris aquatica*), 261
Hartley, Fred, 68
Hartzog, George, 64
hawks, 13, 245
heritage herd, 223–25. *See also* horses
Hester, Gene, 142–43
Hickel, Walter, 68
Hodel, Donald, 125
hog cholera, 238
hog raising, 22. *See also* pigs (feral)
honeybees, 276
hook-and-line technology, 17. *See also* fishing
horses, 22, 23, 25, *129*, 223–25, 356n61
Horton, Chris, 145–46
Howald, Gregg, 233
H.R. 1696 (1997), 191
H.R. 2029 (2007), 273
H.R. 2975 (1979), 80
H.R. 3757 (1979), 81–82, 87
H.R. 4059 (1996), 216–17
H.R. 4236 (1996), 217
H.R. 5122 (2007), 271–72
H.R. 8935 (1957), 58

Huddleston, Jim, 182
Huffman, William E., 132
Hughes, Elden, 187
Hunter, Duncan, 271–72, 273
hunting, 20; in early California, 18–19; of elephant seals, 15; on Santa Cruz Island, 131, 132, 136–37, 204–5, 207, 209, 212, 219–20, 222; on Santa Rosa Island, 85, 126, 128, 178–79, 181, 192, 196, 197, 270–72, 301, 311
Huse, Brian, 188
Huvelle, Ellen Segal, 236–37
Hyder, Alvin, 22
hyperpredation, 246–47

iceplants, 27, 28, 93, 104–5, *279*
Ickes, Harold, 34, 35, 36
I&M (inventory and monitoring) programs, 93–101, 139–45, 147, 152–59, 181, 244–46, 289
In Defense of Animals (organization), 262
Indian paintbrush (*Castilleja mollis*), 188, 195, 196, 268, 271
Ingram, Trudy, 184
inheritance tax, 85, 133, 211–12, 331n51
insects, 13
Institute for Wildlife Studies, 249, 251, 256, 257, 360n44
International Union for the Conservation of Nature (IUCN), 293, 294
Inuits, 111
invasive species. *See* nonnative species
"Inventory and Monitoring Guideline" (NPS-75, 1992), 145
Island Adventures, 136–37, 138, 212–15, 218–21

Index 393

Island Chumash. *See* Chumash
Island Conservation and Ecology Group (ICEG), 233, 358n12
Island Fox Conservation Working Group, 247, 248–49, 255, 256–57, 264
island ironwood (*Lyonothamnus floribundus ssp. aspleniifolius*), 13, 172, 210
island manzanita (*Arctostaphylos tomentosa var. insulicola*), 172, 188, 195, 268, 271
island night lizard (*Xantusia riversiana*), 13, 32
island oak (*Quercus tomentella*), 12, 13, 128, 172, *175*, 177, 210, 239, 280
Island of the Blue Dolphins (O'Dell), 1
Island Packers Company, 62, 130, 229, 283, 298, 356n60
island scrub-jay (*Aphelocoma insularis*), 13, 203, 279–80, 289
island spotted skunk (*Spilogale gracilis amphiala*), 14, 303
isolation, 12, 13, 32

James, W. C., 53
Japanese brown alga (*Undaria pinnatifida*), 294–95, 307
Japanese diving, 19
Japanese trade market, 291
Jarvis, Jonathan, 261, 264, 297
Johnson, Fred W., 51
Johnson, Lyndon, 59
Johnsons Lee, 122, 127, 128, 130, 176, 297
Jones, John C., 25
Joshua Tree National Monument, 62, 101
Joshua Tree National Park, 121

Katz, Elliott, 262
kayaking, 18, 297
Kelco Company, 78, 83–84, 94
Kelp Forest Monitoring Program, 109
kelp forests, 68, *153*, 159, 291; abalone and, 343n41; about, 9–10; El Niño and, 290, 294; fish diversity and, 15; as habitat, 12, 152, 156; harvesting of, 19, 20, 78, 94; monitoring programs on, 88, 109, 154, *155*; Setchell on, 32; spiny lobster and, 153–54. *See also* giant bladder kelp (*Macrocystis pyrifera*)
Kennedy, John F., 59, 60
Kennedy, Roger, 146, 219
kikuyu grass (*Pennisetum clandestinum*), 27, 285, 288
Kittredge, Frank, 42, 44
Klinger, Rob, 226
Krantz, Brian, 218, 219, 220, 355n49
Krist, John, 224
Ku, Jack, 220
Kuchel, Thomas, 60
Kushner, David, 292, 293, 294

Lagomarsino, Richard A., 132
Lagomarsino, Robert, *268*; Channel Islands bills by, 79–81, 82, 83, 86, 96, 125, 310; P.L. 93–477 act and, 72; on Santa Cruz Island raid, 219; on Vail & Vickers ranching phase-out, 193–94, 273
Land and Water Conservation Fund Act (1965), 337n11
landbirds, 13–14, 32, 278–80. *See also specific species*
land grants, 20, 23, 25
land protection plan (LPP), 121

Lane, Franklin, 171
La Niña, 11–12, 289. *See also* climate; El Niño
Lassen Volcanic National Park, 94
Latham and Watkins firm, 189
Latta, Brian, 246
Laughrin, Lyndal, 132, 209, 243, 284
Leahy, William, 37–38
leaseback: about, 81, 123, 171–72; with Vail & Vickers, 122–27, 192
LeBoeuf, Burney, 115
LeDreau, Raymond "Frenchy," 21, 40, 44, 45
Lee, Martha J., 300
Leeworthy, Vernon R., 164
Leopold, A. Starker, 76, 103, 115–16
Leopold Report (1963), 91–92, 312, 314, 369n2
Lester, Herbert, 23, 40
Levine, Neil, 188, 190
Life Magazine, 68
lighthouses, xiv, 20, 21, 22
Littler, Mark M., 108, 109
livestock. *See* cattle ranching; sheep ranching
Lobo Canyon, Santa Rosa Island, 177, 186, *198*, 299
Local Coastal Plan (LCP), 69–71, 213
Lombardo, Carmen, 239
Long, Wayne, 85, 240, 274
long-term resource monitoring. *See* I&M (inventory and monitoring) programs
Los Padres National Forest, 149, 281

MacDonald, Jack, 124
Magnuson-Stevens Act (1972), 71, 169
Makarian, Michael, 260–61

Man and the Biosphere Program, 158
Manassas National Historic Battlefield, 354n37
Manbey, Bernard F., 34
marine botany, 32
marine conservation areas, 166–67, 169, 305, 345n73
Marine Ecosystem Dynamics Monitoring Project, 109
marine harvest refugia, 157–58
Marine Mammal Commission, 76, 115
Marine Mammal Protection Act (1972), 69, 109, 115, 329n13
Marine Mammal Research Center, San Miguel Island, 77
marine protected areas (MPAs), 158, 165, 168, 289, 294
marine reserves, state, 159–69, 293, 313. *See also* Channel Islands National Marine Sanctuary (CINMS); coastal zones
Marine Reserve Working Group (MRWG), 161–67. *See also* Sanctuary Advisory Council (SAC)
marine sanctuaries, 332nn59–61. *See also* Channel Islands National Marine Sanctuary (CINMS)
marine species: about, 14–15, 18–19, 32; managing the habitat of, 107–16, 153–59, 289–96. *See also specific species*
market squid (*Doryteuthis opalescens*), 290
Martin, Mike, 285
Mather, Stephen, 29
McEachern, Kathryn, 188
McGinness, Ilda, 136, 211, 212, 215, 217
McKinsey, Tippy, 225
Meek Construction, 229

Index   395

Mendoza, Antonio de, 17–18
Menke, John, 195, 197, 269
Merck & Co., 78
Mexico, 15, 18
Migratory Bird Treaty Act (1918), 236
Mills, Dave, 219
Minerals Management Service, 88
mining, 16, 21
Miocene Period, 2
missile testing and tracking, 1, 23, 48–49, 51, 52, 88, 311, 325n90
Mission 66, 56–58
Mission San Buenaventura, 17
missions and missionaries, 17, 18
mite (*Varroa jacobsoni*), 228
Monterey Bay, 332n59
Montrose Chemical Corporation, 253–54, 256
Moore, J. R., 23
More, Thomas Wallace, 25–26, 177
Morgando, John, 221, 353n27
Morris, Don, 148, 239
Morrison, Scott, 280
Morrison & Foerster LLP, 261
Multiple Use Management (MUM), 85, 197, 240, 274, 275

National Biological Survey (NBS), 146, 188, 342n22. *See also* U.S. Geological Survey (USGS)
National Environmental Policy Act (NEPA), 68, 102, 106, 141, 189, 221, 236, 262–63
National Historic Preservation Act (1966), 221
National Marine Fisheries Service (NMFS), 69, 71, 77, 100, 152, 161, 167, 329n21, 330n28
National Marine Sanctuaries Act (1972), 71
National Marine Sanctuary Program, 167
National Oceanic and Atmospheric Administration (NOAA), 69, 159, 161, 169, 252; CINMS and, 88–89
National Parks and Conservation Association (NPCA), 126, 183, 185, 188, 190, 248
National Parks and Recreation Act (1978), 331n44
National Park Service (NPS): acquisition of Channel Islands by, xiv–xv, 21, 29; CINMS and, 88–89; federal study on land acquisition by, 119–21; Gherini family and, 24–25, 63–65, 122, 136–38, 211–15; *Leopold Report* and, 91–92; LPPs by, 121; Mission 66 of, 56–57; purchase of East Santa Cruz Island by, 211–12, 215; relations and purchase of Santa Rosa Island by, 122–28, 171–72, 174–76; site visits and reports by, 30–33, 34. *See also* Channel Islands National Monument; Channel Islands National Park; *specific islands*
National Parks Omnibus Act (1998), 145
National Register of Historic Places, 284
National Rifle Association, 273
Native American artifacts, 218–19
native endemic species, overview, 12–13. *See also* ecological restoration; nonnative species; *specific species*
native gumplant (*Grindelia camporum*), 227, 228
Natural Resource Condition Assessment (NRCA), 278, 301–7

natural resource management plan (NRMP), 40, 91, 108, 128, 139–40, 150, 189–94. *See also* general management plan (GMP); resource management plan (RMP)

Natural Resources Inventory and Monitoring Initiative (1987), 141

The Nature Conservancy (TNC): co-management by, xi, xiv, 201–5, 211, 229–30, 249, 275–77; establishment of, 135; on Gherini plan, 63; island acreage owned by, 5; lawsuit by, 206–7; nonnative species eradication by, 219–20, 221, 258; purchase of Santa Cruz Island, 79, 81, 133–36, 309; relations with Stanton, 205–9, 352n10. *See also* ecological restoration

Naval Air Missile Test Center (NAMTC), 51. *See also* U.S. Navy

New York Zoological Society, 114

Nichols, James R., Jr., 223, 224

Nidever, George, 18–19, 22, 37

Nixon, Richard, 69

NOAA Fisheries. *See* National Marine Fisheries Service (NMFS)

Nofziger, James, 126

nonnative species: about, xiv–xv, 12, 26–28; Argentine ants, 277–78; burros, 101–3; cats (feral), 14, 22, 40, 43–44, 105, 232; deer and elk, 85, 128, 179, 181, 194, 198; fennel, 27, 225–26, 230, 258–59, 261, 288, 314; horses, 22, 23, 25, *129*, 223–25, 356n61; pigs (feral), 85, 178, 202, 207, 226; rabbits, 13–14, 22, 40, 43, 53, 93, 103–7; rats, 232–38; sheep (feral), 202–9, 210, 220–22; sheep ranching and, 19–26, 37, 40, 43, 47. *See also* ecological restoration; species eradication; *specific species*

Noon, Kevin, 283

Northern anchovy (*Engraulis mordax*), 290

northern elephant seal (*Mirounga angustirostris*), 15, 19, 44, 111, 112, 115. *See also* pinnipeds

northern fur seal (*Callorhinus ursinus*), 15, 111. *See also* pinnipeds

North Pacific Blob, 290

North Pacific Fur Seal Convention, 111, 336n47

NPS. *See* National Park Service (NPS)

Oberman, Mark, 207, 209

oceanic features, overview, 8–10

oil and gas development, 67–68, 71, 88, 329n22, 332n58

oil shipping traffic, 110

oil spills, 68, 96, 107, 232, 233, 328n7

olive trees, 261

Omnibus Appropriation, Fiscal Year 2007, 273

Oregon, 114

Organic Act (1916), 171, 180, 190, 237, 311–12, 315

organochlorines, 96, 252–54, 255

Orr, Philip, 16, 49

Our Nation and the Sea report (1969), 67

Our Vanishing Shoreline report (1955), 58

Outer Continental Shelf (OCS), 67–68, 88, 120, 329n12

overfishing, 95, 107, 114, 154, 165, 307, 343n39. *See also* fishing

Ovington, Earle, 30

Owens, Doris, 138

Index 397

Owens, Duane, 137, 138, 213
Owens, Jaret, 136–37, 212–15
owls, 13

Pacific Coast Recreation Area Survey (1959), 58
Pacific eelgrass (*Zostera pacifica*), 291
Pacific sardine (*Sardinops sagax*), 290
Pacific Wool Growing Company, 22
pallid bat (*Antrozous pallidus pacificus*), 14
Paralyzed Veterans of America, 271
Parker, David, 155
Parker, S. V., 42
Partnership for Interdisciplinary Studies of Coastal Oceans (PISCO), 160, 289, 293
Patton Escarpment, 3
PCBS, 96, 252
pelagic cormorant (*Phalacrocorax pelagicus*), 357n7
peregrine falcon (*Falco peregrinus*), 14, 248, 255
pesticides, 96, 252–53, 255
Peters, Clay, 94
Peterson, O. A., 51
Peterson, Richard, 115
Peterson, William "Pete," 136, 213
Philbrick, Ralph, 28, 103, 105
physiography, 2–5
Pickett, Matt, 167
Pierce, Franklin, 20
pigeon guillemot (*Cepphus columba*), 238, 357n7
pigs (feral): damage by, 227, 231; eradication of, 178, 204, 220, 230, 238–41, 258–63, 361n67; golden eagles and, 246–47; hunting of, 207, 209; introduction of, 22, 85; proliferation of feral, 226. *See also* hog raising
pink abalone (*Haliotis corrugata*), 154–55, 157, 158, 292. *See also* abalone
pinnipeds, 14–15, 19, 44–45, 74, 98, 100, 110–15. *See also specific species*
Pleistocene era, xiii, 1, 3, 35
Point Bennett, San Miguel Island, 6; pinniped rookery on, 45, 46, 74, 98, 100, 115–16, 152, 296
Point Reyes National Seashore, 171, 332n61
Point Reyes National Seashore Act (1976), 60
Point Reyes National Seashore Bill (S. 476), 60
Power, Dennis, 76
Power, Paula, 285
Presidential Proclamation No. 2281 (1938), 36
Primack, R. B., 231
Prince Island, 58, 76, 163, 279, 330n29
Prisoners Harbor, Santa Cruz Island, 287, 288; invasive species and, 27, 277; NPS control of, 229, 297, 299, 310; private management of, 282, 284; visitor experience at, 289; wetland restoration at, 276, 282–84. *See also* Santa Cruz Island
Proclamation No. 2825 (1949), 52
Pro Hunt, 261–62, 263
Proposition 20 (California), 69
public laws: Public Law 31 (1953), 52–53; Public Law 74-351 (1935), 21; Public Law 93-378 (1974), 141; Public Law 93-477 (1974), 72;

Public Law 96-199 (1980), 87, 93, 179; Public Law 104-333 (1996), 217, 354n41; Public Law 109-364 (2006), 272; Public Law 110-161 (2007), 273
Puddicombe, Robert, 235-36, 237, 262, 369n3
purple sea urchins (*Strongylocentrotus purpuratus*), 156, *157*, 291-92
Putnam, George R., 29-30
pygmy mammoth, xiii, 231

rabbits, 13-14, 22, 40, 43, 47, 50, 53-54, 93, 103-7
Radanovich, George, 184, 189, 191, 348n39
Ralls, Katherine, 247
Rambouillet Merino sheep, 24
ranching, 80-84, 124-27, 171-72, 178-88, 190-94, 197-98. *See also* cattle ranching; sheep ranching; *specific ranches*
range management plan, 128-29
rats, 93, 139, 232-38, 298, 358n10
Rea, William, 191-93, 194
Reagan, Ronald, 119, 354n38
Reber Plan, 67
red abalone (*Haliotis rufescens*), 154-55, *157*, 292. *See also* abalone
Red New Zealand rabbits, 47, 103. *See also* rabbits
red sea urchins (*Strongylocentrotus franciscanus*), 156, 291
red-tailed hawks, 245
Redwood National Park, 145
relevé sampling, 172, 346n3
reservation of use and occupancy (RUO): defined, 122-23; with Gherini family, 212, 215, 216; with Vail &

Vickers, 81-82, 85, 122-28, 171-72, 178, 191, 192, 197, 212, 267, 273, 310
resource management division, 147-48. *See also* general management plan (GMP)
resource management plan (RMP), 91-92, 108, 139, 189, 190-94, 196. *See also* natural resource management plan (NRMP)
Resource Protection Case Study (1982), 120
restoration ecology. *See* ecological restoration
Reynolds, John J., 167, 269
rhinoceros auklet (*Cerorhinca monocerata*), 278
Rhodes, H. W., 22, 30
rice grass (*Piptatherum miliacea*), 27
Richards, Dan, 155
Rick, Torben, 271
Ringrose, Marie, 136, 211, 212, 215, 217
Risebrough, Robert W., 253
Roberson, Emily, 185
Robertson, William B., 95
Robinson, Don, 53, 61, 62, 64-65, 72, 107
Rocky Intertidal Monitoring Program, 109
Roemer, Gary, 244, 246
Rogers, David Banks, 30, 33
Romero, Freddie, 284
Roosevelt, Franklin D., 23, 36, 41
Roosevelt, Theodore, 22
Rothrock, J. T., 173
Roybal, Edward, 60
Rubenstein Law Group, 262-63
Ruckelshaus, William, 253
RUO. *See* reservation of use and occupancy (RUO)

Russian seafarers, 18
Russian thistle (*Salsola iberica*), 27

S. 1104 (1979), 82–83
S. 1209 (2007), 273
Salazar, Ken, 332n60
salt, 27, 129, 181
San Clemente Island: description of, 31; island fox on, 242, 243; land use history of, 29; naval missile testing on, 1; nonnative species on, 294; park history of, 29, 33–34. *See also* Channel Islands
San Clemente Island fox (*Urocyon littoralis clementae*), 242
Sanctuary Advisory Council (SAC), 161–62, 166, 169, 344n57. *See also* Marine Reserve Working Group (MRWG)
San Miguel Island, 7, 39; about, 1, 2, 5–7, 13, 15; bird species on, 279, 280; Daisy Cave, 16, 17; as Environmental Protection Subzone, 76–77; fires on, 149, 151; island foxes on, 242, 244–46, 248–49, 257; land use history of, 19, 22–23, 29, 37, 47–48; Management Advisory Committee, 76; naval use of, 1, 23, 48–49, 51, 52, 61–62, 76, 88, 115–16, 152, 300–301, 311, 325n90; nonnative species eradication on, 101–3, 262, 267; NPS–U.S. Navy MOA on, 61, 74, 76; ocean habitat around, 293; park history of, xiv, 29, 33–34, 37, 58, 76, 311; pinnipeds on, 45, 46, 74, 98, 100, 111, 112, 114, 115, 115–16, 152, 296; status of natural resources on, 304; U.S. Navy use of, 23, 48–49, 61–62, 152, 300, 311. *See also* Channel Islands; Point Bennett, San Miguel Island
San Miguel Island fox (*Urocyon littoralis littoralis*), 14, 242
San Miguel Island milk vetch (*Astragalus miguelensis*), 21
San Nicolas Island, 1; fires on, 147–48; naval use of, 1, 33–34; park history of, 29, 33–34; pinnipeds on, 110–11. *See also* Channel Islands
San Nicolas Island fox (*Urocyon littoralis dickeyi*), 242
Santa Ana winds, 11
Santa Barbara Botanic Garden, 105
Santa Barbara Channel, 17, 30, 67, 71, 87, 96, 108, 156, 160, 290, 295, 332n60
Santa Barbara County Planning Commission, 62, 64
Santa Barbara Gyre, 9, 19
Santa Barbara Island, 1, 7–8, 13, 75; bird species on, 38, 43, 232, 279; fires on, 149; land use history of, 22, 29, 43, 47; park history of, xiv, 29, 34, 45–46, 309; pinnipeds on, 45, 50, 112, 115; rabbits on, 47, 103–7; status of natural resources on, 304–5, 314; U.S. Navy and, 47, 103. *See also* Channel Islands
Santa Barbara Museum of Natural History (SBMNH), 30, 49, 76, 119, 135, 259, 278
Santa Barbara song sparrow. *See* Channel Islands song sparrow (*Melospiza melodia graminea*)
Santa Catalina Island: invasive species on, 294; island fox on, 242, 243;

land use and ownership history of, 1, 29, 31, 309. *See also* Channel Islands
Santa Catalina Island fox (*Urocyon littoralis catalinae*), 242
Santa Cruz Island, 1, *4*, *5*, *134*; bird species on, 279, 280; co-management of, xiv, 201–9, 211, 229–30; eagles on, 256; Eastside, 136–38, 211–25, 229–30, 310; fires on, 149, 226–27; heritage herd on, 223–25; Island Adventures and, 136–37, 138, 212–15; island foxes on, 242, 249, 256–57, 258; land sales of, 34, 79, 133–36, 211–12, 215, 229–30, 309–10, 340n66; land use history of, 20, 23–25, 29, 48, 130–31, 309, 319n48; nonnative species on, 26–27, 225–29, 262–63; park history of, xiv, 56, 74, 120, 121; Restoration Plan, 258–63; sheep ranching on, 20, 23–24, 130–31, 136–37; Smugglers Ranch, 63, 136–38, 212, 297, 299, 353n27; status of natural resources on, 302–3, 314; U.S. Navy and, 88, 229. *See also* Channel Islands; Prisoners Harbor, Santa Cruz Island; Stanton, Carey; The Nature Conservancy
Santa Cruz Island buckwheat (*Eriogonum arborescens*), 28
Santa Cruz Island Company (SCIC), 23–24, 132–33, 135, 201, 205–7, 210, 351n1
"Santa Cruz Island Ecological Management Strategy 2015–2025" (2015), 276
Santa Cruz Island Foundation (SCIF), 191, 216, 223–24, 229, 283, 284
Santa Cruz Island fox (*Urocyon littoralis santacruzae*), 14, 242
Santa Cruz Island harvest mouse (*Reithrodontomys megalotis santacruzae*), 14
Santa Cruz Island Hunt Club, 132, 133, 137, 204–6, 207
Santa Cruz Island ironwood (*Lyonothamnus floribundus* var. *asplenifolius*), 172
Santa Cruz Island pine (*Pinus remorata*), 172
Santa Cruz Island scrub jay (*Aphelocoma coerulescens insularis*), 203
Santa Cruz Predatory Bird Research Group, 246, 251
Santa Monica Mountains National Recreation Area, 79–80, 281
Santarosae Island, 1, *3*, *5*, 35, 243, 280
Santa Rosa Island: about, 1, 5, *6*; bird species on, 280; Cleanup or Abatement Order for, 186–89; DCP for, 176–77; eagles on, 251–52; fires on, 149, 151; inclusion in the park act, 80–86; island foxes on, 242, 249, *250*, 256–57, 258; land use history of, 16, 20, 25–26, 29, 48, 70, 85, 172–76, 309; nonnative species eradication on, 238–41, 267; NPS purchase of, 122–28, 171–72, 310; park history of, xiv, 120, 121, 176–81, 309; private-park co-management of, 127–30; ranching on, 26, 124–29, 181–89, 194, 197–98; RMP for, 189, 190–94; shorebirds on, 13; status of natural resources on, 303–4. *See also* Channel Islands; Vail & Vickers Company

Santa Rosa Island fox (*Urocyon littoralis santarosae*), 14, 242
Santa Rosa Island live forever (*Dudleya blochmaniae ssp. insularis*), 151
Santa Rosa Island manzanita (*Arctostaphylos confertiflora*), 188, 195, 196, 268
Santa Ynez Band of Mission Indians, 285
Sargassum horneri, 294, 307
Save the Heritage Herd, 223, 356n61
Schreiner, Ed, 195, 269
Schumacher, Paul, 22
Schwemm, Cathy, 244
Scorpion Ranch, Santa Cruz Island, 27, 63, 122, 136–38, 213, 218, 297
Scoyen, Eivind, 40–41, 44–46, 47, 49, 50, 58, 322n40
Scripps Institute of Oceanography, 107
Scripps's murrelet (*Synthliboramphus scrippsi*), 14, 43, 232, 234, 235, 237–38, 255, 278, 313
seabirds, 13–14, 20, 41, 45, 255, 278–80, 357n7. *See also specific species*
sea cucumber (*Parastichopus sp.*), 292
A Sea-Dominated National Park (1963), 60
Seagars, Dana, 108
seagrass, 15
sea lions, 14–15, 19, 41, 109, 111, 112–14, 155, 290. *See also* pinnipeds
seals, 14–15, 18–19, 44, 111–13. *See also* pinnipeds
sea otter hunting, 18–19, 110
sea otters (*Enhydra lutris*), 110–11
sea stars (*Pycnopodia helianthoides*), 15, 290, 291, 292, 306, 343n41
Seastrand, Andrea, 184, 186, 189, 215–16

sea urchins (*Strongylocentrotus purpuratus*), 108–9, 156, *157*, 159, 291–92, 343n41
Sebelius, Keith, 86
Senate Committee on Energy and Natural Resources, 86, 120
Senning, Mark, 138
Sequoia National Park, 40–41, 46, 171, 322n40
Setchell, William A., 31–32
Setnicka, Tim, *268*; leadership roles of, 145–47; outhouse incident with, 214; purchase of East Santa Cruz Island and, 215–16; ranching issue and, 181, 189, 193, 199; on species monitoring and eradication, 220, 262, 263; transfer and retirement of, 264–65; Vail family and, 126, 128
settlement agreement (SA), 194–97, 267–69, 275, 311
Shaver, Charles "Mack," *268*; burro issue and, 101–2; as park superintendent, 146, 176, 187; pig eradication and, 240; retirement of, 147; Santa Cruz Island and, 211, 213–14; on Vails & Vickers SUP, 73–74, 128, 180–81
Shaw, James, 319n48
sheep (feral), 62, 202–6, 210, 220–22, 258
sheep ranching: on Anacapa Island, 21; Rothrock on, 173; on San Miguel Island, 19, 22–23, 37; on Santa Barbara Island, 22, 43; on Santa Cruz Island, 20, 23–24, 130–31, 136–37, *203*; on Santa Rosa Island, 20, 25–26; Sumner on, 40, 47
Sherman, Lynne, 223

shorebirds, 13–14
shoreline surveys, 58–59
Sierra Club, 63, 187
silver bird's-foot trefoil (*Lotus argophyllus niveus*), 210
Slattery, Harry, 37
Smith, Dick, 102
Smithsonian Institution, 247
Smugglers Ranch, Santa Cruz Island, 63, 136–38, 212, 297, 299, 353n27. *See also* Santa Cruz Island
Soil Conservation Service, 38
sooty tern (*Onychoprion fuscatus*), 95
South Atlantic Fisheries Management Council, 161
Southern California Bight, 2, 3, 16, 108, 253–54
Southern California Countercurrent, 8–9, 12, 163, 290
Southwick, Robert, 165
Spanish settlements, 17–18, 20
special use permit (SUP), 125–28, 172, 176, 178–82, 189–90, 269–70, 274
species eradication: burros, 101–3, 262, 334n23; cats (feral), 43–44; European honey bees, 227–29; pigs (feral), 178, 220, 230, 238–41, 258–63, 361n67; rabbits, 53–54, 103–7; rats, 93, 139, 232–38, 358n10; sheep (feral), 62, 202–6, 210, 220–22, 258; turkeys, 263. *See also* ecological restoration; nonnative species
spiny cocklebur (*Xanthium spinosum*), 27
spiny lobster (*Panulirus interruptus*), 77, 153, 290, 291, 293, 294
sportfishing. *See* fishing
SS *Winfield Scott*, 21

Standards and Guidelines, 142–43
Stanton, Carey, 75; death of, 209; Ehorn and, 73–74, 149; inheritance of ranch, 56, 131–32; on Marine Mammal Commission, 76; relations with TNC, 202, 205–9, 352n10; Robinson and, 64–65; sale of land by, 79, 133–36, 331n51; SCIC, 23–24, 132–33, 201; scientific research and, 202, 337n6, 352n5
Stanton, Edwin, III, 131, 132, 135
Stanton, Edwin L., 25, 34, 54, 56, 64, 130
Stanton, Evelyn, 131, 132
Starbard, Paul, 218
State of the Parks report (1980), 141
Status of Resources on Santa Rosa Island report (1995), 188
Steller sea lion (*Eumetopias jubatus*), 15, 109, 111, 112, 113
sterilization programs, 259
stone pine (*Pinus pinea*), 261, 282
Storke, Thomas, 59–60
Stratton, Susan K., 285
Stratton Commission, 67, 69
Submerged Lands Act (1953), 52–53, 79
"A Suggested Plan for the Management and Protection of Values of San Miguel Island" (1966), 61–62
Sullivan, Jeff, 218
Sumner, E. Lowell, Jr., 38–44, 47–48, 50, 103–5, 232, 321n31
Sumner Report, 38, 39–40, 43
sunflower sea stars (*Pycnopodia helianthoides*), 291, 292
SUP. *See* special use permit (SUP)
Superfund Act (1980), 254
Sutil Island, 49–50
Swain, Todd, 218

tall fescue (*Festuca arundinacea*), 27
tamarisk (*Tamarix aphylla*), 27
Tax Reform Act (1986), 124
Tentler, Richard, 220, 221, 355n51
Terra Marine Research & Education, 223, 356n60
Tershy, Bernie, 233
Tevrizian, Dickran, Jr., 263
Thompson, Alpheus B., 25
threaded abalone (*Haliotis assimilis*), 292. *See also* abalone
TNC. *See* The Nature Conservancy (TNC)
Tobin, Daniel, 84
Toll, Roger, 21, 30–33, 109
Toll Report, 32, 33
Tolson, Hillory, 48, 49
Tomlinson, Owen, 47, 50
tomols, 16, 18
toolmaking, 16–17
Torrey pine (*Pinus torryeana ssp. insularis*), 13, 127, 130, *131*, 280
Townsend's western big-eared bat (*Corynorhinus townsendii townsendii*), 14
trade economy, 16–17
trails, 62, 76–77, 289, 296–97, 300
Treaty of Guadalupe Hidalgo (1848), 20, 22
Truman, Harry S., 52, 311
Tumamait-Stenslie, Julie, 218, 284
turkeys, 263, 276

Udall, Stewart, 65, 91
Ugolini, Frank, 139, 148, 232, 233, 358n10
underwater archaeological sites, 5
unexploded ordnances (UXO), 152, 300–301

Union Oil, 67–68, 107
United Anglers of Southern California, 165
United States v. California, 52–53
United States v. Montrose et al., 254–55
University of California, 133, 283
University of California, Berkeley, 31
University of California, Davis, 98, 172
University of California, Santa Barbara (UCSB), 76, 132, 243
urchin barrens, 292, 294
U.S. Bureau of Commercial Fisheries, 113
U.S. Bureau of Lighthouses, xiv, 21, 29, 30, 33–34. *See also* lighthouses
U.S. Coast Guard, 42, 61, 88, 117
U.S. Coast Survey, 22
U.S. Commission on Marine Science, 67
U.S. Department of Agriculture, 114, 240–41
U.S. Department of Commerce, 34
U.S. Department of Interior (DOI), 38, 58, 61, 78, 88, 119
U.S. Fish and Wildlife Service (USFWS): about, 69; ESA listings by, 184, 232; interagency cooperation of, 187, 269; on island fox recovery, 257; prescribed burns and, 151; sea otter relocation by, 110; on wetland restoration, 285
U.S. Fish Commission, 114
U.S. Forest Service (USFS), 140, 141, 177
U.S. Geological Survey (USGS), 270, 283, 342n22
U.S. Navy: CINMS and, 88; on coastal boundary, 52, 325n90; co-management by, xiv, 115–16; NAMTC, 51; petroleum reserve of, 58; San Clemente Island base of, 1;

San Miguel Island and, 23, 37–38, 48–49, 61–62, 76, 102, 115–16, 152, 300–301, 311; San Nicolas Island base of, 1, 33–34; Santa Barbara Island and, 47, 103; Santa Cruz Island and, 229; USS *Tortuga* incident and, 152
USS *Tortuga*, 152

Vail, Al, 74, *75*, 83, 84–85, 123, 177
Vail, Mary, 199
Vail, Nita, 176, 269
Vail, N. R., 238–39
Vail, Russell, *75*, 85, 123, 269
Vail, Timothy, 269, 270, 271, 274
Vail family, 26, 275
Vail Family LLC, 269
Vail & Vickers Company: about, 26, 337n18; cervid control and, 269–75; development plans of, 70; Ehorn and, 74, 174–76, 178, 189, 197, 310; on island fox I&M program, 244; lawsuit against NPS by, 191–93, 310–11; RUO with, 81–82, 85, 122–28, 172, 178, 191, 192, 197, 267, 273, 310; sale of land by, 121–25, 128, 172, 310; SA with NPS, 194–97, 267–71, 275; strained relations with NPS of, 176–77, 181–91; SUP of, 125–28, 172, 178–81; on wild pig eradication, 178, 238. *See also* Santa Rosa Island
Van Vuren, Dirk, 202, 203
Vasquez, Larry, 300
Ventura County Fish and Game Commission, 160
Vermeer, Lotus, 262, 284
Vickers, John, 26
Vickers family, 275

Vickers LLC, 269
Vint, Thomas, 30, 31, 32, 33, 35

Walker, Joseph, 18–19
Wardlaw, Kim, 224
warty sea cucumber (*Parastichopus parvimensis*), 292–93
water pollution, 68, 96, 186–88, 233–34, 253, 362n81, 362n84
Waters, William G., 23
Watersipora subtorquata, 295
Watt, James, 119
Watts, David D., 206
weeds, 27
Wenner, Adrian, 228, 260, 277
Werger, Barbara, 356n62
western gull (*Larus occidentalis*), 14, *118*, 357n7
western harvest mice, 284
western snowy plover (*Charadrius alexandrinus nivosus*), 181, *183*, 188–89, 279
wetland restoration, 276, 282–84
Whalen, William, 83, 178, 215, 310, 346n18
whales, 19, 110
Whelan, Nick, 106
Whetsell, Earl, 137
White, John, 40, 46, 322n40
white abalone (*Haliotis sorenseni*), 154, 156, 292, 343n39. *See also* abalone
Wilderness Act (1964), 59, 298
wilderness designation, 87, 122, 206, 297–300, 311
Wild Horse Sanctuary, 225
wild oats (*Avena*), 27, 28
Wiley, Peter C., 164

Wilson, Pete, 181
Wirth, Conrad, 56–57
Woolley, John, 185–86
Woolley, Margaret, 85
Woolley, Will, 269
Work, Hubert, 171
World War I, 32, 78, 171
World War II, 46–47, 103

Xantus's murrelet. *See* Scripps's murrelet (*Synthliboramphus scrippsi*)

Yeager, Dorr, 49
yellow star thistle (*Centaurea solstitialis*), 227, 228
Yellowstone National Park, 171, 281, 332n1
Young, Don, 273

Zinke, Ryan, 301
zooids, 295

IN THE AMERICA'S PUBLIC LANDS SERIES

Restoring Nature: The Evolution of Channel Islands National Park
Lary M. Dilsaver and Timothy J. Babalis

To order or obtain more information on these or other University of Nebraska Press titles, visit nebraskapress.unl.edu.

www.ingramcontent.com/pod-product-compliance
Lightning Source LLC
Chambersburg PA
CBHW030235240426
43663CB00037B/487